VOLUME FORTY SEVEN

ADVANCES IN EXPERIMENTAL
SOCIAL PSYCHOLOGY

SERIES EDITORS

VOLUME FORTY SEVEN

Advances in Experimental
SOCIAL PSYCHOLOGY

Edited by

PATRICIA DEVINE
Psychology Department
University of Wisconsin
Madison, USA

ASHBY PLANT
Department of Psychology
Florida State University
Tallahassee, FL, USA

AMSTERDAM • BOSTON • HEIDELBERG • LONDON
NEW YORK • OXFORD • PARIS • SAN DIEGO
SAN FRANCISCO • SINGAPORE • SYDNEY • TOKYO
Academic Press is an imprint of Elsevier

Academic Press is an imprint of Elsevier
525 B Street, Suite 1800, San Diego, CA 92101-4495, USA
225 Wyman Street, Waltham, MA 02451, USA
32, Jamestown Road, London NW1 7BY, UK
The Boulevard, Langford Lane, Kidlington, Oxford, OX5 1GB, UK
Radarweg 29, PO Box 211, 1000 AE Amsterdam, The Netherlands

First edition 2013

Notice
No responsibility is assumed by the publisher for any injury and/or damage to persons
or property as a matter of products liability, negligence or otherwise, or from any use
or operation of any methods, products, instructions or ideas contained in the material
herein. Because of rapid advances in the medical sciences, in particular, independent
verification of diagnoses and drug dosages should be made

British Library Cataloguing in Publication Data
A catalogue record for this book is available from the British Library

Library of Congress Cataloging-in-Publication Data
A catalog record for this book is available from the Library of Congress

ISBN: 978-0-12-407236-7
ISSN: 0065-2601

For information on all Academic Press publications
visit our website at store.elsevier.com

Printed and bound in USA
13 14 15 16   10 9 8 7 6 5 4 3 2 1

CONTENTS

CONTRIBUTORS

Jason K. Clark
Department of Psychology, University of Iowa, Iowa City, Iowa, USA

Nilanjana Dasgupta
Department of Psychology, University of Massachusetts, Amherst, Massachusetts, USA

Peter H. Ditto
School of Social Ecology, University of California, Irvine, California, USA

Barbara L. Fredrickson
University of North Carolina, Chapel Hill, North Carolina, USA

Jesse Graham
Department of Psychology, University of Southern California, Los Angeles, California, USA

Jonathan Haidt
Stern School of Business, New York University, New York, USA

Ravi Iyer
Department of Psychology, University of Southern California, Los Angeles, California, USA

Sena Koleva
Department of Psychology, University of Southern California, Los Angeles, California, USA

Yuri Miyamoto
Department of Psychology, University of Wisconsin-Madison, Madison, Wisconsin, USA

Matt Motyl
Department of Psychology, University of Virginia, Charlottesville, Virginia, USA

Duane T. Wegener
Department of Psychology, Ohio State University, Columbus, Ohio, USA

Sean P. Wojcik
School of Social Ecology, University of California, Irvine, California, USA

CHAPTER ONE

Positive Emotions Broaden and Build

Barbara L. Fredrickson

University of North Carolina, Chapel Hill, North Carolina, USA

Contents

Abstract

This contribution offers a review, comprehensive to date, of a 15-year research program on the broaden-and-build theory of positive emotions. Although centered on evidence that has emerged from Fredrickson's Positive Emotions and Psychophysiology Laboratory (PEP Lab), it features key findings from other laboratories as well. It begins with a description of 10 representative positive emotions, alongside approaches for assessing them, both directly with the modified Differential Emotions Scale and indirectly through physiological and implicit measures. Next, it offers the seeds of the broaden-and-build theory, including work on the undo effect of positive emotions. It then reviews the state of the evidence for the twin hypotheses that stem from the broaden-and-build theory, the broaden hypothesis and the build hypothesis, including a focus on upward spiral dynamics. It touches next on new frontiers for the theory, including deeper investigations into the biological resources that positive emotions build as well as clinical and

Advances in Experimental Social Psychology, Volume 47
ISSN 0065-2601
http://dx.doi.org/10.1016/B978-0-12-407236-7.00001-2

1

organizational applications. Finally, this contribution closes with a brief presentation of two offshoots from the broaden-and-build theory, namely, the upward spiral model of lifestyle change and work on love as positivity resonance between and among people. Both are targets of increasing work in the PEP Lab.

From its very start, psychology has harbored an inferiority complex. Despite the fact that behavioral scientists rely on the scientific method and strivings for valid and reliable measures just as fervently as do those working in the natural sciences, this complex persists. Psychology has too often played the social comparison game, looking up to the natural sciences and medicine, pressing its nose against the glass ceiling of these high-prestige enterprises, while trying to climb away from and distinguish itself from the humanities and other social sciences, claiming greater empirical validity and relevancy. The recent trend to rename academic departments of "Psychology" as departments of "Psychological Science" or "Psychology and Brain Science" may well reflect this insecurity (Kihlstrom, 2012).

One outward legacy of this deep-seated inferiority complex has been to stay clear of topics that fall under the umbrella of human behavior and experience that are deemed too soft, frivolous, or ethereal. However intriguing they may be, experiences marked by levity or delight were long ignored by psychologists, perhaps for fear that they might somehow spoil an outward impression of rigor or objectivity. For psychology to be taken seriously as a science, it seemed required not only that it *be* rigorous and objective—by following the principles of the scientific method—but that it also *appear* rigorous and objective by tackling problems of grave nature, like mental illness, violence, or social ostracism.

It is true that emotion, a concept often cast as ethereal, was an early topic within psychology (e.g., Cannon, 1929; James, 1884). Yet emotional phenomena were eventually cordoned off in the zeitgeist of behaviorism, whose proponents cataloged them as irrelevant and misleading epiphenomena (Skinner, 1974), and derided those who studied them as mentalists. Although a few unorthodox psychologists ventured off the beaten path to study emotions nevertheless (e.g., Tomkins, 1962, whose work inspired Paul Ekman, Carroll Izard, among others), emotions science did not emerge as an organized subspecialty until the mid-1980s, as marked by the formation of the *International Society for Research on Emotions* (ISRE) in 1984, the first multidisciplinary professional association for scholars specializing in this area. It is fair to say that in the 30 years since, research on emotions has exploded.

Yet even decades after emotions became a rigorous and accepted topic of scientific inquiry, psychology's inferiority complex held sway to keep the focus on the most serious of emotions, namely, fear, anger, sadness, and the like. Even disgust made its way to the fore (e.g., Rozin & Fallon, 1987). It was as if the light-hearted emotions within the human repertoire might somehow weaken the fibers of the cloak of rigor that has been so important for psychology to don. This is my sense of how psychology could exist as a science *for an entire century* before psychologists were allowed to take a close empirical look at positive emotions without jeopardizing their reputations.

I have had the good fortune to work on the leading edge of the new and amply rigorous science of positive emotions. Together with the students and collaborators who have worked with me in my *Positive Emotions and Psychophysiology Laboratory* (PEP Lab, first at the University of Michigan and now at the University of North Carolina at Chapel Hill), I have sought to create an evidence-based understanding of light-hearted moments, charting their variety, the ways they change how the human mind works, and how, little-by-little, they change people's lives. This was not an easy program of research to launch. My first empirical work on positive emotions was in fact rejected countless times over the span of 7 years before it saw publication (i.e., Fredrickson & Levenson, 1998). While serial rejections are never pleasant, this early resistance taught me important lessons both about scholarly precision and about resilience and persistence. The purpose of this chapter is to review the now longstanding PEP Lab research program on positive emotions, centered on my broaden-and-build theory, with discussion of relevant studies from other laboratories as well. I begin with a description of the various affective phenomena my collaborators and I target.

1. TEN REPRESENTATIVE POSITIVE EMOTIONS

I set the stage for this review by briefly describing 10 key positive emotions. This is by no means an exhaustive list. I choose to focus on these 10 emotions not only because they are the targets of increasing research but also because evidence from the PEP Lab suggests that these 10 are experienced relatively frequently in people's daily life. With one important exception, I describe them in the order of their relative frequency, starting with the positive emotions people appear to feel most often and moving on to those that they feel more rarely. The exception is love, which in our studies emerges as the most frequently experienced positive emotion. As described below, I see good reason to describe it last.

Like all emotions, positive emotions are brief, multisystem responses to some change in the way people interpret—or appraise—their current circumstances. When this multisystem response registers that circumstances are somehow bad for the self, a negative emotion arises; when it registers good prospects or good fortune, a positive emotion arises. To foreshadow the broaden-and-build theory, for each of these 10 positive emotions, I describe (a) the appraisal patterns that trigger it, (b) the broadened thought–action repertoire it sparks, and (c) the durable resources that it helps to build. Table 1.1 offers these in summary form across its first four columns.

Joy. Joy emerges when one's current circumstances present unexpected good fortune. People feel joy, for instance, when receiving good news or a pleasant surprise. Joy creates the urge to play and get involved, or what Frijda (1986) termed *free activation*, defined as an "aimless, unasked-for readiness to engage in whatever interaction presents itself" (p. 89). The durable resources created through play are the skills acquired through the experiential learning it prompts.

Gratitude. Gratitude emerges when people acknowledge another person as the source of their unexpected good fortune. Joy becomes gratitude, for instance, when awareness of one's own good fortune is combined with admiration for another person for thoughtfully going out of their way to create that good fortune (Algoe, 2012). Gratitude creates the urge to creatively consider new ways to be kind and generous oneself. The durable resources accrued when people act on this urge are new skills for expressing kindness and care to others.

Serenity. Also called contentment, serenity emerges when people interpret their current circumstances as utterly cherished, right, or satisfying. People feel serenity, for instance, when they feel comfortable, at ease in, or at one with their situation. Serenity creates the urge to savor those current circumstances and integrate them into new priorities or values. The durable resources created through savoring and integrating include a more refined and complex sense of oneself and of one's priorities.

Interest. Interest arises in circumstances appraised as safe but offering novelty. People feel interest, for instance, when they encounter something that is mysterious or challenging, yet not overwhelming. Interest creates the urge to explore, to learn, to immerse oneself in the novelty and thereby expand the self (Izard, 1977; Silvia, 2008). The knowledge so gained becomes a durable resource.

Hope. Whereas most positive emotions arise in circumstances appraised as safe, hope is the exception. Hope arises in dire circumstances in which people fear the worst yet yearn for better (Lazarus, 1991). People feel hope, for instance, in grim situations in which they can envision at least a chance that things might change for the better. Hope creates the urge to draw on one's own capabilities and inventiveness to turn things around. The durable resources it builds include optimism and resilience to adversity.

Table 1.1 Ten representative positive emotions

Emotion label	Appraisal theme	Thought–action tendency	Resources accrued	Core trio in mDES item
Joy	Safe, familiar unexpectedly good	Play, get involved	Skills gained via experiential learning	Joyful, glad, or happy
Gratitude	Receive a gift or benefit	Creative urge to be prosocial	Skills for showing care, loyalty, social bonds	Grateful, appreciative, or thankful
Serenity (a.k.a., contentment)	Safe, familiar, low effort	Savor and integrate	New priorities, new views of self	Serene, content, or peaceful
Interest	Safe, novel	Explore, learn	Knowledge	Interested, alert, or curious
Hope	Fearing the worst, yearning for better	Plan for a better future	Resilience, optimism	Hopeful, optimistic, or encouraged
Pride	Socially valued achievement	Dream big	Achievement motivation	Proud, confident, or self-assured
Amusement	Nonserious social incongruity	Share joviality, laugh	Social bonds	Amused, fun-loving, or silly
Inspiration	Witness human excellence	Strive toward own higher ground	Motivation for personal growth	Inspired, uplifted, or elevated
Awe	Encounter beauty or goodness on a grand scale	Absorb and accommodate	New worldviews	Awe, wonder, amazement
Love	Any/all of the above in an interpersonal connection	Any/all of the above, with mutual care	Any/all of the above, especially social bonds	Love, closeness, or trust

Pride. Pride emerges when people take appropriate credit from some socially valued good outcome. People feel pride, for instance, when they accomplish an important goal (Tracy & Robins, 2007). Pride creates the urge to fantasize about even bigger accomplishments in similar arenas. The big dreams sparked by pride contribute to the durable resource of achievement motivation (Williams & DeSteno, 2008).

Amusement. Amusement occurs when people appraise their current circumstances as involving some sort on nonserious social incongruity. It can erupt, for instance, in the wake of a harmless speech error or physical blunder. Amusement creates urges to share a laugh and find creative ways to continue the joviality. As people follow these urges, they build and solidify enduring social bonds (Gervais & Wilson, 2005).

Inspiration. Inspiration arises when people witness human excellence in some manner. People feel inspired, for instance, when they see someone else do a good deed or perform at an unparalleled level. Inspiration creates the urge to excel oneself, to reach one's own higher ground or personal best. The durable resource it builds is the motivation for personal growth (Algoe & Haidt, 2009; Thrash & Elliot, 2004).

Awe. Awe emerges when people encounter goodness on a grand scale. People feel awe, for instance, when overwhelmed by something (or someone) beautiful or powerful that seems larger than life. The experience of awe compels people to absorb and accommodate this new vastness they have encountered. The durable resources awe creates are new worldviews (Shiota, Keltner, & Mossman, 2007).

Love. Love, which appears to be the positive emotion people feel most frequently, arises when any other of the positive emotions is felt in the context of a safe, interpersonal connection or relationship. I will offer a richer description of love later in this chapter when I discuss positivity resonance as an offshoot of the broaden-and-build theory. For now, suffice it to say that, as an amalgam of other positive emotions, love broadens thought–action repertoires both in an "all of the above" manner and by creating momentary perceptions of social connection and self-expansion. Likewise, love builds a wide range of enduring resources, especially social bonds and community.

2. ASSESSMENT APPROACHES

My empirical approach has been to assess each of these positive emotions via people's self-reports of their own subjective experiences, whether in response to (a) an emotion induction presented in the laboratory, (b) a repeated end-of-day survey of their experiences over the past 24 h, or (c) a questionnaire inquiring about their emotional experiences over the past 2 weeks. To do this, the PEP Lab uses a variant of the *modified Differential Emotions Scale* (mDES, see Appendix; Fredrickson, Tugade, Waugh, & Larkin, 2003) selected to fit the temporal frame of a given study design. The mDES[1] expanded on the *Differential Emotions Scale* (DES; Izard, 1977) to include a far wider set of positive emotions. I created the mDES to be a more encompassing measure of positive emotions than the more commonly used PANAS, which exclusively targets high activation positive affective states (Watson, Wiese, Vaidya, & Tellegen, 1999). Like the DES before it, the mDES uses a trio of emotion adjectives to capture each emotion. The fifth column in Table 1.1 presents the particular trio used in the mDES for each of the 10 positive emotions in turn. Based on evidence that people are better at recalling peak emotional experiences than they are at aggregating across multiple affective episodes (Fredrickson & Kahneman, 1993; Kahneman, Fredrickson, Schreiber, & Redelmeier, 1993), we typically ask respondents to indicate "the *greatest amount* that you've experienced each of the following feelings" (response options: 0, not at all; 1, a little bit; 2, moderately; 3, quite a bit; and 4, extremely). At times, however, we inquire about the frequency of experience, by asking respondents "How often did you feel _____?" (response options: 0, never; 1, rarely; 2, some of the time; 3, often; 4, most of the time). Depending on our empirical approach, we ask respondents to think back to a particular laboratory procedure (e.g., a given film or activity), the past 24 h, or the past 2 weeks. In all cases, each of 20 distinct emotions is represented by a trio of affective adjectives. Those for the positive emotions are supplied in Table 1.1 (researchers interested in using the mDES may download various versions from the PEP Lab Web site, www.PositiveEmotions.org). While at times my collaborators and I examine individual items of the mDES to explore the effects of specific emotions or laboratory inductions, most often we aggregate the 10 positive and 10 negative emotion items separately to create independent positive and negative emotion scores, respectively. These scales yield high internal reliability, ranging from 0.82 to 0.94 (Cohn, Fredrickson, Brown, Mikels, & Conway, 2009; Fredrickson, Cohn, Coffey, Pek, & Finkel, 2008).

---

[1] In my book, *Positivity* (2009, Crown), written for a general audience, I refer to the mDES as the Positivity Self Test. The Web site that accompanies that book, www.PositivityRatio.com, offers a free version of this test along with online tools for tracking people's changes in positivity, negativity, and positivity ratios over time.

Beyond the explicit self-reports of emotion experience captured by the mDES, in our laboratory-based studies my PEP Lab regularly uses facial electromyography (EMG) to capture the frequency of Duchenne smiles, using a new data-reduction technique developed by former students Kareem Johnson and Christian Waugh (Johnson, Waugh, & Fredrickson, 2010). To further circumvent demand effects, we have also used a range of implicit measures of positive affect (e.g., lexical decision task, LDT, Niedenthal, Halberstadt, & Setterlund, 1997; affect misattribution procedure, AMP, Payne, Cheng, Govorun, & Stewart, 2005). We also deploy a version of Russell's Affect Grid (Russell, Weiss, & Mendelsohn, 1989) especially when in need of densely repeated measures of emotion within a single laboratory visit. We modify the Affect Grid by revising the emotion adjectives that appear around the grid's perimeter to best fit our current empirical objectives. I direct readers interested in a deeper discussion of emotion measurement to a chapter Randy Larsen and I wrote on this topic for an edited volume on well-being (Larsen & Fredrickson, 1999).

3. SEEDS OF THE BROADEN-AND-BUILD THEORY

3.1. The undo effect of positive emotions

I began my formal study of emotions as a postdoctoral fellow in the early 1990s, supported by the NIMH training grant on emotions led by Paul Ekman and Richard Lazarus. My intellectual curiosity about positive emotions was piqued by the simple fact that they were so rarely discussed in the existing empirical literature. Working with Robert Levenson at UC Berkeley, I became captivated by the two sentences Levenson had devoted to positive emotions in a chapter he had written on best practices for investigating whether specific discrete emotions carried unique autonomic signatures. In discussing the crucial issue of how to select an appropriate baseline against which to examine the physiological effects of distinct emotions, he wrote ". . . the evolutionary meaning of positive emotions such as happiness might be to function as efficient 'undoers' of states of ANS [autonomic nervous system] arousal produced by certain negative emotions. To test this hypothesis, a reasonable baseline condition for the investigation of ANS concomitants of happiness would be one that produces a prior state of fear, anger or sadness" (Levenson, 1988, p. 25). Indeed, prior work by Levenson and colleagues had examined the autonomic effects of "happiness" assessed against the more commonly used baseline of neutral affect (Levenson, Carstensen, Friesen, & Ekman, 1991; Levenson, Ekman, & Friesen,

1990). Results of this earlier work showed essentially no autonomic signature whatsoever for this positive emotion, which seemed a puzzle.

So at the start of my postdoctoral fellowship, in the fall of 1990, Levenson and I designed an initial laboratory experiment to test this *undo hypothesis* (Fredrickson & Levenson, 1998). As Levenson had proposed, we examined the effects of positive emotions against the backdrop of a negative emotion, in this case, fear. We did, of course, also include a prior neutral baseline to establish the effects of our fear induction. We used a short video clip that capitalized on a fear of heights, to create a common negative emotion in all participants, who were female students at the University of Berkeley. The clip showed a man inching along the outer ledge of a high-rise, hugging the side of the building; at one point, he loses his footing, grasps at whatever he can and dangles high above traffic, struggling to keep from dropping to his certain death.

From pretesting, we knew that this short clip, just 83-s long, was effective in inducing fear specifically. Participants in this experiment reported their own subjective experiences of emotion by manipulating a rating dial whose pointer moved on a continuous 180° scale, labeled from "very negative" (0) to "neutral" (~4.5) to "very positive" (9). During their prevideo resting baseline period, mean rating dial reports were near five (very slightly positive), whereas during this high-rise ledge clip participants' ratings dropped to about three (negative). More importantly for testing the undo hypothesis, participants also experienced significant cardiovascular reactivity to this video clip, with three of four cardiovascular measures showing significant change relative to resting baseline, namely, heart rate; finger pulse amplitude, an index of peripheral vasoconstriction; and pulse transmission time to the ear, a correlate of blood pressure. Pulse transmission time to the finger was also measured but did not show significant change during the fear clip and so was not used within our aggregate index of cardiovascular recovery in this initial study.

We tested the undo hypothesis by randomly assigning participants to view one of four different short video clips immediately following the fear-inducing ledge clip. From pretesting, we knew that two of the four clips evoked two different positive emotions, amusement and contentment. These clips presented images of a puppy playing and ocean waves, respectively. A third was known to be neutral, eliciting no emotion whatsoever by presenting a 1990s-era computer screensaver, and a fourth was known to elicit sadness by showing a boy crying at the death of his father. Importantly, the two positive and the neutral clips, when viewed following a standard resting baseline, produce virtually no cardiovascular signatures whatsoever (Fredrickson, Mancuso, Branigan, & Tugade, 2000, Study 2). That is, there is no way that anyone could know, just by looking at the ensuing physiological responses, whether someone were watching puppies, waves, or a simple screensaver. We chose sadness as an additional comparison condition because although it produces small increases in sympathetic activation (Fredrickson et al., 2000), unlike other negative emotions, it is not associated with any high-action motor program (Fredrickson & Levenson, 1998), like fight or flight that co-opts the sympathetic nervous system. Most often, it is associated with inactivity or disengagement and as such, one might expect it, too, to speed cardiovascular recovery.

So although positive emotions do not appear to "do" anything to the cardiovascular system, when viewed against the backdrop of pronounced negative emotional arousal, the positive emotions clearly stood out in their ability to "undo" lingering cardiovascular activation. Compared to either those in the neutral condition, who took about 40 s to recover, or those in the sad conditions, who took about 60 s to recover, those in the amusement and contentment conditions showed the fastest cardiovascular recovery, recovering within about 20 s each (Fredrickson & Levenson, 1998, Study 1).

Across two subsequent experiments, conducted in my own newly established laboratory at the University of Michigan, my students and I replicated this exact pattern of results using samples more diverse in age, gender, and ethnicity. We also used a more active and self-relevant way to induce the initial negative emotion by having participants prepare to deliver a speech on "Why you are a good friend" under considerable time pressure, which, they were told, would be videotaped for later evaluation by students in another study. We also instructed participants that there was a 50–50 chance that "the computer" would select them to give their speech or not. If "by chance" they were not selected to give their speech, a video clip would begin on the monitor that was placed before them. In actuality, no participants were asked to deliver their prepared speeches. This cover story was developed both to boost the anxiety of the speech preparation task and to justify the quick switch to an unrelated video clip. While our later experiments used the same clips to elicit amusement, contentment, neutrality, and sadness as the original Fredrickson–Levenson experiment, we expanded the array of cardiovascular measures we tracked to include beat-by-beat assessments of both systolic and diastolic blood pressure.

The speech task produced clear and pronounced experiences of anxiety, as indicated both by participants' self-reports of their subjective experience and by significant changes across the entire set of six cardiovascular measures we tracked, each in the direction of heightened sympathetic arousal (Fredrickson et al., 2000, Study 1, Samples 1 and 2). Notably, using different samples, different cardiovascular measures, and a different initial negative emotion from which to recover, two distinct positive emotions again yielded significantly faster recovery from the cardiovascular sequelae of negative emotions.

Using archival data that I had collected in Levenson's lab at UC Berkeley, I also tested the undo hypothesis using a more spontaneous and ecologically valid pairing of negative and positive emotions. People vary in their responses to negative experiences. For whatever reasons, some people smile in the face of sadness and adversity whereas others do not. We explored whether those who smiled during a notably sad film clip (the funeral scene from Steel Magnolias, clipped prior to the humorous interchanges), would show faster cardiovascular recovery after the clip ended. Those who smiled at least once during the sad clip, the data suggested, recovered about 20 s faster than those who never smiled (Fredrickson & Levenson, 1998, Study 2).

Whereas Levenson had supplied the original hypothesis that launched our research on the undo effect of positive emotions, my contribution was to develop a time-based measure of cardiovascular recovery with fine-grained temporal resolution. As was standard in Levenson's lab, we had extracted second-by-second data on participants' responses during the resting baseline as well as during the film sequences they saw. Using these data, I calculated a confidence interval around each participant's baseline level of activation defined by their mean activation over the past 60 s of a 2-min resting baseline period, plus and minus one standard deviation of that mean. This confidence interval was used to characterize each participant's own state of emotional quiescence. During the fear clip, all participants' responses moved out of this relaxed state, as would be expected with the experience of fear. Then, at the start of the randomly assigned secondary video clips, I calculated the time, in seconds, for each participant's cardiovascular responses to return to within the confidence interval that represented their own relaxed state and remain within this interval for 5 of 6 consecutive seconds. I did this for each cardiovascular measure that had shown reactivity in response to the initial negative emotion and then aggregated the recovery times across distinct cardiovascular measures. This data reduction approach was, at the time, novel. Most investigators assessed recovery indirectly, by reassessing the magnitude of a cardiovascular response some minutes later and then inferring recovery from any evident reductions in reactivity. Our more sensitive time-based measure of cardiovascular recovery preceded the later and eventually more sophisticated appreciation for affective chronometry, the investigation of the temporal course of emotion experiences (e.g., Davidson, 1998; Waugh, Hamilton, & Gotlib, 2010).

An offshoot of this early work on the undo effect of positive emotions emerged as an auxiliary branch of research on resilience. Using Block and Kremen's 14-item self-report measure of Ego-Resilience (ER89; Block & Kremen, 1996), we discovered that people who score higher on this index of trait resilience appear to spontaneously harness the undo effect of positive emotions to regulate their own negative emotional experiences. For instance, when faced with the same anxiety-producing speech preparation task, people who score higher on resilience showed significantly faster cardiovascular recovery. Moreover, their quicker recovery was mediated by their greater tendency to experience positive emotions in response to the task, intermixed with their anxiety (Tugade & Fredrickson, 2004, Study 1).

In a second study, by random assignment we had some participant reframe the speech preparation task as an interesting challenge to overcome versus a threat. Under the typical threat instructions, we replicated the effect wherein people who score higher on Block and Kremen's resilience measure showed faster cardiovascular recovery. By contrast, under challenge instruction, we found that people who scored lower on resilience show the same swift cardiovascular recovery as their high resilient counterparts. Moreover, their speedy recovery was mediated by the greater positive emotions they experienced in response to the task alongside their anxiety. Data from both studies bolster the undo effect of positive emotions by suggesting that positive emotions serve as useful resources for regulating negative emotional experiences in daily life. Beyond promoting cardiovascular quiescence, positive emotions have also been found to (a) help resilient people find positive meaning in difficult life circumstances (Tugade & Fredrickson, 2004, Study 3); (b) buffer against depressive symptoms and fuel postcrisis growth in the wake of the September 11th, 2001 terrorist attacks (Fredrickson et al., 2003); and (c) help people effectively recover from stress both in daily life and during bereavement (Ong, Bergeman, Bisconti, & Wallace, 2006).

3.2. The birth of the broaden-and-build theory

The transition in my own thinking from the undo effect to the broaden-and-build theory of positive emotions carries an interesting lesson about the importance of having an appropriate balance of positive to negative emotions for generative thinking. As my first work targeting positive emotions, my studies on the undo effect ignited my fascination with the evolutionary origins of these light-hearted states. Within the still new renaissance of emotions science, very little work targeted emotions with a pleasant subjective feel. This made positive emotions largely uncharted terrain, which presented my favorite kind of intellectual landscape. Although it is not always wise to toil in areas unplowed by others, it certainly provides vast areas to freely explore and ponder.

In our first musings about how existing emotion theory was perhaps unsuitable for the positive emotions, Levenson and I pointed out that the lynchpin theory that specific emotions activate specific action tendencies did not neatly extend to the positive emotions (Fredrickson & Levenson, 1998). The concept of specific action tendencies had become so central within emotions science because it simultaneously explained not only why emotions evoke bodily changes (to support specific action urges) but also why emotions exist (because these specific actions helped human ancestors survive specific and recurring threats to life and limb).

In the stretch of years during which our initial chapter on the undo effect was repeatedly submitted and rejected, I had the opportunity to present my research at the ISRE meeting in 1996, held in Toronto. The invitation to present in this context was itself unprecedented because (at the time) ISRE meetings were open to members only and membership required having at least five publications within emotions research. Although I was starting my second assistant professor position (having just moved from Duke University to the University of Michigan), I scarcely had five publications, let alone five publications on emotions. Motivated in part by the stringent membership rules of ISRE, a number of my peers had formed a parallel academic organization, the *Emotions Research Group (ERG)*, expressly as a forum for early-career emotions researchers to help cultivate and refine each other's work. As ERG gained momentum, the leadership at ISRE decided to make an exception to their standard membership requirement and deemed all members of ERG to be members of ISRE. In so doing, James Gross, then ERG president, was invited to organize a symposium on "New Voices in Emotions Research" for the 1996 ISRE meeting. It was unprecedented for a collection of such junior researchers to have a reasonably large audience at this meeting. It was based on this symposium that Peter Salovey, then editor of the new APA journal, *Review of General Psychology*, invited those of us who presented to put together a Special Issue on emotions research for Volume 2 of his new journal.

Although our "New Voices" symposium was well received, it was not without sharp criticism. The sharpest of which, as I recall, was directed at me. After presenting my data on the undo hypothesis, I had raised the possibility that the central concept of specific action tendencies simply did not apply to the positive emotions. Whereas anger and fear spark the urge to fight or flee, respectively, alongside attendant autonomic activation, amusement and contentment do not appear to evoke any particular actions or autonomic activation. What then, I wondered aloud, might be their evolved function? The function of positive emotions, I speculated, may well be to undo the physiological aftereffects of negative emotions and I suggested that the data that I had presented reflected this undoing function.

A senior scientist in attendance challenged me with no small amount of emotion in his voice. He claimed that I had no basis to describe undoing as a function of positive emotions. At best, he argued, I could call it an "effect." Both his words and intonation hit me hard, and I left the podium with less confidence and more doubts than I had had when I approached it.

The unknown critic's words lingered with me for months.[2] As I was preparing to write my contribution to the invited RGP Special Issue, I set my goal to develop a proper evolutionary argument for the function of positive emotions. I read the evolutionary psychologists of the day (particularly Barkow, Cosmides, & Tooby, 1992; Nesse, 1990; Tooby & Cosmides, 1990) and gathered up as many of the disparate strands of evidence that had then accumulated about positive emotions as I could find. This included work by Mihalyi Csikszentmihalyi, Alice Isen, and others. I puzzled over how my own evidence for the undo effect might fit together with Isen's work that showed that positive emotions "give rise to an enlarged cognitive context" (Isen, 1987, p. 222) and with Csikszentmihalyi's suggestion that flow, a form of positive emotion akin to interest, is marked by a momentary loss of self, and yet over time paradoxically augments the self (Csikszentmihalyi, 1990). Guided by the logic of evolutionary theorists, I paid close attention to the circumstances in which positive emotions occur, and the ancestrally recurrent problems of adaptation for which positive emotions might have served as a well-designed solution. Cataloging the wide range of situations that evoked positive emotions made it clear to me that the simplistic pairing of negative emotions with survival and positive emotions with reproduction was inadequate. In the end, I also decided that the

---

[2] The 1996 Toronto meeting was my first ISRE meeting, and as a junior scholar, I did not recognize many senior scholars by sight. I had the chance to give a keynote on my positive emotions research a decade later at the 2006 ISRE meeting and asked if anyone in the audience was or knew of this "unknown critic" because I wished to thank him personally. No one came forward, so the mystery continues. If you can help me solve this mystery, please do.

unknown critic was right. Undoing was unlikely to be the evolved function of positive emotions. It looked instead be the byproduct of a far more consequential function.

The function of positive emotions, as shaped over millennia by natural selection, I came to conclude, was to build an individual's resources for survival. The means by which this build function was achieved was by a momentarily broadened scope of awareness, creating a form of consciousness within individuals that included a wider array of thoughts, actions, and percepts than typical. This meant that negative and positive emotions alike came to be part of our universal human nature through selective pressures related to survival, albeit on vastly different timescales. Negative emotions carried adaptive significance in the moment that our human ancestors' experienced them as their associated action urges—for example, to fight, flee, or spit—drove behaviors that saved life and limb. Positive emotions, by contrast, carried adaptive significance for our human ancestors over longer timescales. Having a momentarily broadened mindset is not a key ingredient in the recipe for any quick survival maneuver. It is, however, in the recipe for discovery, discovery of new knowledge, new alliances, and new skills. In short, broadened awareness led to the accrual of new resources that might later make the difference between surviving and succumbing to various threats. Resources built through positive emotions also increased the odds that our ancestors would experience subsequent positive emotions, with their attendant broaden-and-build benefits, thus creating an upward spiral toward improved odds for survival, health, and fulfillment. Figure 1.1 provides a graphic summary of this broaden-and-build theory of positive emotions.

This is what I offered as a new account of the evolved adaptive function of positive emotions in that RGP Special Issue (Fredrickson, 1998). It stated that positive emotions have been useful and preserved over human evolution because having recurrent, yet unbidden moments of expanded awareness proved useful for developing resources for survival. Little-by-little micromoments of positive emotional experience, although fleeting, reshape who people are by setting them on trajectories of growth and building their enduring resources for survival. The broaden-and-build theory describes the form of positive emotions as to broaden awareness and their function as to build resources.

From the perspective of the freshly articulated broaden-and-build theory, the undoing effect of positive emotions was a by-product of the broaden effect. To the extent that positive emotions broadened an individual's accessible repertoire of thoughts and action urges, they would also serve to loosen

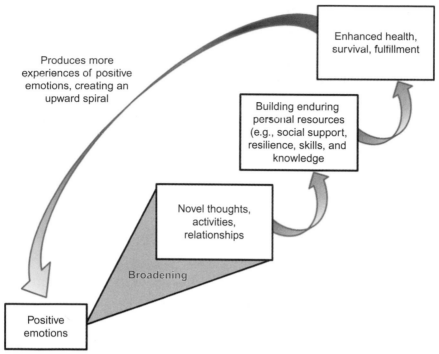

Figure 1.1 The broaden-and-build theory of positive emotions. *Adapted from Fredrickson and Cohn (2008, Fig. 48.1)*

the hold that any particular negative emotion might gain on an individual's mindset by virtue of its associated urge for specific action. One marker of the body's preparation for specific action is cardiovascular activation. If, by broadening people's mindsets, positive emotions can dismantle preparation for specific actions, they should also serve as efficient antidotes for the cardiovascular sequelae of negative emotions.

Another strand of evidence that swayed me from taking undoing to be the evolved function of positive emotions was the wide array of contexts in which positive emotions occur. If the undo effect captured the function of positive emotions, then the occurrence of positive emotions in contexts not characterized by prior negativity would need special explanation. Given that most positive emotions are experienced independently from negative emotions, it seemed that should be the rule to be explained rather than the exception to the rule.

So the broaden-and-build theory was itself evoked by pointed criticism and my own initial negative emotional responses to it. Yet my wish to be open to that criticism and learn from it coaxed me to expand the scope of my thinking about positive emotions, which allowed me to discover more of their unsung value. The sharp words from that senior scholar at ISRE, then, became the irritating grain of sand that commanded my focus until it emerged as something more appealing and useful. Indeed I have come to view the development of the broaden-and-build theoretical framework as my pearl for having generated a string of hypotheses. It marked a turn away from near exclusive focus on the undo effect of positive emotions and toward a more encompassing focus on their abilities to broaden mindsets and build resources.

4. EVIDENCE FOR THE BROADEN-AND-BUILD THEORY

4.1. The broaden hypothesis

The *broaden hypothesis*, drawn from the broaden-and-build theory, states that positive emotions, relative to negative emotions and neutral states, widen the array of thoughts, action urges, and percepts that spontaneously come to mind. This hypothesis was consistent with—and indeed inspired by—the extensive research program of the late Alice Isen and her collaborators. Isen and colleagues' work was exemplary for two reasons. First, she did not assume that positive and negative emotions were "opposites" and as such always compared the effects of positive emotions to the effects of neutral states in tightly controlled laboratory experiments. Second is bolstering generalizability; across studies she and her colleagues used a wide range of techniques to induce positive emotions, ranging from having participants read a list of positive words, view cartoons or a short comedy clip, hear success feedback, or having them receive a small bag of candy as an unexpected gift. From Isen's experiments, we can conclude that people experiencing positive emotions show patterns of thought that are notably unusual (Isen, Johnson, Mertz, & Robinson, 1985), flexible and inclusive (Isen & Daubman, 1984; see also Bolte, Goschke, & Kuhl, 2003; Compton, Wirtz, Pajoumand, Claus, & Heller, 2004; Dreisbach & Goschke, 2004), creative (Isen, Daubman, & Nowicki, 1987; see also Phillips, Bull, Adams, & Fraser, 2002; Rowe, Hirsh, & Anderson, 2007), integrative (Isen, Rosenzweig, & Young, 1991), open to information (Estrada, Isen, & Young, 1997), forward-looking and high-level (Pyone & Isen, 2011), and efficient (Isen & Means, 1983; Isen et al., 1991). Isen and colleagues' work also provides evidence that positive emotions broaden people's action urges, with experiments showing increased preferences for variety and openness to a wider array of behavioral options (Kahn & Isen, 1993; see also Renninger, 1992).

From the perspective of the broaden-and-build theory, I reasoned that the cognitive and behavioral effects of positive emotions that Isen and colleagues had previously uncovered were the downstream consequences of a more basic cognitive shift, one in which the boundaries of awareness stretch open a bit further during positive emotional experiences, enabling people to connect the dots between disparate ideas and thereby act creatively, flexibly, and with greater sensitivity to future time horizons. Although a slim amount of prior evidence supported the view that positive emotions broaden the scope of attention (see Basso, Schefft, Ris, & Dember, 1996; Derryberry & Tucker, 1992; each described in Fredrickson, 1998; see also Gasper & Clore, 2002), conclusiveness was limited because this prior work did not include neutral comparison conditions. Noting this, my students and I set out to test the broaden hypothesis adopting methods from cognitive psychology that captured the breadth momentary awareness.

One experiment that I conducted in collaboration with Christine Branigan, for instance, used short film clips to induce positive, negative, and neutral states in University student participants using a between-participants design (Fredrickson & Branigan, 2005, Study 1). One strength of this work is that we tested the effects of two distinct positive emotions (amusement and contentment) and two distinct negative emotions (anger and anxiety), each relative to a neutral state. Our dependent measure of the scope of participants' attention was a variant of a global–local visual processing task, first developed by Navon (1977) (see Fig. 1.2). Immediately

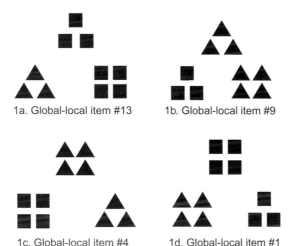

1a. Global-local item #13   1b. Global-local item #9

1c. Global-local item #4   1d. Global-local item #1

Figure 1.2 Sample global–local items used to test the broaden hypothesis. *Adapted from Fredrickson and Branigan (2005, Fig. 1)*

after viewing the randomly assigned video clip, participants were shown a trio of figures and asked to choose which of two comparison figures (on the bottom) was most similar to the target figure (the top). While there are no right or wrong answers, one comparison figure always resembled the target figure in its global configuration (see lower left choice in each item shown in Fig. 1.2), whereas the other comparison figure always resembled the target figure in its local detail elements (see lower right choice in each item shown in Fig. 1.2). Past work had shown that personality traits associated with negative emotions—namely, anxiety and depression—correlated with a bias to choose the local option, consistent with a narrowed scope of attention, whereas traits associated with positive emotions—namely, subjective well-being and optimism—correlate with a bias to choose the global option, consistent with a broadened scope of attention (Basso et al., 1996). Although our results for negative emotions were inconclusive, those for positive emotions clearly demonstrated that temporary states of two distinct positive emotions broaden the scope of attention: Participants in both the amusement condition and the contentment condition chose the global option significantly more often than those in the neutral condition (Fredrickson & Branigan, 2005, Study 1).

In a second experiment that used the same sample and same five video clips to induce positive, negative, and neutral states, we examined the breadth of participants' action urges using a thought listing task (Fredrickson & Branigan, 2005, Study 2). Specifically, after the video clip ended, participants were asked to describe, in a word or two, the strongest emotion they felt while viewing the clip. Then, they were asked to step away from the specifics of the video clip and imagine being in a situation in which this particular emotion would arise, and then "*given this feeling*, please *list* all the things you would like to do *right now*." Participants were then given a form with 20 blank lines that began with "I would like to _____." We simply tallied the number of statements completed as an index of the breadth of participants' thought–action repertoire. Figure 1.3 presents the results. We found that positive emotions, relative to both the neutral state and the negative emotions, broadened people's repertoire of action urges. In this second experiment, we also found marginal evidence that negative emotions, relative to the neutral state, narrowed people's repertoire of action urges (Fredrickson & Branigan, 2005, Study 2).

In later studies, again with University students, we used facial EMG to measure the frequency of participants' Duchenne (genuine) smiles during emotion inductions and related smile frequency to changes in their performance on cognitive tests of attentional breadth and attentional flexibility (Johnson et al., 2010). In the first of two studies, we examined facial

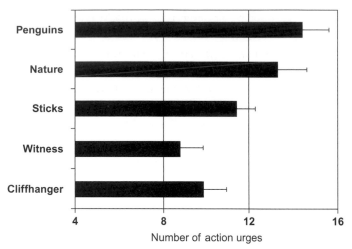

Figure 1.3 Thought–action repertoire size by emotion condition. *Note*: Penguins and Nature elicited amusement and contentment, respectively. Witness and Cliffhanger elicited anger and fear, respectively. Sticks elicited no particular emotion whatsoever. *Adapted from Fredrickson and Branigan (2005, Fig. 3)*

EMG data while participants viewed one of several randomly assigned video clips known to elicit the positive emotions of joy or contentment, the negative emotions of anger or sadness, or emotional neutrality. The dependent measure in this study was a reaction-time-based measure of global–local visual processing administered at baseline and then again following the emotion induction. In this task, participants were shown a large "T" (presented upright, inverted, or oriented toward the right or the left) made up of smaller images of the letter "T" (all also either upright, inverted, or oriented to the right or the left). Participants were to indicate, as quickly and accurately as possible, whether either the large or smaller letters were upright or inverted. Results showed that participants with frequent Duchenne smiles showed a significantly larger change (relative to their own baseline scores) in their bias toward global targets (Johnson et al., 2010, Experiment 1). In a second study, we used facial EMG to identify the Duchenne smiles emitted while participants read a series of 25 self-relevant statements written to induce elation, anger, or neutrality while listening to emotionally consistent music. The dependent measure in this study was a covert attentional orienting task, developed by Posner (1980), again administered both at baseline and following the emotion induction. Participants' task was to respond, as quickly and as accurately as possible, to targets that appeared on either side of a central fixation point. On some trials, these targets were uncued, whereas on other trials, they were preceded by a brief visual cue that was either valid or invalid, meaning that it appeared either on the same or opposite side as the ensuing target, respectively. Changes in attentional flexibility were indexed by changes in the validity effect, calculated as the difference between reaction times to targets preceded by valid versus invalid cues. Results showed that participants with frequent Duchenne smiles showed the greatest increases in attentional flexibility (Johnson et al., 2010, Experiment 2).

Taken together, these two studies provide evidence that positive emotions, as indexed by the frequent expression of genuine (Duchenne) smiles, forecast broadened cognition, namely, holistic processing and attentional flexibility. Notably, although the randomly assigned emotion induction did not predict cognitive shifts in either of these two experiments, these inductions did predict the frequency of Duchenne smiles. In turn, frequent Duchenne smiles predicted cognitive shifts. Importantly, our strategy of assessing cognitive processing at both baseline and following the emotion induction allowed us to conclude that smiling *per se* appears to drive the observed cognitive shifts rather than any stable personality traits associated with frequent smiling. So even in cases in which people's self-reported emotions do not forecast changes in the scope of their attention, we see that fleeting changes in facial muscle activity do. Smiling, then, does not just open the face, but it also opens the mind.

Investigators in other laboratories have also found evidence to support the broaden hypothesis. Wadlinger and Isaacowitz (2006), for instance, used an eye-tracking apparatus to record the location and duration of participants' gaze 60 times per second as they viewed a sequence of 25 arrays of images from the International Affective Picture System (IAPS). Each array included one central image and two peripheral images in various locations. Within any single array, images were of the same affective valence, but between arrays, the images were selected to evoke positive, negative, or neutral affect states. Using Isen's classic technique, by random assignment, university student participants were induced to feel either a positive emotion or a neutral state by receiving a small bag of candy either before or after the eye-tracking task. Specifically, they were asked to take in the slide show "naturally, viewing whatever interests you—as if you were watching a television show." Compared to those in the neutral control condition, participants in a positive emotional state changed the focus of their gaze more frequently, and spent more total time looking at peripherally located images. These data suggest that positive emotions broaden the scope of people's visual attention.

In a conceptually related experiment, Rowe et al. (2007) examined the effects of positive and neutral states, induced through music, on breadth of visual and semantic attention. They found that, relative to sad and neutral states, positive states not only increased the scope of semantic access on a remote associates test (replicating classic work by Isen et al., 1987) but also increased the scope of visuospatial attention on a flanker task. Moreover, within the positive emotion condition, Rowe and colleagues observed a significant association between the span of visuospatial attention and the span of semantic attention, suggesting that broadened visual attention undergirds broadened semantic access (Rowe et al., 2007).

Particularly, compelling evidence for the broaden effect of positive emotions comes from an elegant brain imaging experiment conducted by Schmitz, De Rosa, and Anderson (2009). Their empirical approach rested on well-validated evidence from cognitive neuroscience that one particular brain area, the extrastriate fusiform face area, reliably responds to human faces, whereas a distinct brain area, the parahippocampal place area (PPA) reliably responds to place processing. They assessed the breadth of participants' field of view in visual cortical encoding by showing them a series of compound images that featured human faces in a central location surrounded by images of houses. Participants were asked to indicate whether the face in each compound image was male or female, while ignoring the house that surrounded the face. Positive, negative, or neutral states were induced in alternating blocks using IAPS images. The physiological indicator of emotion-related changes in scope of participants' field of view was the changes in blood flow within the PPA. Consistent with the broaden hypothesis, results showed greater activation in the PPA in the positive emotion conditions, relative to the neutral condition, suggesting that when under the influence of positive emotions, participants cannot help but take in more of the contextual surround. Notably, this study also found decreased activation in the PPA in the negative emotion condition, relative to the neutral condition, consistent with the hypothesis that negative emotions narrow people's field of view (Schmitz et al., 2009).

Intriguing evidence consistent with the broaden hypothesis has also emerged in studies of stroke patients with visual neglect due to lesions in their parietal cortex. These patients are unable to perceive and act on information presented within the visual field opposite the brain lesion. Using both controlled behavioral tasks as well as brain imaging, researchers discovered that when such patients listen to pleasant music, they overcome their loss of awareness. That is, they are temporarily able to see and act on information that simply does not register for them while not listening to music, or when listening to music they do not like (Soto et al., 2009).

Positive emotions have also been linked with better steering performance for participants in a driving simulator, consistent with the theory that broadened visual awareness contributes favorably to steering performance (Trick, Brandigampola, & Enns, 2012). Experiments also show that relative to negative emotions and neutral states, positive emotions are associated with better task switching, especially when encountering novel information (Wang & Guo, 2008).

Evidence also suggests that the broaden effect of positive emotions extends into the social domain. Relative to those experiencing neutral states, people induced to feel positive emotions expand their circle of trust (Dunn & Schweitzer, 2005). They are also more likely to form inclusive social categories (Dovidio, Gaertner, Isen, & Lowrance, 1995; Isen, Niedenthal, & Cantor, 1992) and common in-group identities such that they are more likely to see "them" as "us" (Dovidio, Isen, Guerra, Gaertner, & Rust, 1998). Likewise, Johnson and I found that under the influence of induced positive emotions the own-race bias in face perception disappears completely (Johnson & Fredrickson, 2005). Consistent with these data, Nelson (2009) found that, compared to those in neutral states or negative emotions, people experiencing positive emotions show greater perspective-taking and compassion for a person from a dissimilar cultural background. The experience of positive emotions also predicts the breadth of connection, assessed as self–other overlap, incoming college students feel with their new roommates, as well as greater perspective-taking in their understanding of their roommates' actions (Waugh & Fredrickson, 2006).

Beyond expanding the scope of people's visual, semantic, and social awareness, positive emotions also appear to broaden people's physical demeanor. In studies conducted with Melissa Gross, we used effort-shape and kinematic assessments to characterize people's body moments during different emotional states. Participants wore close-fitting exercise clothes with 31 lightweight spherical markers taped over anatomical landmarks and then engaged in a range of warm-up activities. In a large laboratory equipped with six motion capture cameras, each participant walked across the room as they relived positive, negative, or neutral emotional memories (Gross, Crane, & Fredrickson, 2012). This study included two distinct positive emotions—joy and contentment—and each was marked by a more expansive torso shape, compared to neutral, and a more extended neck and thorax, compared to sadness. Conceivably, an upright posture of the upper body and neck would enable a wider scope of visual information and more freedom of movement than a flexed spine. Expanded bodies may thereby support expanded mindsets and behavioral repertoires. These commonalities also raise the possibility of a common neurological source for the embodiment of the open hearts and open minds that are characteristic of positive emotions.

Boundary conditions of the broaden effect have been uncovered as well. Work by Gable and Harmon-Jones (2008), for instance, examined participants' reaction times to respond to global–local visual targets after viewing either neutral images or images of delicious desserts. Having found less global focus of attention after people view desserts, these authors argue that approach-related positive affect reduces the breadth of attention, as people narrowly focus on obtaining the object of their desire. These data are consistent with the speculation that I have made that positive emotions are distinct from physical pleasures (Fredrickson, 2001). While both carry a pleasant subjective feeling state, I posit that only positive emotions broaden awareness. By consequence, then, it may be that only positive emotions (and not physical pleasures) are capable of having a long-term impact on the accrual of personal and social resources. Possibly consistent with this reasoning, researchers who have tested for the broaden effect following the pleasures induced by massage therapy have found no evidence for it (Finucane & Whiteman, 2007). Of course, null results are inherently ambiguous, so my speculations about the psychological differences between positive emotions and physical pleasures await further and more rigorous empirical test.

4.2. The build hypothesis

Evidence that supports the broaden effect of positive emotions provides initial support for the broaden-and-build theory. The form of the experience of positive emotions, this evidence suggests, is expansive. Under the influence of positive emotions, people have wider perceptual access, wider semantic reach, more inclusive and connected social perceptions, and more relaxed and expansive bodily comportment. While the connections between and among these various forms of the broaden effect await further investigation, the broaden-and-build theory posits that the function of the expansive form of positive emotions is to spur the development of resources, placing people on positive trajectories of growth (Fredrickson, 1998, 2001, 2005). Consistent with this *build hypothesis*, ample research has shown that people who experience and express positive emotions more frequently than others are more resilient (Fredrickson et al., 2003), resourceful (Lyubomirsky, King, & Diener, 2005), socially connected (Mauss et al., 2011), and more likely to function at optimal levels (Fredrickson & Losada, 2005; Mauss et al., 2011).

Extending beyond such correlational evidence linking positive emotion experience to resourcefulness and optimal functioning, prospective evidence more specifically links positive emotional experience with future increases in resourcefulness and optimal functioning. Notably, the broaden-and-build theory posits that positive emotions, although fleeting, accumulate and compound over time in ways that incrementally build people's enduring resources. As such, tests of the build hypothesis defy test within one-time laboratory studies, requiring instead the frequent recurrence of positive emotional experiences plus sufficient time for resources to accrue. A number of studies that have met these criteria have uncovered evidence consistent with the build hypothesis. My students and I found, for instance, that daily experiences of positive emotions predict increases over time in trait resilience, which are in turn associated with improved life satisfaction (Cohn et al., 2009). Relatedly, Gable and colleagues found that positive emotional exchanges between partners within close relationships prospectively predict increases in relational resources over a 2-month period (Gable, Gonzaga, & Strachman, 2006; see also Algoe, Fredrickson, & Gable, 2013). Studying a sample of multiple sclerosis patients, Hart and colleagues found that positive emotions predict increases in the ability to find benefit in adversity (Hart, Vella, & Mohr, 2008).

A key extension of the prospective correlational approach to testing the build hypothesis has been to explore whether an upward spiral dynamic is produced by reciprocal prospective relations between positive emotionality and increased personal resources. That is, just as experiences of positive emotions forecast increases in personal resources, personal resources may reciprocally forecast increases over time in positive emotions. This mutual influence represents the upward spiral, depicted in Fig. 1.1, that leads to higher levels of well-being and functioning over time.

In an initial investigation into positivity-triggered upward spiral processes, Thomas Joiner and I examined the reciprocal relations between positive emotional experience and the psychological resource of broad-minded coping, which captures the degree to which people can step back from their current problems and approach them from a big picture perspective. Results revealed both that positive emotions predicted increases over time in broad-minded coping and that broad-minded coping predicted increases over time in positive emotions. Further analyses revealed that these two variables serially influenced each other. That is, initial levels of positive emotionality predicted later levels of positive emotionality in part through changes in broad-minded coping; likewise, initial levels of broad-minded coping predicted later levels of broad-minded coping in part through changes in positive emotionality (Fredrickson & Joiner, 2002).

Subsequent work has replicated and extended this initial evidence for an upward spiral dynamic between positive emotions and personal and social resources in multiple ways. Continuing my collaboration with Joiner's research team, we found that a more encompassing, factor-analytically derived index of positive coping showed the predicted reciprocal and serial relations with positive emotions over time as did an index of interpersonal trust (Burns et al., 2008). Exploring the benefits of mindfulness training, Eric Garland, Susan Gaylord, and I also found support for upward spiral dynamics in the reciprocal relations among positive reappraisals, trait mindfulness, and emotional well-being (Garland, Gaylord, & Fredrickson, 2011). In a longitudinal assessment of 258 secondary school teachers, Salanova and colleagues found that positive emotions at work (indexed as flow and intrinsic motivation) were reciprocally related both to personal resources (indexed as self-efficacy beliefs) and to organizational resources (indexed as social support and clear goals) in an upward spiral dynamic (Salanova, Bakker, & Llorens, 2006; see related work on "gain cycles" described in Ouweneel, Le Blanc, and Schaufeli (2011), Salanova, Schaufeli, Xanthopoulou, and Bakker (2010), and Salanova, Llorens, and Schaufeli (2011)).

Taking a deeper look into how today's optimal functioning begets future increases in optimal functioning through the experience of positive emotions, Lahnna Catalino and I examined the prospective and reciprocal relations among flourishing mental health, positive emotionality, and the cognitive resource of mindfulness (Catalino & Fredrickson, 2011). We found that people who flourish stand apart from their nonflourishing peers in the magnitude of the positive emotional boost they get out of everyday pleasant events, such as helping others, interacting, playing, learning, and spiritual activity. These bigger "boosts" in day-to-day positive emotion forecast greater gains over time in the cognitive resource of mindfulness, which in turn predicts increased levels of flourishing in an upward spiral dynamic.

In our first attempt to investigate the physiological substrate of upward spiral dynamics, Bethany Kok and I looked at the prospective and reciprocal relations between positive emotionality and the physical resource of cardiac vagal tone (Kok & Fredrickson, 2010). Vagal tone is assessed as the very slight yet functional arrhythmia in heart rate associated with respiration, marked by a decrease in heart rate during exhalation relative to inhalation (Grossman, 1983). As a key measure of parasympathetic influence on the heart, vagal tone is of particular interest not only because it has been related to trait positive emotionality (Oveis et al., 2009) but also because of its strong ties to both physical and mental health (Porges, 2007; Thayer & Sternberg, 2006). That is, vagal tone functions as a personal physical resource with implications for both cardiovascular and metabolic functioning as well as emotional and social well-being. Supporting the upward spiral hypothesis, our results demonstrated that vagal tone prospectively predicted increases in positive emotions over the span of 2 months and, reciprocally, that these increases in positive emotions prospectively predicted increases in vagal tone (Kok & Fredrickson, 2010). Taking vagal tone as a marker of physical health, these data show that people can become physically healthier through their experience of positive emotions.

The most decisive tests of the build hypothesis not only require longitudinal assessments together with measured (or presumed) positive emotional recurrence but also the ability to randomly assign people to distinct emotional trajectories and to link these emotional trajectories to longitudinal increments in resources. Together with my students, I made two initial attempts to reach this level of empirical rigor, yet each failed to provide the opportunity to test the build hypothesis experimentally because the interventions used, namely, finding positive meaning in daily life events, did not reliably boost positive emotional experiences (e.g., see Footnote 3 in Cohn et al., 2009; see Footnote 3 in Fredrickson & Losada, 2005). With no differences in positive emotions between experimental groups, a causal test of the build hypothesis was not possible. In late 2004, while on the lookout for a more potent and reliable intervention to increase people's daily experiences of positive emotions, I was first exposed to loving-kindness meditation (LKM; Salzberg, 1995) in a faculty seminar on integrative medicine at the University of Michigan Medical School (led by Dr. Rita Benn). Emboldened by emerging empirical interest in the long-range effects of mind-training techniques (e.g., Davidson et al., 2003), and with grant support from NIMH, I launched an initial longitudinal field experiment of the effects of learning LKM on the experience of positive emotions and resource-building (Fredrickson et al., 2008).

In the context of a workplace wellness program, we offered a 7-week meditation workshop to employees of a large computer company. The workshop was presented as an opportunity to learn techniques to "reduce stress." Two hundred and two volunteers completed an initial survey that assessed their life satisfaction, depressive symptoms, and their status on a wide range of personal resources. They were then randomly assigned to either our LKM meditation workshop or a monitoring waitlist control group. Over the next 9 weeks, both groups completed daily reports of their emotion experiences and meditation practice. About 2 weeks after the workshop ended, participants completed a final survey that reassessed their life satisfaction, depressive symptoms, and status on the same personal resources measured previously. At this same time, participants also provided a detailed account of the emotions they had experienced on that particular weekday (up to and including lunch) using the Day Reconstruction Method (DRM, Kahneman, Krueger, Schkade, Schwarz, & Stone, 2004).

First and most pivotally, our results showed that, compared to waitlist participants, people randomly assigned to learn LKM did in fact experience increasing levels of positive emotions across the 9 weeks of daily reporting. Figure 1.4 depicts this increase. Interestingly, we observed the predicted Time X Experimental Condition effect not only for our aggregate positive emotion score (computed from the mDES) but also for each of the nine specific positive emotions we assessed (inspiration was not yet an item on the mDES at the time of this study). In addition to random assignment to experimental condition, we found that individual effort, assessed as time spent meditating, also significantly predicted the daily experience of positive emotions, and did so increasingly over the 9 weeks of assessment. Indeed, we observed that for participants in the LKM group, the dose–response relationship between the time they spent meditating and the positive emotional

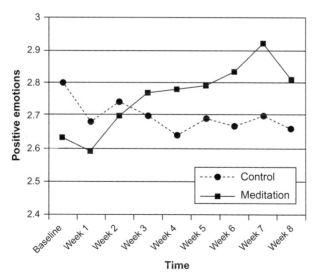

Figure 1.4 Week-by-week positive emotions by experimental condition. *Note*: Meditation training centered on loving-kindness meditation. Positive emotions were computed as the mean across all positive states on the mDES, rated on a scale from 0 to 4. *Adapted from Fredrickson et al. (2008, Fig. 2)*

yield for their invested effort *tripled* over the course of the study. No comparable or inverse effects emerged for negative emotions whatsoever, suggesting that the effects of LKM are specific to positive emotions. Additionally, the DRM data revealed that the total number of hours spent in meditative activity over the previous 9 weeks predicted the amount of positive (but not negative) emotions experienced on a typical week day morning, especially when interacting with others.

The evidence that LKM reliably increased positive emotions was pivotal because it created the necessary platform from which we could test the build hypothesis. To do so, we combined a growth model for positive emotions with an SEM path analysis to test for mediation, as depicted in Fig. 1.5, and tested it for each of the 18 resources assessed pre-and postworkshop. That is, we tested whether the slope of positive emotions predicted increases in resources (path B in Fig. 1.5). We made our test of the build hypothesis more stringent by also requiring that any increase in resources produced by increasing positive emotions be consequential as evidenced by an increase in life satisfaction or a decrease in depressive symptoms (path C in Fig. 1.5). Using these conjoint criteria, we found that 9 of the 18 resources we assessed provided support for the build hypothesis, including cognitive resources (i.e., mindfulness, pathways thinking, and the ability to savor the future), psychological

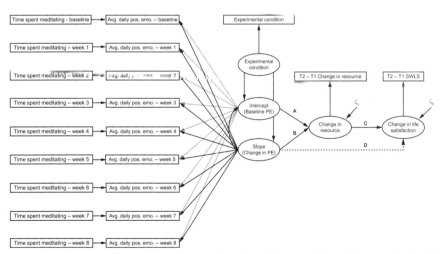

Figure 1.5 Combined latent trajectory and path-analysis model used to test the build hypothesis in the context of meditation training. Avg. daily pos. emo., Average daily positive emotions; PE, positive emotions; SWLS, satisfaction with life. Paths labeled B and C are central to tests of the build hypothesis, whereas those labeled A and D serve as statistical controls. *Adapted from Fredrickson et al. (2008, Fig. 3)*

resources (i.e., environmental mastery, self-acceptance, and purpose in life), social resources (i.e., social support received and positive relations with others), and physical resources (i.e., a reduction in self-reported illness symptoms). These were the first experimental data to support the build hypothesis.

In subsequent work using this same longitudinal experimental design, my collaborators and I have added objective measures of physical resources, most notably by measuring cardiac vagal tone before and after people learn LKM. As noted previously, vagal tone has been related both to trait positive emotionality (Oveis et al., 2009) and to physical and mental health (Porges, 2007; Thayer & Sternberg, 2006). Our primary aim was to test the hypothesis that learning to self-generate positive emotions would serve to augment vagal tone. In addition, because people with high vagal tone have been shown to be better able to regulate their attention and emotions (Porges, Doussard-Roosevelt, & Maiti, 1994), a secondary hypothesis was that these individuals would be poised to get the most out of their efforts to learn LKM.

Beyond extending our evidence for the build hypothesis into objective measures, this second field experiment on the effects of LKM allowed us to test whether the broaden effect of positive emotions accounts for its build effect. To do this, we added assessments of social connection following the daily reports of meditation practice and emotion experience. Specifically, participants called to mind their three longest social interactions of the day and, considering them as a set, rated how "in tune" and "close" they felt to the person/s in those interactions. Based on our previous evidence that positive emotions broaden people's felt social connections as indexed by perceptions of self–other overlap (Waugh & Fredrickson, 2006), we consider these daily ratings as offering an index of broadened social awareness.

Our results replicated the finding that participants randomly assigned to the LKM workshop effectively learned to self-generate increasingly more positive emotions in daily life. In addition, results showed that preworkshop vagal tone moderated this effect, supporting our hypothesis that participants with higher vagal tone would experience the largest increases in positive emotions. Moreover, the upward slope in week-by-week positive emotions also predicted an upward slope in week-by-week reports of social connection. Plus, the two experimental groups differed in their change in vagal tone over the course of the study, with those in the LKM group, on average, showing a significantly larger increase. We tested the plausible causal pathways of this effect on vagal tone by using a variant of a mediational, parallel process latent curve model. The overall model fit provided strong support for the build hypothesis as well as for mediation by broadening and moderation by initial vagal tone. In other words, the upward slope in positive emotions accounted for the upward slope in broadened reports of social connection, and positive emotions and social broadening in turn mediated the effect of LKM on the increase in vagal tone, all of which was moderated by initial vagal tone. This is the first experimental evidence that supports both aspects of the broaden-and-build theory: that positive emotions build consequential resources, in this case, vagal tone, through the effect they have on broadened awareness, in this case, by making people feel closer, more connected, and in tune with others in daily life (Kok et al., 2012).

In more recent experimental work, Kok and I tested whether a very minimal social connection intervention might produce similar effects on positive emotions and vagal tone as does the more intensive LKM workshop (Kok & Fredrickson, in press). The intervention in this case was simply the two questions to which people were asked to respond concerning their longest social interactions of the day, as used in the previous study. Specifically, participants rated how "close to" and "in tune with" their interaction partners they felt each day for 49 consecutive days. We were inspired to test this very minimal intervention because our first longitudinal study that included these two questions daily was the first study in which we had ever found that daily positive emotions increased for all participants—even for those within the waitlist control group—and this increase predicted an increase in vagal tone. I described these findings earlier, as reflecting an upward spiral between positive emotions and vagal tone (Kok & Fredrickson, 2010). To test whether merely reflecting on social connections might *cause* upswings in positive emotions with attendant increases in vagal tone, we randomly assigned participants to reflect either on these two social connection questions or on two placebo questions that inquired how "useful" and "important" their three longest tasks that day had been for them. As hypothesized, participants randomly assigned to the social connection condition reported significantly greater week-by-week increases in their positive emotions (with no parallel or opposing pattern for their negative emotions). In addition, experimental condition produced increases in vagal tone, an effect mediated by the upswing in positive emotions. As in our past work, we also found that initial levels of vagal tone moderated these effects, yet this time, participants with low vagal tone were the ones to experience the biggest positive emotion uplift from the intervention. We speculate that because low vagal tone is associated with lower social skill and lesser ability to regulate one's own attention and emotions, this very minimal intervention may have matched the skill levels for people low on vagal tone, but may have been too elementary, and therefore more frustrating, for those high in vagal tone (Kok & Fredrickson, in press). In any case, in support of the build hypothesis, it appears that when people learn to self-generate more frequent positive emotions—either through meditation or through more elemental shifts in their attention—they launch themselves onto positive trajectories of growth.

5. NEW FRONTIERS FOR THE BROADEN-AND-BUILD THEORY

5.1. Deeper investigations into biological resources built

Some of the latest evidence from my PEP Lab documents that people who can cultivate more frequent positive emotions can shift their characteristic cardiovascular patterns toward health, as indexed by increases in vagal tone (Kok et al., in press). Inspired by these data, the PEP Lab is now engaged in testing whether people's efforts to increase their daily diets of positive emotions build other biological resources for health as well. In a project currently underway (funded by the National Institute for Nursing Research through the NIH initiative to advance the Science of Behavior Change), we are investigating whether, in addition to increasing vagal tone, a stable rise in positive emotions also yields enduring increases in tonic oxytocin levels, as assessed in urine samples gathered over a 24-h period, and enduring reductions in systolic and diastolic blood pressure. Karen Grewen and Kathleen Light are key PEP Lab collaborators on this work. Previously, oxytocin could only be assessed reliably in humans from plasma or cerebral spinal fluid. Recent breakthroughs have led to new methods to assay oxytocin noninvasively, through enzyme immunoassay of urine samples, a procedure pioneered by Grewen and Light (Grewen, Girdler, Amico, & Light, 2005; Grewen, Light, Mechlin, & Girdler, 2008; Light, Grewen, & Amico, 2005; Light et al., 2004). Our approach of collecting 24-h urine samples as people behave normally in their home environments allows us to infer characteristic and presumably stable levels of oxytocin. We conceptualize higher tonic levels of oxytocin as a biological resource for health based on past evidence that higher oxytocin levels predict lower blood pressure and reduced stress.

In this same project, we also venture into social genomics by investigating whether a stable rise in positive emotions also produces reliable changes in gene expression, particular within genes related to the immune system's regulation of inflammatory processes. Our interest in inflammation was inspired by the cytokine theory of depression, which asserts that basal production levels of inflammatory mediators in peripheral tissues signal the brain to produce "sickness behaviors" including decreased positive affect and motivation and increased negative affect and social withdrawal (Dantzer, 2001; Dantzer & Kelley, 2007). Steve Cole is a key PEP Lab collaborator on this work. Cole's pioneering bioinformatics approach to social genomics has linked the increased expression of proinflammatory cytokine genes to various circumstances replete with chronic negative affect such as loneliness (Cole et al., 2007), social stress (Miller et al., 2008; Miller, Rohleder, & Cole, 2009), low socioeconomic status (Chen et al., 2009), and general social adversity (Cole et al., 2010). Our current work not only extends human social genomics into the domain of positive emotions but also expands it from correlational to experimental designs, which will substantially enhance understanding of how people's patterns of emotion experience and expression may alter their patterns of gene expression, with attendant consequences for physical health. We are thus poised to discover whether and to what extent positive emotions function to build cellular resources.

5.2. Clinical and organizational applications

Putting the broaden-and-build theory to use with aims to alleviate psychological disorders or optimize organizational functioning has become a growing interest. One line of clinical application emerged following a presentation I made on the PEP Lab's first LKM field experiment to the Clinical Psychology Doctoral Program at the University of North Carolina—Chapel Hill. Noting that LKM increased people's ability to savor future events (Fredrickson et al., 2008), my UNC colleague and schizophrenia expert, David Penn, suspected that it might also be particularly helpful for individuals experiencing the negative symptoms of schizophrenia. Unlike the positive symptoms of schizophrenia, which include hallucinations and delusions, negative symptoms involve a variety of intertwined emotional and behavioral deficits, including anhedonia (diminished pleasure), avolition (diminished motivation), asociality (diminished interest in or desire for interpersonal interactions), alogia (diminished speech), and blunted affect (diminished expression of affect). Negative symptoms are especially vexing because they are resistant to treatment and greatly diminish the quality of life. Ann Kring, a schizophrenia researcher at UC Berkeley, has proposed that individuals with schizophrenia experience normal levels of positive emotions, or consummatory pleasure, when they directly engaged in enjoyable activities, yet suffer disturbances in the experience of positive emotions in relation to future activities, or anticipatory pleasure (Kring, 1999). Both self-report and fMRI data support this distinction (Gard, Kring, Gard,

Horan, & Green, 2007; Juckel et al., 2006). Penn, together with David Johnson, a graduate student at that time, put Kring's proposal together with the PEP Lab's finding on savoring the future and suggested that we collaborate to explore whether LKM, used as an adjunctive treatment to medication, could reduce negative symptoms for individuals with schizophrenia. To pilot this idea, we conducted an open trial across two LKM group-based workshops with 18 outpatients at the University of North Carolina Hospitals. Our results were promising. First, the overall attendance rate was 84%, which is remarkable for clients with negative symptoms who are known to have difficulties with motivation and social interaction. More importantly, however, clients showed significant improvements in their negative symptoms as well as their positive emotions and life satisfaction, all of which maintained at 3-month follow-up (Johnson et al., 2011; see also Johnson et al., 2009).

Extending from these promising initial data on schizophrenia, I have worked with Eric Garland and colleagues to articulate more precisely how the upward spiral dynamics triggered by positive emotions might be used to counter the downward spiral dynamics of negativity that characterize a number of emotion dysfunctions and deficits in psychopathology (Garland & Fredrickson, in press; Garland et al., 2010). Emotions, we point out, are self-organizing systems that operate to maximize and maintain their own existence. Despair, for example, triggers narrowed, ruminative, and pessimistic patterns of thought alongside behavioral withdrawal and sluggishness, thought–action tendencies that serve to increase the odds that despair will continue and exacerbate in a self-destructive cycle. Positive emotions, by contrast, trigger broadened, curious, and optimistic patterns of thought together with more spontaneous and energetic behavior. These thought–action tendencies increase the odds that people find positive meaning in their future circumstances in ways that seed further positive emotions that decrease stress, provide emotional uplift, and support resilience. Figure 1.6 depicts this process. We propose that upward and downward spirals are not mirror opposites. Beyond their differences in valence and direction, upward spirals are more open, permeable, flexible, and social than downward spirals. These distinctions may thus make positive emotion, and the broadened thought–action repertoires and upward spirals they trigger, linchpins in the prevention and treatment of the inertia often observed among those with clinical disorders, particularly depression and anxiety.

The broaden-and-build theory has also been applied within organizations with an eye toward creating workplace climates that foster innovative

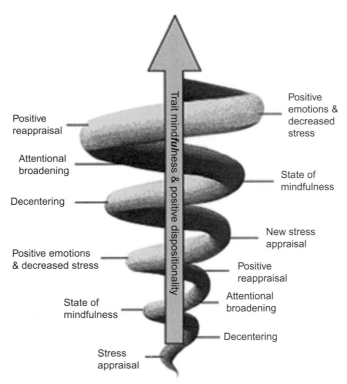

Figure 1.6 Upward spirals of positive emotions that can counter downward spirals of negativity. *Adapted from Garland et al. (2010, Fig. 2)*

ways to build more sustainable business practices that both promote workers' health and inspire their productivity (Vacharkulksemsuk, Sekerka, & Fredrickson, 2011). As just one example, in a study of workers from a broad range of organizations with their immediate supervisors, Carson and colleagues found that the positive emotions that supervisors have at the intersections of their work and family lives cross over to create similar positive experiences for their subordinates. This positive contagion effect was found to be mediated by subordinates' perceptions of greater autonomy in setting their work schedules, and ultimately led to improvements in their job performance (Carlson, Kacmar, Zivnuska, Ferguson, & Whitten, 2011). Another, massive organizational intervention, based in part on broaden-and-build principles, is now underway in the U.S. Army, under the auspices of the army-wide Comprehensive Soldier Fitness initiative (Cornum, Matthews, & Seligman, 2011). Training soldiers in basic skills associated emotional fitness, including the ability to increase the frequency and duration of positive emotions, is part of the Army's overall efforts to build greater resilience to the inevitable adversity and trauma that soldiers experience during deployment to war zones (Algoe & Fredrickson, 2011; see also Luthans, Vogelgesang, & Lester, 2006).

6. OFFSHOOTS FROM THE BROADEN-AND-BUILD THEORY

6.1. The upward spiral theory of lifestyle change

A current overarching goal of my PEP Lab is to investigate whether and how positive emotions alter people's bodily systems and nonconscious motives in ways that ultimately reinforce lifestyle change, defined as sustained adherence to positive health behaviors. The U.S. National Cancer Institute recently put forth the question "Why don't more people alter behaviors known to increase the risk of cancers?" (NIH RFA-CA-11-011). The need to address this question is enormous, given that the American Cancer Society estimates that 62% of all cancers could be prevented altogether through lifestyle change. Yet the question has long defied a rigorous and satisfying answer because too often we have assumed that knowledge is power. People *know* that their daily behavioral choices—about their physical activities and intake of food, tobacco, and alcohol—accumulate and compound to set their risks for cancer and other chronic diseases that shorten lives. Armed with this knowledge, millions resolve to make changes each year. Yet most attempts at lifestyle change fail because knowledge is not powerful enough to override implicit nonconscious desires.

An intriguing association between positive emotions and lifestyle change first emerged in my lab when my former student and collaborator Michael Cohn conducted a follow-up to our initial study (Fredrickson et al., 2008) of the effects of learning how to self-generate more frequent positive emotions through LKM. Our results, presented in Fig. 1.7, showcase the substantial power of positive emotions to predict sustained behavior change: Individuals one standard deviation above the mean in their positive emotional response to their newly adopted health behavior of LKM were ~4.5 times more likely to main that behavior 15 months later, compared to those one standard deviation below the mean (Cohn & Fredrickson, 2010). The extent of people's early positive emotional reactivity to LKM was the sole psychological predictor of whether, more than 1 year later, they voluntarily choose to continue meditating as a regular habit.

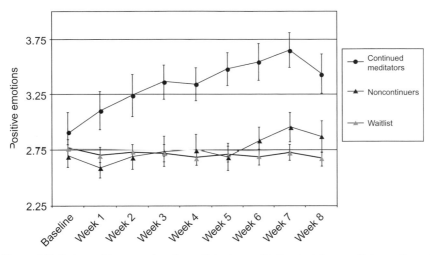

Figure 1.7 Early positive emotional reactivity to meditation training predicts continued meditation at 15-month follow-up. *Adapted from Cohn and Fredrickson (2010, Fig. 1)*

These and other data inspired me to develop a new theoretical offshoot of the broaden-and-build theory, one that I call the *upward spiral model of lifestyle change*. This model states that positive emotions can both knit people to new positive health behaviors and also raise their overall psychological propensity for a suite of wellness behaviors. Positive emotions achieve what New Year's resolutions cannot by motivating sustained adherence to health behaviors by the carrot of flexible, nonconscious desire rather than the whip of rigid, conscious willpower. The upward spiral model of lifestyle change expands on the broaden-and-build theory substantially by articulating key roles for (a) nonconscious motives sparked by positive emotions; (b) a range of wellness behaviors through which individuals become more active, curious, and socially engaged, and ultimately healthier and more resilient; and (c) individual differences in mutable resources, both biological (e.g., oxytocin, cardiac vagal tone, inflammation) and psychological (e.g., resilience, other-focus, mindfulness), that predispose certain people to successful long-term lifestyle change by moderating the positive emotion yield of their wellness behaviors.

The spiral frame of this new model rests on evidence that the relations between emotions and lifestyle-relevant resources are reciprocal. For example, whereas Co-Investigator Cole's past work suggests that negative emotionality prompts proinflammatory processes, experimental work by Eisenberger and colleagues documents the reverse causal pathway, from inflammation to affect (Eisenberger, Inagaki, Rameson, Mashal, & Irwin, 2009). Specifically, these investigators randomly assigned healthy adult volunteers to receive either an inflammatory challenge (i.e., an injection of endotoxin) or a placebo injection. Those under the influence of endotoxin reported increased feelings of social disconnection, which in turn increased depressed mood. In line with the cytokine theory of depression, this and other work suggests that inflammation by itself can alter the affective properties of social and other wellness behaviors. Evidence for such reciprocal and mutual influence can explain the downward spiral dynamic that emerges between negative emotions and negative health behaviors that can lead to the further entrenchment of inflammation-related chronic diseases, such as type II diabetes, cardiovascular disease (both hypertension and stroke), and arthritis.

Preliminary evidence supports my hypothesis that an opposing upward spiral dynamic can emerge between positive emotions and positive health behaviors. As described earlier, a range of biological and psychological resources—namely, vagal tone, oxytocin, resilience, other-focus, and mindfulness—not only predict enhanced positive emotions, but also have been shown to increase with enhanced positive emotion (Burns et al., 2008; Cohn et al., 2009; Fredrickson et al., 2008; Holt-Lunstad, Birmingham, & Light, 2008; Kok & Fredrickson, 2010; Oveis et al., 2009; Waugh & Fredrickson, 2006). This reciprocal causality sets the stage for upward spiral processes to unfold that can further reinforce adherence to positive health behaviors.

Another key driver of the upward spiral dynamic between positive emotions and positive health behaviors posited by the upward spiral model is the nonconscious incentive salience or "wanting" that any past pleasant experience engenders. This aspect of the theory stems from recent advances in behavioral neuroscience that unpacks the complex reward system into separate "liking" and "wanting" systems, fueled by opioid and dopamine activation, respectively (Berridge, 2007). Over time, "liking" a given activity—the situated experience of positive affect—precedes and produces cue-triggered "wanting" for that same activity—which in turn motivates decisions to repeat that activity, even nonconsciously. Through such dopaminergic Pavlovian learning, cues associated with past pleasant experiences gain nonconscious incentive salience and become intrinsically alluring as if covered in eye-catching glitter dust. In the case of drug addictions, "wanting" becomes decoupled from "liking" as addicts attempting recovery experience intense cravings triggered by behavior-related cues (e.g., drug paraphernalia) even though the drug no longer provides pleasure (Robinson & Berridge, 2003). The novel premise of the upward spiral model is that the same nonconscious, biologically based processes that underlie people's unbidden cravings to enact unhealthy lifestyles can be harnessed to foster similar, yet positive cravings to enact healthy lifestyles, making cues to positive health behaviors sparkle with incentive salience that nonconsciously prompts behavioral adherence. Whereas both physical pleasures and positive emotions carry the pleasant subjective feel that sparks nonconscious incentive salience, or "wanting," as I suggested earlier, it appears that only positive emotions—and not pleasures—broaden cognition. As such, positive emotions appear to have unique psychological properties beyond triggering approach-related motivation. Perhaps most significantly, positive emotions, in widening people's awareness, engender flexible and creative behavioral choices rather than rigidly pursued behavioral addictions.

Figure 1.8 provides a conceptual depiction of the upward spiral model. This new model incorporates the broaden-and-build theory as the outer loop of a dual-layered spiral. This layer, as this chapter has shown, rests on the now substantial evidence that positive emotions broaden cognition and build resources. The inner loop of the dual-layered spiral incorporates Berridge's perspectives on liking versus wanting and positions nonconscious motives rooted in positive emotions (as distinct from physical pleasures) as key drivers of flexible—and therefore sustainable—decisions to maintain wellness behaviors. Tethering the outer and inner loops together, the model posits that certain biological and psychological resources, known to be built up through repeated experiences of positive emotions, also serve to increase the subsequent positive emotion yield of a range of wellness behaviors. According

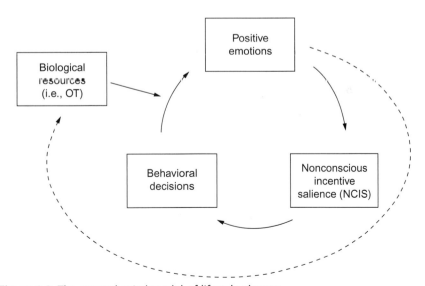

Figure 1.8 The upward spiral model of lifestyle change.

to the upward spiral model, to the extent that a new wellness behavior evokes positive emotions, engaging in that behavior generates both (a) cue–triggered nonconscious motives that shape subsequent behavioral decisions, represented by the inner loop depicted in Fig. 1.8, and (b) increases in key biological and psychological resources that boost the subsequent positive emotion yield of that wellness behavior, as represented by the outer loop of the spiral, and most critically, by the causal arrow that runs between the inner and outer loops (see Fig. 1.8). The PEP Lab has a series of longitudinal studies underway (supported by NINR and NCI) to test this new theoretical offshoot of the broaden-and-build theory.

7. POSITIVITY RESONANCE: BROADEN-AND-BUILD IN SYNC WITH OTHERS

Back in my initial presentation of the broaden-and-build theory (Fredrickson, 1998), I included love as one of four positive emotions featured, the others being joy, interest, and contentment. Love is complex, however, in that most theorists acknowledge that love is not a single emotion and that people experience varieties of it (e.g., romantic or passionate love vs. companionate love vs. nurturant love vs. attachment love). Moreover, love experiences need to be distinguished from love relationships. Whereas the latter might last a lifetime, the former, my focus here, last only moments. Back in 1998, I adopted a perspective on love that I had found in Izard (1977) work, that love comprises any other positive emotion that is felt in the context of people's connections with others. As Izard put it, "acquaintances or friends renew your interest by revealing new aspects of themselves and the resulting increase in familiarity (deeper knowledge of the person) brings joy [and contentment]. In lasting friendships or love relationships, this cycle is repeated endlessly." (1977, p. 243).[3] So as I forecast earlier and in Table 1.1, my initial theorizing on broaden-and-build processes presented love as an "all of the above" positive emotion. To the extent that love triggered the more specific moments of interest, contentment, joy, and the like, it also broadened people's thought–action repertoires and build their enduring personal resources, particularly their social bonds.

Viewing love as any positive emotions shared between two or more people is a reasonable initial description of love to be sure. Looking back,

---

[3] Note that interest and joy were the only two positive emotions about which Izard wrote. He did, however, describe a low arousal state of "mild or receptive joy" that I think is better characterized as contentment or serenity.

however, I see that it does not go nearly far enough to fully describe what happens in those potent interpersonal moments of shared positivity. In my most recent theorizing on love (Fredrickson, 2013), I add two further defining attributes of this most ubiquitous and consequential positive emotion, in addition to shared positivity. These are biobehavioral synchrony and mutual care.

Biobehavioral synchrony refers to the mirroring across people's behaviors, bodies, and brains that each moment of shared positive emotional connection creates. Studying the nonverbal gestures of two people just getting to know one another, Tanya Vacharkulksemsuk and I have found that nonverbal behavioral synchrony is a key mechanism through which self-disclosure produces an embodied sense of rapport (Vacharkulksemsuk & Fredrickson, 2012). Studying changes in oxytocin within parents and their infants engaged in face-to-face play, Ruth Feldman and colleagues have discovered that positivity-infused behavioral synchrony—the degree to which a mother, through eye contact and affectionate touch, laughs, smiles, and coos in time together with her infant—predicts a synchrony between the oxytocin surges evident within both her and her infant. The same pattern of oxytocin synchrony also emerges for fathers and their infants (Feldman, Gordon, & Zagoory-Sharon, 2010). Another indication of biological synchrony can be drawn from the brain imaging work of Uri Hasson and colleagues. Using fMRI of people's brains while either telling or listening to an engaging story, Hasson and colleagues find widespread brain coupling between speaker and listener, especially during emotional moments and for pairs for whom communication is particularly effective (Hasson, 2010; Hasson, Nir, Levy, Fuhrmann, & Malach, 2004; Stephens, Silbert, & Hasson, 2010). It appears, then, that when people share a positive emotional state, they also share gestural, biochemical, and neural patterns. A biobehavioral unity or oneness unfolds.

Like all emotions, love sparks motivational changes. Beyond the thought–action tendencies associated with whichever particular positive emotion is at that moment shared, love motivates mutual care. Each person, in a moment of shared positivity, becomes momentarily invested in the other's well-being. This is an idea I draw from crossing emotions science with relationship science. The momentary experience of love brings an urge to focus on the other person, holistically, with care and concern for his or her well-being, a motive that momentarily eclipses any tendency toward self-absorption. And this caring motive is mutual, reflected back and forth between the two. Whereas relationship scientists cast caring and responsive investment in the well-being of another for his or her own sake as a hallmark of intimate and loving relationships (Hegi & Bergner, 2010; Reis, Clark, & Holmes, 2004), I see mutual care as a momentary state that rises and falls in step with changes in context and emotion.

I call this trio of occurrences *positivity resonance* (Fredrickson, 2013). Within moments of interpersonal connection that are characterized by this amplifying synchrony—of shared positive emotions, biobehavioral synchrony, and mutual care—resource-building positivity resonates between and among people. This back-and-forth reverberation of positive emotional energy sustains itself—and can even grow stronger—until the momentary connection inevitably wanes.

Indeed, I posit sensory and temporal connection as a fundamental precondition for moments of positivity resonance to emerge (Fredrickson, 2013). Neither abstract nor mediated, connection like this is physical and unfolds in real time, as gained through eye contact, touch, shared voice, or mirrored body movements.

Eye contact appears to be especially powerful (Farroni, Csibra, Simion, & Johnson, 2002; Niedenthal, Mermillod, Maringer, & Hess, 2010). Eye contact, studies show, is necessary for facial mimicry to unfold (Schrammel, Pannasch, Graupner, Mojzisch, & Velichkovsky, 2009), and facial mimicry, in turn, is needed to accurately decode what another person is feeling (Maringer, Krumhuber, Fischer, & Niedenthal, 2011). According to Niedenthal and colleagues' *Simulation of Smiles* (*SIMS*) *model* (Niedenthal et al., 2010), brain coupling mediates the effect of facial mimicry on decoding accuracy, whereas eye contact moderates the effect.

Extending the ideas on embodied cognition presented in the SIMS model, I have proposed that the evolved adaptive function of spontaneous and genuine smiles—what have been termed Duchenne smiles—goes beyond what other theorists have suggested. Following Darwin (1872), Ekman and colleagues contend that such smiles evolved as an outward expression of a person's otherwise unseen inner subjective state (Ekman, Davidson, & Friesen, 1990). An opposing view shifts the focus onto the recipient of a smile and proposes that smiles evolved not because they provided readouts of positive emotional states, but instead because they evoked positive emotions in those who meet a smiling person's gaze (Owren & Bachorowski, 2003; see also Gervais & Wilson, 2005). Maintaining the focus on the person who meets the smiler's gaze, the embodied cognition perspective of the SIMS model suggests that, through neural simulation, smiles tune an observer toward a better understanding of the smiler's subjective experience and motives (Niedenthal et al., 2010). Each of these accounts of the function of genuine smiles seems viable, albeit I have argued that each remains incomplete by remaining anchored too exclusively within an individual-level psychology.

Stepping up to the dyadic level, in which both the smiler and the smile recipient play equal and important roles, I have proposed that the function of Duchenne smiles is to create a moment of intersubjectivity characterized by positivity resonance, as reflected by the trio of love's features: a now shared positive emotion, biobehavioral synchrony, and an orientation toward mutual care (Fredrickson, 2013). Harkening back to the broaden-and-build theory, to the extent that positivity resonance builds resources in individuals and in dyads, genuine smiles may have evolved to spur positive psychosocial development and improved physical health in individuals, relationships, and indeed whole communities. Casting love as a moment of positivity resonance, then, offers a detailed evolutionary perspective on how genuine smiles do good both within the body and within society.[4]

Recalling the recent evidence (from my PEP Lab) that shows that positive emotions improve physical health, as indexed by increases in cardiac vagal tone, *through people's experiences of social connection* (Kok et al., in press), leads me to speculate that love, defined as a form of social connection marked by positivity resonance, may perhaps be the most generative and consequential of all positive emotions. That is, I hypothesize that love broadens and builds to a greater degree than other, individually experienced positive emotions. Love, then, may not be just another positive emotion. By virtue of being a single state, distributed across and reverberating between the brains and bodies of two (or more) individuals, love's ability to broaden mindsets and build resources may have substantially greater reach.

8. CLOSING COMMENTS

The science of positive emotions has matured greatly since the 1990s, when I first began work in this area. This maturity is reflected in the emergence of the first and second edited volumes devoted exclusively to empirical

---

[4] Although for simplicity I have depicted positivity resonance here as a property of dyads, I see it as equally able to account for communal experiences of shared positivity, or what Haidt and colleagues refer to as an innate *hive psychology* which periodically propels humans to lose themselves enjoyably in a much larger social organism, like the crowd at a football game, music festival, or religious revival (Haidt, Seder, & Kesebir, 2008). Through physical co-presence and behavioral synchrony, positivity resonance thus can spread from dyads to whole crowds or communities (e.g., Fowler & Christakis, 2009).

research on positive emotions, namely, the *Handbook of Positive Emotions*, edited by Michele Tugade, Michelle L. Shiota, and Leslie Kirby, forthcoming from Guilford Press, and the *Dark and Light Sides of Positive Emotions*, edited by June Gruber and Judith Moskowitz, forthcoming from Oxford University Press. It has been equal parts gratifying and humbling to see that the broaden-and-build theory has offered one generative framework for sustained empirical contributions in this now-active area of emotions science.

Perhaps the most pivotal nudge that the broaden-and-build perspective has offered the field is to fully untether our collective scientific imagination about the value of positive emotions. Evidence for the broaden and undo effects of positive emotions demonstrates that fruitful advances can be made by looking beyond the emotional rewards that good feelings bring. Likewise, evidence for the build effect of positive emotions shows that it pays to look beyond the experiential moment to understand the function of these positive states over the long term. Now, new theorizing about positivity resonance suggests that we may also need to look beyond the familiar individual-level psychological processes to better grasp the full potential of positive emotions.

To be sure, the empirical discoveries made thus far about positive emotions raise many more questions. Additional empirical work is still needed. We have only the slimmest empirical literature, for instance, on the neuroscience of positive emotions (for exemplary contributions see work by Adam Anderson's lab at the University of Toronto and Tor Wager's lab at the University of Colorado at Boulder). We also need to expand further into epigenetics, to chart how positive emotional processes build cellular resources (social genomics pioneer Steve Cole collaborates with my PEP Lab in this area). We also need far more work on the differences and similarities in the ways positive emotions shape, and are shaped by, distinct cultures around the globe (for exemplary contributions, see work by Jeanne Tsai's lab at Stanford University and Shigehiro Oishi's lab at the University of Virginia; see also Lee, Lin, Huang, & Fredrickson, 2012). Finally, although many of the momentary and downstream effects of positive emotions are beneficial, we cannot assume that they are exclusively or invariably so. Additional studies are needed to explore the boundary conditions of the benefits of positive emotions as well as their potential dark sides (for exemplary work in this vein, see work by June Gruber's lab at Yale University; see also McNulty & Fincham, 2012; Vincent, Emich, & Gonalo, in press).

When I consider the current cadre of creative and impeccably trained early-career scientists who have already devoted considerable empirical attention to the science of positive emotions, I feel confident that the light-hearted aspects of human experience will never again be cast out of psychological science. With continued application of the most rigorous empirical approaches, our empirical understanding of positive emotions will broaden and build and perhaps even yield discoveries important enough to rid psychology of its long-held inferiority complex once and for all. Time and data will tell.

APPENDIX

modified Differential Emotions Scale

Instructions: Please think back to how you have felt during the past 24 h. Using the 0–4 scale below, indicate the *greatest amount* that you have experienced each of the following feelings.

Not at all	A little bit	Moderately	Quite a bit	Extremely
0	1	2	3	4

_____ 1. What is the most **amused, fun-loving**, or **silly** you felt?

_____ 2. What is the most **angry, irritated**, or **annoyed** you felt?

_____ 3. What is the most **ashamed, humiliated**, or **disgraced** you felt?

_____ 4. What is the most **awe, wonder**, or **amazement** you felt?

_____ 5. What is the most **contemptuous, scornful**, or **disdainful** you felt?

_____ 6. What is the most **disgust, distaste**, or **revulsion** you felt?

_____ 7. What is the most **embarrassed, self-conscious**, or **blushing** you felt?

_____ 8. What is the most **grateful, appreciative**, or **thankful** you felt?

_____ 9. What is the most **guilty, repentant**, or **blameworthy** you felt?

_____ 10. What is the most **hate, distrust**, or **suspicion** you felt?

_____ 11. What is the most **hopeful, optimistic**, or **encouraged** you felt?

_____ 12. What is the most **inspired, uplifted**, or **elevated** you felt?

_____ 13. What is the most **interested, alert**, or **curious** you felt?

_____ 14. What is the most **joyful, glad**, or **happy** you felt?

_____ 15. What is the most **love, closeness**, or **trust** you felt?

_____ 16. What is the most **proud, confident**, or **self-assured** you felt?

_____ 17. What is the most **sad, downhearted**, or **unhappy** you felt?

_____ 18. What is the most **scared, fearful**, or **afraid** you felt?

_____ 19. What is the most **serene, content**, or **peaceful** you felt?

_____ 20. What is the most **stressed, nervous**, or **overwhelmed** you felt?

Based on Fredrickson (2009) and Fredrickson et al. (2003. Scoring: Use single items to assess specific emotions, or create overall positive and negative emotion scores by computing the mean of 10 positive and 10 negative emotions, respectively. Instructions can be modified to assess emotions in response to specific incidents (e.g., laboratory manipulations or episodes recalled using the Day Reconstruction Method). Scale can be modified to capture emotions experienced over the past 2 weeks by changing the instructions to "how often you've experienced...," the items to "How often have you felt _____?" and the response options to 0, never; 1, rarely; 2, some of the time; 3, often; 4, most of the time.

REFERENCES

Algoe, S. B. (2012). Find, remind, and bind: The functions of gratitude in everyday relationships. *Social and Personality Psychology Compass, 6*(6), 455–469.

Algoe, S. B., & Fredrickson, B. L. (2011). Emotional fitness and the movement of affective science from lab to field. *American Psychologist, 66*(1), 35–42.

Algoe, S. B., Fredrickson, B. L., & Gable, S. L. (in press). The social functions of gratitude via expression. *Emotion*.

Algoe, S. B., & Haidt, J. (2009). Witnessing excellence in action: The "other-praising" emotions of elevation, gratitude, and admiration. *The Journal of Positive Psychology, 4*(2), 105–127.

Barkow, J. H., Cosmides, L., & Tooby, J. (1992). *The adapted mind: Evolutionary psychology and the generation of culture*. New York: Oxford University Press.

Basso, M. R., Schefft, B. K., Ris, M. D., & Dember, W. N. (1996). Mood and global-local visual processing. *Journal of the International Neuropsychological Society, 2*(3), 249–255.

Berridge, K. C. (2007). The debate over dopamine's role in reward: The case for incentive salience. *Psychopharmacology, 191*(3), 391–431.

Block, J., & Kremen, A. M. (1996). IQ and ego-resiliency: Conceptual and empirical connections and separateness. *Journal of Personality and Social Psychology, 70*(2), 349–361.

Bolte, A., Goschke, T., & Kuhl, J. (2003). Emotion and intuition: Effects of positive and negative mood on implicit judgments of semantic coherence. *Psychological Science, 14* (5), 416–421.

Burns, A. B., Brown, J. S., Sachs-Ericsson, N., Plant, E. A., Curtis, J. T., Fredrickson, B. L., et al. (2008). Upward spirals of positive emotion and coping: Replication, extension, and initial exploration of neurochemical substrates. *Personality and Individual Differences, 44*(2), 360–370.

Cannon, W. B. (1929). *Bodily changes in pain, hunger, fear, and rage*. New York: D. Appleton & Co.

Carlson, D., Kacmar, K. M., Zivnuska, S., Ferguson, M., & Whitten, D. (2011). Work-family enrichment and job performance: A constructive replication of affective events theory. *Journal of Occupational Health Psychology, 16*(3), 297–312.

Catalino, L. I., & Fredrickson, B. L. (2011). A Tuesday in the life of a flourisher: The role of positive emotional reactivity in optimal mental health. *Emotion, 11*(4), 938–950.

Chen, E., Miller, G. E., Walker, H. A., Arevalo, J. M., Sung, C. Y., & Cole, S. W. (2009). Genome-wide transcriptional profiling linked to social class in asthma. *Thorax, 64*(1), 38–43.

Cohn, M. A., & Fredrickson, B. L. (2010). In search of durable positive psychology interventions: Predictors and consequences of long-term positive behavior change. *The Journal of Positive Psychology, 5*(5), 355–366.

Cohn, M. A., Fredrickson, B. L., Brown, S. L., Mikels, J. A., & Conway, A. M. (2009). Happiness unpacked: Positive emotions increase life satisfaction by building resilience. *Emotion*, *9*(3), 361–368.

Cole, S. W., Arevalo, J. M. G., Takahashi, R., Sloan, E. K., Lutgendorf, S. K., Sood, A. K., et al. (2010). Computational identification of gene-social environment interaction at the human IL6 locus. *Proceedings of the National Academy of Sciences of the United States of America*, *107*(12), 5681–5686.

Cole, S. W., Hawkley, L. C., Arevalo, J. M., Sung, C. Y., Rose, R. M., & Cacioppo, J. T. (2007). Social regulation of gene expression in human leukocytes. *Genome Biology*, *8*(9), R189.

Compton, R. J., Wirtz, D., Pajoumand, G., Claus, E., & Heller, W. (2004). Association between positive affect and attentional shifting. *Cognitive Therapy and Research*, *28*(6), 733–744.

Cornum, R., Matthews, M. D., & Seligman, M. E. P. (2011). Comprehensive soldier fitness: Building resilience in a challenging institutional context. *American Psychologist*, *66*(1), 4–9.

Csikszentmihalyi, M. (1990). *Flow: The psychology of optimal experience*. New York: Harper and Row.

Dantzer, R. (2001). Cytokine-induced sickness behavior: Where do we stand? *Brain, Behavior, and Immunity*, *15*(1), 7–24.

Dantzer, R., & Kelley, K. W. (2007). Twenty years of research on cytokine-induced sickness behavior. *Brain, Behavior, and Immunity*, *21*(2), 153–160.

Darwin, C. (1872). *On the importance of emotional expression for survival and adaptation*. London: John Murray Publishers.

Davidson, R. J. (1998). Affective style and affective disorders: Perspectives from affective neuroscience. *Cognition and Emotion*, *12*(3), 307–330.

Davidson, R. J., Kabat-Zinn, J., Schumacher, J., Rosenkranz, M., Muller, D., Santorelli, S. F., et al. (2003). Alterations in brain and immune function produced by mindfulness meditation. *Psychosomatic Medicine*, *65*(4), 564–570.

Derryberry, D., & Tucker, D. M. (1992). Neural mechanisms of emotion. *Journal of Consulting and Clinical Psychology*, *60*(3), 329–338.

Dovidio, J. F., Gaertner, S. L., Isen, A. M., & Lowrance, R. (1995). Group-representations and intergroup bias: Positive affect, similarity, and group-size. *Personality and Social Psychology Bulletin*, *21*(8), 856–865.

Dovidio, J. F., Isen, A. M., Guerra, P., Gaertner, S. L., & Rust, M. (1998). Positive affect, cognition, and the reduction of intergroup bias. In C. Sedikides (Ed.), *Intergroup cognition and intergroup behavior* (pp. 337–366). Mahwah, NJ: Erlbaum.

Dreisbach, G., & Goschke, T. (2004). How positive affect modulates cognitive control: Reduced perseveration at the cost of increased distractibility. *Journal of Experimental Psychology. Learning, Memory, and Cognition*, *30*(2), 343–353.

Dunn, J. R., & Schweitzer, M. E. (2005). Feeling and believing: The influence of emotion on trust. *Journal of Personality and Social Psychology*, *88*(5), 736–748.

Eisenberger, N. I., Inagaki, T. K., Rameson, L. T., Mashal, N. M., & Irwin, M. R. (2009). An fMRI study of cytokine-induced depressed mood and social pain: The role of sex differences. *NeuroImage*, *47*(3), 881–890.

Ekman, P., Davidson, R. J., & Friesen, W. V. (1990). The Duchenne smile: Emotional expression and brain physiology. II. *Journal of Personality and Social Psychology*, *58*(2), 342–353.

Estrada, C. A., Isen, A. M., & Young, M. J. (1997). Positive affect facilitates integration of information and decreases anchoring in reasoning among physicians. *Organizational Behavior and Human Decision Processes*, *72*(1), 117.

Farroni, T., Csibra, G., Simion, F., & Johnson, M. H. (2002). Eye contact detection in humans from birth. *Proceedings of the National Academy of Sciences of the United States of America*, *99*(14), 9602–9605.

Feldman, R., Gordon, I., & Zagoory-Sharon, O. (2010). The cross-generation transmission of oxytocin in humans. *Hormones and Behavior*, *58*(4), 669–676.

Finucane, A. M., & Whiteman, A. C. (2007). Positive emotions induced by massage do not broaden attention and cognition. *Irish Journal of Psychology*, *28*, 139–152.

Fowler, J. H., & Christakis, N. A. (2009). Dynamic spread of happiness in a large social network: Longitudinal analysis over 20 years in the Framingham Heart Study. *British Medical Journal*, *338*, 1–13.

Fredrickson, B. L. (1998). What good are positive emotions? *Review of General Psychology*, *2*(3), 300–319.

Fredrickson, B. L. (2001). The role of positive emotions in positive psychology. The broaden-and-build theory of positive emotions. *American Psychologist*, *56*(3), 218–226.

Fredrickson, B. L. (2005). The broaden-and-build theory of positive emotions. In F. A. Huppert, N. Baylis & B. Keverne (Eds.), *The Science of Well-Being* (pp. 217–238). New York: Oxford University Press.

Fredrickson, B. L. (2009). *Positivity*. New York, NY: Crown Publishers.

Fredrickson, B. L. (2013). *Love 2.0*. New York: Hudson Street Press.

Fredrickson, B. L., & Branigan, C. (2005). Positive emotions broaden the scope of attention and thought-action repertoires. *Cognition and Emotion*, *19*(3), 313–332.

Fredrickson, B. L., & Cohn, M. A. (2008). Positive emotions. In M. Lewis, J. Haviland-Jones & L. F. Barrett (Eds.), *Handbook of emotions* (pp. 777–796). (3rd ed.). New York: Guilford Press.

Fredrickson, B. L., & Kahneman, D. (1993). Duration neglect in retrospective evaluations of affective episodes. *Journal of Personality and Social Psychology*, *65*(1), 45–55.

Fredrickson, B. L., Cohn, M. A., Coffey, K. A., Pek, J., & Finkel, S. M. (2008). Open hearts build lives: Positive emotions, induced through loving-kindness meditation, build consequential personal resources. *Journal of Personality and Social Psychology*, *95*(5), 1045–1062.

Fredrickson, B. L., & Joiner, T. (2002). Positive emotions trigger upward spirals toward emotional well-being. *Journal of Personality and Social Psychology*, *65*(1), 45–55.

Fredrickson, B. L., & Levenson, R. W. (1998). Positive emotions speed recovery from the cardiovascular sequelae of negative emotions. *Cognition and Emotion*, *12*(2), 191–220.

Fredrickson, B. L., & Losada, M. F. (2005). Positive affect and the complex dynamics of human flourishing. *American Psychologist*, *60*(7), 678–686.

Fredrickson, B. L., Mancuso, R. A., Branigan, C., & Tugade, M. M. (2000). The undoing effect of positive emotions. *Motivation and Emotion*, *24*(4), 237–258.

Fredrickson, B. L., Tugade, M. M., Waugh, C. E., & Larkin, G. R. (2003). What good are positive emotions in crises? A prospective study of resilience and emotions following the terrorist attacks on the United States on September 11th, 2001. *Journal of Personality and Social Psychology*, *84*(2), 365–376.

Frijda, N. H. (1986). *The emotions*. Cambridge, UK: Cambridge University Press.

Gable, S. L., Gonzaga, G. C., & Strachman, A. (2006). Will you be there for me when things go right? Supportive responses to positive event disclosures. *Journal of Personality and Social Psychology*, *91*(5), 904–917.

Gable, P. A., & Harmon-Jones, E. (2008). Approach-motivated positive affect reduces breadth of attention. *Psychological Science*, *19*(5), 476–482.

Gard, D. E., Kring, A. M., Gard, M. G., Horan, W. P., & Green, M. F. (2007). Anhedonia in schizophrenia: Distinctions between anticipatory and consummatory pleasure. *Schizophrenia Research*, *93*(1–3), 253–260.

Garland, E. & Fredrickson, B.L. (in press). Positive emotions, mindfulness, and ACT. In T. B. Kashdan & J. Ciarrochi (Eds.) *Linking Acceptance and Commitment Therapy and positive psychology: A practioner's guide to a unifying framework*. Oakland, CA: New Harbinger.

Garland, E. L., Fredrickson, B., Kring, A. M., Johnson, D. P., Meyer, P. S., & Penn, D. L. (2010). Upward spirals of positive emotions counter downward spirals of negativity: Insights from the broaden-and-build theory and affective neuroscience on the treatment of emotion dysfunctions and deficits in psychopathology. *Clinical Psychology Review, 30* (7), 849–864.

Garland, E. L., Gaylord, S. A., & Fredrickson, B. L. (2011). Positive reappraisal mediates the stress-reductive effects of mindfulness: An upward spiral process. *Mindfulness, 2*(1), 59–67.

Gasper, K., & Clore, G. L. (2002). Attending to the big picture: Mood and global versus local processing of visual information. *Psychological Science, 13*(1), 34–40.

Gervais, M., & Wilson, D. S. (2005). The evolution and functions of laughter and humor: A synthetic approach. *The Quarterly Review of Biology, 80*(4), 395–430.

Grewen, K. M., Girdler, S. S., Amico, J., & Light, K. C. (2005). Effects of partner support on resting oxytocin, cortisol, norepinephrine, and blood pressure before and after warm partner contact. *Psychosomatic Medicine, 67*(4), 531–538.

Grewen, K. M., Light, K. C., Mechlin, B., & Girdler, S. S. (2008). Ethnicity is associated with alterations in oxytocin relationships to pain sensitivity in women. *Ethnicity & Health, 13*(3), 219–241.

Gross, M. M., Crane, E. A., & Fredrickson, B. L. (2012). Effort-shape and kinematic assessment of bodily expression of emotion during gait. *Human Movement Science, 31*(1), 202–221.

Grossman, P. (1983). Respiration, stress, and cardiovascular function. *Psychophysiology, 20*(3), 284–300.

Haidt, J., Seder, J. P., & Kesebir, S. (2008). Hive psychology, happiness, and public policy. *The Journal of Legal Studies, 37*, S133–S156.

Hart, S. L., Vella, L., & Mohr, D. C. (2008). Relationships among depressive symptoms, benefit-finding, optimism, and positive affect in multiple sclerosis patients after psychotherapy for depression. *Health Psychology, 27*(2), 230–238.

Hasson, U. (2010). I can make your brain look like mine. *Harvard Business Review, 88*(12), 32–33.

Hasson, U., Nir, Y., Levy, I., Fuhrmann, G., & Malach, R. (2004). Intersubject synchronization of cortical activity during natural vision. *Science, 303*(5664), 1634–1640.

Hegi, K. E., & Bergner, R. M. (2010). What is love? An empirically-based essentialist account. *Journal of Social and Personal Relationships, 27*(5), 620–636.

Holt-Lunstad, J., Birmingham, W. A., & Light, K. C. (2008). Influence of a "warm touch" support enhancement intervention among married couples on ambulatory blood pressure, oxytocin, alpha amylase, and cortisol. *Psychosomatic Medicine, 70*(9), 976–985.

Isen, A. M. (1987). Positive affect, cognitive processes, and social behavior. *Advances in Experimental Social Psychology, 20*, 203–253.

Isen, A. M., & Daubman, K. A. (1984). The influence of affect on categorization. *Journal of Personality and Social Psychology, 47*, 1206–1217.

Isen, A. M., Daubman, K. A., & Nowicki, G. P. (1987). Positive affect facilitates creative problem solving. *Journal of Personality and Social Psychology, 52*(6), 1122–1131.

Isen, A. M., Johnson, M. M. S., Mertz, E., & Robinson, G. F. (1985). The influence of positive affect on the unusualness of word associations. *Journal of Personality and Social Psychology, 48*(6), 1413–1426.

Isen, A. M., & Means, B. (1983). The influence of positive affect on decision-making strategy. *Social Cognition, 2*(1), 18–31.

Isen, A. M., Niedenthal, P. M., & Cantor, N. (1992). An influence of positive affect on social categorization. *Motivation and Emotion, 16*(1), 65–78.

Isen, A. M., Rosenzweig, A. S., & Young, M. J. (1991). The influence of positive affect on clinical problem solving. *Medical Decision Making: An International Journal of the Society for Medical Decision Making, 11*(3), 221.

Izard, C. E. (1977). *Human emotions*. New York: Springer.

James, W. E. (1884). What is an emotion? *Mind*, *9*, 188–205.

Johnson, K. J., & Fredrickson, B. L. (2005). "We all look the same to me": Positive emotions eliminate the own-race in face recognition. *Psychological Science*, *16*(11), 875–881.

Johnson, D. P., Penn, D. L., Fredrickson, B. L., Kring, A. M., Meyer, P. S., Catalino, L. I., et al. (2011). A pilot study of loving-kindness meditation for the negative symptoms of schizophrenia. *Schizophrenia Research*, *129*(2–3), 137–140.

Johnson, D. P., Penn, D. L., Fredrickson, B. L., Meyer, P. S., Kring, A. M., & Brantley, M. (2009). Loving-kindness meditation to enhance recovery from negative symptoms of schizophrenia. *Journal of Clinical Psychology*, *65*(5), 499–509.

Johnson, K. J., Waugh, C. E., & Fredrickson, B. L. (2010). Smile to see the forest: Facially expressed positive emotions broaden cognition. *Cognition and Emotion*, *24*(2), 299–321.

Juckel, G., Schlagenhauf, F., Koslowski, M., Wüstenberg, T., Villringer, A., Knutson, B., et al. (2006). Dysfunction of ventral striatal reward prediction in schizophrenia. *NeuroImage*, *29*(2), 409–416.

Kahn, B. E., & Isen, A. M. (1993). The influence of positive affect on variety seeking among safe, enjoyable products. *Journal of Consumer Research*, *20*(2), 257–270.

Kahneman, D., Fredrickson, B. L., Schreiber, C. A., & Redelmeier, D. A. (1993). When more pain is preferred to less: Adding a better end. *Psychological Science*, *4*(6), 401–405.

Kahneman, D., Krueger, A. B., Schkade, D. A., Schwarz, N., & Stone, A. A. (2004). A survey method for characterizing daily life experience: The day reconstruction method. *Science*, *306*(5702), 1776–1780.

Kihlstrom, J. F. (2012). *Let psychology be psychology!*. [Comment on "Identity Shift" by Eric Jaffe, APS Observer, September 2011].

Kok, B. E., Coffey, K. A., Cohn, M. A., Catalino, L. I., Vacharkulksemsuk, T., Algoe, S. B., et al. (in press). How positive emotions build physical health: Perceived positive social connections account for the upward spiral between positive emotions and vagal tone. *Psychological Science*.

Kok, B. E., & Fredrickson, B. L. (2010). Upward spirals of the heart: Autonomic flexibility, as indexed by vagal tone, reciprocally and prospectively predicts positive emotions and social connectedness. *Biological Psychology*, *85*(3), 432–436.

Kok, B. E., & Fredrickson, B. L. (in press). How positive emotions broaden and build. In J. J. Froh & A. Parks-Sheiner (Eds.), *Positive psychology in higher education: A practical workbook for the classroom*. Washington DC: American Psychological Association.

Kring, A. M. (1999). Emotion in schizophrenia: Old mystery, new understanding. *Current Directions in Psychological Science*, *8*(5), 160–163.

Larsen, R. J., & Fredrickson, B. L. (1999). Measurement issues in emotion research. In D. Kahneman, E. Diener & N. Schwarz (Eds.), *Well-being: Foundations of hedonic psychology* (pp. 40–60). New York: Russell Sage.

Lazarus, R. S. (1991). *Emotion and adaptation*. Oxford: Oxford University Press.

Lee, Y., Lin, Y.-C., Huang, C.-L., & Fredrickson, B. L. (2012). The construct and measurement of peace of mind. *Journal of Happiness Studies*, 1–20. http://dx.doi.org/10.1007/s10902-012-9343-5. Advance online publication.

Levenson, R. W. (1988). Emotion and the autonomic nervous system: A prospectus for research on autonomic specificity. In H. L. Wagner (Ed.), *Social psychophysiology and emotion: Theory and clinical applications* (pp. 17–42). London: John Wiley and Sons Ltd.

Levenson, R. W., Carstensen, L. L., Friesen, W. V., & Ekman, P. (1991). Emotion, physiology, and expression in old age. *Psychology and Aging*, *6*(1), 28–35.

Levenson, R. W., Ekman, P., & Friesen, W. V. (1990). Voluntary facial action generates emotion-specific autonomic nervous system activity. *Psychophysiology*, *27*(4), 363–384.

Light, K. C., Grewen, K. M., & Amico, J. A. (2005). More frequent partner hugs and higher oxytocin levels are linked to lower blood pressure and heart rate in premenopausal women. *Biological Psychology, 69*(1), 5–21.

Light, K. C., Grewen, K. M., Amico, J. A., Boccia, M., Brownley, K. A., & Johns, J. M. (2004). Deficits in plasma oxytocin responses and increased negative affect, stress, and blood pressure in mothers with cocaine exposure during pregnancy. *Addictive Behaviors, 29*(8), 1541–1564.

Luthans, F., Vogelgesang, G. R., & Lester, P. B. (2006). Developing the psychological capital of resiliency. *Human Resource Development Review, 5*(1), 25–44.

Lyubomirsky, S., King, L., & Diener, E. (2005). The benefits of frequent positive affect: Does happiness lead to success? *Psychological Bulletin, 131*(6), 803–855.

Maringer, M., Krumhuber, E. G., Fischer, A. H., & Niedenthal, P. M. (2011). Beyond smile dynamics: Mimicry and beliefs in judgments of smiles. *Emotion, 11*(1), 181–187.

Mauss, I. B., Shallcross, A. J., Troy, A. S., John, O. P., Ferrer, E., Wilhelm, F. H., et al. (2011). Don't hide your happiness! Positive emotion dissociation, social connectedness, and psychological functioning. *Journal of Personality and Social Psychology, 100*(4), 738–748.

McNulty, J. K., & Fincham, F. D. (2012). Beyond positive psychology? Toward a contextual view of psychological processes and well-being. *American Psychologist, 67*(2), 101.

Miller, G. E., Chen, E., Sze, J., Marin, T., Arevalo, J. M. G., Doll, R., et al. (2008). A functional genomic fingerprint of chronic stress in humans: Blunted glucocorticoid and increased NF-kappaB signaling. *Biological Psychiatry, 64*(4), 266.

Miller, G. E., Rohleder, N., & Cole, S. W. (2009). Chronic interpersonal stress predicts activation of pro- and anti-inflammatory signaling pathways 6 months later. *Psychosomatic Medicine, 71*(1), 57–62.

Navon, D. (1977). Forest before trees: The precedence of global features in visual perception. *Cognitive Psychology, 9*(3), 353–383.

Nelson, D. W. (2009). Feeling good and open-minded: The impact of positive affect on cross cultural empathic responding. *The Journal of Positive Psychology, 4*(1), 53–63.

Nesse, R. M. (1990). Evolutionary explanations of emotions. *Human Nature, 1*(3), 261–289.

Niedenthal, P. M., Halberstadt, J. B., & Setterlund, M. B. (1997). Being happy and seeing "happy": Emotional state mediates visual word recognition. *Cognition and Emotion, 11*(4), 403–432.

Niedenthal, P. M., Mermillod, M., Maringer, M., & Hess, U. (2010). The Simulation of Smiles (SIMS) model: Embodied simulation and the meaning of facial expression. *The Behavioral and Brain Sciences, 33*(6), 417–433.

Ong, A. D., Bergeman, C. S., Bisconti, T. L., & Wallace, K. A. (2006). Psychological resilience, positive emotions, and successful adaptation to stress in later life. *Journal of Personality and Social Psychology, 91*(4), 730–749.

Ouweneel, E., Le Blanc, P. M., & Schaufeli, W. B. (2011). Flourishing students: A longitudinal study on positive emotions, personal resources, and study engagement. *The Journal of Positive Psychology, 6*(2), 142–153.

Oveis, C., Cohen, A. B., Gruber, J., Shiota, M. N., Haidt, J., & Keltner, D. (2009). Resting respiratory sinus arrhythmia is associated with tonic positive emotionality. *Emotion, 9*(2), 265–270.

Owren, M. J., & Bachorowski, J.-A. (2003). Reconsidering the evolution of nonlinguistic communication: The case of laughter. *Journal of Nonverbal Behavior, 27*(3), 183.

Payne, B. K., Cheng, C. M., Govorun, O., & Stewart, B. D. (2005). An inkblot for attitudes: Affect misattribution as implicit measurement. *Journal of Personality and Social Psychology, 89*(3), 277–293.

Phillips, L. H., Bull, R., Adams, E., & Fraser, L. (2002). Positive mood and executive function: Evidence from stroop and fluency tasks. *Emotion (Washington, D.C.), 2*(1), 12–22.

Porges, S. W. (2007). The polyvagal perspective. *Biological Psychology*, *74*(2), 116–143.

Porges, S. W., Doussard-Roosevelt, J. A., & Maiti, A. K. (1994). Vagal tone and the physiological regulation of emotion. *Monographs of the Society for Research in Child Development*, *59*(2/3), 167–186.

Posner, M. I. (1980). Orienting of attention. *The Quarterly Journal of Experimental Psychology*, *32*, 3–25.

Pyone, J. S., & Isen, A. M. (2011). Positive affect, intertemporal choice, and levels of thinking: Increasing consumers' willingness to wait. *Journal of Marketing Research*, *48*(3), 532–543.

Reis, H., Clark, M. S., & Holmes, J. G. (2004). Perceived partner responsiveness as an organizing construct in the study of intimacy and closeness. In D. J. Masheck & A. P. Aron (Eds.), *Handbook of closeness and intimacy* (pp. 201–225). Mahwah, NJ: Lawrence Erlbaum.

Renninger, K. A. (1992). Individual interest and development: Implications for theory and practice. In K. A. Renninger, S. Hidi & A. Krapp (Eds.), *The role of interest in learning and development* (pp. 361–395). Hillsdale, NJ: Erlbaum.

Robinson, T. E., & Berridge, K. C. (2003). Addiction. *Annual Review of Psychology*, *54*(1), 25–53.

Rowe, G., Hirsh, J. B., & Anderson, A. K. (2007). Positive affect increases the breadth of attentional selection. *Proceedings of the National Academy of Sciences of the United States of America*, *104*(1), 383–388.

Rozin, P., & Fallon, A. E. (1987). A perspective on disgust. *Psychological Review*, *94*(1), 23–41.

Russell, J. A., Weiss, A., & Mendelsohn, G. A. (1989). Affect grid: A single-item scale of pleasure and arousal. *Journal of Personality and Social Psychology*, *57*(3), 493–502.

Salanova, M., Bakker, A. B., & Llorens, S. (2006). Flow at work: Evidence for an upward spiral of personal and organizational resources. *Journal of Happiness Studies*, *7*(1), 1–22.

Salanova, M., Llorens, S., & Schaufeli, W. B. (2011). "Yes, I can, I feel good, and I just do it!" On gain cycles and spirals of efficacy beliefs, affect, and engagement. *Applied Psychology*, *60*(2), 255–285.

Salanova, M., Schaufeli, W. B., Xanthopoulou, D., & Bakker, A. B. (2010). The gain spiral of resources and work engagement: Sustaining a positive work life. In M. P. Leiter & A. B. Bakker (Eds.), *Work engagement: A handbook of essential theory and research* (pp. 118–131). New York: Psychology Press.

Salzberg, S. (1995). *Lovingkindness: The revolutionary art of happiness*. Boston: Shambhala.

Schmitz, T. W., De Rosa, E., & Anderson, A. K. (2009). Opposing influences of affective state valence on visual cortical encoding. *The Journal of Neuroscience*, *29*(22), 7199–7207.

Schrammel, F., Pannasch, S., Graupner, S.-T., Mojzisch, A., & Velichkovsky, B. M. (2009). Virtual friend or threat? The effects of facial expression and gaze interaction on psychophysiological responses and emotional experience. *Psychophysiology*, *46*(5), 922.

Shiota, M. N., Keltner, D., & Mossman, A. (2007). The nature of awe: Elicitors, appraisals, and effects on self-concept. *Cognition and Emotion*, *21*(5), 944–963.

Silvia, P. J. (2008). Interest: The curious emotion. *Current Directions in Psychological Science*, *17*(1), 57–60.

Skinner, B. F. (1974). *About behaviorism*. New York: Vintage.

Soto, D., Funes, M. J., Guzmán-García, A., Warbrick, T., Rotshtein, P., & Humphreys, G. W. (2009). Pleasant music overcomes the loss of awareness in patients with visual neglect. *Proceedings of the National Academy of Sciences of the United States of America*, *106*(14), 6011–6016.

Stephens, G. J., Silbert, L. J., & Hasson, U. (2010). Speaker-listener neural coupling underlies successful communication. *Proceedings of the National Academy of Sciences of the United States of America*, *107*(32), 14425–14430.

Thayer, J. F., & Sternberg, E. (2006). Beyond heart rate variability: Vagal regulation of allostatic systems. *Annals of the New York Academy of Sciences*, *1088*(1), 361–372.

Thrash, T. M., & Elliot, A. J. (2004). Inspiration: Core characteristics, component processes, antecedents, and function. *Journal of Personality and Social Psychology, 87*(6), 957–973.

Tomkins, S. S. (1962). *Affect, imagery, consciousness, vol. 1: The positive affects*. New York: Springer.

Tooby, J., & Cosmides, L. (1990). The past explains the present. *Ethology and Sociobiology, 11*(4), 375–424.

Tracy, J. L., & Robins, R. W. (2007). Emerging insights into the nature and function of pride. *Current Directions in Psychological Science, 16*(3), 147–150.

Trick, L. M., Brandigampola, S., & Enns, J. T. (2012). How fleeting emotions affect hazard perception and steering while driving: The impact of image arousal and valence. *Accident Analysis and Prevention, 45*, 222–229.

Tugade, M. M., & Fredrickson, B. L. (2004). Resilient individuals use positive emotions to bounce back from negative emotional experiences. *Journal of Personality and Social Psychology, 86*(2), 320–333.

Vacharkulksemsuk, T., & Fredrickson, B. L. (2012). Strangers in sync: Achieving embodied rapport through shared movements. *Journal of Experimental Social Psychology, 48*(1), 399–402.

Vacharkulksemsuk, T., Sekerka, L. E., & Fredrickson, B. L. (2011). Establishing a positive emotional climate to create 21st-century organizational change. In N. M. Ashkanasy, C. P. M. Wilderom & M. F. Peterson (Eds.), *The handbook of organizational culture and climate* (pp. 101–118). (2nd ed.). Thousand Oaks, CA: Sage.

Vincent, L., Emich, K., & Gonalo, J. (in press). Stretching the moral gray zone: Positive affect, moral disengagement, and dishonesty. *Psychological Science*.

Wadlinger, H. A., & Isaacowitz, D. M. (2006). Positive mood broadens visual attention to positive stimuli. *Motivation and Emotion, 30*(1), 87–99.

Wang, Y., & Guo, D. (2008). The effects of positive emotions on task switching. *Acta Psychologica Sinica, 40*, 301–306.

Watson, D., Wiese, D., Vaidya, J., & Tellegen, A. (1999). The two general activation systems of affect: Structural findings, evolutionary considerations, and psychobiological evidence. *Journal of Personality and Social Psychology, 76*(5), 820–838.

Waugh, C. E., & Fredrickson, B. L. (2006). Nice to know you: Positive emotions, self-other overlap, and complex understanding in the formation of a new relationship. *The Journal of Positive Psychology, 1*(2), 93–106.

Waugh, C. E., Hamilton, J. P., & Gotlib, I. H. (2010). The neural temporal dynamics of the intensity of emotional experience. *NeuroImage, 49*, 1699–1707.

Williams, L. A., & DeSteno, D. (2008). Pride and perseverance: The motivational role of pride. *Journal of Personality and Social Psychology, 94*(6), 1007–1017.

CHAPTER TWO

Moral Foundations Theory: The Pragmatic Validity of Moral Pluralism

Jesse Graham*, Jonathan Haidt†, Sena Koleva*, Matt Motyl‡, Ravi Iyer*, Sean P. Wojcik§, Peter H. Ditto§
*Department of Psychology, University of Southern California, Los Angeles, California, USA
†Stern School of Business, New York University, New York, USA
‡Department of Psychology, University of Virginia, Charlottesville, Virginia, USA
§School of Social Ecology, University of California, Irvine, California, USA

Contents

Advances in Experimental Social Psychology, Volume 47
ISSN 0065-2601
http://dx.doi.org/10.1016/B978-0-12-407236-7.00002-4

Abstract

Where does morality come from? Why are moral judgments often so similar across cultures, yet sometimes so variable? Is morality one thing, or many? Moral Foundations Theory (MFT) was created to answer these questions. In this chapter, we describe the origins, assumptions, and current conceptualization of the theory and detail the empirical findings that MFT has made possible, both within social psychology and beyond. Looking toward the future, we embrace several critiques of the theory and specify five criteria for determining what should be considered a foundation of human morality. Finally, we suggest a variety of future directions for MFT and moral psychology.

"The supreme goal of all theory is to make the irreducible basic elements as simple and as few as possible without having to surrender the adequate representation of a single datum of experience." (Einstein, 1934, p. 165)

"I came to the conclusion that there is a plurality of ideals, as there is a plurality of cultures and of temperaments. . .There is not an infinity of [values]: the number of human values, of values which I can pursue while maintaining my human semblance, my human character, is finite—let us say 74, or perhaps 122, or 27, but finite, whatever it may be. And the difference this makes is that if a man pursues one of these values, I, who do not, am able to understand why he pursues it or what it would be like, in his circumstances, for me to be induced to pursue it. Hence the possibility of human understanding." (Berlin, 2001, p. 12)

Scientists value parsimony as well as explanatory adequacy. There is, however, an inherent tension between these two values. When we try to explain an aspect of human nature or behavior using only a single construct, the gain in elegance is often purchased with a loss of descriptive completeness. We risk imitating Procrustes, the mythical blacksmith who forced his guests to fit into an iron bed exactly, whether by stretching them out or by cutting off their legs. Einstein, in our opening quote, warns against this Procrustean overvaluation of parsimony.

In this chapter, we ask: How many "irreducible basic elements" are needed to represent, understand, and explain the breadth of the moral domain? We use the term *monist* to describe scholars who assert that the answer is: *one*. This *one* is usually identified as justice or fairness, as Lawrence Kohlberg asserted: "Virtue is ultimately one, not many, and it is always the same ideal form regardless of climate or culture. . . The name of this ideal form is justice" (Kohlberg, 1971, p. 232; see also Baumard, André, & Sperber, 2013). The other common candidate for being the one foundation of morality is sensitivity to harm (e.g., Gray, Young, & Waytz, 2012), or else related notions of generalized human welfare or happiness (e.g., Harris, 2010). Monists generally try to show that all manifestations of morality are derived from an underlying psychological architecture for implementing the one basic value or virtue that they propose.

Other theorists—whom we will call *pluralists*—assert that the answer is: *more than one*. William James's (1909/1987) extended critique of monism and absolutism, *A Pluralistic Universe*, identifies the perceived messiness of pluralism as a major source of intellectual resistance to it:

> *Whether materialistically or spiritualistically minded, philosophers have always aimed at cleaning up the litter with which the world apparently is filled. They have substituted economical and orderly conceptions for the first sensible tangle; and whether these were morally elevated or only intellectually neat, they were at any rate always aesthetically pure and definite, and aimed at ascribing to the world something clean and intellectual in the way of inner structure. As compared with all these rationalizing pictures, the pluralistic empiricism which I profess offers but a sorry appearance. It is a turbid, muddled, gothic sort of an affair, without a sweeping outline and with little pictorial nobility. (p. 650)*

Aristotle was an early moral pluralist, dismissed by Kohlberg (1971) for promoting a "bag of virtues." Gilligan (1982) was a pluralist when she argued that the "ethic of care" was not derived from (or reducible to) the ethic of justice. Isaiah Berlin said, in our opening quotation, that there are a finite but potentially large number of moral ideals that are within the repertoire of human beings and that an appreciation of the full repertoire opens the door to mutual understanding.

We are unabashed pluralists, and in this chapter, we will try to convince you that you should be, too. In the first two parts of this chapter, we present a pluralist theory of moral psychology—Moral Foundations Theory (MFT). In part three, we will provide an overview of empirical results that others and we have obtained using a variety of measures developed to test the theory. We will show that the pluralism of MFT has led to discoveries that had long been missed by monists. In part four, we will discuss criticisms of the theory and future research directions that are motivated in part by those criticisms. We will also propose specific criteria that researchers can use to decide what counts as a foundation. Throughout the chapter, we will focus on MFT's *pragmatic validity* (Graham et al., 2011)—that is, its scientific usefulness for both answering existing questions about morality and allowing researchers to formulate new questions.

We grant right at the start that our particular list of moral foundations is unlikely to survive the empirical challenges of the next several years with no changes. But we think that our general approach is likely to stand the test of time. We predict that 20 years from now moral psychologists will mostly be pluralists who draw on both cultural and evolutionary psychology to examine the psychological mechanisms that lead people and groups to hold divergent moral values and beliefs.

We also emphasize, at the outset, that our project is descriptive, not normative. We are not trying to say who or what is morally right or good. We are simply trying to analyze an important aspect of human social life. Cultures vary morally, as do individuals within cultures. These differences often lead to hostility, and sometimes violence. We think it would be helpful for social psychologists, policy makers, and citizens more generally to have a language in which they can describe and understand moralities that are not their own. We think a pluralistic approach is necessary for this descriptive project. We do not know how many moral foundations there really are. There may be 74, or perhaps 122, or 27, or maybe only 5, but certainly more than one. And moral psychologists who help people to recognize the inherent pluralism of moral functioning will be at the forefront of efforts to promote the kind of "human understanding" that Berlin described.

1. THE ORIGINS OF MFT

For centuries, people looked at the map of the world and noted that the east coast of South America fits reasonably well into the west coast of Africa. The two coasts even have similar rock formations and ancient plant fossils. These many connections led several geologists to posit the theory of continental drift, which was confirmed in the early 1960s by evidence that the sea floor was spreading along mid-oceanic ridges.

Similarly, for decades, social scientists noted that many of the practices widely described by anthropologists fit reasonably well with the two processes that were revolutionizing evolutionary biology: kin selection and reciprocal altruism. When discussing altruism, Dawkins (1976) made occasional reference to the findings of anthropologists to illustrate Hamilton's (1964) theory of kin selection, while Trivers (1971) reviewed anthropological evidence illustrating reciprocity among hunter-gatherers. So the idea that human morality is derived from or constrained by multiple innate mental systems, each shaped by a different evolutionary process, is neither new nor radical. It is accepted by nearly all who write about the evolutionary origins of morality (e.g., de Waal, 1996; Joyce, 2006; Ridley, 1996; Wright, 1994). The main question up for debate is: how many mental systems are there?

Kohlberg (1969) founded the modern field of moral psychology with his declaration that the answer was one. He developed a grand theory that unified moral psychology as the study of the progressive development of the child's understanding of justice. Building on the work of Piaget (1932/1965), Kohlberg proposed that moral development in all cultures is driven forward by the process of role-taking: as children get more practice at taking each other's perspectives, they learn to transcend their own position and appreciate when and why an action, practice, or custom is fair or unfair. If they come to respect authority or value group loyalty along the way (stage 4), this is an unfortunate way-station at which children overvalue conformity and tradition. But if children get more opportunities to role-take, they will progress to the postconventional level (stages 5 and 6), at which authority and loyalty might sometimes be justified, but only to the extent that they promote justice.

The deficiencies of Kohlberg's moral monism were immediately apparent to some of his critics. Gilligan (1982) argued that the morality of girls and women did not follow Kohlberg's one true path but developed along *two* paths: an ethic of justice and an ethic of care that could not be derived from the former. Kohlberg eventually acknowledged that she was right (Kohlberg, Levine, & Hewer, 1983). Moral psychologists in the cognitive-developmental tradition have generally been comfortable with this dualism: justice *and* care. In fact, the cover of the *Handbook of Moral Development* (Killen & Smetana, 2006) shows two images: the scales of justice and African statues of a mother and child.

Turiel (1983) allowed for both foundations in his widely cited definition of the moral domain as referring to "prescriptive judgments of justice, rights, and welfare pertaining to how people ought to relate to each other." (Justice and rights are the Kohlbergian foundation; the concern for "welfare" can encompass Gilligan's "care.") Kohlberg, Gilligan, and Turiel were all united in their belief that morality is about how *individuals* ought to relate to, protect, and respect other individuals.

But what if, in some cultures, even the most advanced moral thinkers value groups, institutions, traditions, and gods? What should we say about local rules for how to be a good group member, or how to worship? If these rules are not closely linked to concerns about justice or care, then should we distinguish them from true moral rules, as Turiel did when he labeled such rules as "social conventions?" Shweder (1990) argued that the cognitive-developmental tradition was studying only a subset of moral concerns, the ones that are most highly elaborated in secular Western societies. Shweder argued for a much more extensive form of pluralism based on his research in Bhubaneswar, India (Shweder, Much, Mahapatra, & Park, 1997). He proposed that around the world, people talk in one or more of *three* moral languages: the ethic of autonomy (relying on concepts such as harm, rights, and justice, which protect autonomous individuals), the ethic of community (relying on concepts such as duty, respect, and loyalty, which preserve institutions and social order), and the ethic of divinity (relying on concepts such as purity, sanctity, and sin, which protect the divinity inherent in each person against the degradation of hedonistic selfishness).

So now we are up to three. Or maybe it's four? Fiske (1991) proposed that moral judgment relies upon the same four "relational models" that are used to think about and enact social relationships: Communal Sharing, Authority Ranking, Equality Matching, and Market Pricing (see also Rai & Fiske, 2011).

Having worked with both Fiske and Shweder, Haidt wanted to integrate the two theories into a unified framework for studying morality across cultures. But despite many points of contact, the three ethics and four relational models could not be neatly merged or reconciled. They are solutions to different problems: categorizing explicit moral discourse (for Shweder) and analyzing interpersonal relationships (for Fiske). After working with the two theories throughout the 1990s—the decade in which evolutionary psychology was reborn (Barkow, Cosmides, & Tooby, 1992)—Haidt sought to construct a theory specifically designed to bridge evolutionary and anthropological approaches to moral judgment. He worked with Craig Joseph, who was studying cultural variation in virtue concepts (Joseph, 2002).

The first step was to broaden the inquiry beyond the theories of Fiske and Shweder to bring in additional theories about how morality varies across cultures. Schwartz and Bilsky's (1990) theory of values offered the most prominent approach in social psychology. Haidt and Joseph also sought out theorists who took an evolutionary approach, trying to specify universals of human moral nature. Brown (1991) offered a list of human universals including many aspects of moral psychology, and de Waal (1996) offered a list of the "building blocks" of human morality that can be seen in other primates.

Haidt and Joseph (2004) used the analogy of taste to guide their review of these varied works. The human tongue has five discrete taste receptors (for sweet, sour, salt, bitter, and umami). Cultures vary enormously in their cuisines, which are cultural constructions shaped by historical events, yet the world's many cuisines must ultimately please tongues equipped with just five innate and universal taste receptors. What are the best candidates for being the innate and universal "moral taste receptors" upon which the world's many cultures construct their moral cuisines? What are the concerns, perceptions, and emotional reactions that consistently turn up in moral codes around the world, and for which there are already-existing evolutionary explanations?

Haidt and Joseph identified five best candidates: Care/harm, Fairness/cheating, Loyalty/betrayal, Authority/subversion, and Sanctity/degradation.[1] We believe that there are more than five; for example, Haidt

---

[1] Prior to 2012, we used slightly different terms: Harm/care, Fairness/reciprocity, Ingroup/loyalty, Authority/respect, and Purity/sanctity.

(2012) has suggested that Liberty/oppression should be considered a sixth foundation (see Section 4.1 for other candidate foundations). We will explain the nature of these foundations in the next section, and we will offer a list of criteria for "foundationhood" in Section 4.2. But before we do, the broader theoretical underpinnings of MFT need to be explained.

2. THE CURRENT THEORY

MFT can be summarized in four claims. If any of these claims is disproved, or is generally abandoned by psychologists, then MFT would need to be abandoned, too.

2.1. Nativism: There is a "first draft" of the moral mind

Some scholars think that evolutionary and cultural explanations of human behavior are competing approaches—one reductionist, one constructivist—but MFT was created precisely to integrate the two (see also Fiske, 1991; Richerson & Boyd, 2005). Our definition of nativism makes this clear: Innate means *organized in advance of experience*. We do not take it to mean hardwired or insensitive to environmental influences, as some critics of nativism define innateness (e.g., Suhler & Churchland, 2011). Instead, we borrow Marcus's (2004) metaphor that the mind is like a book: "Nature provides a first draft, which experience then revises...'Built-in' does not mean unmalleable; it means 'organized in advance of experience'" (pp. 34 and 40). The genes (collectively) write the first draft into neural tissue, beginning in utero but continuing throughout childhood. Experience (cultural learning) revises the draft during childhood, and even (to a lesser extent) during adulthood.

We think it is useful to conceptualize the first draft and the editing process as distinct. You cannot infer the first draft from looking at a single finished volume (i.e., one adult or one culture). But if you examine volumes from all over the world, and you find a great many specific ideas expressed in most (but not necessarily all) of the volumes, using different wording, then you would be justified in positing that there was some sort of common first draft or outline, some common starting point to which all finished volumes can be traced. Morality is innate *and* highly dependent on environmental influences.

The classic study by Mineka and Cook (1988) is useful here. Young rhesus monkeys, who showed no prior fear of snakes—including plastic snakes—watched a video of an adult monkey reacting fearfully (or not) to a plastic snake (or to plastic flowers). The monkeys learned from a single exposure to snake-fearing monkey to be afraid of the plastic snake, but a single exposure to a flower-fearing monkey did nothing. This is an example of "preparedness" (Seligman, 1971). Evolution created something "organized in advance of experience" that made it easy for monkeys—and humans (DeLoache & LoBue, 2009)—to learn to fear snakes. Evolution did not simply install a general-purpose learning mechanism which made the monkeys take on all the fears of adult role models equally.

We think the same is likely true about moral development. It is probably quite easy to teach kids to want revenge just by exposing them to role models who become angry and vengeful when treated unfairly, but it is probably much more difficult to teach children to love their enemies just by exposing them, every Sunday for 20 years, to stories about a role model who loved his enemies. We are prepared to learn vengefulness, in a way that we are *not* prepared to learn to offer our left cheek to those who smite us on our right cheek.

How can moral knowledge be innate? Evolutionary psychologists have discussed the issue at length. They argue that recurrent problems and opportunities faced by a species over long periods of time often produce domain-specific cognitive adaptations for responding rapidly and effectively (Pinker, 1997; Tooby & Cosmides, 1992). These adaptations are often called modules, which evolutionary theorists generally do not view as fully "encapsulated" entities with "fixed neural localizations" (Fodor, 1983), but as *functionally specialized mechanisms* which work together to solve recurrent adaptive problems quickly and efficiently (Barrett & Kurzban, 2006). There is not one general-purpose digestion organ, and if there ever was such an organ, its owners lost out to organisms with more efficient modular designs.

The situation is likely to be the same for higher cognition: there is not one general-purpose thinking or reasoning organ that produces moral judgments, as Kohlberg seemed to suppose. Rather, according to the "massive modularity hypothesis" (Sperber, 1994, 2005), the mind is thought to be full of small information-processing mechanisms, which make it easy to solve—or to learn to solve—certain kinds of problems, but not other kinds.

Tooby, Cosmides, and Barrett (2005) argue that the study of valuation, even more than other areas of cognition, reveals just how crucial it is to posit innate mental content, rather than positing a few innate general learning mechanisms (such as social learning). Children are born with a preference (value) for sweetness and against bitterness. The preference for candy over broccoli is not learned by socialization and cannot be undone by role models, threats, or education about the health benefits of broccoli. Tooby et al. (2005) suggest that the same thing is true for valuation in all domains, including the moral domain. Just as the tongue and brain are designed to yield pleasure when sweetness is tasted, there are cognitive modules that yield pleasure when fair exchanges occur, and displeasure when one detects cheaters. In the moral domain, the problems to be solved are social and the human mind evolved a variety of mechanisms that enable individuals (and perhaps groups) to solve those problems within the "moral matrices"—webs of shared meaning and evaluation—that began to form as humans became increasingly cultural creatures during the past half-million years (see Haidt, 2012, chapter 9, which draws on Richerson & Boyd, 2005; Tomasello, Carpenter, Call, Behne, & Moll, 2005).

MFT proposes that the human mind is organized in advance of experience so that it is prepared to learn values, norms, and behaviors related to a diverse set of recurrent adaptive social problems (specified below in Table 2.1). We think of this innate organization as being implemented by sets of related modules which work together to guide and constrain responses to each particular problem. But you do not have to embrace modularity, or any particular view of the brain, to embrace MFT. You only need to accept that there is a first draft of the moral mind, organized in advance of experience by the adaptive pressures of our unique evolutionary history.

2.2. Cultural learning: The first draft gets edited during development within a particular culture

A dictum of cultural psychology is that "Culture and psyche make each other up" (Shweder, 1990, p. 24). If there were no first draft of the psyche, then groups would be free to invent utopian moralities (e.g., "from each according to his ability, to each according to his need"), and they would be able to pass them on to their children because all moral ideas would be equally learnable. This clearly is not the case (e.g., Pinker, 2002; Spiro, 1956). Conversely, if cultural learning played no formative role, then the first draft would be the final draft, and there would be no variation across cultures.[2] This clearly is not the case either (e.g., Haidt, Koller, & Dias, 1993; Shweder, Mahapatra, & Miller, 1987).

The cognitive anthropologist Dan Sperber has proposed a version of modularity theory that we believe works very well for higher cognition, in general, and for moral psychology, in particular. Citing Marler's (1991) research on song learning in birds, Sperber (2005) proposes that many of

---

[2] Other than those due to individual development, for example, some cultures might offer more opportunities for role-taking, which would cause their members to be more successful in self-constructing their own moralities. This is how Kohlberg (1969) explained cultural differences in moral reasoning between Western and non-Western nations.

the modules present at or soon after birth are "learning modules." That is, they are innate templates or "learning instincts" whose function is to generate a host of more specific modules as the child develops. They generate "the working modules of acquired cognitive competence" (p. 57). They are a way of explaining phenomena such as preparedness (Seligman, 1971).

For example, children in traditional Hindu households are frequently required to bow, often touching their heads to the floor or to the feet of revered elders and guests. Bowing is used in religious contexts as well, to show deference to the gods. By the time a Hindu girl reaches adulthood, she will have developed culturally specific knowledge that makes her automatically initiate bowing movements when she encounters, say, a respected politician for the first time. Note that this knowledge is not just factual knowledge—it includes feelings and motor schemas for bowing and otherwise showing deference. Sperber (2005) refers to this new knowledge—in which a pattern of appraisals is linked to a pattern of behavioral outputs—as an acquired module, generated by the original "learning module." But one could just as well drop the modularity language at this point and simply assert that children acquire all kinds of new knowledge, concepts, and behavioral patterns as they employ their innately given moral foundations within a particular cultural context. A girl raised in a secular American household will have no such experiences in childhood and may reach adulthood with no specialized knowledge or ability to detect hierarchy and show respect for hierarchical authorities.

Both girls started off with the same sets of universal learning modules—including the set we call the Authority/subversion foundation. But in the Hindu community, culture and psyche worked together to generate a host of more specific authority-respecting abilities (or modules, if you prefer). In the secular American community, such new abilities were not generated, and the American child is more likely to hold anti-authoritarian values as an adult. An American adult may still have inchoate feelings of respect for some elders and might even find it hard to address some elders by first name (see Brown & Ford, 1964). But our claim is that the universal (and incomplete) first draft of the moral mind gets filled in and revised so that the child can successfully navigate the moral "matrix" he or she actually experiences.

This is why we chose the architectural metaphor of a "foundation." Imagine that thousands of years ago, extraterrestrial aliens built 100 identical monumental sites scattered around the globe. But instead of building entire buildings, they just built five solid stone platforms, in irregular shapes, and left each site like that. If we were to photograph those 100 sites from the air today, we had probably be able to recognize the similarity across the sites, even though at each site people would have built diverse structures out of local materials. *The foundations are not the finished buildings*, but the foundations constrain the kinds of buildings that can be built most easily. Some societies might build a tall temple on just one foundation, and let the other foundations decay. Other societies might build a palace spanning multiple foundations, perhaps even all five. You cannot infer the exact shape and number of foundations by examining a single photograph, but if you collect photos from a few dozen sites, you can.

Similarly, *the moral foundations are not the finished moralities*, although they constrain the kinds of moral orders that can be built. Some societies build their moral order primarily on top of one or two foundations. Others use all five. You cannot see the foundations directly, and you cannot infer the exact shape and number of foundations by examining a single culture's morality. But if you examine ethnographic, correlational, and experimental data from a few dozen societies, you can. And if you look at the earliest emergence of moral cognition in babies and toddlers, you can see some of them as well (as we will show in Section 4.2). MFT is a theory about the universal first draft of the moral mind and about how that draft gets revised in variable ways across cultures.

2.3. Intuitionism: Intuitions come first, strategic reasoning second

Compared to the explicit deliberative reasoning studied by Kohlberg, moral judgments, like other evaluative judgments, tend to happen quickly (Zajonc, 1980; see review in Haidt, 2012, chapter 3). Social psychological research on moral judgment was heavily influenced by the "automaticity revolution" of the 1990s. As Bargh and Chartrand (1999, p. 462) put it: "most of a person's everyday life is determined not by their conscious intentions and deliberate choices but by mental processes that are put into motion by features of the environment that operate outside of conscious awareness and guidance." They noted that people engage in a great deal of conscious thought, but they questioned whether such thinking generally *causes* judgments or *follows along* after judgments have already been made. Impressed by the accuracy of social judgments based on "thin slices" of behavior (Ambady & Rosenthal, 1992), they wrote: "So it may be, especially for evaluations and judgments of novel people and objects, that what we think we are doing while consciously deliberating in actuality has no effect on the outcome of the judgment, as it has already been made through relatively immediate, automatic means" (Bargh & Chartrand, 1999, p. 475).

Drawing on this work (including Nisbett & Wilson, 1977; Wegner & Bargh, 1998), Haidt (2001) formulated the Social Intuitionist Model (SIM) and defined moral intuition as:

> *the sudden appearance in consciousness, or at the fringe of consciousness, of an evaluative feeling (like–dislike, good–bad) about the character or actions of a person, without any conscious awareness of having gone through steps of search, weighing evidence, or inferring a conclusion. (Haidt & Bjorklund, 2008, p. 188, modified from Haidt, 2001)*

In other words, the SIM proposed that moral evaluations generally occur rapidly and automatically, products of relatively effortless, associative, heuristic processing that psychologists now refer to as System 1 thinking (Kahneman, 2011; Stanovich & West, 2000; see also Bastick, 1982; Bruner, 1960; Simon, 1992, for earlier analyses of intuition that influenced the SIM). Moral evaluation, on this view, is more a product of the gut than the head, bearing a closer resemblance to esthetic judgment than principle-based reasoning.

This is not to say that individuals never engage in deliberative moral reasoning. Rather, Haidt's original formulation of the SIM was careful to state that this kind of effortful System 2 thinking, while seldom the genesis of our moral evaluations, was often initiated by social requirements to explain, defend, and justify our intuitive moral reactions to others. This notion that moral reasoning is done primarily for socially strategic purposes rather than to discover the honest truth about who did what to whom, and by what standard that action should be evaluated, is the crucial "social" aspect of the SIM. We reason to prepare for social interaction in a web of accountability concerns (Dunbar, 1996; Tetlock, 2002). We reason mostly so that we can support our judgments if called upon by others to do so. As such, our moral reasoning, like our reasoning about virtually every other aspect of our lives, is motivated (Ditto, Pizarro, & Tannenbaum, 2009; Kunda, 1990). It is shaped and directed by intuitive, often affective processes that tip the scales in support of desired conclusions. Reasoning is more like arguing than like rational, dispassionate deliberation (Mercier & Sperber, 2010), and people think and act more like intuitive lawyers than intuitive scientists (Baumeister & Newman, 1994; Ditto et al., 2009; Haidt, 2007a, 2007b, 2012).

The SIM is the prequel to MFT. The SIM says that most of the action in moral judgment is in rapid, automatic moral intuitions. These intuitions were shaped by development within a cultural context, and their output can be edited or channeled by subsequent reasoning and self-presentational concerns. Nonetheless, moral intuitions tend to fall into families or categories. MFT was designed to say exactly what those categories are, why we are so morally sensitive to a small set of issues (such as local instances of unfairness or disloyalty), and why these automatic moral intuitions vary across cultures. And this brings us to the fourth claim of MFT.

2.4. Pluralism: There were many recurrent social challenges, so there are many moral foundations

Evolutionary thinking encourages pluralism. As Cosmides and Tooby (1994, p. 91) put it: "Evolutionary biology suggests that there is no principled reason for parsimony to be a design criterion for the mind." Evolution has often been described as a tinkerer, cobbling together solutions to challenges out of whatever materials are available (Marcus, 2008). Evolutionary thinking also encourages functionalism. Thinking is for doing (Fiske, 1992; James, 1890/1950), and so innate mental structures, such as the moral foundations, are likely[3] to be responses to adaptive challenges that faced our ancestors for a very long time.

Table 2.1 lays out our current thinking. The first row lists five longstanding adaptive challenges that faced our ancestors for millions of years, creating conditions that favored the reproductive success of individuals who could solve the problems more effectively. For each challenge, the most effective modules were the ones that detected the relevant patterns in the social world and responded to them with the optimal motivational profile. Sperber (1994) refers to the set of all objects that a module was "designed"[4] to detect as the *proper domain* for that module. He contrasts the proper domain with the *actual domain*, which is the set of all objects that nowadays happens to trigger the module. But because these two terms are sometimes hard for readers to remember, we will use the equivalent terms offered by Haidt (2012): the *original triggers* and the *current triggers*.

We will explain the first column—the Care/harm foundation, in some detail, to show how to read the table. We will then explain the other four foundations more briefly. We want to reiterate that we do not believe these are the only foundations of morality. These are just the five we began with— the five for which we think the current evidence is best. In Section 4.2, we will give criteria that can be used to evaluate other candidate foundations.

2.4.1 The Care/harm foundation

All mammals face the adaptive challenge of caring for vulnerable offspring for an extended period of time. Human children are unusually dependent, and for an unusually long time. It is hard to imagine that in the book of human nature,

---

[3] Spandrels aside (Gould & Lewontin, 1979).

[4] Evolution *is* a design process; it is just not an intelligent design process. See Richerson and Boyd (2005).

Table 2.1 The original five foundations of intuitive ethics

Foundation	Care/harm	Fairness/cheating	Loyalty/betrayal	Authority/subversion	Sanctity/degradation
Adaptive challenge	Protect and care for children	Reap benefits of two-way partnerships	Form cohesive coalitions	Forge beneficial relationships within hierarchies	Avoid communicable diseases
Original triggers	Suffering, distress, or neediness expressed by one's child	Cheating, cooperation, deception	Threat or challenge to group	Signs of high and low rank	Waste products, diseased people
Current triggers	Baby seals, cute cartoon characters	Marital fidelity, broken vending machines	Sports teams, nations	Bosses, respected professionals	Immigration, deviant sexuality
Characteristic emotions	Compassion for victim; anger at perpetrator	Anger, gratitude, guilt	Group pride, rage at traitors	Respect, fear	Disgust
Relevant virtues	Caring, kindness	Fairness, justice, trustworthiness	Loyalty, patriotism, self-sacrifice	Obedience, deference	Temperance, chastity, piety, cleanliness

Adapted from Haidt (2012).

the chapter on mothering is completely blank—not structured in advance of experience—leaving it up to new mothers to learn from their culture, or from trial and error, what to do when their baby shows signs of hunger or injury. Rather, mammalian life has always been a competition in which females whose intuitive reactions to their children were optimized to detect signs of suffering, distress, or neediness raised more children to adulthood than did their less sensitive sisters. Whatever functional systems made it easy and automatic to connect perceptions of suffering with motivations to care, nurture, and protect are what we call the Care/harm foundation.

The original triggers of the Care/harm foundation are visual and auditory signs of suffering, distress, or neediness expressed by one's own child. But the perceptual modules that detect neoteny can be activated by other children, baby animals (which often share the proportions of children), stuffed animals and cartoon characters that are deliberately crafted to have the proportions of children, and stories told in newspapers about the suffering of people (even adults) far away. There are now many ways to trigger feelings of compassion for victims, an experience that is often mixed with anger toward those who cause harm.

But these moral emotions are not just private experiences. In all societies, people engage in gossip—discussions about the actions of third parties that are not present, typically including moral evaluations of those parties' actions (Dunbar, 1996). And as long as people engage in moral discourse, they develop virtue terms. They develop ways of describing the character and actions of others with reference to culturally normative ideals. They develop terms such as "kind" and "cruel" to describe people who care for or harm vulnerable others. Virtues related to the Care foundation may be highly prized and elaborated in some cultures (such as among Buddhists); less so in others (e.g., classical Sparta or Nazi Germany; Koonz, 2003).

2.4.2 The Fairness/cheating foundation

All social animals face recurrent opportunities to engage in nonzero-sum exchanges and relationships. Those whose minds are organized in advance of experience to be highly sensitive to evidence of cheating and cooperation, and to react with emotions that compel them to play "tit for tat" (Trivers, 1971), had an advantage over those who had to figure out their next move using their general intelligence. (See Frank, 1988, on how rational actors cannot easily solve "commitment problems," but moral emotions can.) The original triggers of the Fairness/cheating foundation involved acts of cheating or cooperation by one's own direct interaction partners, but the current triggers of the foundation can include interactions with inanimate objects (e.g., you put in a dollar, and the machine fails to deliver a soda), or interactions among third parties that one learns about through gossip. People who come to be known as good partners for exchange relationships are praised with virtue words such as fair, just, and trustworthy.

2.4.3 The Loyalty/betrayal foundation

Chimpanzee troops compete with other troops for territory (Goodall, 1986); coalitions of chimps compete with other coalitions within troops for rank and power (de Waal, 1982). But when humans developed language, weapons, and tribal markers, such intergroup competition became far more decisive for survival. Individuals whose minds were organized in advance of experience to make it easy for them to form cohesive coalitions were more likely to be part of winning teams in such competitions.[5] Sherif, Harvey, White, Hood, & Sherif (1961/1954) classic Robber's Cave study activated (and then deactivated) the original triggers of the loyalty foundation. Sports fandom and brand loyalty are examples of how easily modern consumer culture has built upon the foundation and created a broad set of current triggers.

2.4.4 The Authority/subversion foundation

Many primates, including chimpanzees and bonobos, live in dominance hierarchies, and those whose minds are structured in advance of experience to navigate such hierarchies effectively and forge beneficial relationships upward and downward have an advantage over those who fail to perceive or react appropriately in these complex social interactions (de Waal, 1982; Fiske, 1991). The various modules that comprise the Authority/subversion foundation are often at work when people interact with and grant legitimacy to modern institutions such as law courts and police departments, and to bosses and leaders of many kinds. Traits such as obedience and deference are virtues in some subcultures—such as among social conservatives in the United States—but can be seen as neutral or even as vices in others— such as among social liberals (Frimer, Biesanz, Walker, & MacKinlay, in press; Haidt & Graham, 2009; Stenner, 2005).

---

[5] There is an intense debate as to whether this competition of groups versus groups counts as group-level selection, and whether group-level selection shaped human nature. On the pro side, see Haidt (2012), Chapter 9. On the con side, see Pinker (2012).

2.4.5 The Sanctity/degradation foundation

Hominid history includes several turns that exposed our ancestors to greater risks from pathogens and parasites, for example, leaving the trees behind and living on the ground; living in larger and denser groups; and shifting to a more omnivorous diet, including more meat, some of which was scavenged. The emotion of disgust is widely thought to be an adaptation to that powerful adaptive challenge (Oaten, Stevenson, & Case, 2009; Rozin, Haidt, & McCauley, 2008). Individuals whose minds were structured in advance of experience to develop a more effective "behavioral immune system" (Schaller & Park, 2011) likely had an advantage over individuals who had to make each decision based purely on the sensory properties of potential foods, friends, and mates. Disgust and the behavioral immune system have come to undergird a variety of moral reactions, for example, to immigrants and sexual deviants (Faulkner, Schaller, Park, & Duncan, 2004; Navarrete & Fessler, 2006; Rozin et al., 2008). People who treat their bodies as temples are praised in some cultures for the virtues of temperance and chastity.

In sum, MFT is a nativist, cultural-developmentalist, intuitionist, and pluralist approach to the study of morality. We expect—and welcome— disagreements about our particular list of foundations. But we think that our general approach to the study of morality is well justified and is consistent with recent developments in many fields (e.g., neuroscience and developmental psychology, as we will show in Section 4). We think it will stand the test of time.

As for the specific list of foundations, we believe the best method for improving it is to go back and forth between theory and measurement. In the next section, we will show how our initial five foundations have been measured and used in psychological studies.

3. EMPIRICAL FINDINGS

In this chapter, we argue for the pragmatic validity of MFT, and of moral pluralism in general. Debates over our theoretical commitments— such as nativism and pluralism—can go on for centuries, but if a theory produces a steady stream of novel and useful findings, that is good evidence for its value. MFT has produced such a stream of findings, from researchers both within and outside of social psychology. Through its theoretical constructs, and the methods developed to measure them, MFT has enabled empirical advances that were not possible using monistic approaches. In this section, we review some of those findings, covering work on political ideology, relations between foundational concerns and other psychological constructs, cross-cultural differences, intergroup relations, and implicit processes in moral cognition.

3.1. Methods and measures

In a provocative article titled "There is nothing so theoretical as a good method," Greenwald (2012) argued that while theory development can bring about new methods, method development is just as crucial (if not more so) for the advancement of psychological theory. While MFT's origins were in anthropology and evolutionary theory, its development has been inextricably linked with the creation and validation of psychological methods by which to test its claims (and, when necessary, revise them accordingly). In fact, we see MFT's current and future development being one of *method-theory coevolution*, with theoretical constructs inspiring the creation of new ways to measure them, and data from the measurements guiding development of the theory.

Although a detailed description of all methods and measures created to test MFT's constructs is beyond the scope of this chapter, researchers interested in what tools are available can find brief descriptions and references in Table 2.2. As the table indicates, four kinds of MFT measures have been developed: (1) *Self-report surveys*—Although MFT is fundamentally about moral intuitions, these have been the most widely used by far, mostly to describe individual and cultural differences in endorsed moral concerns. (We note that according to most definitions of intuition, including the one we gave in Section 2.3, intuitions are available to consciousness and explicit reporting; it is the

Table 2.2 Methods developed to measure MFT's constructs

Method	Description	References
Self-report scales		
Moral Foundations Questionnaire	Ratings of the moral relevance of foundation-related considerations (part 1); agreement with statements supporting or rejecting foundation-related concerns	Graham, Nosek, Haidt, Iyer, Koleva, and Ditto (2011)
Moral Foundations Sacredness Scale	Reports of how much one would need to be paid to violate the foundations in different ways (including an option to refuse the offer for any amount of money)	Graham and Haidt (2012)

Table 2.2 Methods developed to measure MFT's constructs—cont'd

Method	Description	References
Implicit measures		
Evaluative priming	Foundation-related vice words (hurt, cruel, cheat, traitor, revolt, sin) used as primes flashed for 150 ms before positive or negative adjective targets	Graham (2010) (adapted from Ferguson, 2007)
Affect Misattribution Procedure	Pictures representing foundation-related virtues and vices flashed for 150 ms before Chinese characters, which participants rate as more or less positive than other characters	Graham (2010) (adapted from Payne, Cheng, Govorun, & Stewart, 2005)
Foundation Tradeoff Task	Quick dichotomous responses to "which is worse?" task pitting foundation violations against each other	Graham (2010)
Psychophysiological and neuroscience methods		
Facial electromyography	Measurement of affective microexpressions while hearing sentences describing actions supporting or violating foundations	Cannon, Schnall, and White (2011)
Time-specified stimuli for psychophysiological studies	Sentences presented one word at a time, with critical word indicating moral opinion supporting or rejecting a foundation	Graham (2010) (adapted from van Berkum, Holleman, Nieuwland, Otten, & Murre, 2009)
Neuroimaging vignettes	Scenarios describing possible violations of Care (assault) or Sanctity (incest), varying intent and outcome, for use in fMRI studies	Young and Saxe (2011)
Text analysis		
Moral Foundations Dictionary	Dictionary of foundation-related virtue and vice words, for use with Linguistic Inquiry and Word Count program (Pennebaker, Francis, & Booth, 2003)	Graham, Haidt, and Nosek (2009)

mechanisms that give rise to the intuition that are inaccessible.) (2) *Implicit measures*—Reaction time and other methods of implicit social cognition have been modified to bypass self-report and capture reactions to foundation-related words, sentences, and pictures (see Section 3.5.1). (3) *Psychophysiological and neuroscience methods*—These are also intended to bypass self-report, and measure nonconscious and affective reactions more directly, via facial micro-expressions, event-related potentials, or neuroimaging (see Section 3.5.2). (4) *Text analysis*—The *Moral Foundations Dictionary* has been useful for measuring foundation-related word use in a wide range of applications and disciplines, from computer science analyses of blogs (Dehghani, Gratch, Sachdeva, & Sagae, 2011) to digital humanities analyses of eighteenth-century texts (Pasanek, 2009) to political science analyses of the discourse of political elites (Clifford & Jerit, in press). The many methods developed have provided initial convergent and discriminant validity for our pluralistic model (see e.g., Graham et al., 2011), and several of them demonstrate the intuitive nature of moral judgment. Materials for most of the methods described in Table 2.2 can be found at www.MoralFoundations.org.

3.2. Moral foundations and political ideology

In his 1992 speech to the Republican National Convention, Pat Buchanan declared that the United States was engaged in a "cultural war" that was "as critical to the kind of nation we shall be as the Cold War itself." Exemplifying a thesis laid out in less polemic terms a year earlier by Hunter (1991), Buchanan described a battle between two competing moral visions for America. The first championed the virtues of American exceptionalism, traditional families and institutions, and Judeo-Christian sexual propriety (Hunter called this the "orthodox" worldview). The second vision, in Buchanan's dismissive portrayal, was determined to undermine these time-tested institutions and values with support for gay and abortion rights, a squeamish relationship with American power and moral authority, and a penchant for favoring corrosive welfare policies and the habitats of spotted owls over the homes and jobs of hardworking Americans (Hunter called this the "progressive" worldview). In the three decades, since Buchanan's opening salvo, there can be little doubt that this cultural divide between conservative and liberal moral sensibilities has only become deeper and more entrenched in American politics.

MFT was created for research in cultural psychology, not political psychology. Haidt and Joseph (2004) focused on variation in virtue concepts across cultures and eras. The list of foundations was not reverse-engineered from known differences between American liberals and conservatives. Yet the theory mapped on closely and easily to the two sides of the culture war described by Buchanan and by Hunter (1991). These were the first empirical findings produced with MFT (Haidt & Graham, 2007), and these are the findings for which the theory is best known today, so we begin our review with them.

3.2.1 Ideology in five dimensions

MFT's deepest roots are in the work of Richard Shweder, who showed that the moral domain is broader in India than among educated respondents in the United States (Shweder et al., 1987). Now that we have the terminology of Henrich, Heine, and Norenzayan (2010), we can say that the moral domain in WEIRD cultures (Western, Educated, Industrialized, Rich, and Democratic) is fairly narrow, comparatively speaking. It focuses on protecting individuals from harm and exploitation. In most traditional societies, however, the moral domain is broader, including concerns about protecting groups, institutions, traditions, and the moral order more generally. Haidt et al. (1993) confirmed Shweder's basic finding and showed that it holds across social classes in the United States and Brazil: richer people have a narrower moral domain. Haidt and Hersh (2001) provided the first evidence that Shweder's basic argument applied across the political spectrum too: in a small sample of college students who were interviewed about sexual morality, conservatives had a broader moral domain, making greater use of Shweder's ethics of community and divinity.

Shweder's three ethics translate directly into the five foundations (which were derived in part from those three ethics), leading Haidt and Graham (2007) to make the simple prediction that liberals would show greater reliance than conservatives upon the Care and Fairness foundations (which support the moral discourse of the ethics of autonomy), whereas conservatives would show greater reliance upon the Loyalty and Authority foundations (which support Shweder's ethic of community) and the Sanctity foundation (Shweder's ethic of divinity). To test this prediction, Graham, Haidt, and Nosek (2009) created an early draft of the Relevance scale (see Table 2.2; see also Graham et al., 2011). They found support for their prediction, and this basic pattern has been found in many subsequent studies, using many different methods (see Figure 2.1). Haidt and Graham (2007) suggested that MFT could help to explain many aspects of the culture war, including the specific issues that become battlefields, the intractability of the debates, and the inability of the two sides to even understand each other (because their moral visions were based on deep differences—differences

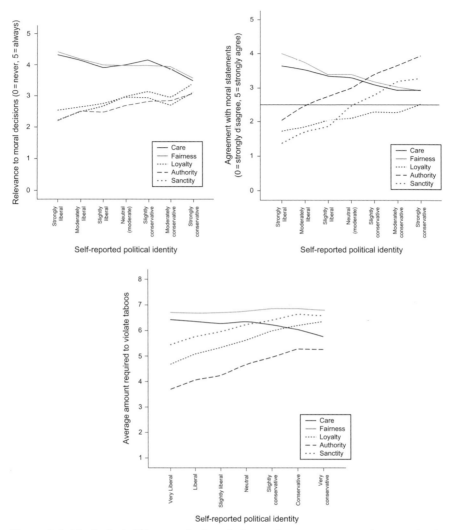

Figure 2.1 Ideological differences in foundation endorsement across three methods. *Adapted from Graham, Haidt, and Nosek (2009).*

in the very foundations upon which moral arguments could rest). Consistent with the intuitionist tradition, arguments about culture-war issues such as gay marriage, abortion, art, and welfare spending should not be expected to influence or convince people on the other side, because attitudes about specific issues are based on deep intuitions, not on the specific reasons put forth during a debate.

A number of studies using a variety of different methods and samples, conducted by several different research groups, have now replicated that first empirical finding. Graham et al. (2009), for example, used four different methods and consistently found that liberals valued Care and Fairness more than did conservatives, whereas conservatives valued Loyalty, Authority, and Sanctity more than did liberals (see Figure 2.1). Using a simple self-report political orientation scale (*very liberal* to *very conservative*) and examining large Internet samples, Graham et al. (2009) show this pattern in explicit judgments of moral relevance (upper left panel, Figure 2.1), agreement with foundation-relevant moral statements (upper right panel, Figure 2.1), and willingness to engage in foundation-related "taboo" acts for money (bottom panel, Figure 2.1). In each case, care and fairness are valued highly across the political spectrum, with liberals on average endorsing them slightly more than conservatives. Loyalty, Authority, and Sanctity, in contrast, show a clear linear increase in importance moving from extreme liberals to extreme conservatives. In a fourth study, Graham et al. (2009) found the same pattern of liberal–conservative differences comparing the frequency of foundation-related words used in the sermons of liberal and conservative churches (see Table 2.2).

Additional evidence of the robustness of this basic pattern of foundation differences is reported by Graham, Nosek, and Haidt (2012), who obtained the same results in a representative sample of U.S. citizens. Graham et al. (2011) have also replicated this ideological pattern using respondents at YourMorals.org from 11 different world regions (see Section 3.4 and Table 2.3).

Finally, McAdams et al. (2008) conducted life narrative interviews with a group of highly religious and politically engaged adults and coded their responses for themes related to the five moral foundations. They found what they characterized as "strong support" for MFT:

> When asked to describe in detail the nature and development of their own religious and moral beliefs, conservatives, and liberals engaged in dramatically different forms of moral discourse. Whereas conservatives spoke in moving terms about respecting authority and order, showing deep loyalty to family and country, and working hard to keep the self pure and good, liberals invested just as much emotion in describing their commitments to relieve the suffering of others and their concerns for fairness, justice, and equality. (McAdams et al., 2008, p. 987).

3.2.2 Personality–morality–ideology linkages

MFT views individual and group differences in reliance on the various moral foundations as emerging from the interactions of differences in biology, cultural socialization, and individual experience (see Haidt, 2012, chapter 12). A useful framework for conceptualizing these interactions is McAdams' three-level model of personality (1995) (McAdams & Pals, 2006). At Level 1

Table 2.3 Foundation correlations with political ideology by world area

	USA	UK	Canada	Australia	Western Europe	Eastern Europe	Latin America	Africa	Middle East	South Asia	East Asia	Southeast Asia	Average
N	80,322	2579	4314	1563	3766	888	1345	153	575	884	479	550	
Care	−0.35	−0.25	−0.31	−0.28	−0.22	−0.17	−0.16	−0.04	−0.19	−0.14	−0.19	−0.12	−0.20
Fairness	−0.44	−0.40	−0.36	−0.38	−0.33	−0.28	−0.33	−0.35	−0.32	−0.21	−0.24	−0.29	−0.32
Loyalty	0.47	0.42	0.34	0.44	0.35	0.35	0.32	0.39	0.42	0.33	0.28	0.33	0.37
Authority	0.56	0.51	0.50	0.53	0.47	0.43	0.46	0.51	0.56	0.42	0.37	0.48	0.48
Sanctity	0.58	0.46	0.47	0.52	0.46	0.45	0.48	0.51	0.51	0.45	0.42	0.49	0.49

Adapted from Graham et al. (2011)

are *dispositional traits* such as the Big 5. These are global, decontextualized traits that describe broad patterns of cognitive or emotional responding. At Level 2 are what McAdams calls *characteristic adaptations*, including values, goals, and moral strivings that are often reactions (or adaptations) to the contexts and challenges an individual encounters. Characteristic adaptations are therefore more conditional and domain-specific than dispositional traits and are thus more variable across life stages and situational contexts. Finally, at Level 3 in McAdams's framework are *integrative life stories*—the personal narratives that people construct to make sense of their values and beliefs. For many people, these life stories include an account of the development of their current moral beliefs and political ideology. Haidt, Graham, and Joseph (2009) elaborated McAdams' third level for work in political psychology by pointing out that many such stories are not fully self-authored, but rather are often "borrowed" from ideological narratives and stereotypes commonly held in the culture.

We view the moral and personality traits measured by our various methods (as summarized in Table 2.2) as Level 2 characteristic adaptations, linked closely to particular dispositional traits (Level 1). We cannot measure moral foundations directly—we cannot see the "first draft" of the moral mind. All we can do is read the finished books and quantify the differences among individuals and groups. All we can do is measure the morality of a person and quantify the degree to which that person's morality is based on each foundation. (We sometimes say that a person scored high on a particular foundation, but that is a shorthand way of saying that their morality, as we measure it, relies heavily on virtues and concepts related to that foundation.) An individual's morality is constructed as they grow up in a particular culture, with particular life experiences. But two siblings who bring different dispositional traits to otherwise similar contexts and experiences will develop different moral and political characteristic adaptations. As young adults, they will then find different ideological narratives compelling and may come to self-identify as members of different political parties.

For example, substantial evidence suggests that political conservatism is associated with personality characteristics that incline individuals toward a general resistance to novelty and change. In a comprehensive meta-analysis of the psychological correlates of conservatism, Jost, Glaser, Kruglanski, and Sulloway (2003) found that, compared to liberals, conservatives have higher needs for order, structure, and closure, and report lower levels of openness to experience. Conservatives have been found to respond less positively to novel stimuli at physiological and attentional levels as well (Amodio, Jost,

Master, & Yee, 2007; Hibbing & Smith, 2007; Oxley et al., 2008; Shook & Fazio, 2009). Similarly, a growing body of literature has revealed a relation between greater political conservatism and heightened levels of disgust sensitivity (Dodd et al., 2012; Helzer & Pizarro, 2011; Inbar, Pizarro, & Bloom, 2009; Inbar, Pizarro, Iyer, & Haidt, 2012; Smith, Oxley, Hibbing, Alford, & Hibbing, 2011). Together, this constellation of dispositional tendencies may provide the emotional infrastructure underlying conservative reverence for long-established institutions and highly structured systems of social hierarchy and sexual propriety. Conversely, individuals with lower need for structure, greater openness to experience, and dampened disgust sensitivity should be less anxious about challenging traditional authority structures, lifestyle, and sexual practices. These dispositional tendencies may in turn afford greater attraction to liberal policy positions seeking to "reform" traditional values and institutions to reflect greater equality for historically oppressed social groups and a less restrictive view of sexual purity and moral contamination more generally.

Providing empirical support for the causal connections between personality characteristics, moral concerns, and political ideology is a challenging task, and more research in this area is clearly needed. A small set of studies, however, have directly examined these types of associations. Lewis and Bates (2011) measured the Big Five personality traits, moral foundations, and political ideology and found that higher scores on Care–Fairness were related to greater openness, neuroticism, and agreeableness, and that higher Loyalty–Authority–Sanctity scores were associated with greater conscientiousness and extraversion, and lower levels of neuroticism. Importantly, and consistent with McAdams' three-level personality model, moral foundation endorsements mediated the relationship between Big Five traits and political ideology.

In a similar study, Hirsh, DeYoung, Xu, and Peterson (2010) used a more fine-grained measure of the Big Five personality traits that separates each trait into two separate "aspects" (DeYoung, Quilty, & Peterson, 2007). Like Lewis and Bates (2011), they found an overall measure of agreeableness to be a significant predictor of greater endorsement of the Care and Fairness foundations, but that when examined at the level of aspects, this relation was limited to the aspect of agreeableness they term compassion. The other aspect of agreeableness, politeness, was not related to Care–Fairness scores but was, in fact, predictive of higher scores on the Authority foundation. Also, where Lewis and Bates (2011) found openness to be a significant predictor of Care–Fairness, Hirsh et al. (2010) found no significant relation, but they did find a negative relation between openness (particularly the intellect aspect) and the Authority and Sanctity foundations. Hirsh et al. (2010) also found an association between greater overall conscientiousness and endorsement of Loyalty, Authority, and Sanctity foundations, but these relations were driven only by the orderliness (not the industriousness) aspect of that trait. Subtle differences between these and the Lewis and Bates (2011) findings notwithstanding, the Hirsh et al. (2010) findings are consistent with the general thrust of MFT, and their study again provides evidence that moral foundation endorsements mediated the relationships between personality factors and political ideology.

Finally, in an attempt to integrate research on conservative sensitivity to threatening stimuli with MFT, Van Leeuwen and Park (2009) examined whether a conservative pattern of moral foundation endorsement mediated the relationship between perceived social dangers and political conservatism. They found that the tendency to emphasize Loyalty, Authority, and Sanctity over Care and Fairness was related to both explicit and implicit conservatism in the expected directions, and that it also partially mediated the relationship between Belief in a Dangerous World and conservatism. The authors argue that these results suggest that a basic inclination to perceive the environment as dangerous may lead to greater endorsement of the Loyalty, Authority, and Sanctity foundations, perhaps due to the perceived protection these group-oriented values seem to provide.

3.2.3 Political stereotypes and interpersonal judgment

It has often been said that politics is perception. Do the relations between moral foundations and political ideology have implications for how people perceive and make judgments about groups and individuals? Do people recognize the moral differences between liberals and conservatives? Do liberal and conservative moral profiles predict what characteristics they will view favorably in others?

Graham et al. (2011) addressed some of these questions by examining whether people favored or disfavored members of social groups that were conceptually related to the five moral foundations. The researchers began by categorizing 27 social groups according to the moral foundations they exemplify, for example, ACLU members (Fairness), police officers (Authority), and virgins (Sanctity). They found that participants' attitudes toward these groups were predicted most strongly by their endorsement of the corresponding moral foundations, even when controlling for political ideology. In other words, knowing a person's MFQ scores gives you important information, over and above their ideology, about their social group prejudices. These results speak to the tight relationship between social and moral judgment, while also demonstrating the predictive and discriminant validity of the five foundations.

Graham, Nosek, et al. (2012) used MFT to examine the moral stereotypes liberals and conservatives hold about each other. Participants filled out the MFQ either normally, or else as a "typical" liberal, or else as a "typical" conservative. Overall, participants correctly simulated the general liberal-conservative pattern predicted by MFT. That is, the typical liberal scores were higher than the typical conservative scores on Care and Fairness, and the typical conservative scores were higher than the typical liberal scores on Loyalty, Authority, and Sanctity. However, participants' estimations of these differences were exaggerated. In fact, the differences in moral foundation scores that participants reported for the typical liberal and the typical conservative were significantly larger than the actual differences observed between even the most extreme partisans. Although participants who identified as liberals, moderates, and conservatives all exaggerated these stereotypes, they did so to varying degrees. Liberals, more than conservatives and moderates, reported the most exaggerated stereotypes of political partisans when estimating all five foundations. Most importantly, conservatives tended to be relatively accurate in their beliefs about how much liberals valued Care and Fairness, but liberals estimated that conservatives valued these foundations far less than they actually did. MFT's pluralistic approach thus allows not only for a better understanding of the moral differences between liberals and conservatives but also for a more nuanced understanding of the moral stereotypes that contribute to the seemingly intractable nature of partisan conflict.

In terms of judgments of individuals rather than groups, Federico, Weber, Ergun, and Hunt (in press) asked two groups of respondents (professors solicited from liberal and conservative colleges and visitors to Mechanical Turk) to evaluate the extent to which 40 of the most influential people of the twentieth century were "moral exemplars." A moral exemplar was defined simply as "a highly moral person." The target individuals had previously been rated by a separate sample of social science professors as to how much each individual embodied each of the five moral foundations. The results were generally quite consistent with the predictions of MFT, although subtle and important differences did emerge. Overall, there was substantial agreement across the ideological spectrum on what led an individual to be perceived as virtuous, with both liberal and conservative respondents relying most heavily in their moral evaluations on the targets' embodiment of the Care, Fairness, and Sanctity foundations. Ideological agreement regarding the moral importance of Care and Fairness follows directly from MFT, but the importance liberals placed on the Sanctity foundation is more surprising (although it was only a significant predictor of liberal moral evaluations in the academic sample). Also consistent with MFT, liberals were more likely than conservatives to favor those individuals who espoused virtues related to the Care and Fairness foundations, while conservatives were more likely than liberals to favor those who personified virtues related to Authority and Sanctity. The most important divergence from the predictions of MFT was that target individuals' embodiment of Loyalty and Authority had no significant effect on judgments of virtuousness, even for conservative respondents. In fact, Authority was actually found to be a negative predictor of liberals' moral evaluations, suggesting that those on the political left may perceive the embodiment of Authority as more vice than a virtue. Frimer et al. (in press) conclude from their findings that Care, Fairness, and Sanctity are core foundations of moral evaluation but that Loyalty and Authority may play more complicated, interactive roles that need to be unpacked by future research.

MFT has even been useful in understanding preferences for individual political candidates. Iyer, Graham, Koleva, Ditto, and Haidt (2010) compared two similar groups of Democrats during the 2008 Democratic Primary: supporters of Hillary Clinton and supporters of Barack Obama. Although both candidates were Democrats with only subtle policy differences, their supporters differed on several individual difference measures (psychopathic personality, moral relativism, empathy, and global concern for others). Most importantly, endorsement of the moral foundations predicted which candidate participants were more likely to favor, even when controlling for age, gender, education, and self-placement on the liberal-conservative dimension. Specifically, Clinton supporters showed a more "conservative" profile of moral foundation endorsement, as greater endorsement of both the Loyalty and Authority foundations predicted Clinton favorability. Relative favorability toward Obama, on the other hand, was predicted by greater endorsement of the Fairness foundation. This pattern makes sense given that Clinton polled better with the relatively conservative white working class.

3.2.4 Beyond liberal and conservative

The research discussed thus far describes ideological differences in reliance on the moral foundations as if all individuals fit neatly along a single liberal-conservative continuum. However, political ideology is a complex and multifaceted construct that can be understood along multiple dimensions. For example, one popular method is to distinguish economic and social political preferences (Conover & Feldman, 1981; Duckitt, 2001; McClosky & Zaller, 1984; Weber & Federico, 2007). MFT offers the opportunity to create a five-dimensional space, and then to examine whether people tend to cluster into some regions and not others.

Haidt et al. (2009) investigated this possibility by performing a cluster analysis of over 20,000 American participants who completed the Moral Foundations Questionnaire. They found support for a four-cluster solution, which identified four groups with distinct moral profiles (see Figure 2.2). The first group, labeled "secular liberals," scored the highest on Care and Fairness, and they scored very low on Loyalty, Authority, and Sanctity. This group also scored the highest on Openness to Experience and lowest on Right Wing Authoritarianism and Social Dominance Orientation, a pattern that typically exemplifies American liberalism. They also reported high levels of atheism. By contrast, the group labeled "social conservatives" showed a nearly opposite profile of results. Social conservatives were lowest on the Care and Fairness foundations and very high on the other three. They were low on Openness to Experience, high on both Right Wing Authoritarianism and Social Dominance Orientation, and they reported the most frequent religious attendance.

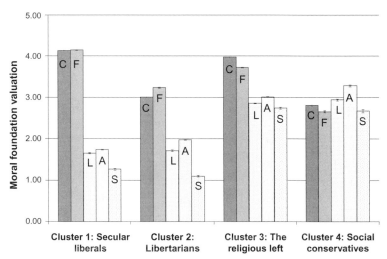

Figure 2.2 Cluster analysis of Moral Foundations Questionnaire responses. *Note*: C, Care; F, Fairness; L, Loyalty; A, Authority; S, Sanctity. *N*s for each cluster are as follows: 5946 (cluster 1), 5931 (cluster 2), 6397 (cluster 3), 2688 (cluster 4). Error bars represent ±2 S.E. *Adapted from Haidt et al. (2009).*

These two clusters offered no surprises. They are just what you had expect from our common stereotypes about liberals and conservatives, and from the findings of Graham et al. (2009) and Jost et al. (2003). However, the other two groups were different. The third group, dubbed "libertarians," scored low on all five moral foundations, and they tended to highly value hedonism and self-direction on the Schwartz Values Scale (Schwartz & Bilsky, 1990), and they showed high levels of atheism. The fourth group, labeled "religious left," scored relatively high on all five foundations, on religious participation, and on the Schwartz values of benevolence, tradition, conformity, security, and spirituality. Importantly, neither the libertarians nor the religious left fits neatly into the categories of "liberal" or "conservative," but their unique moral and psychological identity was detectable when their moralities were analyzed using the five scores of the MFQ. The left-right dimension is indeed useful as a first pass (Jost, 2006). But the pluralism of MFT gives us greater resolution and detects groups that do not fit well on that one dimension.

In a similar vein, Weber and Federico (in press) used a mixed model latent class analysis to argue for a more heterogeneous approach to understanding political ideology after identifying six discrete ideological groups (consistent liberals, libertarians, social conservatives, moderates, consistent conservatives, inconsistent liberals). They found each group to have unique sets of economic and social policy preferences that were reflected in distinct patterns of moral foundation endorsement. Further, Care and Fairness concerns were most related to an ideological preference dimension of equality–inequality, while Loyalty, Authority, and Sanctity were most aligned with the ideological preference dimension of openness-conformity (Federico et al., in press).

The most extensive examination of an ideological subgroup that cannot be easily placed along a simple liberal-conservative dimension is the work of Iyer, Koleva, Graham, Ditto, and Haidt (2012) that set out to identify the cognitive, affective, and moral characteristics of self-identified libertarians. Libertarians are an increasingly influential group in American politics, with their ideological positions gaining attention through the popularity of the Tea Party movement and media coverage of the Presidential campaign of Congressman Ron Paul (R-TX). Libertarian values, however, presented a challenge for MFT, as the primary value that libertarians espouse— individual liberty—was not well captured by the existing five foundations. Indeed, the original conception of MFT (Haidt & Joseph, 2004) took Shweder's ethic of autonomy and created foundations that represented the liberal vision of positive liberty, where individual freedom is defined by opportunity, rather than the libertarian vision of negative liberty, where individual freedom is defined by a lack of obstruction (see Berlin, 1969, for a broader discussion of negative vs. positive liberty).

Iyer et al. (2012) compared a large sample of self-identified libertarians ($N = 11{,}994$) to self-identified liberals and conservatives across dozens of measures, looking in particular at measures that would shed light on the moral values of Libertarians. They also created a set of MFQ-like items designed specifically to measure endorsement of liberty as a moral value. In the cluster analysis described above (from Haidt et al., 2009), the cluster containing the largest number of libertarians reported relatively weak endorsement on all five foundation subscales of the MFQ. Iyer et al. similarly found that self-described libertarians showed relatively weak endorsement of all five foundations; both the relatively weaker endorsement of Care and Fairness concerns typical of conservatives, as well as the relatively weaker endorsement of Loyalty, Authority, and Sanctity concerns typical of liberals (see Figure 2.3).

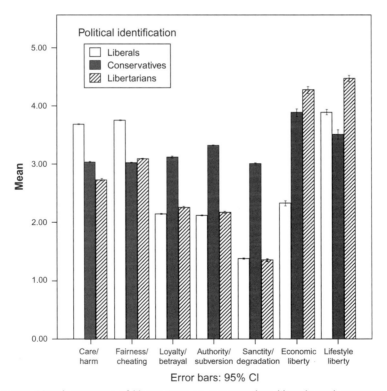

Figure 2.3 Moral concerns of libertarians as compared to liberals and conservatives. *Adapted from Iyer et al. (2012).*

Does that mean that libertarians have no morality—or, at least, less concern with moral issues than liberals or conservatives? Or might it be that their core moral value was simply not represented among the five foundations measured by the MFQ? Consistent with the latter position, when Iyer et al. examined the items tapping the value placed on liberty as a moral concern, they found that libertarians did indeed score higher than both liberals and conservatives. This relative valuation of liberty was found both on items tapping concerns about economic and property-related freedoms (typically valued by political conservatives more than liberals) as well as lifestyle freedoms (typically valued by political liberals more than conservatives). Similar findings emerged from the Good Self measure (Barriga, Morrison, Liau, & Gibbs, 2001), where libertarians reported valuing being independent more than other groups, as well as from the Schwartz Values Scale (Schwartz, 1992), on which libertarians scored highest of all groups on valuing self-direction.

Iyer et al. also identified a number of other interesting psychological characteristics of their libertarian sample. Perhaps reflecting the emotional underpinnings of their focus on individual liberty, libertarians scored higher than liberals or conservatives on a scale measuring psychological reactance (Brehm & Brehm, 1981; Hong, 1996). Libertarians also showed a relatively cerebral as opposed to emotional cognitive style (e.g., high in need for cognition, low empathizing, and high systematizing [Baron-Cohen, 2009]) and lower interdependence and social relatedness (e.g., low collectivism, low on all three subscales of the Identification with All of Humanity Scale).

Together, these findings paint a consistent portrait of the moral psychology of libertarianism. Libertarians—true to their own descriptions of themselves—value reason over emotion and show more autonomy and less interdependence. Their central moral value, therefore, is one that grants people the right to be left alone. MFT's five moral foundations appeared to be inadequate in capturing libertarians' moral concerns, but the approach that gave birth to these foundations served us well in examining this new group, and stimulated us to consider Liberty/oppression as a candidate for addition to our list of foundations (see Section 4.1.5, and further discussion in Haidt, 2012, chapter 8).

3.3. Moral foundations and other psychological constructs

One of the liveliest areas of current moral psychology is the intersection of moral judgment, attitudes, and emotion. Many of these studies have also focused on ideology variables, either as predictors or as outcomes of situational and individual variation in moral intuition and emotion.

3.3.1 Attitudes

Koleva, Graham, Iyer, Ditto, and Haidt (2012) illustrated the utility of MFT's pluralistic framework for understanding the psychological underpinnings of specific policy issues. In two web studies ($N = 24,739$), we used scores on the MFQ to predict moral disapproval and attitude stands on 20 hot-button issues, such as same-sex marriage, abortion, torture, and flag desecration/protection. We found that MFQ scores predicted attitudes on these issues, even after partialling out participants' ideology, gender, religiosity, and other demographic variables. We expected that the foundations would predict variation based on overlapping content—for example, people who scored high on the Care foundation would be particularly sensitive to issues involving violence or cruelty, and this was indeed true, in general. But unexpectedly, the Sanctity foundation emerged as the strongest predicting foundation for most issues. For example, people who score high on the loyalty foundation tend to be more patriotic, and therefore more strongly in favor of "protecting" the flag from desecration, but scores on the Sanctity foundation were even more predictive. Some people see the flag as merely a piece of cloth; others see it as a sacred object, containing a nonmaterial essence that must be protected. These findings about the importance of Sanctity in ongoing political controversies could not have been obtained using moral theories that limited the moral domain to issues of Care or Fairness.

Another advantage of using a multifaceted approach like MFT is that it helps us understand how a person could hold different attitudes across issues that appear to engender similar moral concerns. For example, even though abortion, euthanasia, and the death penalty all evoke arguments for the sanctity of life, opposition to the first two was best predicted by Sanctity, whereas opposition to the third was best predicted by Care scores. This may help explain why liberals, who score low on Sanctity concerns (Graham et al., 2009; Haidt & Graham, 2007), do not generally oppose access to abortion and euthanasia, but do tend to oppose the death penalty.

Aside from refining our understanding of ideological opinions, these findings suggest novel approaches to persuasion and attitude change. For example, Feinberg and Willer (2013) showed that framing messages about the environment in terms of Sanctity, rather than just Care, increased conservatives' support for environmental policies, presumably because this framing triggers intuitions which resonate with conservatives.

3.3.2 Emotion

In a related line of inquiry, researchers have examined the interplay between morality and emotion, particularly the emotion of disgust, in shaping moral judgments and ideological attitudes and self-identification. Much of this work has either explicitly drawn on MFT or offers indirect evidence that supports its premises. For example, Horberg, Oveis, Keltner, and Cohen (2009) showed that an individual's trait propensity toward feeling disgust, an emotion that is related to Sanctity concerns (Rozin et al., 2008), as well as experimental inductions of disgust, intensified the moral importance of maintaining physical and spiritual purity. This effect was specific: other emotions, such as trait or state anger, fear, or sadness did not have an effect on judgments related to purity, and disgust did not affect nonpurity moral judgments, such as Care/harm or justice. Finally, Preston and Ritter (2012) showed that the concepts of religion and cleanliness are linked such that priming religion increased the mental accessibility of cleanliness-related concepts and the desirability of cleaning products, whereas priming thoughts of personal cleanliness increased ratings of the value ascribed to religious beliefs. This work underscores the relevance of experiences with and concerns about the Sanctity foundation to moral judgment.

Building on the finding that conservatives tend to moralize Sanctity concerns more than liberals (Graham et al., 2009). Helzer and Pizarro (2011) reported two experiments in which subtle reminders of physical purity—standing by a hand sanitizer and using hand wipes—led participants to report being more politically conservative and more disapproving of sexual purity violations, like incest or masturbation. Similarly, Inbar, Pizarro, and Bloom (2011) found that experimental inductions of disgust led participants to report more negative attitudes toward gay men but not toward lesbians or other outgroups. However, unlike Helzer and Pizarro (2011), these researchers did not find a general effect of disgust on political attitudes or on self-identification. Finally, Inbar, Pizarro, Iyer, and Haidt (2012) showed that self-identified conservatives, both in the United States and around the world, reported greater propensity toward feeling contamination disgust, and that disgust sensitivity predicted voting patterns in the United States. Interestingly, Jarudi (2009) found that conservatives were more sensitive to purity concerns about sex (e.g., anal sex), but not about food (e.g., eating fast food), even though disgust sensitivity was related to disapproval in both domains.

Finally, several studies have examined the role of anger and contempt, in addition to disgust, in response to foundation-related violations. For example, Russell and Giner-Sorolla (2011) gave participants scenarios that depicted violations of Care, Fairness, or Sanctity and assessed their moral judgments, anger, and disgust. Next, participants were asked to generate circumstances that could change their opinion and then to reevaluate the scenarios assuming these new circumstances. Whereas ratings of disgust did not change during reevaluation, anger for the harm and fairness violations was decreased and this change in emotion predicted a change in moral judgment. These findings suggest that moral anger is a more flexible emotion that is sensitive to context, whereas moral disgust appears to be less so.

Another study on the role of anger, contempt, and disgust in moral judgment showed that even violations outside the Sanctity domain elicit strong moral disgust, suggesting a domain-general function for this emotion (Hutcherson & Gross, 2011). However, the authors also found that moral violations that entail direct harm to the self-elicited anger more than disgust, and that contempt was the strongest emotional response to nonmoral violations attributed to low competence. Taken together, these studies suggest that anger and disgust are common responses to moral transgressions, but that anger is, in a sense, more open to reason and revision based on new information.

The ability to contrast multiple moral emotions, operating with respect to multiple sets of moral issues, is greatly enhanced by the pluralism and intuitionism of MFT, compared to moral theories that are either monist or rationalist. Among the most important discoveries has been the powerful and until-recently underappreciated role of disgust, and related intuitions about sanctity, in moral judgment, political attitudes, and even voting behavior.

3.3.3 Moral character

In addition to attitudes and emotion, several studies have now explored the moral foundations' association with variables related to moral character. For example, in a large community sample, individuals scoring higher on non-diagnostic psychopathic trait measures indicated less concerns about care and fairness as measured by the MFQ (Glenn, Iyer, Graham, Koleva, & Haidt, 2009); these associations were mediated by their weaker empathic concern. Psychopathic personality was also associated with high endorsement of loyalty, which was mediated by greater social dominance orientation. However, when morality was measured with the Sacredness Scale (see Table 2.2), those high in psychopathic personality indicated greater willingness to violate *all five* foundations for money, suggesting that such individuals might be generally similar to those low in psychopathy in terms of their abstract moral evaluations, but are more willing to (hypothetically) violate moral concerns in exchange for a salient reward like money.

Finally, the moral foundations have been examined not just in relation to participants' own character but also in relation to how they infer others' traits. Specifically, Clifford and Jerit (in press) found that foundation scores predicted relevant traits' accessibility when describing politicians (e.g., Care scores were positively related to how many Harm-related traits, e.g., kind and compassionate, were brought to mind). Furthermore, a politician's known position on an issue interacted with the individuals' own position in affecting trait-inferences related to the foundation assumed to motivate the position (e.g., if one opposes the death penalty due to strong harm concerns, one will rate a politician who supports the death penalty as low on harm traits).

3.3.4 Other psychological constructs

In addition to these studies of attitudes, emotion, and character, researchers have used MFT to examine a variety of other constructs. For example, using an evolutionary framework, Kurzban and colleagues found that participants' Care and Sanctity scores related to their opposition to recreational drug use, which the authors argue to be driven by unrestricted views on sexuality (Kurzban, Dukes, & Weeden, 2010).

Similarly, building on an evolutionary perspective of sports fandom as a by-product of adaptations that evolved in the context of small-scale warfare, Winegard and Deaner (2010) found that participants' endorsement of moral concerns about group loyalty predicted the extent to which they identified with their favorite sports team. Furthermore, men scored higher on Loyalty than women, and this difference partially explained their higher sports fandom compared to women's.

Within the field of communication, Tamborini and colleagues recently examined the link between moral sensitivity to harm and fairness and perceptions and appeal of violent media (Tamborini, Eden, Bowman, Grizzard, & Lachlan, 2012). Their findings indicated that higher Care scores predicted perceptions of a film narrative that contained gratuitous violence as more graphic and less appealing. Similarly, higher Fairness scores predicted greater appeal of a film narrative that contained strong justification of violence.

Finally, a recent study in environmental and agricultural ethics explored individuals' free associations with the phrases "ethical/morally right food" and "unethical/morally wrong food" and categorized them as relating to the moral foundations (Makiniemi, Pirttila-Backman, & Pieri, in press). Results suggested that the free associations were dominated by concepts related to the Care and Sanctity foundations, followed by Fairness, Loyalty, and Authority concerns.

3.4. Cross-cultural differences and intergroup relations

For any theory that claims to be rooted in human nature, the theory must be tested in diverse samples and across different cultures. While MFT is in its toddlerhood, great progress has already been made in examining the moral foundations in several cultures. In this section, we describe how MFT has been used so far to investigate cultural differences in morality and phenomena related to intergroup relations more generally.

3.4.1 East-West cultural differences

Using a large international sample, Graham et al. (2011) showed that the moral foundations model was a good fit to the data across world regions. They also found that even after controlling for various demographic variables, world region was a significant predictor of foundation-related concerns. Specifically, participants in Eastern cultures (South Asia, East Asia, and Southeast Asia) expressed slightly greater Loyalty- and Sanctity-related moral concerns than did participants in Western cultures (United States, Canada, United Kingdom, and other Western European countries), which are consistent with established cultural differences in collectivism (Triandis, 1995) and the role of purity concerns in daily life and religious practices (Shweder et al., 1997). Furthermore, compared to the liberal versus conservative differences in the United States, these cross-cultural differences were small—consistent with the theory that variation within cultures exceeds variation between cultures (e.g., Vauclair & Fischer, 2011).

However, the findings of Graham et al. (2011) come with two important caveats: they are based on data collected in English and from participants with access to the Internet. Thus, these findings likely come from Westernized (or even WEIRD) segments of these populations. Fortunately, researchers in dozens of countries have been translating and back-translating moral foundations measures (translations available at MoralFoundations.org), and collecting data with them among native speakers in various countries (see e.g., Bobbio, Nencini, & Sarrica, 2011; Kim, Kang, & Yun, 2012; Van Leeuwen & Park, 2009). For example, as of June 2012, the MFQ has been translated into Amharic, Arabic, Bahasa Indonesian, Bengali, Chinese (Cantonese and Mandarin), Croatian, Dari (Afghan Persian), Dutch, Farsi (Persian), French, French Canadian, German, Greek, Hebrew, Hindi, Indonesian, Italian, Japanese, Kiswahili, Korean, Lithuanian, Malay, Nepali, Polish, Portuguese, Portuguese (Brazilian), Romanian, Russian, Serbian, Spanish, Spanish-Castilian, Swedish, Tagalog, Thai, Turkish, Ukrainian, Urdu, Vietnamese, and Yoruba (Nigeria). Field work in Nicaragua has enabled foundation measurement among social groups who do not typically speak English or have access to the Internet (migrant field workers, residents of the Managua city dump, sex workers), and further field work is planned for India, Iran, Morocco, and Lebanon. This work will be crucial not only for detecting cross-cultural differences in reliance on the foundations but also for exploring within-culture variation as well.

3.4.2 Other cultural differences

Within both Eastern and Western cultures, there are a number of consistent patterns of moral concerns. Evolutionary perspectives (e.g., Neuberg, Kenrick, & Schaller, 2010; Van Vugt & Park, 2009) note that pathogens are among the principle existential threats to organisms, so those who could best avoid pathogens would have enhanced evolutionary fitness. Van Vugt and Park contend that human groups develop unique practices for reducing pathogen exposure—particularly in how they prepare their foods and maintain their hygiene. When groups are exposed to the practices of a foreign culture, they may perceive its members as especially likely to carry pathogens that may contaminate one's ingroup. This contamination fear may lead people to place greater emphasis on Sanctity, which Haidt and Joseph (2007) describe as originating in an anti-pathogen system. In a recent analysis, Van Leeuwen, Park, Koenig, and Graham (2012) demonstrated that historical pathogen prevalence at the country level is a significant predictor not only of Sanctity but also of Loyalty and Authority as well. Specifically, there was a positive relationship between country-level historical pathogen prevalence and individual-level endorsement of these three foundations, even after statistically controlling for national gross domestic product and individual demographic variables. In addition to providing support for the proposal that Sanctity intuitions are related to mechanisms for combating pathogenic disease, these findings also suggest that pathogen prevalence and contamination fears may enhance group cohesion, collectivism, and adherence to group norms, as a means to minimize the contamination threat.

The threat that other cultures engender may lead to individual differences within Eastern and Western cultures, too. Van Leeuwen and Park (2009) conducted a study showing that perceiving the social world as dangerous predicts increased adherence to the binding moral foundations, which predicts increased conservatism on measures of political orientation. Furthermore, adherence to these binding foundations mediated the relationship between perceptions of a dangerous world and political conservatism.

The link between moral foundations and political orientation appears robust across cultures (see Table 2.3). Graham et al. (2011) found that across the 12 world regions for which data were available, liberals consistently valued Care and Fairness concerns more than conservatives, whereas conservatives consistently valued Loyalty, Authority, and Sanctity more than liberals. Further, they found that these political orientation patterns were robust across national and cultural contexts, both in terms of direction (i.e., a negative relationship between conservatism and valuation of Care and Fairness and a positive relationship between conservatism and Loyalty, Authority, and Sanctity) and magnitude (i.e., correlations were consistently stronger for Authority and Sanctity, and weakest for Care). Van Leeuwen and Park (2009) found a similar relationship between moral foundations and political orientation among a sample of Dutch participants, providing further evidence of the robustness of this pattern across national and cultural contexts. The relative predictive power of the Authority and Sanctity foundations across studies and across cultures suggests that the most intractable of political conflicts are particularly likely to involve disagreements about respect for tradition, authority, and spiritual purity.

3.4.3 Intergroup relations

Moral differences often lead to poor intergroup relations. Kesebir and Pyszczynski (2011) (see also Motyl & Pyszczynski, 2009; Pyszczynski, Motyl, & Abdollahi, 2009) argue that the mere awareness of groups with different moral intuitions and worldviews is existentially threatening and may engender hostility and violence. In one series of studies, McGregor et al. (1998) showed that when participants read a passage that disparaged their political views as amoral and sickening they were more aggressive and administered more hot sauce to their critic. In related work, Rosenblatt, Greenberg, Solomon, Pyszczynski, and Lyon (1989) found that threats led to increased punitiveness toward moral transgressors. The punishments were greatest when judging prostitutes, whose behavior violates the Sanctity foundation. Together, these findings suggest that disagreement on moral intuitions is especially likely to lead to increased intergroup aggression and conflict.

Intergroup moral conflicts are particularly intractable. As the moral issues at the core of these conflicts are rooted in different intuitions, people on opposing sides of these conflicts simply do not understand how anyone can hold different moral intuitions (Ditto & Koleva, 2011). This empathy gap leads people to view adherents of different moral worldviews as less warm than adherents of similar moral worldviews (Bruneau, Dufour, & Saxe, 2012). Similarly, this empathy gap for moral and political adversaries can make intergroup violence more likely, as adversaries can more easily view each other as not deserving moral rights (Waytz, Epley, & Cacioppo, 2010).

3.5. Implicit moral cognition

Although MFT is at base a theory about the intuitive nature of moral concerns, work on the implicit processes involved in foundation-related judgments is still in its infancy. Nevertheless, MFT's pluralist approach can provide a theoretical framework to organize and explain disparate findings connecting morality and automaticity. As discussed in Section 3.3.2, incidental disgust (caused by bad smells in the air or dirty surroundings) has been shown to increase the harshness of moral judgments (Schnall, Haidt, Clore, & Jordan, 2008), even when the disgust was induced via hypnotic suggestion that participants could not consciously recall afterward (Wheatley & Haidt, 2005). Similarly, individual differences in disgust sensitivity have been shown to predict intuitive negativity toward gays, measured both by an Implicit Association Test and by intentionality assessments (Inbar, Pizarro, Knobe, & Bloom, 2009). Such unconscious effects are not only a blow to our collective self-image as rational moral decision-makers, they are also difficult to explain with monist theories treating all morality as harm (Gray et al., 2012), fairness (Baumard et al., 2013), or innate rules of grammar (Mikhail, 2007). In this section, we show examples of how MFT is beginning to shed light on automatic or otherwise nonconscious reactions to moral stimuli.

3.5.1 Implicit morality across ideology

Just as the methods of implicit social cognition have begun to transform moral psychology, they have begun to transform the study of political ideology as well (Nosek, Graham, & Hawkins, 2010). In one of the first explorations of how ideology relates to explicit foundation endorsement, Graham et al. (2009; Study 2) used an implicit measure of ideological orientation: a liberal-conservative/self-other Implicit Association Test. They found that while implicit ideology added little predictive power beyond explicit ideology in predicting abstract assessments of the moral relevance of foundation-related concerns, it did uniquely predict agreement with moral foundation judgment statements over and above explicit ideology. This finding suggests that while participants' self-reports of political ideology are sufficient to predict what they might *say* they consider morally relevant, their implicit political identities give you additional information about the foundation-related judgments they will actually make.

Given all the work on self-reported differences in foundation endorsement between liberals and conservatives (see Figure 2.1), a question naturally emerges: how "deep" do those differences go? Do people on opposite ends of the political spectrum have different automatic reactions to various moral cues, or do they experience the same intuitive moral reactions and differentially endorse them? A number of studies suggest that liberals' implicit reactions "look like" the endorsed opinions of conservatives but that liberals then suppress or correct these first reactions when reporting their explicit opinions. For instance, Skitka, Mullen, Griffin, Hutchinson, and Chamberlin (2002) found that when liberals were tired, distracted, or under cognitive load, they showed levels of personal attributions such as victim-blaming akin to those of conservatives. The authors posited "motivated correction" as the process liberals undergo to bring these automatic reactions in line with their conscious egalitarian goals and values. Similarly, Eidelman, Crandall, Goodman, and Blanchar (2012) found that low-effort thought (induced by cognitive load, time pressure, or alcohol) increased aspects of conservatism such as acceptance of hierarchy and preference for the status quo.

Graham (2010) tested whether MFT could provide an organizing framework for such findings, with the hypothesis that liberals intuitively respond to Loyalty, Authority, and Sanctity cues more strongly than would be suggested by their explicitly endorsed moral opinions. Using several implicit measures of reactions to foundation-related stimuli—evaluative priming, the AMP, and event-related brain potentials using EEG (see Table 2.2)—the authors found support for this hypothesis and found no evidence of such implicit–explicit discrepancy for conservatives. Moreover, when randomly assigned to give their first "gut" reactions on the MFQ, participants across the political spectrum indicated that their answers were the same as their consciously endorsed opinions, indicating that liberals are unaware of the discrepancy between their implicit and explicit moralities. In contrast to these studies, Wright and Baril (2011) found that cognitive load or ego depletion manipulations decreased MFQ endorsements of Loyalty, Authority, and Sanctity among conservatives. Although two large studies using different samples have failed to replicate this effect, more work needs to be done to test whether conservatives also have implicit–explicit discrepancies in their moralities, particularly for Care and Fairness concerns.

3.5.2 Psychophysiological pluralism

We do not expect that anyone will find five distinct and discrete patterns of physiological activity related to the five foundations. Foundations are not spots in the brain (see discussion of modularity in Section 2.1), nor are they each identified by one specific physiological signature. Nonetheless, when you broaden the moral domain beyond Care and Fairness and you begin considering a broader range of moral intuitions, it stands to reason that you might find a broader range of central and peripheral psychophysiological responses to moral stimuli. Using facial EMG (see Table 2.2), Cannon et al. (2011) showed that levator activity (disgust microexpression) was highest for Sanctity violations and second highest for Fairness violations, while corrugator activity (angry microexpression) was highest for violations of Care. Moreover, muscle activity differentially predicted severity of explicit moral judgments for different types of concerns, with disgust expressions predicting harsher Sanctity and Fairness judgments, anger expressions predicting harsher Care judgments, and smiling predicting less harsh Loyalty judgments.

In a vignette study contrasting judgments about Care (accidental vs. intentional assault) and Sanctity (accidental vs. intentional incest), Young and Saxe (2011) found that intentionality was central to the Care judgments but was much less crucial for Sanctity judgments. They followed up this finding with an fMRI study and found that the right temporoparietal junction (TPJ)—an area implicated in theory of mind reasoning, and hence intentionality judgments—was more involved in Care judgments than in Sanctity judgments.

Two other studies have looked for links between moral foundations and brain structures or responses. Lewis, Kanai, Bates, and Rees (2012) gave subjects the MFQ and then collected structural MRI brain scans. They found a variety of significant and interpretable relationships, including: (1) Scores on the Care and Fairness foundations (combined) were associated with larger gray-matter volume in the dorsomedial prefrontal cortex (DMPFC, an area associated with mentalizing and empathy) and (2) Sanctity scores were associated with more gray-matter volume in the left anterior insula (a region active in several moral emotions including disgust). They also found that high scores on the Authority and Sanctity foundations were associated with more gray-matter volume in the subcallosal gyrus, although they did not know how to interpret this finding.

Parkinson et al. (2011) wrote vignettes to trigger a range of moral intuitions, inspired partly by MFT, and then carried out an fMRI study. They found that stories about people committing intentional physical harm preferentially activated regions associated with understanding and imagining actions; stories about sexual deviance preferentially activated many areas associated with affective processing (including the amygdalae and the anterior insula); and stories about dishonesty preferentially activated brain areas associated with reasoning about mental states (including the DMPFC and the TPJ). Their interpretation of these results was strongly supportive of the pluralist approach we emphasize in this chapter:

> *These results provide empirical support for philosophical arguments against the existence of a functional or anatomical module common and peculiar to all moral judgments. . . .Separate systems were found to characterize different kinds of moral*

judgment. . .It is likely that moral judgment is even more multidimensional than what is suggested here, given that there remain other domains of morality that were not examined in the current study (e.g., disrespect, betrayal of an in-group, fairness). These results suggest that, just as disparate systems are now understood to subserve aspects of cognitive faculties once thought to be monolithic (e.g., memory, attention), distinct systems subserve different types of moral judgment. Future research may benefit from working toward a taxonomy of these systems as Haidt and Graham (2007) have suggested (Parkinson et al., 2011, p. 3171).

In a massive measurement validation effort, Knutson et al. (2009) compiled standardized ratings for 312 different moral vignettes to be used in behavioral neuroscience research; they explicitly referred to MFT's constructs to categorize vignettes and identify missing areas of moral concern. Although recent work has begun to distinguish the implicit processes involved in Care and Sanctity judgments, much more work is needed to investigate similarities and differences in implicit processing of Fairness, Loyalty, and Authority concerns. To anticipate the next section, we see future investigations of the implicit processes involved in foundation-related concerns, judgments, and reactions as a primary next step not just for MFT, but for moral psychology in general.

4. FUTURE DIRECTIONS

In this section, we look toward the future of moral foundations research, with special attention paid to new areas of inquiry and the evolution of the theory itself. We begin by describing notable recent critiques of MFT, which we see as essential for helping to shape its future development. We then offer five criteria for foundationhood, to guide future discussions of what exactly the list of foundations should be, and what it would take to change or expand our current list. Finally, we give additional consideration to what will characterize the next several years of research in MFT and in moral psychology more generally.

4.1. Criticisms of the theory

Confirmation bias—the tendency to search only for supportive evidence—is powerful, and nobody has yet found a way to train people out of it (Lilienfeld, Ammirati, & Landfield, 2009). The best cure for the confirmation bias is other people—friends, colleagues, and opponents who do not share your biases, and who may even be motivated to find the disconfirming evidence that is sometimes hiding in plain sight. Scientists who create new theories would be well-advised, therefore, to seek out critics in order to improve their thinking.

Criticism is in fact so valuable that it is worth paying for. That, at least, was our thinking in 2007 when we offered the "moral foundations prize"— one thousand dollars to anyone who could "demonstrate the existence of an additional foundation, or show that any of the current five foundations should be merged or eliminated." The challenge was posted at MoralFoundations.org for 2 years. Nobody won the full prize, which required making a theoretical case and backing it up with empirical evidence, but three people or teams were awarded $500 each for nominating strong candidates for "foundationhood" (we will discuss these candidates below).

In the years since 2007, we have been fortunate that many critics have stepped forward and volunteered to criticize MFT for free. These critics have helped us to overcome our confirmation bias, find flawed or under-specified parts of the theory, and make improvements. Most of the criticisms have been directed at one of the four basic claims we made in Section 2: nativism, cultural development, intuitionism, and pluralism. We describe them in that order.

4.1.1 Critiques of nativism

Nobody in psychology today argues that the human mind is truly a "blank slate" at birth, but opinions range widely from minimalist positions, which say that there is hardly any writing on the "first draft" of the mind, to maximalist positions such as massive modularity (Sperber, 2005; Tooby et al., 2005), which say that the mind is to a great degree organized in advance of experience, including hundreds or thousands of functional modules. We are near the maximalist side of the spectrum, although, like Sperber (2005), we temper our nativism with extensive discussions of cultural development and variation (Haidt, 2012; Haidt & Joseph, 2007). The foundations are part of the first draft of the mind, but experience edits that draft extensively.

Critics of nativism tend to be critics of MFT. Suhler and Churchland (2011) argued that all nativist theories must clear a very high bar to be taken seriously. To be more than mere "hand waving," they must "be supported by, or at least consilient with," evidence from genetics, neurobiology, and developmental psychology. (See also Narvaez, 2008, who asked for physiological evidence of modules and asserted that subcortical brain areas include modules but the cerebral cortex does not.) We fully agree that developmental psychology is a crucial testing ground for claims about moral nativism (see Section 4.2.4), but we reject their claim that nativists are obligated to point to specific neural circuits, or to genes for those circuits. Given that nobody can find a set of genes that, collectively, explains 5% of the variance in how *tall* people are (Gudbjartsson et al., 2008), what chance is there that anyone will find a set of genes that code for mental modules such as loyalty or sanctity whose expression is far more subject to cultural influence than is height? To insist that nativists must point to genes is to ban nativism from psychology.

And yet, psychology has made enormous strides in recent years because of a flood of nativist findings. Personality psychology has been transformed by the discovery that nearly all personality traits are heritable (Bouchard, 1994; Turkheimer, 2000). Developmental psychology has been transformed by the discovery that infants have a great deal of innate knowledge about the physical world (Baillargeon, 1987; Spelke, 2000), and even about the social world (Hamlin, Wynn, & Bloom, 2007). These findings have earth-shaking implications for moral psychology, rendering blank slate or pure learning approaches nonstarters. None of these findings were reduced to "hand waving" by their authors' failure to point to specific genes or brain circuits. It may have been a defensible strategy in the 1970s to assume that the mind is a blank slate and then require nativists to shoulder the burden of proof, but nowadays, we believe, the discussion should focus on *how exactly* moral knowledge is innate, not *whether* it is (Tooby et al., 2005).

Nonetheless, Suhler and Churchland do point out places in which our "how exactly" discussion has been vague or underspecified, giving us an opportunity to improve the theory. In response to their critique, we offered a more detailed discussion of moral modularity (Haidt & Joseph, 2011; see also Haidt & Joseph, 2007). We have also tried to be much more specific in this chapter about what exactly a foundation is, and how you know when something is innate (see Section 4.2).

4.1.2 Critiques of cultural learning

Nobody doubts that cultural learning is a part of moral development, but cognitive developmentalists have long argued that morality is to a large extent self-constructed by the child. Piaget (1932/1965) strongly rejected ideas prevalent in his day that children internalized their moral values from society (e.g., Durkheim, 1925/1973) or from their parents (Freud, 1923/1962). Kohlberg (1969) believed that children go through two stages of "conventional" moral judgment, and Turiel argued that children are adept at distinguishing social conventions (which vary by culture) from true morality (which is universally applicable). But both men believed that real morality (postconventional, for Kohlberg; the moral domain, for Turiel) was something the child identified for herself during social interactions with peers, aided by the process of role-taking. Cognitive developmentalists carried out a variety of cross-cultural studies, but the goal of these studies—and their consistent conclusion—was that the fundamental stuff of morality did not vary across cultures (Hollos, Leis, & Turiel, 1986; Kohlberg, 1969). Again, as Kohlberg (1971) asserted: "Virtue is ultimately one, not many, and it is always the same ideal form regardless of climate or culture...The name of this ideal form is justice." Any cross-cultural differences in the ability to reason about justice were explained as *developmental* differences: children in some cultures did not have as many opportunities for role-taking in egalitarian interactions, but if they did have those opportunities, they had reached the same endpoint.

Of MFT's four main claims, cultural learning has received the least direct criticism. Following Piaget, Kohlberg, and Turiel, researchers in the cognitive-developmental tradition could argue that MFT has overstated the role of cultural learning and underplayed the role of self-construction by conscious reasoning about care and fairness. This argument was made by Turiel, Killen, and Helwig (1987) against Shweder et al. (1987). But none have advanced such a critique against MFT yet.

4.1.3 Critiques of intuitionism

Social psychologists and neuroscientists are generally comfortable with the enhanced role that automatic processes (including moral intuition) have played in moral psychology in recent years. Some researchers in those fields, however, favor a slightly different arrangement of reasoning and intuition. In particular, Greene, Morelli, Lowenberg, Nystrom, and Cohen (2008) argue that "cognition" (or emotionless deliberative processing, which involves the dorsolateral prefrontal cortex) is not the servant of the "emotions" (rapid intuitive judgments which more heavily rely upon areas of the brain implicated in emotional responding). In Greene's dual-process model, cognition and emotion are analogized to John Stuart Mill (cool utilitarian reasoning) versus Immanuel Kant (deontological principles, which are, paradoxically, based in emotion), fighting it out in the brain. However, Greene agrees with the basic intuitionist claim that rapid, automatic, affectively laden processing often drives moral reasoning and turns it into rationalization.

Critiques of intuitionism (in the form of the SIM, as well as other intuitionists such as Gigerenzer, 2007) are more common from developmental psychologists, particularly those in the cognitive-developmental tradition (Narvaez, 2008, 2010; Saltzstein & Kasachkoff, 2004). Narvaez (2010) grants that intuitionism has been "a useful corrective to overly rationalistic approaches that have long dominated moral psychology" (p. 165). She also notes that "the vast research showing that humans often operate using implicit processes cannot be true everywhere except in the moral domain" (p. 165). Nonetheless, she argues that intuition and reasoning are best seen as partners in a dance, in which either partner can lead and the other will follow. She makes the important point that moral "expertise," like other forms of expertise, often begins with conscious deliberation that gradually becomes automatic. She charges that "moral intuitionist theories often seem to rely on data from novices using seat-of-the-pants intuition—a quick, prereflective, front-end intuition that novices typically display" (p. 171). As a developmentalist, she is interested in how people arrive at "mature moral functioning," and she is more interested in moral behavior than in moral judgment.

We think that Narvaez is correct that we have focused too much of our attention on the initial moral judgment, and not enough on the processes by which morality develops and improves with experience (see also Bloom, 2010). Given our interest in cultural development and the "revision process," we believe MFT can be elaborated to address her concerns, and we are pleased that a few developmental psychologists have begun to do this, using MFT to study the development of character (Frimer et al., in press), the development of moral reasoning (Baril & Wright, 2012), and the role of morality in adult development, including personal narratives (McAdams et al., 2008).

4.1.4 Critiques of pluralism per se

Much of the criticism of MFT has focused on its pluralism. We first address criticism from monists who reject the very notion of pluralism. Then, we address critics who accept pluralism but argue for a different set of foundations, values, or virtues than the five we first proposed.

The most direct and detailed monist critique of MFT has come from Gray et al. (2012), who argue that all morality can be reduced to perceptions of dyadic harm (intentionally harmful agent plus suffering patient), and so only Care/harm is truly foundational: "A dyadic template suggests that perceived suffering is not only tied to immorality, but that *all* morality is understood through the lens of harm" (p. 108, emphasis added). While it seems reasonable to assert that Care/harm might be the most prototypical moral concern (see discussions of the Care/harm foundation in Haidt & Joseph, 2004, 2007), the reduction of *all* instances of moral judgment to perceptions of dyadic harm illustrates the deficits of moral monism. The idea that every moral judgment occurs through a single mental process (be it perceptions of dyadic harm, fairness intuitions, moral grammar, or another monist account) holds intuitive appeal, and it would certainly be convenient for moral scientists if morality worked this parsimoniously. But such an account quickly becomes Procrustean, cutting off phenomena it cannot explain (e.g., the role of disgust in moral judgments) and stretching its unitary construct to fit everything else (e.g., stretching "harm" to cover anything perceived as morally bad). (For more on this theory, see Ditto, Liu, & Wojcik, 2012; Graham & Iyer, 2012; Koleva & Haidt, 2012.)

A similar harm-based moral monism has also been suggested by Harris (2010):

> Haidt's data on the differences between liberals and conservatives is interesting, but is his interpretation correct? It seems possible, for instance, that his five foundations of morality are simply facets of a more general concern about harm. What, after all, is the problem with desecrating a copy of the Qu'ran? There would be no problem but for the fact that people believe that the Qu'ran is a divinely authored text. Such people almost surely believe that some harm could come to them or to their tribe as a result of such sacrileges—if not in this world, then in the next (p. 89 [see also pages 180–181]).

Harris makes his monist critique in the context of the larger normative argument that science should determine human values and pronounce which moral views are correct based on which ones lead to the greatest happiness (which can be measured in the brain by neuroscientific techniques). For the person morally offended by the desecration of a holy book, Harris suggests simply discarding the incorrect view that any deity exists who would cause harm because of it. Once that illusion is gone, one can correctly see, according to Harris, that desecrating a holy book is morally acceptable because it causes no harm. Moral monism is thus necessary for such a project, which requires a single standard by which to measure moral rightness or wrongness. For Harris, that standard is human welfare, defined in a rather narrow way: the absence of suffering.

But even if one agrees with Harris's normative views, would the reduction of all morality to harm help us understand how morality actually works? Or would it be (to paraphrase William James) another attempt to clean up the litter the world actually contains? A monist model in which all moral judgments (even those based on explicitly harmless transgressions) are produced by a single mental process (perceptions of intentional dyadic harm) cleans up much of the "litter" of empirically observed moral life, and in this cleaning suffers as a scientific description of morality. To name just three examples, such an account cannot explain: why incidental disgust harshens moral judgments (Schnall et al., 2008), why cognitive processes differ for Care- and Sanctity-based moral judgments (Young & Saxe, 2011), or why moral judgments of character can be produced by less harmful (Tannenbaum, Uhlmann, & Diermeier, 2011) or even harmless (Inbar, Pizarro, & Cushman, 2012) actions. Although not as explicitly committed to monism, accounts boiling morality down to fairness (Baumard et al., 2013) or universal grammar (Mikhail, 2007) can suffer from the same deficits in their ability to adequately describe and explain human morality in all its messiness and complexity (see also Graham, 2013).

4.1.5 Alternative pluralisms

MFT has never claimed to offer an exhaustive list of moral foundations. We have tried from the beginning to identify the candidates for which the evidence was strongest, and we have actively sought out arguments and evidence for additional foundations. The first winner of the "moral foundations challenge" was John Jost, who suggested that we were missing concerns about liberty and oppression. As described in Section 4.1.4, we have already begun empirical work testing Liberty/oppression as a possible sixth foundation. The second winner was the team of Elizabeth Shulman and Andrew Mastronarde, who proposed that concerns about waste and inefficiency, particularly when a group is trying to achieve a common goal, produce an emotional reaction that is not related to any of the other foundations. The third winner was Polly Wiessner, an anthropologist who noted that issues of ownership and property arise everywhere, even among the !Kung Bushmen whom she studies, and that concerns about ownership have apparent precursors in animals' ability to recognize and guard their own territories.

We think that Liberty/oppression, Efficiency/waste, and Ownership/theft are all good candidates for foundationhood, and we are conducting further research on those issues, along with Honesty/deception, to determine whether we should add any of them to the current list of five foundations. We think the issue of identifying foundations is rather like the issue of counting planets. There are millions of objects orbiting the sun, but astronomers do not call them all planets. There are six (including the Earth) that are so visible that they were recorded in multiple ancient civilizations, and then there are a bunch of objects further out that were discovered with telescopes. Astronomers disagreed for a while as to whether Pluto and some more distant icy bodies should be considered planets. Similarly, we are content to say that there are many aspects of human nature that contribute to and constrain moral judgment, and our task is to identify the most important ones—the sets of social sensitivities that are most helpful for understanding intercultural and intracultural moral disagreements and for understanding moral thought and behavior, in general.

Although articulated well before the development of MFT, Turiel's (1979, 1983) moral-conventional distinction prefigures one of the most common responses to MFT that we have heard from other researchers: two foundations—Care and Fairness—are legitimately moral, holding for all times and places, while the other three are merely conventional—valued in some times and places, but not in the same way as Care and Fairness. This critique was echoed by Jost (2009), who raised the normative objection that calling Loyalty, Authority, and Sanctity "moral" could legitimize anything from jingoism to blind obedience to prejudice and racism. Jost's objection raises a valid critique of some of our writings (Haidt, 2007b; Haidt & Graham, 2007) that blurred the line between the descriptive and the normative and highlights the importance of carefully distinguishing the two. MFT is designed to provide a purely descriptive understanding of human morality, *not* to provide any normative justification (or condemnation) of any particular moral judgments or concerns. Although the word "moral" can introduce ambiguities because it has both descriptive and normative uses, MFT is about the foundations of morality as it is observed around the world, not about the moral systems that ought to prevail.

In contrast to the critique that MFT has included too much in its mapping of the moral domain, some have criticized it for not including enough. Janoff-Bulman and Sheikh (2012) presented a 2 × 3 matrix of moral motives, based on their work distinguishing approach-based moral prescriptions and avoidance-based moral proscriptions (Janoff-Bulman, Sheikh, & Baldacci, 2008; Janoff-Bulman, Sheikh, & Hepp, 2009) crossed with three contexts: intrapersonal, interpersonal, and intragroup. They argue that the moral foundations cover some of the six cells in this matrix, but fail to cover others—namely, intrapersonal prescriptions and proscriptions, and the intragroup prescriptions that characterize social justice solidarity concerns. Although MFT's treatment of all foundations involves both prescriptions (moral goods to be approached and admired) and proscriptions (moral bads to be condemned and avoided) Janoff-Bulman raises the important point that it is not necessarily the case that Care and Fairness only operate at the individual level, while Loyalty, Authority, and Sanctity (which we have sometimes referred to as the "binding" foundations) always operate at the group level. Graham and Haidt (2010) describe several intrapersonal concerns related to Sanctity (e.g., prescriptions for treating one's body as a temple, proscriptions against masturbation and impure thoughts). Interestingly, our own self-critiques (see below) have also brought up the group-focused fairness concerns we have been missing (e.g., equity and vigilance against free-riders, reciprocal retaliations for outgroup attacks), but unlike social justice concerns (which we see as primarily focused on group members, not the group itself), we predict that these concerns would be endorsed more by conservatives than by liberals. Nevertheless, considering the different fundamental psychological motives (approach/avoid) involved in different moral concerns will be a promising area for future development.

Further, Janoff-Bulman's inclusion of different contexts (intrapersonal, interpersonal, intragroup, and even intergroup) echoes the critique by Rai and Fiske (2011) that MFT does not pay enough attention to *relational context*. Specifically, they propose four moral motives—unity, hierarchy, equality, and proportionality—based on Fiske's (1992) relational models described above in Section 1, and say that these motives can add to MFT "by grounding the foundations in a theory of social relationships and thereby predicting when and how people will rely on one foundation over another" (p. 67). Jarudi (2009) suggests an expansion of the Sanctity domain, distinguishing between sexual purity and food purity. Finally, in addition to their meta-theoretic critiques of MFT's approach (see Section 4.1.1), Suhler and Churchland (2011) suggest other candidate foundations, such as industry and modesty.

Despite the collective coherence suggested by our use of "we" throughout this chapter, we are constantly arguing among ourselves over changes to existing foundations and considerations of new candidate foundations. Iyer (2009) first pointed out that our measures of Fairness concerns centered on equality rather than equity and that concerns about equality are often motivated by care for others, whereas equity concerns may be motivationally distinct (Iyer, Read, & Correia, 2010). Iyer (2009) also questioned the pragmatic utility of separating Loyalty and Authority, suggesting that both concerns could conceptually be considered part of a single foundation concerning subsuming one's interests for one's group. Analyses of libertarians (described in Section 3.2.4) raised the question of whether Liberty/oppression is its own basic moral concern, not reducible to self-interest or existing foundations. And in responses to open-ended questions about what people felt guilty about (or ways in which they were not living up to their values), honesty violations come up more frequently than any other kind of concern (see Iyer, 2010, on treating honesty as a separate foundation). We are currently investigating all of these as part of the method-theory coevolution of MFT.

4.2. Getting specific: What does it take to be a foundation?

One common critique of MFT has been that our list of foundations is arbitrary, chosen originally by Haidt and Joseph (2004) based on their reading of five books and articles. Many scientists would like to see a set of explicit criteria which researchers could use to decide what counts as a foundation. We agree that such a list would be helpful for progress in moral psychology.

We therefore offer a list of five criteria for foundationhood. We looked for guidance to the long-running debate over how many "basic emotions" there are. Ekman, Sorenson, and Friesen (1969) originally offered a list of six emotions, based on their research on facial expressions: joy, sadness, anger, fear, surprise, and disgust. Gradually a few more emotions were added, and eventually Ekman (1992) offered a set of nine criteria for what it takes to be a basic emotion. He made no commitment to parsimony, suggesting that perhaps 17 emotions might eventually qualify as basic emotions (Ekman, 1994). Some emotions, such as fear and anger, meet all of Ekman's criteria very cleanly; they are prototypical emotions, about which there is less debate. Other emotions, such as awe, relief, and contentment, meet most of the criteria to some degree, making them less prototypical exemplars of emotionhood and leaving more room for debate.

We think the same is true of foundationhood. We think that our original list of five foundations did a good job of capturing the most obvious and least debatable foundations, but we acknowledge that there is still room for debate, and, like Ekman, we are confident that our initial list is not the final list.

Here, then, is our list of five criteria (see below and Table 2.4). The first two criteria establish the kinds of phenomena we are studying—intuitive moral judgments. The last three indicate that a content area of morality may be related to an innate but variably expressed foundation. We will illustrate each criterion by discussing the Fairness foundation, which we believe meets all criteria extremely well.

Table 2.4 Criteria for foundationhood, with evidence for the current foundations

Foundation criteria	Care/harm	Fairness/cheating	Loyalty/betrayal	Authority/subversion	Sanctity/degradation
Criterion 1: Common in third-party normative judgments	Playground harm: Nucci and Turiel (1978)	Catching cheaters: Dunbar (1996)	The Black Sheep effect: Marques, Yzerbyt, and Leyens (1988)	Disrespect for authority: Shweder et al. (1987)	Food and sex taboos: Haidt et al. (1993)
Criterion 2: Automatic affective evaluations	To cruelty and violence: Luo et al. (2006), Cannon et al. (2011) and Graham (2010)	To cheating: Sanfey, Rilling, Aronson, Nystrom, and Cohen (2003); to unfairness or inequality: Cannon et al. (2011) and Graham (2010)	To ingroup betrayals: Cannon et al. (2011) and Graham (2010)	To subversion: Cannon et al. (2011) and Graham (2010)	To sexual violations: Parkinson et al. (2011); to degradation: Cannon et al. (2011) and Graham (2010)
Criterion 3: Culturally widespread	Bowlby (1969)	Fiske (1992)	Herdt (1981)	Fiske (1992)	Douglas (1966)
Criterion 4: Evidence of innate preparedness	NHP: Hrdy (2009) and Preston and de Waal (2002); Infants: Hamlin, Wynn, and Bloom (2007)	NHP: Brosnan (2006); Infants: Schmidt and Sommerville (2011) and Sloane, Baillargeon, and Premack (2012)	NHP: De Waal (1982); Infants: Kinzler, Dupoux, and Spelke (2007) and Hamlin et al. (in press)	NHP: Boehm (1999, 2012); Not yet shown in infants	Not yet shown in NHP or infants
Criterion 5: Evolutionary model	Kin selection: Hamilton (1964); Attachment theory: Bowlby (1969)	Reciprocal altruism: Trivers (1971)	Multilevel selection: Wilson (2002); Tribalism: Richerson and Boyd (2005)	Rank and dominance: de Waal (1982) and Boehm (1999)	Disgust: Rozin, Haidt, and McCauley (2008); Behavioral immune system: Schaller and Park (2011)

Note: NHP, nonhuman primates.

4.2.1 Criterion 1: A common concern in third-party normative judgments

One of the most significant steps in the evolution of morality may have occurred when human beings developed "shared intentionality"—the ability of multiple people to hold a shared mental representation of what they are trying to do together (Tomasello et al., 2005). Chimpanzees seem to have some sense of norms for behavior within the group, and they sometimes get upset when they are not treated according to their expectations. The evidence that they react to third parties who violate norms, however, is mixed or anecdotal at best (de Waal, 1996). But when humans developed the capacity for shared intentionality, our capacity to recognize norms began to grow into a passion for enforcing them on each other (Boehm, 2012). Humans began to live in "moral matrices"—the "consensual hallucinations" that provide a common normative framework against which people can and do judge the actions of others, even when those actions have no direct implications for the self (Haidt, 2012).

The sorts of third-party violations that people in a community react to is a good guide to where moral foundations should be sought. If a putatively moral issue never shows up in gossip, even in communities that are said to endorse values related to that foundation, then that is a reason to doubt the existence of such a foundation. Gossip about fairness, for example, is ubiquitous. From hunter-gatherers (Wiessner, 2005) to Chaldean-Iraqui merchants in Michigan (Henrich & Henrich, 2007) to college roommates sharing a kitchen, people gossip frequently about members of their group who cheat, fail to repay favors, or take more than their share. In fact, Dunbar (1996) reports that one of the principle functions of gossip is to catch cheaters and free-riders within groups.

In the first row of Table 2.4, we have listed studies that show people making third-party moral judgments—condemning others for actions that have no direct consequences for the self. These studies show that people in at least some cultural groups make judgments closely related to the content of all five foundations. Our own studies using multiple measures provide ample documentation of people condemning third parties for violations related to each foundation (e.g., Graham et al., 2009).

4.2.2 Criterion 2: Automatic affective evaluations

MFT is an intuitionist theory—it tries to explain the rapid, automatic reactions people have to violations of what they take to be a shared moral order. There is not just one moral intuition—a general flash of "wrongness"—just as there is not one taste receptor on the tongue whose output tells us "delicious!" Rather, we posit that there are a variety of rapid, automatic reactions to patterns in the social world. When we detect such patterns, moral modules fire, and a fully enculturated person has an affectively valenced experience. Not just a feeling of "good!" or "bad!," but an experience with a more specific "flavor" to it, such as "cruel!," "unfair!," "betrayal!," "subversive!," or "sick!" If a moral reaction can be elicited quickly and easily, with a variety of images, bumper-stickers, or one-sentence stories, that is a point in favor of its foundationhood. Reactions to unequal distributions among children are often visible on the face of the disadvantaged child within one second (LoBue, Chiong, Nishida, DeLoache, & Haidt, 2011), and fMRI studies repeatedly show that people have rapid, affectively laden reactions to being cheated, and those reactions tend to activate brain areas related to emotion, including the anterior insula and the orbitofrontal cortex (Rilling et al., 2002; Sanfey et al., 2003). In an fMRI study of economic games, fair offers (compared to unfair offers of the same value) activated neural reward circuitry, while accepting unfair offers activated self-control circuitry (Tabibnia, Satpute, & Lieberman, 2008). It is easy to trigger rapid and affectively laden judgments of unfairness using still photos, bumper stickers, or a single number on a computer screen that reveals one's partner's choice in a cooperative game. The same is true for images of harm or cruelty activating the Care foundation (e.g., Luo et al., 2006), and stories about sexual violations activating the Sanctity foundation (e.g., Parkinson et al., 2011). There has been less research on automatic reactions to violations of Loyalty and Authority, but here too studies have shown split-second reactions to sentences, words, or pictures showing violations of these foundations (Cannon et al., 2011; Graham, 2010).

4.2.3 Criterion 3: Culturally widespread

We have proposed that moral foundations are part of the "first draft" of the moral mind. These drafts get edited during childhood development within a particular culture, and some cultures actively suppress some of the foundations. Examples include the ways that Nazi Germany turned compassion into the vice of "softness" (Koonz, 2003), or the way that egalitarian movements such as Occupy Wall Street have tried to create "horizontal" societal structures that do not rely on the Authority foundation. So it is not necessary that a foundation be shown to underlie morality in *all* human cultures. Innate does not mean universally visible in the adult phenotype. It means "organized in advance of experience," such that we should expect to see it expressed in some form in *most* human cultures.

Additionally, we should not treat all cultures as equally informative. Hunter-gatherer societies should carry added weight because they may more closely resemble lifestyles of the "environment of evolutionary adaptation" (Cosmides & Tooby, 1994) in which the moral foundations presumably evolved. Traditional societies with small-scale agriculture or herding have also existed for long enough periods to have produced genetic adaptations (e.g., for lactose tolerance and starch metabolism, and quite possibly for behavior too; see Cochran & Harpending, 2009). If moral foundations were shaped by gene-culture coevolution (Richerson & Boyd, 2005) in response to long-standing adaptive challenges, then a candidate foundation should be easily visible in anthropological reports from these societies. Modern "WEIRD" societies (Henrich et al., 2010) are arguably the worst places to look for moral foundations because such societies have narrowed the moral domain in order to grant individuals the maximum freedom to pursue their projects. Nonetheless, when similar moral concerns are found across WEIRD societies, agricultural societies, and hunter-gatherer societies, the case for foundationhood gets stronger. Fairness certainly passes this test—nobody has yet identified a society in which reciprocity is not an important moral concern (Brown, 1991; Fiske, 1992). The other foundations also show up widely in anthropological accounts (as shown in the third row of Table 2.4), and in Brown's (1991) list of human universals.

Authority is a particularly interesting case in that hunter-gatherer societies are generally egalitarian. Yet as Boehm (1999) explains, it is not that they lack the innate cognitive and emotional structures for implementing hierarchical relationships because such relationships emerge very rapidly when groups take up agriculture. Rather, hunter-gatherers generally find cultural mechanisms of suppressing the ever-present threat of alpha-male behavior, thereby maintaining egalitarian relationships among adult males in spite of the hierarchical tendencies found among most primates, including humans.

4.2.4 Criterion 4: Evidence of innate preparedness

The fact that a behavior or ability is found in most or all human societies does not prove that anything is innate. All human societies face some similar challenges, and it is quite possible that all societies have hit upon similar solutions using their general-purpose, nondomain-specific intelligence. For example, all societies have invented ways to carry water. Perhaps all societies have invented fairness and turn-taking as efficient solutions to the challenge of dividing scarce resources; perhaps, all societies have invented food taboos in response to the real dangers of toxins and contaminants. Perhaps there are no innate moral foundations.

The case for innateness grows much stronger when a behavior or ability is found in nonhuman primates (particularly chimpanzees and bonobos) and when it can be shown to emerge in young children before they have been exposed to relevant teaching or reinforcement. Contrary to Suhler and Churchland (2011), we do not believe that claims about innateness need to point to specific genes or brain areas. Rather, nativists must offer some reason for believing that a behavior or ability is "organized in advance of experience."

de Waal (1996) has long argued that the "building blocks" of human morality are present in other primates. We believe that such building blocks have been shown for the Care foundation (i.e., empathy and nurturance; Hrdy, 2009; Preston & de Waal, 2002), the Loyalty foundation (coalitional behavior and intercoalitional conflict; de Waal, 1982), and the Authority foundation (rank and deference; Boehm, 1999, 2012). There is some evidence for precursors of Fairness (Brosnan, 2006), but it is more anecdotal, and the limited lab evidence (e.g., Brosnan & de Waal, 2003) has been disputed (Brauer, Call, & Tomasello, 2006; see also Hammerstein, 2003). We know of no evidence that nonhuman primates have any building blocks of the Sanctity foundation, such as the emotion of disgust, or even contamination sensitivity (see Rozin & Fallon, 1987). We presume that Sanctity is the most recently evolved foundation, perhaps coevolving with human religiosity in the past one or two hundred thousand years.

Recent findings in developmental psychology strongly support the nativist claims of MFT. The fourth row of Table 2.2 lists examples of such research. In the past 6 years, infants and young children have been shown to have surprisingly sophisticated social-cognitive abilities, often including affective reactions to third-party violators (i.e., puppets who do bad things to other puppets). For example, infants do not like puppets who harm others, but they do like puppets who help others (Hamlin et al., 2007). Infants are also sensitive to third-party fairness violations (Sloane et al., 2012); interestingly, this sensitivity predicted infants' own altruistic sharing behavior (Schmidt & Sommerville, 2011). Children as young as three are adept at sharing rewards equally, but only when they both cooperated to produce the benefit (Hamann, Warneken, Greenberg, & Tomasello, 2011). Infants notice markers of ingroup membership and prefer members of their ingroup (Kinzler et al., 2007), and even prefer those who help similar others and harm dissimilar others (Hamlin, Mahajan, Liberman, & Wynn, in press). We know of no research on how infants process markers of authority and respect, or of purity, sanctity, or contagion; we hope that such research will be done in the future. But we do note that children's games are often based on a single foundation, giving children the opportunity to practice a portion of their moral repertoire. For example, the game of "Simon Says" appoints a leader who commands followers, and the game of cooties is about contagion and how to remove contagion (i.e., with a "cooties shot"). The concept of "cooties" is not found universally, but it has been identified in several far-flung cultures (Hirschfeld, 2002; Samuelson, 1980), it seems to emerge with no encouragement from adults, and it emerges in Western societies that discourage the use of caste and contagion as moral categories. Importantly, cooties games tend to emerge around the age of 7 or 8 (Opie & Opie, 1969), which is the age at which disgust sensitivity becomes pronounced (Rozin & Fallon, 1987). In other words, these games seem to reflect the *externalization* of children's developing social-emotional abilities, not the *internalization* of prevailing cultural norms.

4.2.5 Criterion 5: Evolutionary model demonstrates adaptive advantage

Anti-nativists often criticize evolutionary psychology as a collection of "just-so" stories. And indeed, given the power of the human imagination and the epistemological predations of the confirmation bias, one could invent an evolutionary story for just about any candidate foundation, especially if one is allowed to appeal to the good of the *group*. But a good evolutionary theory will specify—often with rigorous mathematical models—exactly how a putative feature conferred an adaptive advantage upon *individuals* (or upon other bearers of the relevant genes), in comparison to members of the same group who lacked that feature. A good evolutionary theory will not casually attribute the adaptive advantage to the group (i.e., appeal to group selection) without a great deal of additional work, for example, showing that the feature confers a very strong advantage upon groups during intergroup competition while conferring only a small disadvantage upon the individual bearer of the trait (see Wilson, 2002; and see Haidt, 2012, chapter 9, on group-selection for groupish virtues). If no clear adaptive advantage can be shown, then that is a mark against foundationhood.

Another important safeguard against "just-so" thinking is to rely upon already-existing evolutionary theories. As we said in Section 1, MFT was inspired by the obvious match between the major evolutionary theories and the major moral phenomena reported by anthropologists. We engaged in no *post hoc* evolutionary theorizing ourselves. The fifth row of Table 2.4 shows evolutionary theories that spell out the adaptive advantages of certain innate mechanisms which we posit to be among the modules comprising each foundation. For example, the fairness foundation is largely just an elaboration of the psychology described by Trivers (1971) as the evolved psychological mechanisms that motivate people to play "tit for tat."

In sum, we have offered five criteria for foundationhood. Any moral ability, sensitivity, or tendency that a researcher wants to propose as an expression of an additional moral foundation should meet these criteria. At that point, the researcher will have established that there is something innate and foundational about an aspect of human morality. The only hurdle left to clear to get added to the list of moral foundations is to show that the candidate foundation is distinct from the existing foundations. For example, we do not believe that there is an "equality" foundation, not because we think there is nothing innate about equality, but because we think that equality is already accounted for by our existing foundations. Equality in the distribution of goods and rewards is (we believe) related to the Fairness foundation. Equality is a special case of equity: when all parties contributed equally, then all parties should share equally (Walster, Walster, & Berscheid, 1978). People who take more than their share are cheating. Moral judgments related to *political* equality—particularly the anger at bullies and dominators who oppress others—may be an expression of the candidate Liberty/oppression foundation. (See Haidt, 2012, chapter 8, for further discussion of equality, equity, and liberty.)

4.3. Looking ahead: New directions for moral foundations research

The preceding sections of this chapter give an indication not only of the work that has been done using MFT but also of the work that has yet to be done. For instance, Section 3.1 describes many different methods for measuring foundation-related concerns explicitly and implicitly, and yet the majority of the empirical work described in Section 3 relies on just one of those methods (the MFQ; see Table 2.2). In this penultimate section, we describe the future we see for moral foundations research, for refining the theory itself and applying it to new research questions.

4.3.1 Method-theory coevolution of MFT

We began this Section 4 with a detailed discussion of various critiques of MFT because we see such critiques as crucial for the progress and future shaping of the theory. In our vision of method-theory coevolution, critics are especially needed on the theory side, pointing out problems with existing constructs and offering competing conceptualizations of the moral domain. We expect that work bridging MFT with other theories will be productive, for MFT and for moral psychology overall. Janoff–Bulman and Sheikh (2012) and Rai and Fiske (2011) have both offered expansions or alternate configurations of the moral foundations, and while we may disagree on some particulars, none of these theories are incompatible. They are different ways of approaching the same phenomena. And while a strict moral monism *is* incompatible with MFT, monist critiques such as those offered by Gray et al. (2012) can also advance the science by prompting more work on how different kinds of moral concerns can be similar as well as distinct.

Working out where the theories converge and diverge can help advance our understanding of morality—particularly once competing predictions can be spelled out to testable hypotheses. Given the confirmation bias inevitable when researchers test their own theories, adversarial collaborations (in which the adversaries first agree on terminology, predictions, and what counts as evidence for and against specific claims) may be necessary to avoid the kind of unresolved theoretical stalemates described by Greenwald (2012).

In this vein, tests of alternate foundations will likely characterize the next few years of moral foundations development. We hope that the criteria spelled out in Section 4.2 will be useful for such efforts: what is the existing evidence along these five criteria for the candidate foundations described in Section 4.1, such as liberty, honesty, waste, property, social justice, industry, and modesty? Where is the evidence the strongest, and where does more work need to be done to test candidate foundations? This is not to say that more work will not be done on the five initial foundations. Table 2.4 highlights areas where little evidence is currently available for particular foundations on particular criteria. For instance, might infants show some ability to detect violations of Authority, and to respond to violators negatively? Such work is likely to lead to the creation of new methods as well. Again, the end goal is for competing conceptualizations and theories to be specified and worked out to the point that new methods are developed to marshal evidence for the claims, which will bring new (often unexpected) findings that can in turn lead to new theoretical syntheses and developments.

4.3.2 Applying MFT to new areas, and new questions

Theories typically reflect the strengths and weaknesses of their founders. We (the authors) are all social psychologists with interests in political ideology, and so it should be of no surprise that most of the work described ' Section 4 falls in the realm of political psychology. Nevertheless, we are hopeful that as more and more researchers make use of MFT's methods and constructs, the benefits of moral pluralism can be realized in more and more content areas and disciplines. Here are a few areas we see as particularly fertile.

4.3.2.1 Implicit social cognition

First, we are beginning to see more work by cognitive scientists on how judgment processes differ for different kinds of concerns. This work has mostly contrasted Sanctity with Care or Fairness (e.g., Feinberg & Willer, 2013; Inbar, Pizarro, & Cushman, 2012; Young & Saxe, 2011), but so far much less work has been done on Loyalty and Authority concerns. Recent (see Table 2.2) and future implicit measures of foundation-related intuitions and reactions could be used by social/cognitive psychologists and neuroscientists to learn more about the automatic processes associated with foundation-related judgments.

4.3.2.2 Development

Second, developmental psychologists are just beginning to test the earliest signs of emergence for moral concerns other than care and fairness. There is much fertile research ground here for both infant/toddler studies and lifespan development studies—do the "binding" concerns of Loyalty, Authority, and Sanctity become more important as people get older, become parents, or take on leadership positions at work? What are the different patterns of emergence and developmental trajectories for different foundational concerns?

4.3.2.3 Culture and social ecology

As Shweder (1990) says, each culture is expert in some aspects of human flourishing, but not all. Although we are working with researchers in other nations to explore the morality of other cultures (see Section 3.4), much more work needs to be done to move beyond WEIRD research samples (Henrich et al., 2010). Variations in social ecology (Oishi & Graham, 2010), such as residential mobility, economic structure, or population density, could also be important for predicting foundation endorsements. In one large-scale study, Motyl (2012) found that moral misfits—partisans living in communities which voted heavily against their party's U.S. Presidential candidate—were disproportionately likely to move to a new community. Furthermore, their new communities voted more heavily for the participant's party's candidate. This research suggests that moral values may steer people to live in morally segregated groups, with implications for attitude polarization and intergroup conflict.

4.3.2.4 Beyond moral intuitions

As noted above, research should examine what happens after the initial moral judgment is made. A central but largely understudied component of the SIM (Haidt, 2001) is that while one's initial moral judgment is typically intuitive, explicit moral reasoning plays many important roles as people gossip, argue, and otherwise talk about moral issues with other people. We hope that researchers will study moral disagreements as they play out over the course of many days or months, sometimes shifting in terms of the moral foundations used to justify judgments (e.g., see Koleva et al., 2012).

4.3.2.5 Interpersonal morality

One criticism of MFT, and of morality research in general, is that it largely ignores the role of interpersonal and relational factors (Rai & Fiske, 2011). Do moral judgments based on the moral foundations indeed vary for different relationship contexts? Moreover, what are the interpersonal antecedents and consequences of individual variation in foundation-related concerns? We have recently begun to explore these questions—for example, Koleva (2011) examined the role of moral foundation similarity in romantic ideals and relationship satisfaction, and more recent work is examining the relationships between adult romantic attachment and foundation concerns— but many more questions remain.

4.3.2.6 From moral judgment to moral behavior

The virtues have been central to MFT in theory, but not yet in practice. As Narvaez (2010) asked, what is the relation between moral judgment on one hand, and actual moral behavior on the other? Following Graham, Meindl, and Beall (2012), how can the pluralism of moral judgments and concerns help researchers capture a wider array of morally relevant behaviors? Relatedly, what are the practical real-world implications of MFT for persuasion (e.g., Feinberg & Willer, 2013) or other aspects of moral disagreements?

4.3.2.7 Beyond psychology

Researchers in many departments beyond psychology have begun to apply MFT's methods and constructs to such fields as public policy (Oxley, 2010), media studies (Tamborini, 2011), marketing (Winterich, Zhang, & Mittal, 2012), legal studies (Prince, 2010), climate science (Markowitz & Shariff,

2012), business ethics (Sadler-Smith, 2012), political science (Jones, 2012), genetics (Smith et al., 2011), neuropsychology (Young & Saxe, 2011), neuroanatomy (Lewis et al., 2012), and even agricultural ethics (Makiniemi et al., in press). Given the importance of values in real-world domains such as philanthropy, politics, and business, we hope that MFT proves useful beyond academia as well.

5. CONCLUSION

A cherished maxim in psychology comes from Lewin (1951): "There is nothing so practical as a good theory." Putting this maxim together with Einstein's maxim at the opening of this chapter, we think MFT is a good theory. It is a practical theory—complete with a set of well-validated measurement tools—which has quickly yielded a great variety of new findings, in many fields. It is a non-Procrustean theory which does not force researchers to "surrender the adequate representation" of experience. And it is an open and revisable theory, offering an initial list of foundations along with a list of criteria for how to revise the list. MFT is a theory in motion, a theory to be expanded, constricted, refined, and built upon. Above all, we think it is the right theory for our age—a golden age of cross-disciplinary research in which most scientists studying morality have at least some familiarity with findings in neighboring fields. Conferences on moral psychology nowadays often include researchers who study chimpanzees, psychopaths, infants, hunter-gatherers, or people with brain damage. MFT gives this varied set of researchers a common language for talking about the moral domain. It calms the sometimes-divisive nature-nurture debate by distinguishing the first draft of the moral mind and the experiential editing process.

We think MFT is practical in another way too: it helps researchers as well as the general public look beyond the moral values that are dearest to them, and understand those who live in a different moral matrix. We close with a final quote from Berlin (2001), who explains one reason why pluralism is so practical:

> If I am a man or a woman with sufficient imagination (and this I do need), I can enter into a value system which is not my own, but which is nevertheless something I can conceive of men pursuing while remaining human, while remaining creatures with whom I can communicate, with whom I have some common values—for all human beings must have some common values or they cease to be human, and also some different values else they cease to differ, as in fact

they do. That is why pluralism is not relativism—the multiple values are objective, part of the essence of humanity rather than arbitrary creations of men's subjective fancies.

ACKNOWLEDGMENTS

The authors wish to thank Trish Devine, Jeremy Frimer, Ashby Plant, Linda Skitka, and the USC Values, Ideology, and Morality Lab for helpful comments on a draft of this chapter.

REFERENCES

Ambady, N., & Rosenthal, R. (1992). Thin slices of expressive behavior as predictors of interpersonal consequences: A meta-analysis. *Psychological Bulletin, 111,* 256–274.

Amodio, D. M., Jost, J. T., Master, S. L., & Yee, C. M. (2007). Neurocognitive correlates of liberalism and conservatism. *Nature Neuroscience, 10,* 1246–1247.

Baillargeon, R. (1987). Object permanence in 3 1/2- and 4 1/2-month-old infants. *Developmental Psychology, 23*(5), 655–664.

Bargh, J. A., & Chartrand, T. L. (1999). The unbearable automaticity of being. *American Psychologist, 54,* 462–479.

Baril, G., & Wright, J. C. (2012). Different types of moral cognition: Moral stages versus moral foundations. *Personality and Individual Differences, 53,* 468–473.

Barkow, J., Cosmides, L., & Tooby, J. (Eds.), (1992). *The adapted mind: Evolutionary psychology and the generation of culture.* New York: Oxford University Press.

Baron-Cohen, S. (2009). Autism: The empathizing-systemizing (E-S) theory. *The Year in Cognitive Neuroscience. Annals of the New York Academy of Science, 1156,* 68–80.

Barrett, H. C., & Kurzban, R. (2006). Modularity in cognition: Framing the debate. *Psychological Review, 113,* 628–647.

Barriga, A. Q., Morrison, E. M., Liau, A. K., & Gibbs, J. C. (2001). Moral cognition: Explaining the gender difference in antisocial behavior. *Merrill-Palmer Quarterly, 47,* 532–562.

Bastick, T. (1982). *Intuition: How we think and act.* Chichester, England: Wiley.

Baumard, N., André, J. B., & Sperber, D. (2013). A mutualistic approach to morality. *Behavioral and Brain Sciences, 36,* 59–122.

Baumeister, R. F., & Newman, L. S. (1994). How stories make sense of personal experiences: Motives that shape autobiographical narratives. *Personality and Social Psychology Bulletin, 20,* 676–690.

Berlin, I. (1969). *Four essays on liberty.* USA: Oxford University Press.

Berlin, I. (2001). My intellectual path. In H. Hardy (Ed.), *The power of ideas* (pp. 1–23). Princeton, NJ: Princeton University Press.

Bloom, P. (2010). How do morals change? *Nature, 464,* 490.

Bobbio, A., Nencini, A., & Sarrica, M. (2011). Il Moral Foundation Questionnaire: Analisi della struttura fattoriale della versione italiana. *Giornale di Psicologia, 5,* 7–18.

Boehm, C. (1999). *Hierarchy in the forest: The evolution of egalitarian behavior.* Cambridge, MA: Harvard University Press.

Boehm, C. (2012). *Moral origins: The evolution of virtue, altruism, and shame.* New York: Basic.

Bouchard, T. J. J. (1994). Genes, environment, and personality. *Science, 264,* 1700–1701.

Bowlby, J. (1969). Attachment and loss. *Attachment* Vol. 1. New York: Basic.

Brauer, J., Call, J., & Tomasello, M. (2006). Are apes really inequity averse? *Proceedings of the Royal Society B, 273,* 3123–3128.

Brehm, S. S., & Brehm, J. W. (1981). *Psychological reactance: A theory of freedom and control.* London: Academic Press, Inc.

Brosnan, S. F. (2006). Nonhuman species' reactions to inequity and their implications for fairness. *Social Justice Research, 19*, 153–185.

Brosnan, S. F., & de Waal, F. B. (2003). Monkeys reject unequal pay. *Nature, 425*, 297–299.

Brown, D. E. (1991). *Human universals.* Philadelphia: Temple University Press.

Brown, R. W., & Ford, M. (1964). Address in American English. In D. Hymes (Ed.), *Language in culture and society* (pp. 234–244). New York: Harper & Row.

Bruneau, E. G., Dufour, N., & Saxe, R. (2012). Social cognition in members of conflict groups: Behavioural and neural responses in Arabs, Israelis and South Americans to each other's misfortunes. *Philosophical Transactions of the Royal Society Biological Sciences, 367*, 717–730.

Bruner, J. S. (1960). *The process of education.* Cambridge, MA: Harvard University Press.

Cannon, P. R., Schnall, S., & White, M. (2011). Transgressions and expressions: Affective facial muscle activity predicts moral judgments. *Social Psychological and Personality Science, 2*, 325–331.

Clifford, S., & Jerit, J. (in press). How word do the work of politics: Moral Foundations Theory and the debate over stem-cell research. *Journal of Politics.*

Cochran, G., & Harpending, H. (2009). *The 10,000 year explosion: How civilization accelerated human evolution.* New York: Basic.

Conover, P. J., & Feldman, S. (1981). The origins and meaning of liberal-conservative self-identifications. *American Journal of Political Science, 25*(4), 617–645.

Cosmides, L., & Tooby, J. (1994). Origins of domain specificity: The evolution of functional organization. In L. A. Hirschfeld & S. A. Gelman (Eds.), *Mapping the mind: Domain specificity in cognition and culture* (pp. 85–116). Cambridge, UK: Cambridge University Press.

Dawkins, R. (1976). *The selfish gene.* New York: Oxford University Press.

De Waal, F. (1982). *Chimpanzee politics: Power and sex among apes.* London: Jonathan Cape.

De Waal, F. B. M. (1996). *Good natured: The origins of right and wrong in humans and other animals.* Cambridge, MA: Harvard University Press.

Dehghani, M., Sagae K., Sachdeva, S. & Gratch, J. (in press). Linguistic Analysis of the debate over the Construction of the 'Ground Zero Mosque'. Journal of Information Technology & Politics.

DeLoache, J. S., & LoBue, V. (2009). The narrow fellow in the grass: Human infants associate snakes and fear. *Developmental Science, 12*(1), 201–207.

DeYoung, C. G., Quilty, L. C., & Peterson, J. B. (2007). Between facets and domains: 10 aspects of the Big Five. *Journal of Personality and Social Psychology, 93*, 880–896.

Ditto, P., & Koleva, S. P. (2011). Moral empathy gaps and the American culture war. *Emotion Review, 3*(3), 331–332 (special issue on "Morality and Emotion" edited by Joshua Greene).

Ditto, P. H., Liu, B., & Wojcik, S. P. (2012). Is anything sacred anymore? Commentary on target article. *Mind perception is the essence of morality* (K. Gray, L. Young, & A. Waytz). *Psychological Inquiry, 23*, 155–161.

Ditto, P. H., Pizarro, D. A., & Tannenbaum, D. (2009). Motivated moral reasoning. In B. H. Ross (Series Ed.) & D. M. Bartels, C. W. Bauman, L. J. Skitka, & D. L. Medin (Eds.), *Psychology of learning and motivation: Vol. 50. Moral judgment and decision making* (pp. 307–338). San Diego, CA: Academic Press.

Dodd, M., Balzer, A., Jacobs, C., Gruszczynski, M., Smith, K., & Hibbing, J. (2012). The political left rolls with the good and the political right confronts the bad: Connecting physiology and cognition to preferences. *Philosophical Transactions of the Royal Society B, 367*(1589), 640–649.

Douglas, M. (1966). *Purity and danger.* London: Routledge and Kegan Paul.

Duckitt, J. (2001). A cognitive-motivational theory of ideology and prejudice. In M. P. Zanna (Ed.), *Advances in experimental social psychology: Vol. 33.* (pp. 41–113). San Diego: Academic Press.

Dunbar, R. (1996). *Grooming, gossip, and the evolution of language.* Cambridge, MA: Harvard University Press.

Durkheim, E. (1925/1973). *Moral education* (E. Wilson & H. Schnurer, Trans.). New York: The Free Press.

Eidelman, S., Crandall, C. S., Goodman, J. A., & Blanchar, J. C. (2012). Low-effort thought promotes political conservatism. *Personality and Social Psychology Bulletin, 38,* 808–820.

Einstein, A. (1934). On the method of theoretical physics. *Philosophy of Science, 1,* 163–169.

Ekman, P. (1992). An argument for basic emotions. *Cognition and Emotion, 6,* 169–200.

Ekman, P. (1994). All emotions are basic. In P. Ekman & R. Davidson (Eds.), *The nature of emotion* (pp. 15–19). New York: Oxford University Press.

Ekman, P., Sorenson, E. R., & Friesen, W. V. (1969). Pan-cultural elements in facial displays of emotion. *Science, 164,* 86–88.

Faulkner, J., Schaller, M., Park, J. H., & Duncan, L. A. (2004). Evolved disease-avoidance mechanisms and contemporary xenophobic attitudes. *Group Processes & Intergroup Relations, 7,* 333–353.

Federico, C. M., Weber, C. R., Ergun, D., & Hunt, C. (in press). Mapping the connections between politics and morality: The multiple sociopolitical orientations involved in moral intuition. *Political Psychology.*

Feinberg, M., & Willer, R. (2013). The moral roots of environmental attitudes. *Psychological Science.*

Ferguson, M. J. (2007). On the automatic evaluation of end-states. *Journal of Personality and Social Psychology, 92,* 596–611.

Fiske, A. P. (1991). *Structures of social life: The four elementary forms of human relations: Communal sharing, authority ranking, equality matching, market pricing.* New York: Free Press.

Fiske, S. T. (1992). Thinking is for doing: Portraits of social cognition from daguerreotype to laser photo. *Journal of Personality and Social Psychology, 63,* 877–889.

Fodor, J. A. (1983). *Modularity of mind: An essay on faculty psychology.* Cambridge, MA: MIT Press.

Frank, R. (1988). *Passions within reason: The strategic role of the emotions.* New York: Norton.

Freud, S. (1923/1962). *The ego and the id* (J. Riviere, Trans.). New York: Norton.

Frimer, J. A., Biesanz, J. C., Walker, L. J., & MacKinlay, C. W. (in press). Liberals and conservatives rely on common moral foundations when making moral judgments about influential people. *Journal of Personality and Social Psychology.*

Gigerenzer, G. (2007). *Gut feelings: The intelligence of the unconscious* New York: Viking Press.

Gilligan, C. (1982). *In a different voice: Psychological theory and women's development.* Cambridge, MA: Harvard University Press.

Glenn, A. L., Iyer, R., Graham, J., Koleva, S., & Haidt, J. (2009). Are all types of morality compromised in psychopathy? *Journal of Personality Disorders, 23*(4), 384–398.

Goodall, J. (1986). *The chimpanzees of Gombe: Patterns of behavior.* Cambridge, MA: Belknap Press.

Gould, S. J., & Lewontin, R. C. (1979). The spandrels of San Marco and the Panglossian paradigm: A critique of the adaptationist programme. *Proceedings of the Royal Society of London, 205B,* 581–598.

Graham, J. (2010). Left gut, right gut: Ideology and automatic moral reactions, Doctoral dissertation. Retrieved from ProQuest Dissertations and Theses (AAT 3437423).

Graham, J. (2013). Beyond economic games: A mutualistic approach to the rest of moral life [Commentary on Baumard, André, & Sperber]. *Behavioral and Brain Sciences.*

Graham, J., & Haidt, J. (2010). Beyond beliefs: Religions bind individuals into moral communities. *Personality and Social Psychology Review, 14,* 140–150.

Graham, J., & Haidt, J. (2012). Sacred values and evil adversaries: A Moral Foundations approach. In P. Shaver & M. Mikulincer (Eds.), *The social psychology of morality: Exploring the causes of good and evil.* New York: APA Books.

Graham, J., Haidt, J., & Nosek, B. A. (2009). Liberals and conservatives rely on different sets of moral foundations. *Journal of Personality and Social Psychology, 96*, 1029–1046.

Graham, J., & Iyer, R. (2012). The unbearable vagueness of "essence": Forty-four clarification questions for Gray, Young, and Waytz. *Psychological Inquiry, 23*, 162–165.

Graham, J., Meindl, P., & Beall, E. (2012). Integrating the streams of morality research: The case of political ideology. *Current Directions in Psychological Science, 21*, 373–377.

Graham, J., Nosek, B. A., & Haidt, J. (2012). The moral stereotypes of liberals and conservatives: Exaggeration of differences across the political spectrum. *PLoS One, 7*, e50092.

Graham, J., Nosek, B. A., Haidt, J., Iyer, R., Koleva, S., & Ditto, P. H. (2011). Mapping the moral domain. *Journal of Personality and Social Psychology, 101*, 366–385.

Gray, K., Young, L., & Waytz, A. (2012). Mind perception is the essence of morality. *Psychological Inquiry, 23*, 101–124.

Greene, J. D., Morelli, S. A., Lowenberg, K., Nystrom, L. E., & Cohen, J. D. (2008). Cognitive load selectively interferes with utilitarian moral judgment. *Cognition, 107*, 1144–1154.

Greenwald, A. G. (2012). There is nothing so theoretical as a good method. *Perspectives on Psychological Science, 7*, 99–108.

Gudbjartsson, D. F., Walters, G. B., Thorleifsson, G., Stefansson, H., Halldorsson, B. V., Zusmanovich, P., et al. (2008). Many sequence variants affecting diversity of adult human height. *Nature Genetics, 40*, 609–615.

Haidt, J. (2001). The emotional dog and its rational tail: A social intuitionist approach to moral judgment. *Psychological Review, 108*, 814–834.

Haidt, J. (2007a). The new synthesis in moral psychology. *Science, 316*, 998–1002.

Haidt, J. (2007b). Moral psychology and the misunderstanding of religion. http://www.edge.org/3rd_culture/haidt07/haidt07_index.html Retrieved on July 20, 2012.

Haidt, J. (2012). *The righteous mind: Why good people are divided by politics and religion.* New York: Pantheon.

Haidt, J., & Bjorklund, F. (2008). Social intuitionists answer six questions about moral psychology. In W. Sinnott-Armstrong (Ed.), *Moral psychology, Vol. 2: The cognitive science of morality: Intuition and diversity* (pp. 181–217). Cambridge, MA: MIT Press.

Haidt, J., & Graham, J. (2007). When morality opposes justice: Conservatives have moral intuitions that liberals may not recognize. *Social Justice Research, 20*, 98–116.

Haidt, J., & Graham, J. (2009). Planet of the Durkheimians, where community, authority, and sacredness are foundations of morality. In J. Jost, A. C. Kay & H. Thorisdottir (Eds.), *Social and psychological bases of ideology and system justification* (pp. 371–401). New York: Oxford University Press.

Haidt, J., Graham, J., & Joseph, C. (2009). Above and below left–right: Ideological narratives and moral foundations. *Psychological Inquiry, 20*, 110–119.

Haidt, J., & Hersh, M. A. (2001). Sexual morality: The cultures and reasons of liberals and conservatives. *Journal of Applied Social Psychology, 31*, 191–221.

Haidt, J., & Joseph, C. (2004). Intuitive ethics: How innately prepared intuitions generate culturally variable virtues. *Daedalus, 133*, 55–66.

Haidt, J., & Joseph, C. (2007). The moral mind: How 5 sets of innate intuitions guide the development of many culture-specific virtues, and perhaps even modules. In P. Carruthers, S. Laurence & S. Stich (Eds.), *The innate mind: Vol. 3.* (pp. 367–391). New York: Oxford.

Haidt, J., & Joseph, C. (2011). How moral foundations theory succeeded in building on sand: A response to suhler and churchland. *Journal of Cognitive Neuroscience, 23*, 2117–2122.

Haidt, J., Koller, S., & Dias, M. (1993). Affect, culture, and morality, or is it wrong to eat your dog? *Journal of Personality and Social Psychology, 65*, 613–628.

Hamann, K., Warneken, F., Greenberg, J. R., & Tomasello, M. (2011). Collaboration encourages equal sharing in children but not in chimpanzees. *Nature, 476*, 328–331.

Hamilton, W. D. (1964). The genetical evolution of social behavior. II. *Journal of Theoretical Biology, 7,* 17–52.

Hamlin, J. K., Mahajan, N., Liberman, Z., & Wynn, K. (in press). Not like me = bad: Infants prefer those who harm dissimilar others. *Psychological Science.*

Hamlin, K., Wynn, K., & Bloom, P. (2007). Social evaluation by preverbal infants. *Nature, 450,* 557–559.

Hammerstein, P. (2003). Why is reciprocity so rare in social animals? In P. Hammerstein (Ed.), *Genetic and cultural evolution of cooperation* (pp. 55–82). Cambridge: MIT.

Harris, S. (2010). *The moral landscape: How science can determine human values.* New York: Free Press.

Helzer, E. G., & Pizarro, D. A. (2011). Dirty liberals!: Reminders of physical cleanliness influence moral and political attitudes. *Psychological Science, 22,* 517–522.

Henrich, J., Heine, S. J., & Norenzayan, A. (2010). The weirdest people in the world? *The Behavioral and Brain Sciences, 33,* 61–83.

Henrich, N., & Henrich, J. (2007). *Why humans cooperate: A cultural and evolutionary explanation.* Oxford: New York.

Herdt, G. H. (1981). *Guardians of the flutes.* New York: Columbia University Press.

Hibbing, J. R., & Smith, K. B. (2007). The biology of political behavior. *The Annals of the American Academy of Political and Social Science, 617,* 6–14.

Hirschfeld, L. A. (2002). Why don't anthropologists like children? *American Anthropologist, 104,* 611–627.

Hirsh, J. B., DeYoung, C. G., Xu, X., & Peterson, J. B. (2010). Compassionate liberals and polite conservatives: Associations of agreeableness with political ideology and moral values. *Personality and Social Psychology Bulletin, 36,* 655–664.

Hollos, M., Leis, P., & Turiel, E. (1986). Social reasoning in Ijo children and adolescents in Nigerian communities. *Journal of Cross-Cultural Psychology, 17,* 352–374.

Hong, S. (1996). Refinement of the Hong psychological reactance scale. *Educational and Psychological Measurement, 56,* 173–182.

Horberg, E. J., Oveis, C., Keltner, D., & Cohen, A. B. (2009). Disgust and the moralization of purity. *Journal of Personality and Social Psychology, 97*(6), 963–976.

Hrdy, S. B. (2009). *Mothers and others: The evolutionary origins of mutual understanding.* Cambridge, MA: Harvard.

Hunter, J. D. (1991). *Culture wars: The struggle to define America.* New York: Basic Books.

Hutcherson, C. A., & Gross, J. J. (2011). The moral emotions: A social–functionalist account of anger, disgust, and contempt. *Journal of Personality and Social Psychology, 100,* 719–737.

Inbar, Y., Pizarro, D. A., & Bloom, P. (2009). Conservatives are more easily disgusted than liberals. *Cognition and Emotion, 23,* 714–725.

Inbar, Y., Pizarro, D. A., & Bloom, P. (2011). Disgusting smells cause decreased liking of gay men. *Emotion, 12,* 23–27.

Inbar, Y., Pizarro, D. A., & Cushman, F. (2012). Benefiting from misfortune: When harmless actions are judged to be morally blameworthy. *Personality and Social Psychology Bulletin, 38,* 52–62.

Inbar, Y., Pizarro, D., Iyer, R., & Haidt, J. (2012). Disgust sensitivity, political conservatism, and voting. *Social Psychological and Personality Science, 5,* 537–544.

Inbar, Y., Pizarro, D. A., Knobe, J., & Bloom, P. (2009). Disgust sensitivity predicts intuitive disapproval of gays. *Emotion, 9*(3), 435.

Iyer, R. (2009). What are the basic foundations of morality? http://www.polipsych.com/2009/11/13/what-are-the-basic-foundations-of-morality/ Retrieved on June 26, 2012.

Iyer, R. (2010). The case for honesty as a moral foundation. http://www.polipsych.com/2010/12/07/the-case-for-honesty-as-a-moral-foundation/ Retrieved on June 26, 2012.

Iyer, R., Graham, J., Koleva, S., Ditto, P., & Haidt, J. (2010). Beyond identity politics: Moral psychology and the 2008 Democratic primary. *Analyses of Social Issues and Public Policy*, *10*, 293–306.

Iyer, R., Koleva, S. P., Graham, J., Ditto, P. H., & Haidt, J. (2012). Understanding libertarian morality: The psychological roots of an individualist ideology. *PLoS One*, *7*, e42366.

Iyer, R., Read, S. J., & Correia, J. (2010). Functional justice: Productivity and well-being goals define fairness. Available at SSRN: http://ssrn.com/abstract=1691969 or http://dx.doi.org/10.2139/ssrn.1691969.

James, W. (1890/1950). *The principles of psychology*. New York: Dover.

James, W. (1909/1987). *A pluralistic universe*. New York: Library of America.

Janoff-Bulman, R., & Sheikh, S. (2012). The forbidden, the obligatory, and the permitted: Moral regulation and political orientation. Paper presented to the Society for Personality and Social Psychology annual conference, San Diego, CA.

Janoff-Bulman, R., Sheikh, S., & Baldacci, K. (2008). Mapping moral motives: Approach, avoidance, and political orientation. *Journal of Experimental Social Psychology*, *44*, 1091–1099.

Janoff-Bulman, R., Sheikh, S., & Hepp, S. (2009). Proscriptive versus prescriptive morality: Two faces of moral regulation. *Journal of Personality and Social Psychology*, *96*, 521–537.

Jarudi, I. N. (2009). Everyday morality and the status quo: Conservative concerns about moral purity, moral evaluations of everyday objects, and moral objections to performance enhancement, Doctoral dissertation, Yale University.

Jones, B. (2012). The morality of representation: Constituent moral foundations and position-taking in congress. *Social Science Research Network*. http://ssrn.com/abstract=2018491, http://dx.doi.org/10.2139/ssrn.2018491.

Joseph, C. (2002). Morality and the virtues in Islam, Doctoral dissertation, University of Chicago.

Jost, J. T. (2006). The end of the end of ideology. *American Psychologist*, *61*, 651–670.

Jost, J. T. (2009). Group morality and ideology: Left and right, right and wrong. Paper presented to the Society for Personality and Social Psychology annual conference, Tampa, FL.

Jost, J. T., Glaser, J., Kruglanski, A. W., & Sulloway, F. J. (2003). Political conservatism as motivated social cognition. *Psychological Bulletin*, *129*, 339.

Joyce, R. (2006). *The evolution of morality*. Cambridge, MA: The MIT Press.

Kahneman, D. (2011). *Thinking, fast and slow*. New York: Farrar, Strauss, Giroux.

Kesebir, P., & Pyszczynski, T. (2011). A moral-existential account of the psychological factors fostering intergroup conflict. *Social and Personality Psychology Compass*, *5*, 878–890.

Killen, M., & Smetana, J. G. (2006). *Handbook of moral development*. Mahwah, New Jersey: Erlbaum.

Kim, K. R., Kang, J., & Yun, S. (2012). Moral intuitions and political orientation: Similarities and differences between Korea and the United States. *Psychological Reports*, *111*, 173–185.

Kinzler, K. D., Dupoux, E., & Spelke, E. S. (2007). The native language of social cognition. *Proceedings of the National Academy of Sciences of the United States of America*, *104*(30), 12577–12580. http://dx.doi.org/10.1073/pnas.0705345104.

Knutson, K., Krueger, F., Koenigs, M., Hawley, A., Escobedo, J., Vasudeva, V., et al. (2009). Behavioral norms for condensed moral vignettes. *Social Cognitive and Affective Neuroscience*, *5*(4), 378–384.

Kohlberg, L. (1969). Stage and sequence: The cognitive-developmental approach to socialization. In D. A. Goslin (Ed.), *Handbook of socialization theory and research* (pp. 347–480). Chicago: Rand McNally.

Kohlberg, L. (1971). From is to ought: How to commit the naturalistic fallacy and get away with it in the study of moral development. In T. Mischel (Ed.), *Psychology and genetic epistemology* (pp. 151–235). New York: Academic Press.

Kohlberg, L., Levine, C., & Hewer, A. (1983). *Moral stages: A current formulation and a response to critics*. Basel, Switzerland: Karger.

Koleva, S. (2011). Birds of a moral feather: The role of morality in romantic attraction and relationship satisfaction, Doctoral dissertation. Retrieved from ProQuest Dissertations and Theses (AAT 3472884).

Koleva, S., Graham, J., Iyer, Y., Ditto, P. H., & Haidt, J. (2012). Tracing the threads: How five moral concerns (especially purity) help explain culture war attitudes. *Journal of Research in Personality, 46*(2), 184–194.

Koleva, S., & Haidt, J. (2012). Let's use Einstein's safety razor, not Occam's Swiss Army knife or Occam's chainsaw. Commentary on target article, *Mind perception is the essence of morality* (K. Gray, L. Young, & A. Waytz). *Psychological Inquiry, 23*, 175–178.

Koonz, C. (2003). *The Nazi conscience*. Cambridge, MA: Belknap.

Kunda, Z. (1990). The case for motivated reasoning. *Psychological Bulletin, 108*, 480–498.

Kurzban, R., Dukes, A., & Weeden, J. (2010). Sex, drugs and moral goals: Reproductive strategies and views about recreational drugs. *Proceedings of Biological Sciences, 277* (1699), 3501–3508.

Lewin, K. (1951). *Field theory in social science*. Chicago: University of Chicago Press.

Lewis, G. J., & Bates, T. C. (2011). From left to right: How the personality system allows basic traits to influence politics via characteristic moral adaptations. *British Journal of Psychology, 102*, 1–13.

Lewis, G. J., Kanai, R., Bates, T. C., & Rees, G. (2012). Moral values are associated with individual differences in regional brain volume. *Journal of Cognitive Neuroscience, 24*, 1657–1663.

Lilienfeld, S. O., Ammirati, R., & Landfield, K. (2009). Giving debiasing away: Can psychological research on correcting cognitive errors promote human welfare? *Perspectives on Psychological Science, 4*, 390–398.

LoBue, V., Chiong, C., Nishida, T., DeLoache, J., & Haidt, J. (2011). When getting something good is bad: Even 3-year-olds react to inequality. *Social Development, 2011*, 154–170.

Luo, Q., Nakic, M., Wheatley, T., Richell, R., Martin, A., & Blair, R. J. R. (2006). The neural basis of implicit moral attitude—An IAT study using event-related fMRI. *NeuroImage, 30*, 1449–1457.

Makiniemi, J., Pirttila-Backman, A., & Pieri, M. (in press). The endorsement of the moral foundations in food-related moral thinking in three European countries. *Journal of Agricultural and Environmental Ethics*.

Marcus, G. (2004). *The birth of the mind*. New York: Basic.

Marcus, G. (2008). *Kluge: The haphazard construction of the human mind*. Boston: Houghton Mifflin.

Markowitz, E. M., & Shariff, A. F. (2012). Climate change and Moral Judgement: Psychological challenges and opportunities. *Nature Climate Change, 2*, 243–247.

Marler, P. (1991). The instinct to learn. In S. Carey & R. Gelman (Eds.), *The epigenesis of mind: Essays on biology and cognition*. Mahwah, NJ: Erlbaum.

Marques, J. M., Yzerbyt, V. Y., & Leyens, J. P. (1988). The 'black sheep effect': Extremity of judgments towards ingroup members as a function of group identification. *European Journal of Social Psychology, 18*, 1–16.

McAdams, D. P. (1995). What do we know when we know a person? *Journal of Personality, 63*, 365–396.

McAdams, D., Albaugh, M., Farber, E., Daniels, J., Logan, R., & Olson, B. (2008). Family metaphors and moral intuitions: How conservatives and liberals narrate their lives. *Journal of Personality and Social Psychology, 95*(4), 978–990.

McAdams, D. P., & Pals, J. L. (2006). A new Big Fig: Fundamental principles for an integrative science of personality. *American Psychologist, 61*, 204–217.

McClosky, H., & Zaller, J. (1984). *The American ethos: Public attitudes toward capitalism and democracy.* Cambridge, MA: Harvard University Press.

McGregor, H. A., Lieberman, J. D., Greenberg, J., Solomon, S., Arndt, J., Simon, L., et al. (1998). Terror management and aggression: Evidence that mortality salience motivates aggression against worldview-threatening others. *Journal of Personality and Social Psychology, 74*(3), 590.

Mercier, H., & Sperber, D. (2010). Why do humans reason? Arguments for an argumentative theory. *The Behavioral and Brain Sciences, 34,* 57–74.

Mikhail, J. (2007). Universal moral grammar: Theory, evidence and the future. *Trends in Cognitive Sciences, 11*(4), 143–152.

Mineka, S., & Cook, M. (1988). Social learning and the acquisition of snake fear in monkeys. In T. R. Zentall & J. B. G. Galef (Eds.), *Social learning: Psychological and biological perspectives* (pp. 51–74). Hillsdale, NJ: Lawrence Erlbaum.

Motyl, M. (2012). How moral migration geographically polarizes the electorate. *Invited talk given at the Society for Experimental Social Psychology's annual conference, Austin, TX.*

Motyl, M., & Pyszczynski, T. (2009). The existential underpinnings of the cycle of violence and terrorist and counterterrorist pathways to peaceful resolutions. *International Review of Social Psychology, 22,* 267–291.

Narvaez, D. (2008). The social-intuitionist model: Some counter-intuitions. In W. A. Sinnott-Armstrong (Ed.), *Moral psychology, Vol. 2, The cognitive science of morality: Intuition and diversity* (pp. 233–240). Cambridge, MA: MIT Press.

Narvaez, D. (2010). Moral complexity: The fatal attraction of truthiness and the importance of mature moral functioning. *Perspectives on Psychological Science, 5,* 163–181.

Navarrete, C. D., & Fessler, D. M. T. (2006). Disease avoidance and ethnocentrism: The effects of disease vulnerability and disgust sensitivity on intergroup attitudes. *Evolution and Human Behavior, 27,* 270–282.

Neuberg, S. L., Kenrick, D. T., & Schaller, M. (2010). Evolutionary social psychology. In S. T. Fiske, D. T. Gilbert & G. Lindzey (Eds.), *Handbook of social psychology* (pp. 761–796). (5th ed.). New York: John Wiley & Sons.

Nisbett, R. E., & Wilson, T. D. (1977). Telling more than we can know: Verbal reports on mental processes. *Psychological Review, 84,* 231–259.

Nosek, B. A., Graham, J., & Hawkins, C. B. (2010). Implicit political cognition. In B. Gawronski & B. K. Payne (Eds.), *Handbook of implicit social cognition* (pp. 548–564). New York, NY: Guilford.

Nucci, L., & Turiel, E. (1978). Social interactions and the development of social concepts in preschool children. *Child Development, 49,* 400–407.

Oaten, M., Stevenson, R. J., & Case, T. I. (2009). Disgust as a disease avoidance mechanism. *Psychological Bulletin, 135,* 303-321.

Oishi, S., & Graham, J. (2010). Social ecology: Lost and found in psychological science. *Perspectives on Psychological Science, 5,* 356–377.

Opie, I., & Opie, P. (1969). *Children's games in street and playground.* Oxford, UK: Clarendon Press.

Oxley, D. (2010). Fairness, justice and an individual basis for public policy, Doctoral dissertation, University of Nebraska.

Oxley, D. R., Smith, K. B., Alford, J. R., Hibbing, M. V., Miller, J. L., Scalora, M., et al. (2008). Political attitudes vary with physiological traits. *Science, 321,* 1667–1670.

Parkinson, C., Sinnott-Armstrong, W., Koralus, P. E., Mendelovici, A., McGeer, V., & Wheatley, T. (2011). Is morality unified? Evidence that distinct neural systems underlie judgments of harm, dishonesty, and disgust. *Journal of Cognitive Neuroscience, 23,* 3162–3180.

Pasanek, B. (2009). Ideology and metaphor. Presented to Kellogg School of Management, September 2009.

Payne, B. K., Cheng, C. M., Govorun, O., & Stewart, B. D. (2005). An inkblot for attitudes: Affect misattribution as implicit measurement. *Journal of Personality and Social Psychology*, *89*(3), 277.

Pennebaker, J. W., Francis, M. E., & Booth, R. J. (2003). *Linguistic inquiry and word count: LIWC2001 manual*. Mahwah, NJ: Erlbaum.

Piaget, J. (1932/1965). *The moral judgment of the child*. (M. Gabain, Trans.). New York: Free Press.

Pinker, S. (1997). *How the mind works*. New York: Norton.

Pinker, S. (2002). *The blank slate: The modern denial of human nature*. New York: Viking.

Pinker, S. (2012). *The false allure of group selection*. http://edge.org/conversation/the-false-allure-of-group-selection Retrieved on July 20, 2012.

Preston, S. D., & de Waal, F. B. (2002). Empathy: Its ultimate and proximate bases. *The Behavioral and Brain Sciences*, *25*, 1–72.

Preston, J. L., & Ritter, R. S. (2012). Cleanliness and godliness: Mutual association between two forms of purity. *Journal of Experimental Social Psychology*, *48*, 1365–1368.

Prince, C. (2010). Moral foundation theory and the law. *Seattle University Law Review*, *33*, 1293–1317.

Pyszczynski, T., Motyl, M., & Abdollahi, A. (2009). Righteous violence: Killing for god, country, freedom, and justice. *Behavioral Sciences of Terrorism and Political Aggression*, *1*, 12–39.

Rai, T. S., & Fiske, A. P. (2011). Moral psychology is relationship regulation: Moral motives for unity, hierarchy, equality, and proportionality. *Psychological Review*, *118*, 57–75.

Richerson, P. J., & Boyd, R. (2005). *Not by genes alone: How culture transformed human evolution*. Chicago: University of Chicago Press.

Ridley, M. (1996). *The origins of virtue*. Harmondsworth, UK: Penguin.

Rilling, J., Gutman, D., Zeh, T., Pagnoni, G., Berns, G., & Kilts, C. (2002). A neural basis for social cooperation. *Neuron*, *35*, 395–405.

Rosenblatt, A., Greenberg, J., Solomon, S., Pyszczynski, T., & Lyon, D. (1989). Evidence for terror management theory. I. The effects of mortality salience on reactions to those who violate or uphold cultural values. *Journal of Personality and Social Psychology*, *57*, 681.

Rozin, P., & Fallon, A. E. (1987). A perspective on disgust. *Psychological Review*, *94*, 23.

Rozin, P., Haidt, J., & McCauley, C. R. (2008). Disgust. In M. Lewis, J. M. Haviland-Jones & L. F. Barrett (Eds.), *Handbook of emotions* (pp. 757–776). (3rd ed.). New York: Guilford Press.

Russell, P. S., & Giner-Sorolla, R. (2011). Moral anger is more flexible than moral disgust. *Social Psychological and Personality Science*, *2*(4), 360–364.

Sadler-Smith, E. R. (2012). Before virtue: Biology, brain, behavior, and the 'moral sense'. *Business Ethics Quarterly*, *22*, 351–376.

Saltzstein, H. D., & Kasachkoff, T. (2004). Haidt's moral intuitionist theory: A psychological and philosophical critique. *Review of General Psychology*, *8*, 273–282.

Samuelson, S. (1980). The cooties complex. *Western Folklore*, *39*, 198–210.

Sanfey, A. G., Rilling, J. K., Aronson, J. A., Nystrom, L. E., & Cohen, J. D. (2003). The neural basis of economic decision-making in the ultimatum game. *Science*, *300*, 1755–1758.

Schaller, M., & Park, J. H. (2011). The behavioral immune system (and why it matters). *Current Directions in Psychological Science*, *20*, 99–103.

Schmidt, M. F. H., & Sommerville, J. A. (2011). Fairness expectations and altruistic sharing in 15-month-old human infants. *PLoS One*, *6*, e23223. http://dx.doi.org/10.1371/journal.pone.0023223.

Schnall, S., Haidt, J., Clore, G. L., & Jordan, A. H. (2008). Disgust as embodied moral judgment. *Personality and Social Psychology Bulletin, 34,* 1096–1109.

Schwartz, S. H. (1992). Universals in the content and structure of values. In M. P. Zanna (Ed.), *Advances in experimental social psychology: Vol. 25.* (pp. 1–65). New York: Academic Press.

Schwartz, S. H., & Bilsky, W. (1990). Toward a theory of the universal content and structure of values: Extensions and cross-cultural replications. *Journal of Personality and Social Psychology, 58,* 878–891.

Seligman, M. E. P. (1971). Phobias and preparedness. *Behavior Therapy, 2,* 307–320.

Sherif, M., Harvey, O. J., White, B. J., Hood, W., & Sherif, C. (1961/1954). *Intergroup conflict and cooperation: The Robbers Cave experiment.* Norman, OK: University of Oklahoma Institute of Group Relations.

Shook, N. J., & Fazio, R. H. (2009). Political ideology, exploration of novel stimuli, and attitude formation. *Journal of Experimental Social Psychology, 45*(4), 995–998.

Shweder, R. A. (1990). In defense of moral realism: Reply to Gabennesch. *Child Development, 61,* 2060–2067.

Shweder, R. A., Mahapatra, M., & Miller, J. (1987). Culture and moral development. In J. Kagan & S. Lamb (Eds.), *The emergence of morality in young children* (pp. 1–83). Chicago: University of Chicago Press.

Shweder, R. A., Much, N. C., Mahapatra, M., & Park, L. (1997). The "big three" of morality (autonomy, community, and divinity), and the "big three" explanations of suffering. In A. Brandt, & P. Rozin (Eds.), *Morality and health* (pp. 119–169). New York: Routledge.

Simon, H. (1992). What is an "explanation" of behavior? *Psychological Science, 3,* 150–161.

Skitka, L. J., Mullen, E., Griffin, T., Hutchinson, S., & Chamberlin, B. (2002). Dispositions, scripts, or motivated correction?: Understanding ideological differences in explanations for social problems. *Journal of Personality and Social Psychology, 83*(2), 470.

Sloane, S., Baillargeon, R., & Premack, D. (2012). Do infants have a sense of fairness? *Psychological Science, 23,* 196–204.

Smith, K. B., Oxley, D. R., Hibbing, M. V., Alford, J. R., & Hibbing, J. R. (2011). Linking genetics and political attitudes: Re-conceptualizing political ideology. *Political Psychology, 32,* 369–397.

Spelke, E. S. (2000). Core knowledge. *American Psychologist, 55,* 1233–1243.

Sperber, D. (1994). The modularity of thought and the epidemiology of representations. In L. A. Hirschfeld, & S. A. Gelman (Eds.), *Mapping the mind: Domain specificity in cognition and culture* (pp. 39–67). Cambridge, UK: Cambridge University Press.

Sperber, D. (2005). Modularity and relevance: How can a massively modular mind be flexible and context-sensitive? In P. Carruthers, S. Laurence, & S. P. Stich (Eds.), *The innate mind: Structure and contents: Vol. 1.* (pp. 53–68). New York: Oxford University Press.

Spiro, M. (1956). *Kibbutz: Venture in utopia.* Cambridge, MA: Harvard.

Stanovich, W., & West, R. F. (2000). Individual difference in reasoning: Implications for the rationality debate? *The Behavioral and Brain Sciences, 23,* 645–726.

Stenner, K. (2005). *The authoritarian dynamic.* New York: Cambridge.

Suhler, C. L., & Churchland, P. (2011). Can innate, modular "foundations" explain morality? Challenges for Haidt's moral foundations theory. *Journal of Cognitive Neuroscience, 23*(9), 2103–2116.

Tabibnia, G., Satpute, A. B., & Lieberman, M. D. (2008). The sunny side of fairness: Preference for fairness activates reward circuitry (and disregarding unfairness activates self-control circuitry). *Psychological Science, 19,* 339–347.

Tamborini, R. (2011). Moral intuition and media entertainment. *Journal of Media Psychology: Theories, Methods, and Applications, 23,* 39–45.

Tamborini, R., Eden, A., Bowman, N. D., Grizzard, M., & Lachlan, K. A. (2012). The influence of morality subcultures on the acceptance and appeal of violence. *Journal of Communication*, *62*(1), 136–157.

Tannenbaum, D., Uhlmann, E. L., & Diermeier, D. (2011). Moral signals, public outrage, and immaterial harms. *Journal of Experimental Social Psychology*, *47*, 1249–1254.

Tetlock, P. E. (2002). Social-functionalist frameworks for judgment and choice: The intuitive politician, theologian, and prosecutor. *Psychological Review*, *109*, 451–472.

Tomasello, M., Carpenter, M., Call, J., Behne, T., & Moll, H. (2005). Understanding and sharing intentions: The origins of cultural cognition. *The Behavioral and Brain Sciences*, *28* (5), 675–735.

Tooby, J., & Cosmides, L. (1992). The psychological foundations of culture. In J. H. Barkow, L. Cosmides, & J. Tooby (Eds.), *The adapted mind: Evolutionary psychology and the generation of culture* (pp. 19–136). New York: Oxford.

Tooby, J., Cosmides, L., & Barrett, H. C. (2005). Resolving the debate on innate ideas: Learnability constraints and the evolved interpenetration of motivational and conceptual functions. In P. Carruthers, S. Laurence, & S. Stich (Eds.), *The innate mind: Structure and contents* (pp. 305–337). New York: Oxford.

Triandis, H. C. (1995). *Individualism and collectivism*. Boulder, CO: Westview.

Trivers, R. L. (1971). The evolution of reciprocal altruism. *The Quarterly Review of Biology*, *46*, 35–57.

Turiel, E. (1979). Distinct conceptual and developmental domains: Social-convention and morality. *Nebraska symposium on motivation*, Lincoln, NE: University of Nebraska Press.

Turiel, E. (1983). *The development of social knowledge: Morality and convention*. Cambridge, England: Cambridge University Press.

Turiel, E., Killen, M., & Helwig, C. C. (1987). Morality: Its structure, function, and vagaries. In J. Kagan, & S. Lamb (Eds.), *The emergence of morality in young children* (pp. 155–243). Chicago: University of Chicago Press.

Turkheimer, E. (2000). Three laws of behavior genetics and what they mean. *Current Directions in Psychological Science*, *9*, 160–164.

Van Berkum, J. J. A., Holleman, B., Nieuwland, M., Otten, M., & Murre, J. (2009). Right or wrong? The brain's fast response to morally objectionable statements. *Psychological Science*, *20*(9), 1092–1099.

Van Leeuwen, F., & Park, J. H. (2009). Perceptions of social dangers, moral foundations, and political orientation. *Personality and Individual Differences*, *47*, 169–173.

Van Leeuwen, F., Park, J. H., Koenig, B. L., & Graham, J. (2012). Regional variation in pathogen prevalence predicts endorsement of group-focused moral concerns. *Evolution and Human Behavior*, *33*, 429–437.

Van Vugt, M., & Park, J. H. (2009). Guns, germs, and sex: How evolution shaped our intergroup psychology. *Social and Personality Psychology Compass*, *3*(6), 927–938.

Vauclair, C., & Fischer, R. (2011). Do cultural values predict individuals' moral attitudes? A cross-cultural multilevel approach. *European Journal of Social Psychology*, *41*(5), 645–657.

Walster, E., Walster, G., & Berscheid, E. (1978). *Equity: Theory and research*. Boston: Allyn & Bacon.

Waytz, A., Epley, N., & Cacioppo, J. T. (2010). Social cognition unbound. *Current Directions in Psychological Science*, *19*(1), 58.

Weber, C., & Federico, C. M. (2007). Interpersonal attachment and patterns of ideological belief. *Political Psychology*, *28*(4), 389–416.

Weber, C., & Federico, C. M. (in press). Moral foundations and heterogeneity in ideological preferences. *Political Psychology*.

Wegner, D. M., & Bargh, J. A. (1998). Control and automaticity in social life. In D. Gilbert, S. T. Fiske, & G. Lindzey (Eds.), *Handbook of social psychology: Vol. 1*. (pp. 446–496). (4th ed.). New York: McGraw-Hill.

Wheatley, T., & Haidt, J. (2005). Hypnotic disgust makes moral judgments more severe. *Psychological Science*, *16*, 780–784.

Wiessner, P. (2005). Norm enforcement among the Ju/'hoansi Bushmen. *Human Nature*, *16*, 115–145.

Wilson, D. S. (2002). *Darwin's cathedral: Evolution, religion, and the nature of society*. Chicago: University of Chicago Press.

Winegard, B., & Deaner, R. O. (2010). The evolutionary significance of Red Sox nation: Sport fandom as a byproduct of coalitional psychology. *Evolutionary Psychology*, *8*(3), 432–446.

Winterich, K., Zhang, Y., & Mittal, V. (2012). How political identity and charity positioning increase donations: Insights from Moral Foundations Theory. *International Journal of Research in Marketing: Special Issue on Consumer Identities*, *29*, 346–354.

Wright, R. (1994). *The moral animal*. New York: Pantheon.

Wright, J. C., & Baril, G. (2011). The role of cognitive resources in determining our moral intuitions: Are we all liberals at heart? *Journal of Experimental Social Psychology*, *47*, 1007–1012.

Young, L., & Saxe, R. (2011). When ignorance is no excuse: Different roles for intent across moral domains. *Cognition*, *120*, 202–214.

Zajonc, R. B. (1980). Feeling and thinking: Preferences need no inferences. *American Psychologist*, *35*, 151–175.

CHAPTER THREE

Culture and Analytic Versus Holistic Cognition: Toward Multilevel Analyses of Cultural Influences

Yuri Miyamoto
Department of Psychology, University of Wisconsin-Madison, Madison, Wisconsin, USA

Contents

Abstract

A growing body of literature has documented cultural differences in cognitive processes and also proposed various factors underlying these cultural differences. At the same time, not much attention has been paid to proximal-level processes that connect distal-level societal factors to individuals' cognitive processing. This chapter aims to present a framework to integrate factors at multiple levels to understand cultural influences on cognitive processes. The chapter begins by providing an overview of cultural differences in cognitive processes, including potential moderators of cultural differences. Next, factors underlying cultural differences at multiple levels are outlined, with a focus on proximal-level situational processes. Subsequently, by introducing the case of

Advances in Experimental Social Psychology, Volume 47
ISSN 0065-2601
http://dx.doi.org/10.1016/B978-0-12-407236-7.00003-6

culturally contingent consequences of power, the chapter illustrates how cultural contexts can moderate the effect of a certain factor on cognitive processes, highlighting the
importance of multilevel analyses. Implications of multilevel analyses and directions for
future research are discussed at the end.

Studies on cross-cultural differences in cognitive processes have been rapidly
accumulating over the past decade (Nisbett, 2003; Nisbett & Miyamoto,
2005; Nisbett, Peng, Choi, & Norenzayan, 2001). These studies have demonstrated cultural differences across a wide range of cognitive processes,
including processes which used to be considered universal. For example,
although studies done in Western cultural contexts have repeatedly shown
a robust tendency for people to overestimate internal causes and underestimate external causes of behavior (i.e., the fundamental attribution error;
Ross, 1977), such a tendency has been found to be attenuated or nonexistent
in Asian cultural contexts (e.g., Miller, 1984). Demonstrations of cultural
differences in cognitive processes highlight the crucial role that sociocultural
contexts play in shaping the nature and function of cognitive processes.

As is often the case in social psychological research (Zanna & Fazio,
1982), however, questions guiding cross-cultural research have evolved over
the past decades (Heine & Norenzayan, 2006). First-generation questions
asked "Is there a cultural difference?" and these led to the accumulation
of evidence showing cultural differences in cognitive processes, such as
the studies that showed cultural differences in the fundamental attribution
error. Second-generation questions built on findings of cultural differences
and probed, "When is there such an effect?" (i.e., under what conditions) or
"How does the effect occur?" (i.e., through what processes does culture
shape psychological experience). For example, researchers who asked the
second-generation questions have shown how cultural differences in attribution depend on moderating conditions, such as situational salience
(e.g., Choi & Nisbett, 1998), and how the way people view the self can
shape their cognitive processes (e.g., Kühnen & Oyserman, 2002).

At the same time, even though "when" and "how" questions are closely
related to each other, they have rarely been asked simultaneously. While too
much emphasis on "when" questions can lead to a relatively dispersed
understanding, exclusive focus on "how" questions can reduce the rich
sociocultural phenomena too much (Zanna & Fazio, 1982). To integrate
"when" and "how" questions into a single framework, this chapter proposes
the importance of taking into account factors at multiple levels to understand

cultural influences on cognitive processes, especially by highlighting proximal-level processes through which distal-level societal factors influence and shape individuals' cognitive processes.

Section 1 delineates the nature and scope of cultural differences in cognitive processes by providing an overview of cultural differences in cognitive processes and also reviewing potential moderators of cultural differences. Section 2 outlines multilevel analyses of factors underlying cultural differences by highlighting proximal-level situational factors that bridge the gap between distal-level situational factors and individual psychological factors. Section 3 illustrates how the effect of a proximal-level factor can depend on distal-level factors by introducing studies on culturally contingent consequences of power. Both throughout the chapter and at the end, implications and issues that need to be addressed in future research are discussed.

1. CULTURAL DIFFERENCES IN ANALYTIC VERSUS HOLISTIC COGNITION

Although there are various ways in which cognitive processes can differ across individuals and sociocultural environments (e.g., Müller-Lyer illusion; Segall, Campbell, & Herskovit, 1966), one of the most well-documented cognitive processes that differ across cultures is the extent to which people attend to contextual and relational information (Miyamoto & Wilken, 2013; Nisbett, 2003; Nisbett & Miyamoto, 2005; Nisbett et al., 2001; Witkin, Dyk, Faterson, Goodenough, & Karp, 1974). For example, when presented with a picture of a wolf standing in woods, some people focus on the focal object (i.e., the wolf) without paying much attention to its context (i.e., the woods), whereas other people attend to relationships between the focal object and its context (Masuda & Nisbett, 2001). Also, when explaining why someone engaged in a certain behavior (e.g., cheating behavior), some people tend to attribute the cause to the actor's internal attributes (e.g., competitive personality), whereas other people tend to attribute the cause to contextual factors surrounding the actor (e.g., unemployment; Miller, 1984). The cognitive style of people who focus on an object independently from its context and categorize and explain things based on attributes of the object has been called *analytic* or *field independent*. In contrast, the cognitive style of people who attend to relationships between a focal object and its contexts and categorize and explain things on the basis of such relationship has been called *holistic* or *field interdependent*.

Researchers have suggested that analytic and holistic cognitive styles are closely associated with characteristics of sociocultural environments at a distal level (Fiske, Kitayama, Markus, & Nisbett, 1998; Nisbett, 2003; Nisbett et al., 2001; Varnum, Grossmann, Kitayama, & Nisbett, 2010). In particular, in sociocultural environments characteristic of North America or Western Europe, individuals are considered to be fundamentally independent from social relationships, whereas in sociocultural environments characteristic of East Asia, individuals are considered to be inherently connected to and embedded in social relationships (Markus & Kitayama, 1991; Triandis, 1989). It has been theorized that, in the former, *independent* sociocultural environments, individuals tend to focus on their own goals and their target objects without being too much influenced by surrounding others' demands or contexts, which leads to an analytic cognitive style. In contrast, in the latter, *interdependent* sociocultural environments, it is theorized that individuals need to attend to relationships and to contexts, which leads to a holistic cognitive style.

In this section, I will review evidence demonstrating cultural differences in analytic versus holistic cognition and potential moderators such cultural differences. Most of the studies introduced in this section compare a sample from Western cultures (e.g., North America, Western Europe) with a sample from East Asian cultures (e.g., China, Korea, and Japan) because those two cultures differ from each other on the critical distal-level situational factors (i.e., independent vs. interdependent social structures) assumed to underlie cultural differences in cognitive processes. In addition, comparisons of Western and Eastern cultures have the benefit of allowing researchers to examine cultural differences in cognitive processes while controlling for other factors, such as the level of economic development or modernization. At the same time, it is important to note that cognitive differences are not confined to East–West differences. As will be reviewed in the subsequent section, studies have found that cognitive differences exist between other sociocultural environments that are assumed to differ in terms of independent versus interdependent social structures, such as other regions of the world (e.g., Eastern Europe, West Africa, Northern vs. Southern Italy), religions (e.g., Protestants, Catholic), and social classes (e.g., working-class, middle-class).

1.1. Cultural differences

1.1.1 Attention

One of the core features of analytic and holistic cognition is attention to focal versus contextual information in a visual field. In a pioneering study of cultural differences in attention, Masuda and Nisbett (2001) presented

American and Japanese participants with animated video clips of naturalistic underwater scenes containing focal fish within a background and asked them to describe the scenes. Japanese participants were more likely than American participants to refer to the background and to relationships between focal fish and the background (e.g., "a big fish was swimming toward the green seaweed"). Such cultural differences have also been shown in eye movements. When watching still photos of naturalistic scenes containing a focal object and its background (e.g., a tiger in a jungle), American participants looked at the focal objects sooner and longer than Chinese participants did, and Chinese participants made more saccades to the background than American participants did (Chua, Boland, & Nisbett, 2005). These studies suggest that Westerners and East Asians are actually looking at different things when they are exposed to naturalistic scenes.

Although these findings provide evidence for the existence of cultural differences in attention, such findings could be driven by differences in meanings people ascribe to animals or naturalistic scenes. If there were cultural differences in attention to stimuli stripped of any potential meanings, it would provide stronger evidence for cultural differences in attention. In fact, many studies have found cultural differences using simple geometric figures (e.g., Doherty, Tsuji, & Phillips, 2008; Ji, Peng, & Nisbett, 2000; Kitayama, Duffy, Kawamura, & Larsen, 2003; McKone et al., 2010; Savani & Markus, 2012; Witkin et al., 1954). For example, the Framed-Line Task (FLT; Kitayama et al., 2003; Figure 3.1) measures the ability to incorporate or ignore contextual information (i.e., square frame). Participants were first shown a

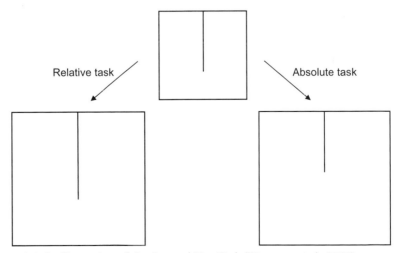

Figure 3.1 An illustration of the Framed-Line Task (Kitayama et al., 2003).

square frame with a vertical line in it and then presented with another square frame of either the same or a different size. In the second square, participants were asked to draw a line that was identical to the first line in either absolute (i.e., absolute task) or relative (to the frame) length (i.e., relative task). Thus, the absolute task required attention to the length of the focal line independently from the contextual frame, whereas the relative task required attention to the relationship between the focal line and the contextual frame. Japanese participants tended to make more errors in the absolute task compared to American participants, whereas American participants tended to make more errors in the relative task compared to Japanese participants. Furthermore, a functional magnetic resonance imaging (fMRI) study showed that working on culturally incompatible tasks (i.e., the relative task for Americans and the absolute task for East Asians) increased activation in regions of the brain associated with attentional control compared to working on culturally compatible tasks did (Hedden, Ketay, Aron, Markus, & Gabrieli, 2008), suggesting that the culturally incongruent task is more challenging.

These cross-cultural results suggest that East Asians are more likely than Americans to attend to contextual information when perceiving visual stimuli that include focal objects and their contexts. Do such cultural differences in attention to contextual information extend to attention to *configural relationships* between objects? Because configural relationships between objects provide context in which each object is located, East Asians may be more likely than Americans to attend to such relationships. By focusing on facial perception, a domain characterized by configural processing (Farah, Wilson, Drain, & Tanaka, 1998), Miyamoto, Yoshikawa, and Kitayama (2011) examined whether East Asians are more sensitive to changes in spatial (configural) relationships between facial features than Americans are. Two sets of faces were created from original faces: the spacing set was created by changing spacing between the features (i.e., the eyes and the mouth) and the featural set was created by replacing the eyes and mouth with those of other faces (see Figure 3.2; Mondloch, Le Grand, & Maurer, 2002). Both Caucasian and Japanese faces as well as female and male faces were used. Participants worked on an identity-matching task where they were presented with two faces sequentially on a computer screen and were instructed to judge whether the two faces were the same or different as accurately and as quickly as possible. The proportion of correct responses was computed for the featural set and the spacing set.

As predicted, an interaction between face set and culture was significant. Although both American participants and Japanese participants performed equally well in the featural set, Japanese participants were more accurate than

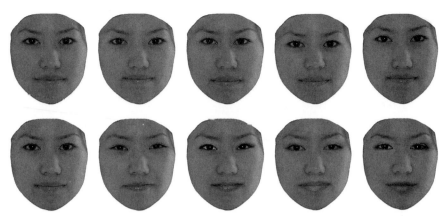

Figure 3.2 Example of spacing and featural sets used in Miyamoto et al. (2011, Study 2). The leftmost face on each row is the original face. The faces on the top row show a spacing set and those on the bottom row show a featural set. The final, definitive version of this paper has been published in *Cognitive Science*, 35/3, April 2011 by Wiley-Blackwell Publishing Ltd. All rights reserved. © 2011 Wiley-Blackwell Publishing Ltd.

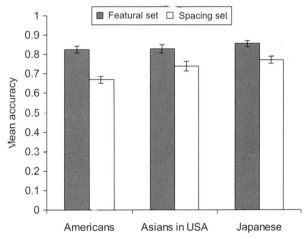

Figure 3.3 Mean accuracy as a function of culture and face set. Error bars represent the standard error (Miyamoto et al., 2011, Study 2). The final, definitive version of this paper has been published in *Cognitive Science*, 35/3, April 2011 by Wiley-Blackwell Publishing Ltd. All rights reserved. © 2011 Wiley-Blackwell Publishing Ltd.

were American participants in the spacing set (see Figure 3.3). In addition, Americans were slower to respond regardless of the type of changes when compared with Japanese, suggesting that cultural differences in accuracy in the spacing set were not due to speed–accuracy trade-offs. Furthermore, after completing the identity–matching task, participants were asked to report the extent to which they focused on various aspects of face. In line with their performance on the identity-matching task, Japanese participants reported attending more to configural aspects, such as configuration and impression, than American participants did. To further explore the effect of culture on cognition, Asian participants in the United States were also recruited to participate in the study. Exposure to American cultural contexts may lead Asian participants in the United States to focus less on configural relationships. Such evidence would suggest the role of culture in shaping face perception. Supporting this possibility, Asian participants in the United States showed the pattern in-between Japanese and American participants in both their accuracy in the spacing set and their self-reported attention to configural aspects of face. Although face processing is known to be highly configural, these findings suggest that cultural contexts can influence the extent to which people attend to configural aspects of face and underscore the robustness of culture's influence on cognition.

1.1.2 Categorization and attribution
The existence of such cultural differences in attentional styles suggests that even if people are presented with the same stimuli, people from different cultures are looking at different aspects of the stimuli. This could have downstream effects on other cognitive processes that build on the attended information, such as categorization and attribution. Specifically, Westerners' attention to the focal objects and their attributes may lead them to categorize objects based on attributes of the objects. In contrast, East Asians' attention to relationships among objects and their context may lead them to categorize objects based on relationships between the objects.

In support of this contention, research has shown cultural differences in object categorization, with some cultures using more taxonomic ways and others using more thematic ways. Taxonomic categorization is based on features shared by the objects (i.e., whether the objects share properties, appearance, or function), whereas thematic categorization is based on spatial, causal, or temporal relationships between the objects (i.e., whether the objects are jointly involved in a theme or context; Markman, 1989; Markman & Hutchinson, 1984). For example, when choosing two objects among three (e.g., a *carrot*, an *eggplant*, and a *rabbit*) that could be grouped together, a *carrot* and an *eggplant* would be grouped together according to taxonomic categorization (because both are vegetables), whereas a *carrot* and a *rabbit* would be grouped together according to thematic categorization (because rabbits eat carrots). Consistent with predictions, American participants were more likely to use taxonomic modes to group objects than to use thematic modes, whereas Chinese participants were more likely to use thematic modes to group objects than to use taxonomic modes (Ji, Zhang, & Nisbett, 2004; for cultural differences in another type of categorization, see Norenzayan, Smith, Kim, & Nisbett, 2002).

Attention can guide not only categorization but also attribution. When people are led to focus on an actor (e.g., by brightly illuminating the actor), people tend to attribute an actor's behavior to dispositional causes more and to situational causes less than when they are not led to focus on the actor (McArthur & Post, 1977). Given that Westerners tend to focus on a focal object (i.e., an actor) and its attributes, they may tend to attribute an actor's behavior to an actor's disposition. In fact, studies conducted in Western cultures have repeatedly shown the robustness of the fundamental attribution error—a tendency to overestimate the internal cause (i.e., properties of focal object) and underestimate the external cause (i.e., contextual or situational factors) of behavior (Ross, 1977). On the other hand, if Asians tend to perceive relationships between a focal object or an event and its contexts, they may tend to attribute behaviors to situational causes and thus show weaker or no fundamental attribution error. Supporting this contention, cross-cultural research has shown that the fundamental attribution error is attenuated or nonexistent in Asian cultures (Choi & Nisbett, 1998; Masuda & Kitayama, 2004; Miller, 1984; Miyamoto & Kitayama, 2002; Morris & Peng, 1994; Norenzayan, Choi, & Nisbett, 2002).

In one of the early demonstrations of cultural differences in causal attribution (Miller, 1984), American and Indian participants were asked to narrate behaviors of a person they knew well in their daily lives and to explain why the behavior was undertaken. When explaining the behavior (e.g., cheating behavior), compared to Indian adults, American adults made more reference to general dispositions (e.g., competitive personality) and less reference to contextual factors (e.g., unemployment social status). Similar cultural differences were found between Americans and Chinese (Morris & Peng, 1994). When weighting factors that caused actual mass murder cases, American participants weighted dispositional factors (e.g., chronic psychological problems) more heavily than Chinese participants did, whereas Chinese participants weighted situational factors (e.g., social change) more heavily than American participants did.

Westerners may also infer the disposition of an actor more readily compared to East Asians. One way to test such a possibility is to examine lexical choices because the type of lexicon people choose to describe a behavior reflects underlying inferences (Semin & Fiedler, 1988). Adjectives (e.g., helpful) convey information about the disposition of the person, whereas verbs (e.g., helps) provide information about the context surrounding the person or the relationship between the person and objects. If Westerners are more likely than East Asians to make dispositional inference, they may use more adjectives. In fact, research has shown that, compared to Japanese, Italians tend to use more adjectives and fewer verbs to describe others (Maass, Karasawa, Politi, & Suga, 2006). Recent research has also provided neural evidence, which suggests that European Americans spontaneously draw dispositional inferences from observing trait-implying behaviors, whereas Asian Americans do not (Na & Kitayama, 2011; see also Zárate, Uleman, & Voils, 2001).

1.1.3 Temporal information

Studies reviewed so far have focused on cultural differences in the extent to which people focus on focal objects versus their contexts. Recent studies have shown that cultural differences extend to attention to *temporal* contexts. In a temporal dimension, events that happen close to the present moment can be considered to be focal, whereas events that will happen in a distant future or happened in a distant past can be considered to be relatively more contextual. Because East Asians pay more attention to contextual information, it is possible that they also pay more attention to temporally distant events compared to Westerners. In fact, Maddux and Yuki (2006) found that whereas Westerners focus on proximal consequences, East Asians tend to perceive indirect, distal consequences of an event. For example, when judging the consequences of a shot in a game of pool on subsequent shots, European Americans perceived that the shot would have a larger impact on the next shot than Asian Americans did, whereas Asian Americans perceived that the shot would have a larger impact in the sixth shot after the focal shot than European Americans did.

Such findings show cultural differences in attention to proximal versus distal events that do not involve the self. However, it is not clear if cultural differences in attention to proximal versus distal events extend to the way individuals perceive and react to proximal or distal events in their own life or if such cultural differences have any consequences for individuals. Previous studies have shown that perceiving that a task is useful for fulfilling one's short-term goals (proximal utility value) or long-term, distal goals (distal utility value) has various motivational benefits (e.g., Hulleman & Harackiewicz, 2009). Given cultural differences in attention to proximal versus distal future events, there may be cultural differences in whether a proximal or distal utility value brings more benefits. Specifically, East Asians may tend to perceive how the present task (e.g., math problems) is connected to accomplishing distal, long-term future goals (e.g., career endeavor), and thus could be motivated by such a distal utility value. In contrast, Westerners may tend to focus on how the present task is useful for accomplishing immediate, short-term goals (e.g., calculating tips), and thus could be motivated by such a proximal utility value.

To test these hypotheses, Shechter, Durik, Miyamoto, and Harackiewicz (2011) asked participants to learn a new math technique (i.e., how to solve two-digit multiplication without using paper and pencil) through reading an instructional notebook and listening to an audio tape that guided them through the notebook. The manipulation of proximal and distal utility value was embedded in the instructional notebook. Participants in the distal utility value condition were told about the usefulness of the technique in the long-term future (e.g., career endeavor, graduate school), whereas participants in the proximal utility value condition were told about the usefulness of the technique in various everyday life situations (e.g., calculating tips, managing personal finances). After learning the math technique, participants worked on multiplication problems. At the end, participants reported the amount of effort they exerted on the problem sets and how interested they were in the math technique on seven-point rating scales from 1 to 7.

Consistent with the hypotheses, as shown in Figure 3.4, East Asian participants found the technique to be more interesting and reported working harder after the distal utility was highlighted than they did after the proximal utility was highlighted, whereas European American participants showed the opposite pattern. These findings not only highlight differences in attention to proximal and distal events but also provide their potential motivational consequences. They suggest that East Asians gain the most motivational benefit from learning distal connections between the task and long-term goals, whereas Westerners gain the most motivational benefit from learning about proximal connections between the task and short-term goals.

Cultural differences in attention to proximal and distal temporal contexts have also shown in attention to proximal and distal *past* events (Ji, Guo, Zhang, & Messervey, 2009). When judging the relevance of factors that happened in the past and in the present to solving a case of theft, Chinese participants rated the past information to be more relevant to solving the case of theft than European Canadians did, whereas both groups of participants rated the present information to be equally relevant. As a whole, these findings suggest that East Asians are more likely than Westerners to attend to both

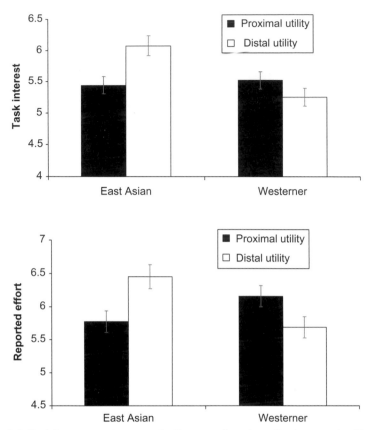

Figure 3.4 Task interest and reported effort as a function of culture and utility value manipulation (Shechter et al., 2011, Study 2). The final, definitive version of this paper has been published in *Personality and Social Psychology Bulletin*, 37/3, March 2011 by SAGE Publications Ltd. All rights reserved. © 2011 SAGE Publications Ltd.

past and future distal events, whereas Westerners are more likely than East Asians to focus on proximal events, and such cultural differences have motivational consequences (Shechter et al., 2011).

1.1.4 Dialectical reasoning

Given East Asians' attention to relationships among objects, they may also perceive relationships between contradictory elements and tolerate contradictions. Research done in a wide range of domains has provided support for such a possibility (for a review see Spencer-Rodgers, Williams, & Peng, 2010). For example, Peng and Nisbett (1999) found that Chinese participants preferred proverbs that contained a contradiction (e.g., "too humble is half proud") more than American participants did, suggesting that contradictions are more accepted and even preferred by Chinese than by Americans. Such a tendency to accept contradictions has been termed "dialectical" thinking (Peng & Nisbett, 1999).

Another feature of dialectical thinking is to perceive that the reality is a process that is constantly changing rather than fixed entities. In one of their studies, Ji, Nisbett, and Su (2001) presented participants with scenarios depicting various individuals and their current situation and asked participants to estimate a probability that things will change in the future. For example, one scenario depicted a high school student who has been the chess champion for 3 years and participants were asked to judge the likelihood that the student will lose in the next game against the strongest opponent. Chinese participants estimated the probability for things to change to be higher than American participants did. This shows that Chinese tend to anticipate larger changes than Americans do.

1.1.5 Clarifying the relationship between analytic versus holistic and local versus global cognition

It is important to note that, although global cognitive processing and holistic cognitive processing are often equated with each other, they are orthogonal constructs (Kimchi, 1992). Global cognitive processing is processing of properties at a hierarchically higher (global) level of structure than properties at a hierarchically lower (local) level (Navon, 1977). For example, according to the action identification theory (Vallacher & Wegner, 1987), one can represent a behavior (e.g., riding a bike) at a hierarchically higher level (e.g., exercising) or at a hierarchically lower level (e.g., pedaling). A higher level representation indicates global processing, whereas a lower level representation indicates local processing (Förster & Dannenberg, 2010). On the other hand, holistic (or configural) cognitive processing is processing of relationships between components and/or contexts (Garner, 1978; Rock, 1986; Treisman, 1986), as exemplified by studies reviewed so far in this section. The independence of global and holistic cognitive processing suggests that holistic cognitive processing can sometimes be associated with global cognitive processing when contextual properties are located at a higher level of hierarchical structure, whereas holistic cognitive processing can sometimes be associated with a local cognitive processing when contextual properties are located at a lower level of hierarchical structure.

Understanding the locus of contextual information at different levels of hierarchical structure could provide an explanation for why East Asians sometimes seem to engage more in *local* cognitive processing and sometimes seem to engage more in *global* cognitive processing when compared with Westerners. When contextual information resides in local properties, East Asians tend to show local cognitive processing. For example, verbs, which convey more contextual information than adjectives do (Semin & Fiedler, 1988), are located at a hierarchically lower level of structure compared to adjectives, and Japanese are more likely than Americans to use verbs to describe others (Maass et al., 2006). Thus, in such tasks, Japanese engage in more local cognitive processing than Americans do.

In contrast, when contextual information exists in global properties, East Asians tend to show global cognitive processing. In fact, in many of the visual attention tasks, contextual information is located in a larger field, which is more global than specific parts that comprise the scene. For example, in the FLT (Kitayama et al., 2003), attending to the relationship between the line and the square frame requires more attention to a hierarchically higher (global) level of information than attending only to the line. As reviewed above, East Asians typically show more global cognitive processing in such visual attention tasks. Furthermore, in Navon's (1977) global–local task, identification of global features (i.e., identifying a large letter consists of smaller letters) requires more attention to configural relationship between smaller letters than does identification of local features (i.e., identifying small letters embedded in a larger letter). Research has that participants who were primed with independence showed facilitated identification of local features compared to identification of global features, whereas those who were primed with interdependence showed the opposite pattern (Kühnen & Oyserman, 2002), suggesting that interdependent cultural constructs can be associated with more global processing when contextual information (e.g., configural relationship) resides in global properties (see also McKone et al., 2010).

These analyses suggest that what characterizes cognitive differences between independent and interdependent cultural environments is the processing of contextual information (and thus holistic or analytic cognitive processing). Cultural differences in global or local cognitive processing seem to depend on the locus of contextual information in the hierarchical structure. This, however, does not rule out the possibility that there might be sociocultural or ecological factors, other than independent and interdependent cultural environments, which influence global or local cognitive processing independently from holistic or analytic cognitive processing. For example, literacy or formal education systems might foster global cognitive processing (e.g., Greenfield, 1972; Scribner & Cole, 1973).

1.2. Moderators of cultural differences

Most of the studies reviewed earlier focused on demonstrating cultural differences in cognitive processing. However, are there any specific conditions or factors that increase or decrease cultural differences? Although not many studies have explored factors that moderate cultural differences in cognition, some moderating factors are proposed in the domain of attitude attribution, especially using the classic attitude attribution paradigm (Jones & Harris, 1967). In this paradigm, participants read an essay either supporting or opposing a certain issue (e.g., Castro's Cuba) and are asked to infer the true attitude of the protagonist who allegedly wrote it. In addition, some of the participants are told that the protagonist chose whether to support or oppose the issue in the essay (i.e., free-choice condition). Not surprisingly, in this condition, participants tend to infer that the protagonist has an attitude that corresponds to the content of the essay. The other participants are told that the protagonist was assigned to a position by the teacher and thus did not have choice over which position to take (i.e., no-choice condition). Although the situational constraints should be enough to explain the behavior in the no-choice condition, previous studies conducted in Western cultural contexts have repeatedly shown that people fail to take the situational constraints into consideration and tend to infer that the protagonist has an attitude that corresponds to the position stated in the essay (Gilbert & Malone, 1995; Jones, 1979). This tendency has been called correspondence bias.

As reviewed in the foregoing section (e.g., Morris & Peng, 1994; Norenzayan, Choi, et al., 2002), East Asians tend to focus more on contextual information and attribute behavior more to situational causes than Westerners do. Because taking situational constraints into consideration should reduce the correspondence bias, it is logical to expect that East Asians would show less correspondence bias compared to Westerners. However, several cross-cultural studies found that East Asians actually exhibit as strong of a correspondence bias as Westerners do in the standard no-choice condition (Choi & Nisbett, 1998; Krull et al., 1999; Masuda & Kitayama, 2004; Miyamoto & Kitayama, 2002). How can this seeming contradiction be resolved? To account for the contradiction, researchers have explored moderators of cultural differences in correspondence bias.

1.2.1 Situational salience

One of the features of the attitude attribution paradigm is that situational constraint information (i.e., the information that the protagonist was assigned to a position by the teacher) is relatively nonsalient compared to behavioral information (i.e., the content of the essay). Thus, if the situational information is made more salient, East Asians might take it more into consideration and show less correspondence bias compared to Westerners. Studies have provided evidence supporting this contention. When participants went through the same situation as the protagonist did by writing an essay defending the position assigned to them before inferring the protagonist's attitude, Korean participants attenuated the degree of correspondence bias compared to the standard paradigm, whereas American participants showed as strong of a correspondence bias as they did in the standard paradigm (Choi & Nisbett, 1998). Similarly, making situational information salient has been shown to increase cultural differences in the correspondence bias even when a different paradigm, where participants played a role in causing the protagonist's behavior, was used (Masuda & Kitayama, 2004; also see Norenzayan, Choi, et al., 2002). These findings suggest that when situational information is made salient, Americans still show the correspondence bias, whereas East Asians tend to take situational information into greater consideration and hence exhibit an attenuated correspondence bias.

1.2.2 Diagnosticity of behavior

Another feature of the attitude attribution paradigm is that the essay used in the standard no-choice condition is reasonably long and persuasive. It is possible that such a behavior is perceived to be highly diagnostic of the protagonist's underlying attitude. Even though the protagonist had no choice over which position to defend, the content of the essay (e.g., length, persuasiveness) provides useful information about the willingness of the protagonist to defend the position. If the essay is long and persuasive, it is reasonable to assume that the essay is diagnostic of the true attitude of the protagonist. However, if the essay is short and unpersuasive, it is probably less diagnostic of the true attitude of the protagonist. Part of the reason why Asians may draw as strong of a correspondence inference as Americans in the standard no-choice condition thus might be because they perceived the willingness of the protagonist to defend the position based on these essay features.

To test this hypothesis, Miyamoto and Kitayama (2002) conducted the standard no-choice condition by recruiting both Americans and Japanese and also manipulated the diagnosticity of the essay. Participants were told that a protagonist was attending a political science seminar and asked by an instructor to write an essay supporting (or opposing, depending on the condition) capital punishment. Half of the participants received an essay which was long and persuasive, thus highly diagnostic of the protagonist's

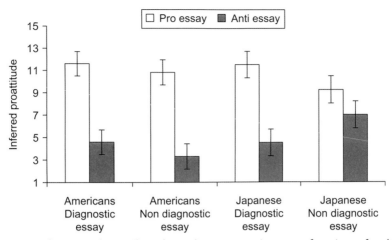

Figure 3.5 The attitude attributed to the protagonist as a function of culture, diagnosticity of essay, and essay direction (Miyamoto & Kitayama, 2002, Study 1). Higher values indicate that participants inferred that the protagonist supported capital punishment, whereas lower values indicate that participants inferred that the protagonist opposed capital punishment.

strong attitude, whereas the other half of the participants received an essay which was short and unpersuasive, thus not diagnostic of the attitude. Based on the information, participants were asked to estimate the real attitude of the protagonist toward capital punishment on a 15-point scale (1 = *very strongly opposing*, 15 = *very strongly supportive*).

The results are presented in Figure 3.5. The degree of correspondence bias is indicated by the difference in inferred attitude between proessay and antiessay conditions. Supporting the hypotheses and replicating other studies, there were no cultural differences in the degree of correspondence bias when the essay was diagnostic of the attitude. Both American and Japanese participants inferred that the protagonist had an attitude that corresponded to the position of the essay when the essay was long and persuasive. On the other hand, when the essay was not diagnostic, American participants still showed the same degree of correspondence bias, whereas correspondence bias was attenuated among Japanese participants, suggesting that when the behavior is not diagnostic of the underlying attitude, Japanese pay more attention to situational constraints and show less correspondence bias compared to Americans.

Taken together, these findings suggest that despite cultural differences in attention to situational information, cultural differences in attitude attribution can be surpassed if there is not enough situational information to which to attend, or if the behavior is so diagnostic of the attitude that it overrides attention to situational information. Although moderators have not been explored much in domains other than attitude attribution, it would be informative for future research to explore potential moderators in other domains as well. For example, recent research (Ito, Masuda, & Hioki, 2012) found no cultural differences in attention to a target object versus contextual information when participants were asked to *categorize* the target's facial emotions as either positive or negative (rather than to *rate the intensity* of the target's facial emotions, as was the case in previous research that found cultural differences using similar stimuli; Masuda, Ellsworth, et al., 2008). This implies the possibility that when contextual information is completely irrelevant to the judgment, even East Asians inhibit their attention to contextual information to the same extent as Americans do. The identification of such moderators sheds light not only on the boundary conditions but also on processes that contribute to cultural differences.

1.3. Summary

In summary, cultural differences in cognition have been demonstrated across various domains. Whereas Westerners tend to focus on focal objects and their properties, categorize objects based on their properties, attribute a cause of a behavior to internal properties, and explain an event by focusing on focal and proximal factors, East Asians tend to focus on relationship between focal objects and their contexts, categorize objects based on their relationships, attribute a cause of a behavior to contextual factors, and explain an event by attending to contextual and distal information. Additionally, the salience of situational information and the diagnosticity of behavioral information have been suggested as moderators of cultural differences in attribution. Further research is needed to elucidate other moderators of cultural differences in cognitive processing.

2. MULTILEVEL ANALYSES OF CULTURAL INFLUENCES ON COGNITION

The preceding summary has shown cultural differences in a wide range of cognitive processes. Such evidence demonstrating cultural differences is essential for understanding the nature and scope of cultural influences. At the same time, the demonstration of cultural differences *per se* does not explain why there are cultural differences. Therefore, various factors underlying cultural differences in cognitive processing have been

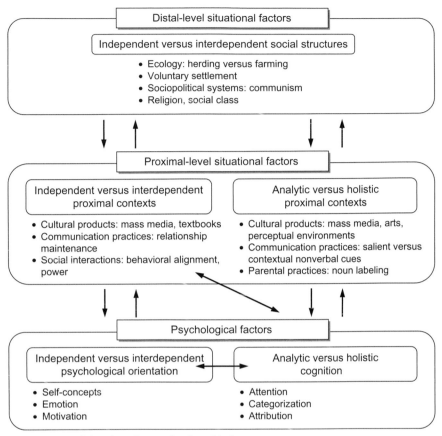

Figure 3.6 Multilevel analyses of cultural influences.

proposed and explored. As illustrated in Figure 3.6, some of the proposed factors are distal-level situational factors that determine the nature of social structures at the level of society, whereas some factors are proximal-level situational factors surrounding individuals in their daily lives, such as cultural practices and products. In addition, some of the factors are also psychological factors. In this section, factors at three different levels will be introduced, highlighting the importance of considering multilevel processes of cultural influences.

2.1. Distal-level situational factors

As introduced in Section 1, various researchers theorize that cultural differences in cognitive processes are rooted in the nature of social environments at a distal level (Fiske et al., 1998; Nisbett, 2003; Nisbett et al., 2001;

Varnum et al., 2010). One of the fundamental ways in which social environments differ across cultures is whether individuals are inherently connected to and embedded in social relationships or if individuals are fundamentally independent from social relationships (i.e., independent vs. interdependent social structures; Fiske et al., 1998; Markus & Kitayama, 1991; Triandis, 1989). Living in social environments where individuals are mutually dependent on others presumably requires attention to relationships and to contexts. On the other hand, living in social environments where individuals are independent from surrounding others may allow individuals to focus on their own goals and their target objects without being overly constrained by surrounding contexts or surrounding others' demands.

Research traces cultural differences to these social structure differences, which have been shaped through the history of each society (e.g., ecology, voluntary settlement, political system; the top box in Figure 3.6). For example, Nisbett and his colleagues have proposed that East–West differences in cognitive processes can be traced back to ecological and sociostructural differences between Ancient Greek and Chinese societies (Nisbett, 2003; Nisbett et al., 2001). Ancient Chinese society was based on large-scale agriculture, which involved cooperation and coordination among a large number of individuals. In such a society, social relations were characterized by interdependence among individuals, which likely has fostered attention to relationships and to the contexts. In contrast, Ancient Greek society was based on herding, fishing, and small-scale agriculture, which did not involve much cooperation or coordination among a large number of individuals. Social relations in such a society were characterized by autonomy and independence of each individual, which might have contributed to focused attention to focal objects.

Several lines of research have provided support for such a link between the modes of social structures and cognitive styles by comparing societies that differ in their social structures due to ecological or sociopolitical factors. For example, ecology and social structures of the community have been linked to cognitive styles (Witkin & Berry, 1975). Individuals living in Canadian Eskimo communities, where people engage in hunting and have flexible social relations, showed more analytic cognitive processing than those who live in Temne communities in West Africa, where people engage in rice farming and emphasize conformity (Berry, 1966). Although such findings are suggestive of the effects ecology has on cognitive processing, Canadian Eskimo communities differ from Temne communities not only in their ecology and social structures but also in various other ways, such as ethnicity or language. A more recent research, thus, has explored whether a similar association between ecology and cognitive styles can be found even when communities within the same nation were examined (Uskul, Kitayama, & Nisbett, 2008). By comparing communities in Turkey, researchers found that people who live in herding communities, where autonomy is emphasized, showed more analytic cognitive processing compared to those who live in farming communities and fishing communities, where close cooperation among the family members is required.

Societies also differ in their social structures due to historical and sociopolitical factors. Among Western cultures, due to the history of feudalism in Southern Italy (Putnam, 1993) and communist regimes in Central and Eastern Europe, social structures in Southern Italy and Central and Eastern Europe have historically been interdependent compared to those in Northern Italy, Western Europe, and the United States. In line with the differences in social structures, southern Italian participants made more thematic categorization, thus showing more holistic cognitive processing, than northern Italian participants did (Knight & Nisbett, 2007), and Russian and Croatian participants attended to more contextual information in a visual task than American participants did (Grossmann & Varnum, 2011; Varnum, Grossmann, Katunar, Nisbett, & Kitayama, 2008). Furthermore, a history of voluntary settlement might have fostered an independent mode of social structure where freedom from constraint and personal agency is promoted (Turner, 1920). If so, living in a "frontier" may foster more analytic cognitive processing. In support of this possibility, people who live in voluntary settlement societies (i.e., the United States or Hokkaido in Japan) show more analytic cognitive styles compared to those who live in nonvoluntary settlement societies (i.e., Western Europe or mainland Japan; Kitayama, Ishii, Imada, Takemura, & Ramaswamy, 2006; Kitayama, Park, Sevincer, Karasawa, & Uskul, 2009).

Religious beliefs and practices also shape the modes of social relations, which in turn could influence cognitive processing. In fact, recent studies found that different religions foster analytic or holistic cognition, depending on the modes of social relations emphasized by the religion. For example, the inward state and beliefs of individuals are emphasized over church rituals in Protestants (Cohen, Hall, Koenig, & Meador, 2005; Weber, 1958). Reflecting such a focus on the inward condition of the soul, Protestants were more likely than Catholics to endorse internal attributions when attributing the cause of behaviors (Li et al., 2012). In addition, religious beliefs have also been shown to influence attention to local versus global features in Navon's task (Colzato, Hommel, van den Wildenberg, & Hsieh, 2010; Colzato, van Beest, et al., 2010). In this task, participants are usually faster to judge global, relational features than to judge local, analytic features, thus showing the global-precedence effect (Navon, 1977). Dutch Calvinists, whose religion emphasizes individual responsibilities, showed a weaker global-precedence effect, thus demonstrating more analytic, focused attention, compared to Dutch Atheists. In contrast, Italian Roman Catholics and Israeli Orthodox Jews, whose religions emphasize social responsibilities, as well as Taiwanese Buddhists, whose religion emphasizes compassion and physical and social contexts, showed a stronger global-precedence effect, thus demonstrating more holistic, relational attention, than did matched seculars in their respective countries.

Lastly, even within the same society, people coming from different social classes are exposed to, and are living in, different social environments. Middle-class environments involve a higher sense of control and more resources to influence the environment, whereas working-class environments involve a lower sense of control and more of a need to adjust to the environment (Lachman & Weaver, 1998; Snibbe & Markus, 2005; Stephens, Markus, & Townsend, 2007). Differences in social structures have been linked to different styles of cognitive processing. Compared to middle-class individuals, working-class individuals tend to prefer situational explanations, make thematic categorization, attend to contextual information in perceptual tasks, and endorse dialectical views (Grossmann & Varnum, 2011; Kraus, Piff, & Keltner, 2009; Miyamoto & Ji, 2011; Na et al., 2010).

2.2. Proximal-level situational factors

These previous studies have demonstrated that individuals who live in societies that have more interdependent social structures tend to show a more holistic cognitive style compared to those who live in societies that have more independent social structures (thus showing a link between the top box and the bottom box in Figure 3.6). However, the process through which such group-level differences in social structures shape and influence the cognitive style of each individual is not clear. In order to understand exactly how living in interdependent (or independent) social environments guides people's attention to contextual and relational (or focal) information, it is crucial to unpack proximal-level processes that bridge the gap between distal-level situational factors and individual's cognitive processing as illus-
      the middle box in Figure 3.6.

Distal-level situational factors shape the core social structure and ideas of a society, which, in turn, shape and become reflected in proximal-level situational factors surrounding individuals in their daily lives, such as social interactions, practices, and products (Fiske et al., 1998; Markus & Kitayama, 1994). Through participation in, and exposure to, such proximal-level situational factors, individuals' cognitive processing is likely to become attuned to the dominant mode of social structure and ideas reflected in these proximal contexts. Prolonged participation in, and repeated exposure to, such proximal factors may shape individuals' habitual style of cognitive processing. At the same time, proximal-level situational factors are collective processes which are shaped and maintained by individuals who participate in them. Thus, proximal contexts, such as social interactions and practices, not only shape and influence individuals but also are shaped and maintained by individuals, suggesting the mutual relations between proximal contexts and individuals' psychological processes (Fiske et al., 1998; Shweder, 1990).

In addition, when considering the relationship between proximal-level contexts and cognitive processing, it is useful to distinguish between two domains of proximal-level contexts: analytic versus holistic domain and independent versus interdependent domain. Some proximal contexts reflect analytic versus holistic cognition prevalent in a given culture, such as the amount of dispositional or situational explanations presented in mass media (Morris & Peng, 1994). Through repeated exposure to such proximal contexts, individuals are likely to attune their cognitive processes to fit the pattern of information that exists in their proximal contexts. At the same time, proximal contexts can also guide cognitive processing through a more indirect route—through interdependent versus independent proximal contexts. Some of the proximal contexts reflect interdependent versus independent modes of social relationships prevalent in a given culture, such as the extent to which textbooks emphasize self-direction or group harmony (Imada, 2012) or the extent to which communication practices place emphasis on relationship maintenance (Miyamoto & Schwarz, 2006). Engaging in interdependent proximal contexts is likely to guide attention to relationships and social contexts, which in turn may lead attention to contextual information in general, thus contributing to holistic cognitive processing. In contrast, engaging in independent proximal contexts is likely to guide attention to the self and to one's goals, which in turn may lead attention to focal information in general, thus contributing to analytic cognitive processing.

Despite the crucial role proximal-level situational factors play in shaping individuals' cognitive processing, compared to the amount of research done on the effects of distal-level factors on cognitive processing, relatively little attention has been given to the processes through which proximal-level situational factors influence cognitive processes. Below, by distinguishing analytic versus holistic and independent versus interdependent domains, processes through which such proximal-level contexts foster cognitive processing are outlined.

2.2.1 Analytic versus holistic proximal contexts

Proximal-level situations can attune and guide cognition by directly channeling individuals' attention to either focal or contextual aspects of environments and inducing corresponding cognitive processing.

Culturally specific styles of cognitive processing can be reflected in various kinds of social practices in which people engage in their daily lives, such as parental practices and linguistic practices. For example, when talking to their infants playing with toys, compared to Japanese mothers, American mothers were more likely to label toys to their infants, thus highlighting the objects (Fernald & Morikawa, 1993; also see Tardif, Gelman, & Xu, 1999). In addition, culturally specific styles of cognition can also be reflected in communication practices (Hall, 1976). For example, when describing a situation in which they engaged in nonverbal communication, American participants reported relying mainly on facial and bodily cues (e.g., facial expressions, body language), which are relatively salient, explicit nonverbal cues, whereas Japanese participants reported taking into account situational cues (e.g., weather, atmosphere) in addition to facial and bodily cues, suggesting that Japanese nonverbal communication requires more attention to less salient contextual cues than American nonverbal communication does (Eggen, Miyamoto, & Uchida, 2012; also see Ishii, Reyes, & Kitayama, 2003; Tanaka et al., 2010).

Cultural differences in cognitive styles are also embodied and reflected in cultural products to which people are exposed in their daily lives (for a meta-analysis, see Morling & Lamoreaux, 2008). For example, American newspapers referred more to dispositional causes than Hong Kong newspapers did when covering sports events (Lee, Hallahan, & Herzog, 1996; also see Morris & Peng, 1994), and American mass media focused more on personal characteristics and less on the backgrounds of athletes than Japanese mass media did when covering Olympic games (Markus, Uchida, Omoregie, Townsend, & Kitayama, 2006). Cultural products are not confined to narratives. The characteristic cognitive style can also be embodied and reflected in the visual properties of products and environments. For example, Eastern traditional paintings, including both portraits and landscapes, tend to include a larger amount of contextual information than do Western counterparts (Masuda, Gonzalez, Kwan, & Nisbett, 2008).

Cognitive styles may be embodied even in the nature of perceptual environments, such as townscapes. Reflecting a holistic cognitive style, objects may not look distinct from each other and may look more complex in Japanese townscapes than in American townscapes. To test this hypothesis, Miyamoto, Nisbett, and Masuda (2006, Study 1) sampled about 1000 townscapes of Japan and the United States by randomly selecting public elementary schools, post offices, and hotels from cities of three different sizes in each culture and taking pictures in front of, and one street behind, each institution (examples are shown in Figure 3.7). When presented with these photos of randomly sampled perceptual environments of Japan and the United States, and asked to judge the complexity and ambiguity of them (e.g., "How ambiguous is the boundary of each object?"), participants rated Japanese perceptual environments to be more complex and ambiguous compared to the American perceptual environments, suggesting cultural differences in the perceptual environments. In addition, to provide an objective measure of complexity, the number of bounded particles in each picture was counted by an image analysis software. In line with the subject judgment, it was found that Japanese perceptual environments contained a larger number of objects than American perceptual environments.

Prolonged and repeated exposure to such culturally divergent perceptual environments may afford culturally specific patterns of attention. If the Japanese perceptual environments are more complex and boundaries between objects are ambiguous, it might be harder to distinguish objects from the background in such perceptual environments and thus attention might be guided more toward the whole field. Repeated exposure to such complex and ambiguous perceptual environments may thus afford holistic cognitive processing, at least temporarily. This hypothesis was tested in the subsequent study (Miyamoto et al., 2006, Study 2). As a cover story, American and Japanese participants were told that the study was about visual image processing and that they would work on two ostensibly different tasks (i.e., a scenery rating task and a change detection task). The scenery rating task, which was introduced to participants as a pretest to select pictures for the future experiment, was the manipulation of exposure to perceptual environments. In this task, participants were randomly assigned to see 95 American or Japanese perceptual environments and asked to imagine that

Figure 3.7 Examples of American perceptual environments and Japanese perceptual environments (Miyamoto et al., 2006). The final, definitive version of this paper has been published in *Psychological Science*, 17/2, February 2006 by SAGE Publications Ltd. All rights reserved. © 2006 SAGE Publications Ltd.

they were placed in the scenery and judge how much they liked it. Subsequently, they worked on the change-blindness task (Masuda & Nisbett, 2006), which was the measure of cognitive processing. In this task, participants were presented with pairs of animated vignettes depicting culturally neutral scenes (e.g., construction site) and asked to detect changes among each pair. Some changes were made in regard to the attributes of focal objects (e.g., the presence or absence of a person on a truck), whereas the other changes were made in regard to contextual information (e.g., the location of the truck, changes in background objects).

Replicating cultural differences in attention (e.g., Masuda & Nisbett, 2001, 2006), Japanese participants detected a larger number of changes in

Table 3.1 The mean number (and standard deviation) of detected changes as a function of culture of participants, culture of scenes, and type of changes (Miyamoto et al., 2006, Study 2)

Culture of participants	Culture of scenes	Focal changes	Contextual changes
American participants	American scenes	1.66 (0.98)	2.07 (0.87)
	Japanese scenes	1.69 (0.84)	2.67 (1.22)
Japanese participants	American scenes	1.75 (0.93)	2.67 (0.96)
	Japanese scenes	1.53 (1.00)	3.17 (1.06)

contextual information than American participants did, whereas there were no cultural differences in the detection of changes in focal objects (see Table 3.1). More importantly, however, those participants who were exposed to Japanese perceptual environments in the first task detected a larger number of changes in contextual information compared to those who were exposed to American perceptual environments. Consistent with the previous finding which found cultural differences only in the detection of contextual changes (Masuda & Nisbett, 2006), there were no effects of perceptual environments on the detection of changes in focal information. These findings suggest that exposure to Japanese perceptual environments can afford attention to contextual information compared to exposure to American perceptual environments, thus providing evidence for the role of proximal-level contexts in channeling cognitive processing (see also Ueda & Komiya, 2012, for a replication of this study using an eye-tracking device).

2.2.2 Independent versus interdependent proximal contexts
Cognitive processing is not only directly guided by exposure to analytic versus holistic proximal contexts but also guided through participation in interdependent versus independent proximal contexts. Through participation in interdependent or independent proximal contexts, individuals may attune their cognitive processing to fit the needs of the proximal contexts, resulting in culturally divergent cognitive processing. Specifically, engagement in interdependent proximal contexts that highlight one's adjustment to social contexts may require attention to surrounding others and social contexts, which in turn may foster attention to contextual information in general (i.e., holistic cognition), whereas engagement in independent proximal contexts that highlight pursuit of one's unique goals may guide attention to the self and to one's goals, which may lead attention to focal information in general (i.e., analytic cognition).

First of all, studies have shown that interdependent or independent modes of social structure are manifested in cultural products (Morling & Lamoreaux, 2008). American textbooks tended to emphasize independent themes, such as self-direction and achievement, whereas Japanese textbooks tended to emphasize interdependent themes, such as conformity and group harmony (Imada, 2012) and American magazine ads tended to emphasize uniqueness compared to Korean magazine ads, whereas Korean magazine ads tended to emphasize harmony compared to American magazine ads (Kim & Markus, 1999).

A recent study has shown that emphasis on uniqueness versus harmony can also be encoded in visual stimuli, such as colorings of geometric patterns, devoid of any explicit verbal messages (Ishii, Miyamoto, Rule, & Toriyama, 2012). In the first step of this study, both American and Japanese students were asked to color patchwork-like geometric patterns using a set of 24 colored pencils. Analyses of visual features of the colored figures revealed that Japanese students were more likely to use lighter colors (e.g., whitish colors or pastels) than American students. Such use of lighter colors is likely to make Japanese colorings look more harmonious. To examine whether Japanese colorings are indeed perceived as more harmonious than American colorings, in the second step, different groups of American and Japanese students were recruited and asked to rate harmoniousness or uniqueness of the colorings made by participants in the first step. Both American and Japanese raters judged Japanese colorings to be more harmonious than American colorings, and American colorings to be more unique than Japanese colorings. Such findings illustrate subtle ways through which interdependent or independent modes of social structure can be represented in cultural products.

Social interactions and practices, such as communication practices, can also reflect the mode of social structure characteristic of the society. Communication serves functions to convey information as well as to maintain relationships in any cultures. However, communication practices in interdependent proximal contexts may be especially likely to require people to focus on the relational function. It thus may be more difficult for people in interdependent proximal contexts to communicate when they have to convey information under a condition where they cannot readily engage in relationship maintenance, such as when leaving a request on an answering machine. To test this hypothesis, Miyamoto and Schwarz (2006) asked Japanese and American participants to role-play a senior student who is on the way to attend a conference to present his/her honors thesis and realized that she or he left an important presentation material on an office desk. Participants were asked to call either a peer or a professor and to make a request (i.e., to send the material to a conference center) on an answering machine. In addition, to measure the amount of cognitive resource left available during the communication, participants were asked to work on a secondary cognitive task on a computer while placing a call.

As hypothesized, Japanese participants attended to relational functions more than American participants did; they tailored their message more to the recipient of the message (i.e., their message was more friendly and less polite when calling a peer than when calling a professor) and left a longer message, presumably reflecting their concern for relationship maintenance. Partly due to Japanese participants' attention to relational functions, Japanese participants had less cognitive resource left available to work on the secondary task and showed lower performance on the secondary task compared to American participants. Interestingly, consistent with such cultural differences in the message length, answering machines made by Japanese manufacturers offered a longer time limit for an incoming message than did those made by American manufacturers. These findings suggest that communication practices in Japan are likely to emphasize the relational function more than communication practices in the United States, whereas communication practices in the United States tend to focus on the informational function more than communication practices in Japan. Cultural differences in relational functions of communication practices have also been shown in the extent of behavioral adjustments—how much people align their behavior to surrounding others. A meta-analysis of conformity studies based on Asch's paradigm across 17 countries found that the conformity rate was higher in countries based on interdependent social structures than in those countries based on independent social structures (Bond & Smith, 1996).

Participation in such interdependent proximal contexts and adjustment to social contexts may require holistic cognitive processing. In support of this, researchers have shown a link between behavioral mimicry and holistic cognitive processing (Van Baaren, Horgan, Chartrand, & Dijkmans, 2004). Those participants who attended more to contextual information in a visual attention task were more likely to mimic nonverbal behaviors of a target person presented in a video clip, suggesting a link between holistic cognitive processing and behavioral alignment to others. Furthermore, when participants' own nonverbal behaviors were mimicked by the experimenter, participants displayed increased recall of objects' locations, suggesting that behavioral mimicry can foster processing of contextual information.

In addition, concerns arising from social interaction issues have also been linked to holistic cognitive processing (Kim & Markman, 2006). Participants who were reminded of a time when they were socially isolated attended more to the relationship between a focal object and its background, presumably because a fear of isolation motivated them to focus on others and social contexts. The type of social concerns matters too. Whereas a self-focused manifestation of social anxiety (i.e., social phobia; e.g., "I get nervous that people are staring at me as I walk down the street") was correlated with relatively better analytic performance on the FLT, an other-focused manifestation of social anxiety (i.e., *taijin kyofusho*; e.g., "I am afraid that I will blush in front of other people and as a result offend them") was correlated with relatively better holistic performance on the FLT (Norasakkunkit, Kitayama, & Uchida, 2012). These findings suggest that engagement in self-focused, independent proximal contexts is linked to, and fosters, analytic cognitive processing, whereas engagement in other-focused, interdependent proximal contexts is linked to, and fosters, holistic cognitive processing.

2.3. Individual-level factors

Another way to understand how distal group-level differences in social structures influence cognitive processes is to examine the link between different modes of social structures and cognitive processing at the individual level, through mediation of psychological orientations at the individual level. This mechanism refers to the following links in Figure 3.6: independent versus interdependent social structures (top box) → independent versus interdependent psychological orientation (bottom left box) → analytic and holistic cognition (bottom right box). A body of cross–cultural literature has documented that interdependent and independent modes of social structures shape and influence interdependent versus independent psychological orientations of individuals, such as self-concepts, emotion, and motivation (Fiske et al., 1998; Markus & Kitayama, 1991, 1994; Triandis, 1995). In turn, these individual psychological orientations may be associated with individual cognitive styles. Thus, researchers have been examining how independent versus interdependent psychological orientations are linked to analytic and holistic cognition (i.e., the link between the bottom left and bottom right boxes in Figure 3.6).

One way to examine this link is to activate or "prime" the ideas associated with interdependent or independent psychological orientations in individuals' minds and examine whether the activated ideas lead to the corresponding cognitive processing. Researchers have proposed various methods to prime interdependent or independent psychological orientations (e.g., Gardner, Gabriel, & Lee, 1999). For example, asking participants to think what makes them different from their family and friends primes' independence, whereas asking participants to think what they have in common with their family and friends primes interdependence (Trafimow, Triandis, & Goto, 1991). Studies have shown that priming the concept of independence or interdependence can foster corresponding styles of cognition (for a meta-analysis, see Oyserman & Lee, 2008). For example, after participants were primed with interdependence by circling first-person plural pronouns (e.g., "we," "us"), they were faster to identify global features in Navon's global-local task and better at recalling objects' location than after they were primed with independence by circling first-person singular pronouns (e.g., "I," "me"; Kühnen & Oyserman, 2002), suggesting that priming the idea of interdependence fosters holistic cognitive processing.

Another way to examine the link between independent or interdependent psychological orientations and cognitive styles is to measure individual differences in each domain and examine correlations between them. However, recent large-scale studies that explored the relationships between individual differences in psychological orientations and individual differences in cognitive styles found only weak correlations between them (Kitayama et al., 2009; Na et al., 2010). In addition, the correlations among tasks within each domain were also weak, suggesting the possibility that psychological orientations and cognitive styles may not exist as coherent sets of traits that differentiate individuals within each culture. This is in stark contrast to the large body of cross-cultural evidence showing that psychological orientations and cognitive styles exist as coherent sets of descriptors of *group* characteristics.

Taking proximal-level processes into consideration may help researchers to understand the dissociation between individual-level and group-level characteristics. It is possible that, even though distal-level social structural differences shape proximal-level contexts, which in turn shape psychological processes of individuals who participate in them, each individual is exposed to only a subset of proximal-level contexts, to which one attunes psychological processes. For example, interdependent social structures in Japan may be reflected in the nature of their proximal-level contexts, such that their mass media may highlight situational causes of behavior, and their communication practices may require more attention to contextual nonverbal cues. Some individuals are likely to be exposed to mass media frequently but do not engage much in communication practices, whereas some other individuals are likely to be engaged in communication practices frequently but are not exposed much to mass media. To the extent that individuals attune their psychological processes to fit the proximal context to which they are exposed, individuals may differ in which specific domains they engage in holistic cognitive processing. The former type of individuals may be holistic in their attributional style, but may not be particularly holistic in other cognitive domains, whereas the latter type of individuals may be holistic in their attentional style, but may not be particularly holistic in other cognitive domains. Thus, there could be multiple ways for people to attune their cognitive styles or psychological orientations to the cultural patterns within the same culture, which could lead to weak correlations *within* each culture at the individual-level but strong associations *across* cultures at the group-level. Although cultural differences are often attributed to individual differences in the study of culture (Shweder, 1973), the contrasting patterns between group-level and individual-level processes indicate the importance of distinguishing different levels of analyses and examining the relationship between them.

The effects of different social structures on cognitive processing have also been examined by focusing on bicultural individuals who have been exposed to two different social structures and thus have internalized two different systems of psychological processes. These bicultural individuals may be able to frame-switch between different systems of psychological processes depending on cultural contexts. Supporting this prediction, Hong Kong Chinese made more situational attributions after being exposed to Chinese cultural icons than after being exposed to American cultural icons (Hong, Morris, Chiu, & Benet-Martínez, 2000). Other research has shown that even European Americans shift their cognitive style after exposure to East Asian cues (e.g., a symbol of yin-yang) by making more dialectical predictions (Alter & Kwan, 2009).

2.4. Summary

A growing body of literature shows that factors at multiple levels underlie cultural differences in cognitive processing. At the most distal level, ecological and sociopolitical environments shape the core social structure of a society. Social structures, in turn, shape and become reflected in proximal-level contexts, in which individuals are located in their daily lives. Through participation in, and exposure to, such proximal-level contexts, cognitive styles of individuals become attuned to the cultural pattern reflected in the proximal-level contexts. In addition, cognitive processing can also be fostered by the activation of corresponding psychological constructs even at the individual level. The role of proximal-level processes underscores the importance of taking a multilevel approach to understand cultural influences on cognitive processing.

3. CULTURALLY CONTINGENT SITUATED COGNITION: A CASE FOR CULTURAL MODERATION OF A PROXIMAL-LEVEL SITUATIONAL FACTOR

Although studies reviewed in the preceding section suggest that various situational factors foster corresponding cognitive processing, effects of factors on cognitive processes may not be deterministic. In a collective system, such as culture, which is comprised of multiple factors at multiple levels that coexist in a state of tension, the effect of a factor depends on the totality of the system (Lewin, 1951; Ross & Nisbett, 1991). This suggests that an analysis of the coexisting factors in the system is important when understanding and predicting the effects of a factor. Thus, in order to predict the effect of a factor on cognitive processes, it is necessary to understand the nature of multilevel structures in which the factor is located.

Furthermore, construal or subjective meaning that actors attach to situational factors may also influence the effect of a factor; the impact of "objective" situational factors depends on how actors construe their meaning (Ross & Nisbett, 1991). To predict the effect of a certain situational factor on the behavior, one thus needs to know how the actors interpret it in relation to their goals, values, and beliefs situated within each cultural context. The same situational factor may lead to different behaviors depending on cultural contexts, if different cultural contexts provide different ways to construe the factor.

Power might be one of such proximal-level factors whose effects particularly depend on distal-level factors in which it is located. Studies conducted in Western cultural contexts have suggested that power plays a crucial role in guiding cognition, emotion, and behavior (Fiske, 1993; Keltner, Gruenfeld, & Anderson, 2003). However, the effects of power on psychological processes could depend on the distal-level social structures in which power is located. In this section, I first describe research that has examined the effects of power on cognition in Western cultural contexts and then describe research that has examined the effects of power across cultures to illustrate how distal-level factors can moderate the effects of power.

Here, power is defined as the capacity to influence others (Dahl, 1957; French & Raven, 1959; Vescio, Snyder, & Butz, 2003). According to French and Raven (1959), the strength of power that person A has over person B is defined as the maximum potential ability of person A to influence person B, such as changing person B's behavior, needs, or values. Thus, for example, bosses typically have power over their subordinates, to the extent that bosses have the potential ability to change subordinates' behavior, needs, or values.

3.1. Cognitive consequences of power in Western cultures
3.1.1 Power fosters processing of goal-relevant information
Previous studies have repeatedly shown the psychological effects of having power or being in positions of power in Western cultural contexts (Fiske, 1993; Fiske & Dépret, 1996; Keltner et al., 2003). One of the central characteristics of power is to allow individuals who are in positions of power to pursue and attain goals related to their own rewards (Keltner et al., 2003). Powerful individuals may thus tend to selectively focus on the information relevant to their goal-pursuit without being distracted by peripheral information. On the other hand, it is harder for individuals without power to pursue their goals. Instead, powerless individuals tend to adjust themselves to others more than powerful individuals do (Anderson, Keltner, & John, 2003). Powerless individuals may thus need to attend not only to information relevant to their goals but also to peripheral, contextual information, in order to adjust themselves.

Supporting this possibility, powerful individuals have been shown to process goal-relevant information more than powerless individuals do (Overbeck & Park, 2001). Participants were assigned to the role of either a professor or a student and engaged in an e-mail role play. Through the e-mail exchanges, the student had to make a request (e.g., arrange a meeting) and the professor could determine the outcome. After the role play, participants were asked to recall information about their partner. Those who were assigned to be a professor were especially more likely to recall information relevant to the task (e.g., the other person has an inflexible schedule) than were those who were assigned to be a student. Furthermore, whereas professor-role participants recalled relevant information more than irrelevant information (e.g., the other person was once on the amateur golf circuit), student-role participants recalled relevant and irrelevant information equally. These findings suggest that exerting power fosters processing of goal-relevant information.

Studies have also shown that power encourages attention to stereotype-confirming information (Fiske & Dépret, 1996; Goodwin, Gubin, Fiske, & Yzerbyt, 2000). For example, in Goodwin and colleagues' studies, participants were presented with information about six applicants for a high school internship program. For the two target applicants, the targets' ethnicity was highlighted. Then, participants received two types of information: information that confirmed stereotypes about the ethnicity and information that disconfirmed stereotypes about the ethnicity. Power was manipulated by telling half of the participants that their evaluations would not affect the final decisions (i.e., no-power condition) and telling the other half of the participants that their evaluations would play a major role in who would be selected (i.e., powerful condition). Participants in the powerful condition more selectively attended to stereotype-confirming information than to stereotype-disconfirming information, whereas participants in the no-power condition attended to both types of information equally. These findings thus support the possibility that power fosters selective attention to information that is focal and consistent with the salient aspect of the target person (i.e., ethnicity).

Power has also been shown to foster processing of "gist" by facilitating attention to stimuli that are primary and relevant to the task, even when nonsocial stimuli are used (Smith, Jostmann, Galinsky, & van Dijk, 2008; Smith & Trope, 2006). Compared to powerless participants, powerful participants tend to perform better on the Embedded Figure Test (EFT; Witkin, Oltman, Raskin, & Karp, 1971), where the task is to find a small figure that is embedded within a larger, complex pattern (Smith & Trope, 2006). Because the small figure is more relevant to the goal of the task than the complex overall pattern, powerful individuals' superior performance on the EFT seems to indicate their focused attention to task-relevant information, whereas powerless individuals' inferior performance on the EFT seems to indicate their divided attention to both task-relevant and task-irrelevant information.

Guinote (2007a) has further suggested that power leads to the selective processing of information relevant to the goal of the task and inhibits processing of peripheral, irrelevant information. For example, one study showed that powerful individuals are better at focusing on central information and ignoring peripheral information compared to powerless individuals (Guinote, 2007b, Experiment 2). Participants were assigned to the role of either a subordinate or a manager. Subsequently, they worked on a stimulus–response compatibility paradigm (Tucker & Ellis, 1998), in which pictures of graspable objects (e.g., a cup) were presented and participants had to judge as fast as possible whether each object was upright or inverted by pressing a left or right response key. Participants who were assigned to be subordinates responded more slowly when the irrelevant dimension (i.e., whether a handle is on a left or right side of the cup) was incompatible with the correct response key (i.e., pressing a left or right response key) than when it was compatible, whereas participants who were assigned to be managers were not influenced by the irrelevant dimension. This suggests that powerless individuals attend to the information irrelevant and peripheral to the task (i.e., direction of the handle), whereas powerful individuals focus on information central to the task (i.e., position of the cup) and ignore peripheral information.

3.1.2 Power fosters analytic cognition

Attention to the target of one's goal (as opposed to peripheral information) is closely linked to attention to focal (as opposed to contextual) information because the target of one's goal is likely focal and not peripheral information. Thus, power may influence not only processing of goal-relevant versus peripheral information but also analytic versus holistic cognitive processing. Specifically, when one is influencing others, objects or people who are the targets of one's goal are more salient than the surrounding contexts. Therefore, exerting power may also facilitate processing of focal objects or people and their central features independently from the surrounding contexts, leading to analytic cognitive processing. On the other hand, being subject to another person's power may facilitate processing of the relationship between focal objects or people and their surrounding contexts, leading to holistic cognitive processing.

The hypothesized link between power and analytic cognition has been shown across different cognitive tasks. One task examined the types of words people use to describe other people. The same person or the same behavior can be described in multiple ways. For example, when describing someone who often snaps at others, one can describe the person as someone who "snaps at others" or "is aggressive." The type of words people use to describe a person conveys different underlying information and inferences about the person (Semin & Fiedler, 1988), as discussed in Section 1.1. Specifically, verbs provide information about the context surrounding the person, whereas adjectives convey information about the disposition of the person that transcends specific contexts. Thus, if being subject to another person's power is linked to more processing of contextual information, people may use more verbs to describe a person when they are subject to the person's power (e.g., when the person is their supervisor) compared to when they are not subject to the person's power (e.g., when the person is their colleague).

One study explored such a possibility in a naturalistic setting (Miyamoto & Schwarz, 2004) by asking American students at a community college to recall two recent interactions they had at their job: one interaction with their supervisor and the other interaction with their colleague (counterbalanced within each participant). They were asked to briefly describe either their supervisor or colleague and their recent interaction. All the sentences in which the target person (either the supervisor or colleague) was the subject of the sentence were coded to examine how frequently the target person was described with verbs or adjectives. For example, as part of the descriptions, one respondent wrote "She [my supervisor] often *tries to guilt* me into doing more than my job requires," which was coded as a verb. Another participant wrote "My colleague is a very *nice* person," which was coded as an adjective. As shown in Figure 3.8, respondents used more verbs to describe their supervisor, who likely had power over them, than to describe their colleague, who likely had less power over them. There were no differences in the amount of adjectives respondents used to describe a supervisor or a colleague, potentially due to the overall low frequency of adjectives when describing a person in interactions. These findings suggest that people tend to use more verbs to describe someone when they are subject to the person's power compared to when they are not subject to the person's power.

The link between power and the use of words was also explored in another study (Miyamoto & Ji, 2011, Study 1). Participants were told that the study involved two ostensibly unrelated tasks (i.e., an episodic memory task and a verbal description task). Power was manipulated by the episodic

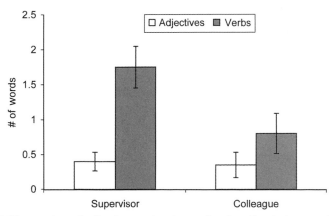

Figure 3.8 The number of adjectives and verbs used to describe their supervisor or their colleague when describing their interactions (Miyamoto & Schwarz, 2004).

memory task, where participants were randomly assigned to one of three conditions: influence, adjustment, and neutral conditions. In the influence condition, participants were asked to recall two situations in which they had influenced or changed the surrounding people according to their own wishes. In the adjustment condition, participants were asked to recall two situations in which they had adjusted themselves to surrounding others. Participants in the neutral condition were asked to recall two situations in which they had interacted with surrounding others. In the subsequent task, participants were asked to work on a verbal description task (Maass et al., 2006), where they were asked to think about a student of the same sex whom they knew very well and to describe what type of person she or he was or what she or he did at school/work.

As shown in Figure 3.9, after recalling situations in which they influenced other people, participants were more likely to use adjectives to describe another student than after recalling situations in which they adjusted to other people, whereas recalling neutral interactions did not differ from either condition. The opposite trend was observed for the use of verbs to describe another student. After recalling situations in which they adjusted to other people, participants were marginally more likely to use verbs to describe another student than after recalling situations in which they influenced other

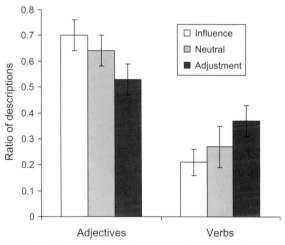

Figure 3.9 The likelihood of using adjectives and verbs to describe another student as a function of the type of incidents they recalled in the preceding task (Miyamoto & Ji, 2011, Study 1). The final, definitive version of this paper has been published in *Personality and Social Psychology Bulletin*, 37/11, November 2011 by SAGE Publications Ltd. All rights reserved. © 2011 SAGE Publications Ltd.

people. These findings suggest that exerting power over others facilitates the use of adjectives (i.e., analytic cognition), whereas adjusting to others facilitates the use of verbs (i.e., holistic cognition).

The link between power and analytic cognition has also been shown in the way in which people categorize objects (Miyamoto & Ji, 2011, Study 2). As introduced in Section 1.1, when presented with a *carrot*, an *eggplant*, and a *rabbit* and asked to choose the two that go together, there are two typical ways in which adults categorize them: taxonomic categorization (i.e., grouping carrot and eggplant because both are vegetables) or thematic categorization (i.e., grouping carrot and rabbit because rabbits eat carrots). Taxonomic categorization is based on features (e.g., properties, appearance, or function) shared by objects, whereas thematic categorization is based on spatial, causal, or temporal relationships between objects (Markman, 1989; Markman & Hutchinson, 1984). Thus, if power facilitates processing of central features of objects independently from the surrounding contexts, power may foster taxonomic categorization.

Following the procedure of the abovementioned study, power was manipulated by the episodic memory task. Participants were asked to recall two situations in which they either influenced or adjusted to other people. Subsequently, participants worked on the categorization task (adapted from Ji et al., 2004), where they were presented with several sets of three words (e.g., *seagull*, *sky*, and *dog*) and asked to indicate which two of the three in each set were most closely related and why. There were 8 critical sets embedded within 12 sets. Based on their grouping and reasoning, participants' responses to each of these eight sets were coded as taxonomic, thematic, or neither.

Consistent with the hypothesis, after recalling situations in which they influenced other people, participants were more likely to make taxonomic categorizations than after recalling situations in which they adjusted to other people. The opposite was the case for thematic categorization. That is, after recalling situations in which they adjusted to other people, participants were more likely to make thematic categorizations than after recalling situations in which they influenced other people. These results suggest that exerting power fosters taxonomic categorization, whereas adjusting to others fosters thematic categorization.

In sum, previous studies conducted in Western cultural contexts provide converging evidence that having power fosters processing of information relevant to the task and of focal objects and their central features independently from the surrounding contexts. On the other hand, not having power or adjusting to others has been shown to facilitate processing of both relevant and irrelevant information and of the relationship between focal objects and their surrounding contexts.

3.2. Culturally contingent cognitive consequences of power

3.2.1 Cultural differences in imperatives

As reviewed in the previous section, studies conducted in Western cultural contexts showed that power fosters goal-relevant, analytic cognitive processing. Does power have the same effects across cultures? In order to predict the effects of power on behavior, one needs to know the nature of distal-level social structures in which power is located and how individuals interpret and exercise power in relation to their goals, values, and beliefs. If different social structures provide different meanings to power and require different tasks for individuals to exercise power, power may have different effects on individuals across cultures.

Cross-cultural theorists have suggested that different sociocultural environments prescribe different tasks and imperatives for individuals (Markus & Kitayama, 1991; Triandis, 1995). In independent cultural contexts, such as the United States, the primary imperative is to pursue self-set goals independently from social contexts. On the other hand, in interdependent cultural contexts, such as Japan, the primary imperative is to fit into one's roles and social contexts by attending to surrounding needs. For example, whereas influencing the surroundings according to one's own goals and wishes is emphasized in independent cultural contexts, adjusting oneself to the surroundings is more emphasized in interdependent cultural contexts (Morling, Kitayama, & Miyamoto, 2002; Weisz, Rothbaum, & Blackburn, 1984).

Given cultural differences in primary imperatives, it is possible that in order to effectively exercise power, individuals need to engage in the imperatives that are emphasized and essential in the particular cultural context. That is, in order to effectively exert power in independent cultural contexts, people may need to focus on pursuing their own goals independently from social contexts. In contrast, in order to effectively exert power in interdependent cultural contexts, people may need to fit into their roles and social contexts by attending to others' needs.

Supporting the contention that power is associated with the pursuit of own goals in independent cultural contexts, studies conducted in Western cultural contexts have suggested that participants primed with high power were more likely to engage in goal-directed behavior (Galinsky, Gruenfeld, & Magee, 2003) and less likely to take the perspective of others

(Galinsky, Magee, Inesi, & Gruenfeld, 2006) compared to those primed with low power. On the other hand, cross-cultural research has shown that when describing the reason why they had influenced another person, Indians mainly focused on promoting the influencee's benefits, whereas Americans mainly focused on promoting their own benefits (Savani, Morris, Naidu, Kumar, & Berlia, 2011). These findings suggest that whereas exerting power in independent cultural contexts involves pursuit of one's own goals, exerting power in interdependent cultural contexts involves more attention to others' needs.

Cross-cultural research on leadership has further suggested that people in positions of power are expected to act in a way consistent with their cultural imperatives (Kohn & Schooler, 1982; Naoi & Schooler, 1985; Smith, Misumi, Tayeb, & Peterson, 1989; Zemba, Young, & Morris, 2006). For example, paternalism is considered to be one of the characteristics of leaders in China, and leaders are thus expected to take care of their subordinates and pay attention to subordinates' needs (Cheng, Chou, Wu, Huang, & Farh, 2004; Fu, Wu, Yang, & Ye, 2008). In addition, culturally contingent expectations about the actions of leaders manifest in how people represent the physical location of the leader in relation to the group (Menon, Sim, Fu, Chiu, & Hong, 2010). In the United States, where leaders are expected to act assertively upon the environment, participants represented leaders as standing ahead of groups (i.e., trailblazing). Alternatively, in Singapore, where leaders are expected to be responsible and protect the group, participants represented leaders as standing behind the group (i.e., trailing-behind). Thus, people seem to expect those who are in positions of power to act in line with their cultural imperatives. Furthermore, such different expectations about people in positions of power can be reflected in the values people in positions of power actually endorse. In large-scale survey studies, those who were in higher hierarchical positions in Japan endorsed more conformity of ideas and less personally responsible standards of morality (Naoi & Schooler, 1985), whereas there were no such associations in the United States (Kohn & Schooler, 1982).

Consistent with these culturally contingent representations of leaders and power, Zhong, McGee, Maddux, and Galinsky (2006) further showed that the concept of power is associated with different constructs across cultures. When the concept of power was activated among European Americans, their responses to words related to entitlement (e.g., earn, entitlement) were facilitated, whereas their responses to words related to responsibility (e.g., duty, responsibility) were inhibited. Asians and Asian Americans showed the opposite pattern: their responses to words related to responsibility were facilitated, whereas their responses to words related to entitlement were inhibited.

3.2.2 Cognitive consequences of power across cultures

The evidence reviewed in the previous section suggests that exerting power requires different imperatives across cultures. Whereas exerting power seems to require the pursuit of one's own goals in Western cultural contexts, exerting power seems to require fitting into one's role and attending to others' needs in Eastern cultural contexts. Such culturally divergent imperatives associated with power are likely to foster different kinds of cognitive processing that serve the particular imperatives. Specifically, in Western, independent social environments, where the primary imperative is to pursue self-set goals, power may foster cognitive processing that helps individuals to focus on their goals without being distracted by peripheral or contextual information (i.e., analytic cognition). Indeed, as reviewed in the above section, previous studies conducted in Western cultural contexts provided support for this contention. On the other hand, in Eastern, interdependent social environments, where the primary imperative is to fit into one's role and social contexts by attending to surrounding needs, power may foster cognitive processing that helps individuals attend not only to their own goals but also to surrounding contextual information (i.e., holistic cognition).

Supporting the possibility that processing of contextual information helps individuals fit into social contexts, studies have shown that attention to contextual information is linked to social adjustments as reviewed in Section 2.2. For example, participants who showed lower performance on the EFT, indicating higher attention to contextual information, also showed the tendency to mimic the nonverbal behavior of a target person (e.g., touching her face; Van Baaren et al., 2004). This suggests that individuals who attend to contextual information are more likely to align their behavior to others compared to those individuals who attend less to contextual information. In addition, processing of contextual information has also been linked to sensitivity to fear of isolation (Kim & Markman, 2006) and an other-focused manifestation of social anxiety (Norasakkunkit et al., 2012). These findings suggest the possibility that attending to contextual information helps individuals fit into social situations better.

Therefore, Miyamoto and Wilken (2010) hypothesized that exerting power in independent social environments would facilitate analytic cognitive processing, allowing people to focus on pursuing their own goals.

On the other hand, exerting power over others in interdependent social environments would foster holistic cognitive processing, allowing people to attend to others and fit into social contexts. To test this contention, the first study was conducted to examine how individual differences in cognitive style are related to individual differences in the orientation to interpersonal influence or adjustment by recruiting both American and Japanese participants (Miyamoto & Wilken, 2010, Study 1). It was predicted that, in the United States, participants who are oriented toward interpersonal influence would show a more analytic cognitive style, whereas in Japan, the association would be absent or even reversed.

The orientation toward interpersonal influence or adjustment was assessed by using the Circumplex Scale of Interpersonal Values (Locke, 2000). The scale consisted of 64 items, and participants were asked to rate how important each of the items was for them when they were in interpersonal situations. Following previous studies (Tsai, Miao, Seppala, Fung, & Yeung, 2007), the tendency to value influencing others was measured by four items (e.g., "I have an impact on them"), while the tendency to value adjusting to others was measured by five items (e.g., "I do what they want me to do"). Cognitive style was assessed by the FLT (Kitayama et al., 2003). In the absolute task, participants had to focus on the length of the focal line independently from the contextual frame, whereas in the relative task, participants had to attend to the relationship between the focal line and the contextual frame.

As hypothesized, interpersonal influence was marginally negatively correlated ($r=-0.21$) with the amount of error on the absolute task in the United States. Such findings indicate that American participants who were more oriented toward interpersonal influence were better able to focus on the focal line independently form the contextual frame and thus showed more analytic cognitive processing compared to those who were less oriented toward interpersonal influence. Such findings are consistent with the previous studies, showing the link between power and analytic cognition in Western cultural contexts. On the other hand, consistent with the prediction, interpersonal influence was positively correlated with the amount of error on the absolute task ($r=0.23$) in Japan, which suggests that Japanese participants who were oriented toward interpersonal influence showed more holistic cognitive processing compared to those who were less oriented toward interpersonal influence. A reversed pattern was observed for interpersonal adjustment: interpersonal adjustment was marginally positively correlated with the amount of error on the absolute task in the United States

($r = 0.21$) but was not correlated in Japan ($r = 0.06$). This suggests that American participants who were more oriented toward interpersonal adjustment showed more holistic cognitive processing, whereas such a link did not exist in Japan. Patterns of correlations for the relative task were also in the predicted directions for each culture, though none of the correlations were significant. These findings suggest that those who are oriented more toward interpersonal influence have divergent cognitive styles across cultures: they tend to have a relatively *analytic* cognitive style in the United States and a relatively *holistic* cognitive style in Japan.

To further test the hypothesis that exerting power facilitates different cognitive processing across cultures, in another study, power was manipulated by assigning American and Japanese participants to different roles through structured interactions (Miyamoto & Wilken, 2010, Study 2). Each participant was paired with another same-gendered participant to work on a structured communication task (Schober & Clark, 1989; Tsai et al., 2007). Participants were seated at opposite ends of a table. A small divider was placed in the middle of the table, which was low enough to allow participants to see their partner's face but high enough to prevent them from seeing their partner's side of the table. Participants were given the same set of cards of Tangram figures and were told that the goal of the task was to sort them in the same order as their partner. Then, they were randomly assigned to the role of either a leader or a matcher. The leader's job was to decide how to order the cards and then to verbally describe them to the matcher. The matcher's job was to figure out how the leader ordered the cards. After they completed the communication task, they worked on an ostensibly unrelated visual task, the FLT (Kitayama et al., 2003).

As a manipulation check, participants were also asked to rate the extent to which they influenced their partner (influence) and the extent to which they were influenced by their partner (adjustment) during the communication task. The manipulation check showed a significant two-way interaction between role (leader or matcher) and question type (influence or adjustment) interaction. Leaders reported influencing matchers more than matchers reported influencing leaders, whereas matchers reported being influenced by leaders more than leaders reported being influenced by matchers. This interaction was more pronounced for Japanese participants than for American participants, indicated by a significant three-way interaction between culture, role, and question type. However, the two-way interaction between role and question type was significant for both groups. This suggests that the manipulation of power worked in both cultures, though it was even more effective for Japanese participants than for American participants.

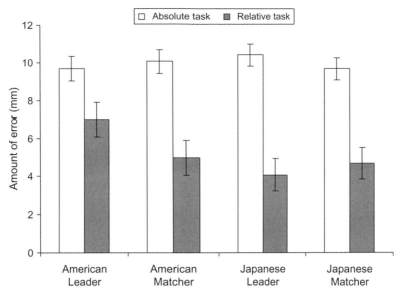

Figure 3.10 Amount of error on the Framed-Line Task (i.e., absolute and relative tasks) as a function of culture and the role participants were assigned to (Miyamoto et al., 2010, Study 2). The final, definitive version of this paper has been published in *Psychological Science*, 21/11, November 2010 by SAGE Publications Ltd. All rights reserved. © 2010 SAGE Publications Ltd.

The amount of error on the FLT is shown in Figure 3.10. If participants were attending to contextual information, they should have made more errors on the absolute task and fewer errors on the relative task. Among American participants, there was a significant interaction between role (leader or matcher) and FLT (absolute or relative). That is, although participants, in general, made more errors on the absolute task than on the relative task, the difference between the absolute and relative task errors was smaller for leaders than it was for matchers, suggesting that leaders showed a more analytic cognitive processing than did matchers. On the other hand, among Japanese participants, there was no effect of role. Leaders showed as holistic cognitive processing as matchers did. Because the results of the manipulation check showed that the manipulation had a larger impact on Japanese participants than on American participants, the lack of manipulation effect on cognitive processing among Japanese is likely not due to the failure of the manipulation for Japanese. These findings show that whereas influencing others fosters an analytic cognitive style in the United States, influencing others fosters a cognitive style at least as holistic as adjusting to others does in Japan.

Taken together, these two studies provide support for the contention that influencing others is linked to the type of cognitive processing that serves the cultural imperative. In American cultural contexts, influencing others fosters an analytic cognitive style, which possibly allows people to focus on the target of their own goals without being distracted by others. On the other hand, in Japanese cultural contexts, influencing others requires a cognitive style at least as holistic as adjusting to others does, which may allow people to attend to the demands of others and to fit into social contexts. Such findings not only illustrate that cognitive styles are shaped by the nature of interpersonal contexts but also show that how they are shaped depends on cultural contexts which prescribe meaning to interactions, providing evidence for culturally contingent situated cognition (Culture × Situation × Person interaction; Cohen, 2007; Hong & Mallorie, 2004).

3.2.3 Future directions for research on culturally contingent cognitive consequences of power

These studies on culturally contingent consequences of power are based on the assumption that cultural differences in primary imperatives partly guide cultural differences in cognitive consequences of power. That is, power fosters analytic cognitive processing in independent cultural environments presumably because in order to effectively exert power in such cultural environments, people need to focus on pursuing their own goals, which should foster analytic cognitive processing. On the other hand, power fosters holistic cognitive processing in interdependent cultural environments, presumably because effectively exerting power in such cultural environments requires people to fit into roles and attend to social contexts, which should foster holistic cognitive processing.

Based on this reasoning, power should lead to holistic cognitive processing even in Western, independent cultural environments when people need to fit into roles and attend to social contexts in order to exert power. Partially supporting this possibility, Goodwin et al. (2000) found that, although powerful participants more selectively paid attention to stereotype-confirming information than to stereotype-disconfirming information, powerful participants increased attention to stereotype-disconfirming information and attended to both types of information equally when they were induced to feel responsible toward others (also see Torelli & Shavitt, 2010). If selective attention to information that is focal and consistent with the salient category partly reflects analytic cognitive processing, such findings imply that activating the need to attend to others diminishes analytic cognitive processing and fosters holistic cognitive processing. It would be informative for future research to directly test such a possibility by manipulating the need to attend to others while exerting influence over others and examining its consequences on holistic cognitive processing.

There could also be a distal sociostructural mechanism underlying cultural differences in cognitive consequences of power. Power was defined here as the capacity to influence others (Dahl, 1957; French & Raven, 1959; Vescio et al., 2003). According to this definition, structural properties of social relations (e.g., asymmetrical control over resources or outcomes; Fiske, 1993; Fiske & Dépret, 1996; Keltner et al., 2003; Thibaut & Kelley, 1959) are considered to be sources of power. It is possible that cultural differences in cognitive consequences of power are partly rooted in cultural differences in structural properties of social relations. That is, in Japanese social structures, those who are in positions of "power" might typically have less control over the outcome of those who are not in positions of "power" compared to the case in the United States. For example, compared to Western countries, the prime minister in Japan plays a smaller role in budget politics, while opinions of lower level bureaucrats occasionally can have large impact on the budget (Campbell, 1977). This suggests that even Japanese individuals may become analytic if they are placed in positions where they have complete control over the outcome and others have no control.

When considering mechanisms, it is also important to distinguish social power from personal power. Social power is about the exercise of power over others in interpersonal relationships, whereas personal power is about one's ability to carry out actions or agency (Overbeck & Park, 2001). In the current theorization, power was mainly conceptualized as social power. Specifically, it was reasoned that exerting power over others fosters holistic cognitive processing in Japan because people need to attend to others and social contexts in order to effectively exert power in interdependent cultural environments. If attention to interpersonal contexts is the main reason for social power to foster holistic cognitive processing in Japan, personal power may not foster holistic cognitive processing even in Japan because there are no interpersonal contexts to which to attend. Thus, regardless of culture, it is possible that when people are exercising personal power, they tend to focus on their own goals, leading to analytic cognitive processing. Consistent with this possibility, recent research showed that, after being deprived of control, a form of personal power, both Chinese and Caucasian participants became analytic in their cognitive style in order to regain control over the environment (Zhou, He, Yang, Lao, & Baumeister, 2012).

Personal power is also related to social class. Middle-class individuals tend to have a higher sense of control and more resources to influence the environment, whereas working-class individuals tend to have a lower sense of control and more of a need to adjust to the environment (Lachman & Weaver, 1998; Snibbe & Markus, 2005). As reviewed in Section 2.1, previous studies have shown an association between social class and cognitive styles (Kraus et al., 2009; Miyamoto & Ji, 2011; Na et al., 2010). For example, using data from a large-scale survey, Miyamoto and Ji (2011, Study 3) showed that individuals with higher educational attainment and higher income made more taxonomic categorization, indicating more analytic cognitive processing, than did individuals with lower educational attainment and lower income, and a sense of agency partially mediated such social class differences in categorization. It would be fruitful for future research to examine whether social class has the same or different cognitive consequences across cultures. If personal power is associated with more analytic cognitive processing across cultures, middle-class individuals are likely to show an analytic cognitive style across cultures. In fact, research done in the United States and Russia found that college students from middle-class backgrounds tend to show a more analytic cognitive style compared to those from working-class backgrounds (Grossmann & Varnum, 2011).

3.3. Summary

In summary, power has been shown to be a proximal-level situational factor that has culturally divergent cognitive consequences. In Western, independent social structures, where the primary imperative is to pursue self-set goals, power fostered analytic cognitive processing, whereas in Eastern, interdependent social structures, where the primary imperative is to be attentive to others' needs and fit in, power fostered holistic cognitive processing. The cultural moderation of the effect of a proximal-level situational factor suggests the importance of taking multiple levels of cultural influences into consideration because the effect of a particular factor can depend on factors at different levels in the larger cultural system.

4. IMPLICATIONS AND FUTURE DIRECTIONS

In this chapter, multilevel analysis of cultural influences is proposed as a useful approach to understand both how distal-level societal factors influence individuals' cognitive processing through proximal-level processes and how factors at different levels interact to influence individuals' cognitive processing. A wide range of studies showing cultural differences in cognitive processes were reviewed in an attempt to illustrate the nature and scope of cultural differences. However, such evidence of cultural differences in cognition does not specify why there are cultural differences in cognition to begin with. To understand how culture influences cognition, multilevel analyses of factors underlying cultural influences were outlined, especially by highlighting the proximal-level processes through which distal societal factors influence individuals' cognitive processes. Lastly, studies on culturally contingent cognitive consequences of power were reviewed in order to illustrate a case where the effect of a proximal-level factor depends on distal-level factors.

Much remains to be learned about relationships between factors at multiple levels. All the arrows in Figure 3.6 are bidirectional, indicating the assumption that factors are mutually shaping and influencing each other. Thus, for example, cognitive processing of individuals is assumed to be not only an outcome of participation in interdependent or independent proximal contexts but also a factor that shapes and influences interdependent or independent proximal contexts. If holistic cognitive processing fosters attention to others and social contexts and if analytic cognitive processing fosters attention to the self, then such divergent cognitive processing is likely to influence social interactions and practices. Consistent with this possibility, one study showed that when primed with holistic cognitive processing, participants were more likely to mimic the non-verbal behavior of an experimenter than they did when they were primed with analytic cognitive processing (Van Baaren et al., 2004). Similar additional future explorations will shed light on the functions of different types of cognition processing in social interactions.

Another direction for future research is to examine the longitudinal effects of exposure to proximal-level situational factors. Most evidence on the effects of proximal contexts on cognitive processes is based on short-term exposure to proximal contexts. It is thus an open question whether prolonged exposure to new proximal contexts can cause chronic changes in cognitive styles. One study found that the length of participation in Oriental medicine training practices, which embody a holistic and dialectical worldview, was associated with a holistic cognitive style (Koo & Choi, 2005), thus showing the long-term effects of a proximal factor. Longitudinal examination of individuals who have moved to different cultural contexts would also provide an opportunity to test whether exposure to new proximal contexts can lead to chronic changes in cognitive styles and thus test the malleability of chronic cognitive styles. Interestingly, studies that examined longitudinal effects of exposure to North American culture on identification with North American culture have found mixed results (Cheung, Chudek, & Heine, 2011; Minoura, 1992). Whereas those who immigrated to North America earlier in their life showed changes in their identification as a function of their exposure to North American culture, those who immigrated later in their adolescence showed no changes in their identification, implying that there might be a sensitive period. Examination of whether and when cognitive processing changes in response to prolonged exposure to a new cultural context will contribute to a better understanding of cultural influences as well as cognitive processes.

As evidence documenting cultural differences in cognitive processes has been accumulated over the past decade, questions guiding research have also evolved. In addition to identifying the existence of cultural differences, researchers have examined moderating factors ("when") and mechanisms ("how") at multiple levels. Although there is much to be learned from asking "when" and "why" questions, exclusive focus on either "when" or "how" questions might lead to an understanding that is either too dispersed or too generalized. Especially, in a complex system like culture that is comprised of multiple levels, how a certain factor influences another factor can be moderated by factors at a different level. By integrating "when" and "how" questions into a single framework through highlighting proximal-level processes and examining how the effect of a proximal-level factor depends on distal-level factors, it is my hope that multilevel analyses provide a fruitful way to understand the cultural grounding of cognition.

REFERENCES

Alter, A. L., & Kwan, V. Y. (2009). Cultural sharing in a global village: Evidence for extracultural cognition in European Americans. *Journal of Personality and Social Psychology*, *96*, 742–760.

Anderson, C., Keltner, D., & John, O. P. (2003). Emotional convergence between people over time. *Journal of Personality and Social Psychology*, *84*, 1054–1068.

Berry, J. W. (1966). Temne and Eskimo perceptual skills. *International Journal of Psychology*, *1*, 207–229.

Bond, R., & Smith, P. B. (1996). Culture and conformity: A meta-analysis of studies using Asch's (1952b, 1956) line judgment task. *Psychological Bulletin*, *119*, 111–137.

Campbell, J. C. (1977). *Contemporary Japanese budget politics*. Berkeley: University of California Press.

Cheng, B., Chou, L., Wu, T., Huang, M., & Farh, J. (2004). Paternalistic leadership and subordinate responses: Establishing a leadership model in Chinese organizations. *Asian Journal of Social Psychology*, *7*, 89–117.

Cheung, B. Y., Chudek, M., & Heine, S. J. (2011). Evidence for a sensitive period for acculturation: Younger immigrants report acculturating at a faster rate. *Psychological Science*, *22*, 147–152.

Choi, I., & Nisbett, R. E. (1998). Situational salience and cultural differences in the correspondence bias and actor-observer bias. *Personality and Social Psychology Bulletin, 24,* 949–960.

Chua, H. F., Boland, J. E., & Nisbett, R. E. (2005). Cultural variation in eye movements during scene perception. *Proceedings of the National Academy of Sciences of the United States of America, 102,* 12629–12633.

Cohen, D. (2007). Methods in cultural psychology. In S. Kitayama, & D. Cohen (Eds.), *Handbook of cultural psychology* (pp. 196–236). New York: Guilford Press.

Cohen, A. B., Hall, D. E., Koenig, H. G., & Meador, K. G. (2005). Social vs. individual motivation: Implications for normative definitions of religious orientation. *Personality and Social Psychology Review, 9,* 48–61.

Colzato, L. S., Hommel, B., van den Wildenberg, W., & Hsieh, S. (2010). Buddha as an eye opener: A link between prosocial attitude and attentional control. *Frontiers in Psychology, 1,* 156.

Colzato, L. S., van Beest, I., van den Wildenberg, W. M., Scorolli, C., Dorchin, S., Meiran, N., et al. (2010). God: Do I have your attention? *Cognition, 117,* 87–94.

Dahl, R. A. (1957). The concept of power. *Behavioral Science, 2,* 201–218.

Doherty, M. J., Tsuji, H., & Phillips, W. A. (2008). The context sensitivity of visual size perception varies across cultures. *Perception, 37,* 1426–1433.

Eggen, A., Miyamoto, Y., & Uchida, Y. (2012). Cultural differences in nonverbal communication. Unpublished manuscript. University of Wisconsin-Madison, Madison, WI.

Farah, M., Wilson, K., Drain, M., & Tanaka, J. (1998). What is 'special' about face perception? *Psychological Review, 105,* 482–498.

Fernald, A., & Morikawa, H. (1993). Common themes and cultural variations in Japanese and American mothers' speech to infants. *Child Development, 64,* 637–656.

Fiske, S. T. (1993). Controlling other people: The impact of power on stereotyping. *The American Psychologist, 48,* 621 628.

Fiske, S. T., & Dépret, E. (1996). Control, interdependence and power: Understanding social cognition in its social context. *European Review of Social Psychology, 7,* 31–61.

Fiske, A., Kitayama, S., Markus, H., & Nisbett, R. E. (1998). The cultural matrix of social psychology. In D. T. Gilbert, S. T. Fiske, G. Lindzey, D. T. Gilbert, S. T. Fiske, & G. Lindzey (Eds.), *The handbook of social psychology: Vols. 1 and 2.* (pp. 915–981). (4th ed.) New York, NY: McGraw-Hill.

Förster, J., & Dannenberg, L. (2010). GLOMOsys: Specifications of a global model on processing styles. *Psychological Inquiry, 21,* 257–269.

French, J. R. P., & Raven, B. (1959). The bases of social power. In D. Cartwright (Ed.), *Studies in social power* (pp. 150–167). Ann Arbor, MI: Institute for Social Research.

Fu, P., Wu, R., Yang, Y., & Ye, J. (2008). Chinese culture and leadership. In J. S. Chhokar, F. C. Brodbeck & R. J. House (Eds.), *Culture and leadership across the world: The GLOBE book of in-depth studies of 25 societies* (pp. 877–907). Mahwah, NJ: Lawrence Erlbaum Associates Publishers.

Galinsky, A. D., Gruenfeld, D. H., & Magee, J. C. (2003). From power to action. *Journal of Personality and Social Psychology, 85,* 453–466.

Galinsky, A. D., Magee, J. C., Inesi, M., & Gruenfeld, D. H. (2006). Power and perspectives not taken. *Psychological Science, 17,* 1068–1074.

Gardner, W. L., Gabriel, S., & Lee, A. L. (1999). "I" value freedom, but "we" value relationships: Self-construal priming mirrors cultural differences in judgment. *Psychological Science, 10,* 321–326.

Garner, W. R. (1978). Aspects of a stimulus: Features, dimensions, and configurations. In E. Rosch & B. B. Lloyd (Eds.), *Cognition and categorization* (pp. 99–133). Hillsdale, NJ: Erlbaum.

Gilbert, D. T., & Malone, P. S. (1995). The correspondence bias. *Psychological Bulletin, 117,* 21–38.

Goodwin, S. A., Gubin, A., Fiske, S. T., & Yzerbyt, V. Y. (2000). Power can bias impression processes: Stereotyping subordinates by default and by design. *Group Processes & Intergroup Relations, 3,* 227–256.

Greenfield, P. M. (1972). Oral or written language: The consequence for cognitive development in Africa, the United States and England. *Language and Speech, 15,* 169–178.

Grossmann, I., & Varnum, M. W. (2011). Social class, culture, and cognition. *Social Psychological and Personality Science, 2,* 81–89.

Guinote, A. (2007a). Behaviour variability and the situated focus theory of power. *European Review of Social Psychology, 18,* 256–295.

Guinote, A. (2007b). Power affects basic cognition: Increased attentional inhibition and flexibility. *Journal of Experimental Social Psychology, 43,* 685–697.

Hall, E. T. (1976). *Beyond culture.* Garden City, New York: Anchor Press/Double Day.

Hedden, T., Ketay, S., Aron, A., Markus, H. R., & Gabrieli, J. D. E. (2008). Cultural influences on neural substrates of attentional control. *Psychological Science, 19,* 12–17.

Heine, S. J., & Norenzayan, A. (2006). Toward a psychological science for a cultural species. *Perspectives on Psychological Science, 1,* 251–269.

Hong, Y. Y., & Mallorie, L. M. (2004). A dynamic constructivist approach to culture: Lessons learned from personality psychology. *Journal of Research in Personality, 38,* 59–67.

Hong, Y. Y., Morris, M. W., Chiu, C. Y., & Benet-Martínez, V. (2000). Multicultural minds: A dynamic constructivist approach to culture and cognition. *The American Psychologist, 55,* 709–720.

Hulleman, C. S., & Harackiewicz, J. M. (2009). Promoting interest and performance in high school science classes. *Science, 326,* 1410–1412.

Imada, T. (2012). Cultural narratives of individualism and collectivism: A content analysis of textbook stories in the United States and Japan. *Journal of Cross-Cultural Psychology, 43,* 576–591.

Ishii, K., Miyamoto, Y., Rule, N., & Toriyama, R. (2012). Physical objects as a vehicle of cultural values: Maintaining harmony and uniqueness through colored geometric patterns. Unpublished manuscript, Kobe University.

Ishii, K., Reyes, J. A., & Kitayama, S. (2003). Spontaneous attention to word content versus emotional tone: Differences among three cultures. *Psychological Science, 14,* 39–46.

Ito, K., Masuda, T., & Hioki, K. (2012). Affective information in context and judgment of facial expression: Cultural similarities and variations in context effects between North Americans and East Asians. *Journal of Cross-Cultural Psychology, 43,* 429–445.

Ji, L. J., Guo, T., Zhang, Z., & Messervey, D. (2009). Looking into the past: Cultural differences in perception and representation of past information. *Journal of Personality and Social Psychology, 96,* 761–769.

Ji, L., Nisbett, R., & Su, Y. (2001). Culture, change, and prediction. *Psychological Science, 12,* 450–456.

Ji, L. J., Peng, K., & Nisbett, R. E. (2000). Culture, control, and perception of relationships in the environment. *Journal of Personality and Social Psychology, 78,* 943–955.

Ji, L. J., Zhang, Z., & Nisbett, R. E. (2004). Is it culture or is it language? Examination of language effects in cross-cultural research on categorization. *Journal of Personality and Social Psychology, 87,* 57–65.

Jones, E. E. (1979). The rocky road from act to disposition. *The American Psychologist, 34,* 107–117.

Jones, E. E., & Harris, V. A. (1967). The attribution of attitudes. *Journal of Experimental Social Psychology, 3,* 1–24.

Keltner, D., Gruenfeld, D., & Anderson, C. (2003). Power, approach, and inhibition. *Psychological Review*, *110*, 265–284.

Kim, H., & Markus, H. R. (1999). Deviance or uniqueness, harmony or conformity? A cultural analysis. *Journal of Personality and Social Psychology*, *77*, 785.

Kim, K., & Markman, A. B. (2006). Differences in fear of isolation as an explanation of cultural differences: Evidence from memory and reasoning. *Journal of Experimental Social Psychology*, *42*, 350–364.

Kimchi, R. (1992). Primacy of wholistic processing and global/local paradigm: A critical review. *Psychological Bulletin*, *112*, 24–38.

Kitayama, S., Duffy, S., Kawamura, T., & Larsen, J. T. (2003). Perceiving an object and its context in different cultures: A cultural look at New Look. *Psychological Science*, *14*, 201–206.

Kitayama, S., Ishii, K., Imada, T., Takemura, K., & Ramaswamy, J. (2006). Voluntary settlement and the spirit of independence: Evidence from Japan's "northern frontier. *Journal of Personality and Social Psychology*, *91*, 369–384.

Kitayama, S., Park, H., Sevincer, A. T., Karasawa, M., & Uskul, A. K. (2009). A cultural task analysis of implicit independence: Comparing North America, Western Europe, and East Asia. *Journal of Personality and Social Psychology*, *97*, 236–255.

Knight, N., & Nisbett, R. E. (2007). Culture, class and cognition: Evidence from Italy. *Journal of Cognition and Culture*, *7*, 283–291.

Kohn, M. L., & Schooler, C. (1982). Job conditions and personality: A longitudinal assessment of their reciprocal effects. *The American Journal of Sociology*, *87*, 1257–1286.

Koo, M., & Choi, I. (2005). Becoming a holistic thinker: Training effect of Oriental medicine on reasoning. *Personality and Social Psychology Bulletin*, *31*, 1264–1272.

Kraus, M. W., Piff, P. K., & Keltner, D. (2009). Social class, the sense of control, and social explanation. *Journal of Personality and Social Psychology*, *97*, 992–1004.

Krull, D. S., Loy, M. H.-M., Lin, J., Wang, C.-F., Chen, S., & Zhao, X. (1999). The fundamental attribution error: Correspondence bias in individualist and collectivist cultures. *Personality and Social Psychology Bulletin*, *25*, 1208–1219.

Kühnen, U., & Oyserman, D. (2002). Thinking about the self influences thinking in general: Cognitive consequences of salient self-concept. *Journal of Experimental Social Psychology*, *38*, 492–499.

Lachman, M. E., & Weaver, S. L. (1998). The sense of control as a moderator of social class differences in health and well-being. *Journal of Personality and Social Psychology*, *74*, 763–773.

Lee, F., Hallahan, M., & Herzog, T. (1996). Explaining real-life events. How culture and domain shape attributions. *Personality and Social Psychology Bulletin*, *22*, 732–741.

Lewin, K. (1951). In D. Cartwright (Ed.), *Field theory in social science: Selected theoretical papers*. New York: Harper.

Li, Y., Johnson, K. A., Cohen, A. B., Williams, M. J., Knowles, E. D., & Chen, Z. (2012). Fundamental(ist) attribution error: Protestants are dispositionally focused. *Journal of Personality and Social Psychology*, *102*, 281–290.

Locke, K. D. (2000). Circumplex scales of interpersonal values: Reliability, validity, and applicability to interpersonal problems and personality disorders. *Journal of Personality Assessment*, *75*, 249–267.

Maass, A., Karasawa, M., Politi, F., & Suga, S. (2006). Do verbs and adjectives play different roles in different cultures? A cross-linguistic analysis of person representation. *Journal of Personality and Social Psychology*, *90*, 734–750.

Maddux, W. W., & Yuki, M. (2006). The 'Ripple Effect': Cultural differences in perceptions of the consequences of events. *Personality and Social Psychology Bulletin*, *32*, 669–683.

Markman, E. (1989). *Categorization and naming in children: Problems of induction*. Cambridge, MA: The MIT Press.

Markman, E., & Hutchinson, J. (1984). Children's sensitivity to constraints on word meaning: Taxonomic versus thematic relations. *Cognitive Psychology, 16,* 1–27.

Markus, H. R., & Kitayama, S. (1991). Culture and the self: Implications for cognition, emotion, and motivation. *Psychological Review, 98,* 224–253.

Markus, H. R., & Kitayama, S. (1994). A collective fear of the collective: Implications for selves and theories of selves. *Personality and Social Psychology Bulletin, 20,* 568–579.

Markus, H. R., Uchida, Y., Omoregie, H., Townsend, S. S. M., & Kitayama, S. (2006). Going for the gold: Models of agency in Japanese and American contexts. *Psychological Science, 17,* 103–112.

Masuda, T., Ellsworth, P. C., Mesquita, B., Leu, J., Tanida, S., & Van de Veerdonk, E. (2008). Placing the face in context: Cultural differences in the perception of facial emotion. *Journal of Personality and Social Psychology, 94,* 365–381.

Masuda, T., Gonzalez, R., Kwan, L., & Nisbett, R. E. (2008). Culture and aesthetic preference: Comparing the attention to context of East Asians and Americans. *Personality and Social Psychology Bulletin, 34,* 1260–1275.

Masuda, T., & Kitayama, S. (2004). Perceiver-induced constraint and attitude attribution in Japan and the US: A case for the cultural dependence of the correspondence bias. *Journal of Experimental Social Psychology, 40,* 409–416.

Masuda, T., & Nisbett, R. E. (2001). Attending holistically versus analytically: Comparing the context sensitivity of Japanese and Americans. *Journal of Personality and Social Psychology, 81,* 922–934.

Masuda, T., & Nisbett, R. E. (2006). Culture and change blindness. *Cognitive Science, 30,* 381–399.

McArthur, L. Z., & Post, D. L. (1977). Figural emphasis and person perception. *Journal of Experimental Social Psychology, 13,* 520–535.

McKone, E., Davies, A., Fernando, D., Aalders, R., Leung, H., Wickramariyaratne, T., et al. (2010). Asia has the global advantage: Race and visual attention. *Vision Research, 50,* 1540–1549.

Menon, T., Sim, J., Fu, J., Chiu, C., & Hong, Y. (2010). Blazing the trail versus trailing the group: Culture and perceptions of the leader's position. *Organizational Behavior and Human Decision Processes, 113,* 51–61.

Miller, J. G. (1984). Culture and the development of everyday social explanation. *Journal of Personality and Social Psychology, 46,* 961–978.

Minoura, Y. (1992). A sensitive period for the incorporation of a cultural meaning system: A study of Japanese children growing up in the United States. *Ethos, 20,* 304–339.

Miyamoto, Y., & Ji, L. J. (2011). Power fosters context-independent, analytic cognition. *Personality and Social Psychology Bulletin, 37,* 1449–1458.

Miyamoto, Y., & Kitayama, S. (2002). Cultural variation in correspondence bias: The critical role of attitude diagnosticity of socially constrained behavior. *Journal of Personality and Social Psychology, 83,* 1239–1248.

Miyamoto, Y., Nisbett, R. E., & Masuda, T. (2006). Culture and the physical environment: Holistic versus analytic perceptual affordances. *Psychological Science, 17,* 113–119.

Miyamoto, Y., & Schwarz, N. (2004). Person perception in hierarchy: An examination using the linguistic category model. *Proceeding of the 45th conference of the Japanese Society of Social Psychology* (in Japanese).

Miyamoto, Y., & Schwarz, N. (2006). When conveying a message may hurt the relationship: Cultural differences in the difficulty of using an answering machine. *Journal of Experimental Social Psychology, 42,* 540–547.

Miyamoto, Y., & Wilken, B. (2010). Culturally contingent situated cognition: Influencing others fosters analytic perception in the U.S. but not in Japan. *Psychological Science, 21,* 1616–1622.

Miyamoto, Y., & Wilken, B. (2013). Cultural differences and their mechanisms. In D. Reisberg (Ed.), *Oxford handbook of cognitive psychology* (pp. 970–985). Oxford: Oxford University Press.

Miyamoto, Y., Yoshikawa, S., & Kitayama, S. (2011). Feature and configuration in face processing: Japanese are more configural than Americans. *Cognitive Science, 35,* 563–574.

Mondloch, C., Le Grand, R., & Maurer, D. (2002). Configural face processing develops more slowly than featural face processing. *Perception, 31,* 553–566.

Morling, B., Kitayama, S., & Miyamoto, Y. (2002). Cultural practices emphasize influence in the United States and adjustment in Japan. *Personality and Social Psychology Bulletin, 28,* 311–323.

Morling, B., & Lamoreaux, M. (2008). Measuring culture outside the head: A meta-analysis of individualism-collectivism in cultural products. *Personality and Social Psychology Review, 12,* 199–221.

Morris, M. W., & Peng, K. (1994). Culture and cause: American and Chinese attributions for social and physical events. *Journal of Personality and Social Psychology, 67,* 949–971.

Na, J., Grossman, I., Varnum, M. E. W., Kitayama, S., Gonzalez, R., & Nisbett, R. E. (2010). Cultural differences are not always reducible to individual differences. *Proceedings of the National Academy of Sciences of the United States of America, 107,* 6192–6197.

Na, J., & Kitayama, S. (2011). Spontaneous trait inference is culture-specific behavioral and neural evidence. *Psychological Science, 22,* 1025–1032.

Naoi, A., & Schooler, C. (1985). Occupational conditions and psychological functioning in Japan. *The American Journal of Sociology, 90,* 729–752.

Navon, D. (1977). Forest before trees: The precedence of global features in visual perception. *Cognitive Psychology, 9,* 353–383.

Nisbett, R. E. (2003). *The geography of thought: How Asians and Westerners think differently. . . and why.* New York: Free Press.

Nisbett, R. E., & Miyamoto, Y. (2005). The influence of culture: Holistic versus analytic perception. *Trends in Cognitive Sciences, 9,* 467–473.

Nisbett, R. E., Peng, K., Choi, I., & Norenzayan, A. (2001). Culture and systems of thought: Holistic versus analytic cognition. *Psychological Review, 108,* 291–310.

Norasakkunkit, V., Kitayama, S., & Uchida, Y. (2012). Social anxiety and holistic cognition: Self-focused social anxiety in the United States and other-focused social anxiety in Japan. *Journal of Cross-Cultural Psychology, 43,* 742–757.

Norenzayan, A., Choi, I., & Nisbett, R. E. (2002). Cultural similarities and differences in social inference: Evidence from behavioral predictions and lay theories of behavior. *Personality and Social Psychology Bulletin, 28,* 109–120.

Norenzayan, A., Smith, E. E., Kim, B. J., & Nisbett, R. E. (2002). Cultural preferences for formal versus intuitive reasoning. *Cognitive Science, 26,* 653–684.

Overbeck, J., & Park, B. (2001). When power does not corrupt: Superior individuation processes among powerful perceivers. *Journal of Personality and Social Psychology, 81,* 549–565.

Oyserman, D., & Lee, S. W. S. (2008). Does culture influence what and how we think? Effects of priming individualism and collectivism. *Psychological Bulletin, 134,* 311–342.

Peng, K., & Nisbett, R. E. (1999). Culture, dialectics, and reasoning about contradiction. *The American Psychologist, 54,* 741–754.

Putnam, R. D. (1993). *Making democracy work.* Princeton, NJ: Princeton university press.

Rock, I. (1986). The description and analysis of object and event perception. In K. R. Boff, L. Kaufman & J. P. Thomas (Eds.), *Handbook of perception and human performance: Vol. 2,* (pp. 33.1–33.71). New York: Wiley.

Ross, L. (1977). The intuitive psychologist and his shortcomings. In L. Berkowitz (Ed.), *Advances in experimental social psychology: Vol. 10.* (pp. 173–220). San Diego: Academic Press.

Ross, L., & Nisbett, R. E. (1991). *The person and the situation: Perspectives of social psychology.* New York: Mcgraw-Hill.

Savani, K., & Markus, H. R. (2012). Evidence for cultural expertise in dynamic visual attention: European Americans outperform Asians in multiple object tracking. *Journal of Experimental Social Psychology, 40,* 766–769.

Savani, K., Morris, M. W., Naidu, N. R., Kumar, S., & Berlia, N. V. (2011). Cultural conditioning: Understanding interpersonal accommodation in India and the United States in terms of the modal characteristics of interpersonal influence situations. *Journal of Personality and Social Psychology, 100,* 84–102.

Schober, M. F., & Clark, H. H. (1989). Understanding by addressees and overhearers. *Cognitive Psychology, 21,* 211–232.

Scribner, S., & Cole, M. (1973). Cognitive consequences of formal and informal education. *Science, 183,* 554–559.

Segall, M. H., Campbell, D. T., & Herskovit, M. J. (1966). *The influence of culture on visual perception.* Indianapolis, IN: Bobbs-Merrill.

Semin, G., & Fiedler, K. (1988). The cognitive functions of linguistic categories in describing persons: Social cognition and language. *Journal of Personality and Social Psychology, 54,* 558–568.

Shechter, O., Durik, A. M., Miyamoto, Y., & Harackiewicz, J. M. (2011). The role of utility value in achievement behavior: The importance of culture. *Personality and Social Psychology Bulletin, 37,* 303–317.

Shweder, R. A. (1973). The between and within of cross-cultural research. *Ethos, 1,* 531–545.

Shweder, R. A. (1990). Cultural psychology: What is it? In J. W. Stigler, R. A. Shweder & G. Herdt (Eds.), *Cultural psychology: Essays on comparative human development* (pp. 1–46). Cambridge, England: Cambridge University Press.

Smith, P. K., Jostmann, N. B., Galinsky, A. D., & van Dijk, W. W. (2008). Lacking power impairs executive functions. *Psychological Science, 19,* 441–447.

Smith, P. B., Misumi, J., Tayeb, M., & Peterson, M. (1989). On the generality of leadership style measures across cultures. *Journal of Occupational Psychology, 62,* 97–109.

Smith, P. K., & Trope, Y. (2006). You focus on the forest when you're in charge of the trees: Power priming and abstract information processing. *Journal of Personality and Social Psychology, 90,* 578–596.

Snibbe, A., & Markus, H. (2005). You can't always get what you want: Educational attainment, agency, and choice. *Journal of Personality and Social Psychology, 88,* 703–720.

Spencer-Rodgers, J., Williams, M. J., & Peng, K. (2010). Cultural differences in expectations of change and tolerance for contradiction: A decade of empirical research. *Personality and Social Psychology Review, 14,* 296–312.

Stephens, N. M., Markus, H., & Townsend, S. M. (2007). Choice as an act of meaning: The case of social class. *Journal of Personality and Social Psychology, 93,* 814–830.

Tanaka, A., Koizumi, A., Imai, H., Hiramatsu, S., Hiramoto, E., & de Gelder, B. (2010). I feel your voice: Cultural differences in the multisensory perception of emotion. *Psychological Science, 21,* 1259–1262.

Tardif, T., Gelman, S. A., & Xu, F. (1999). Putting the "Noun Bias" in context: A comparison of English and Mandarin. *Child Development, 70,* 620–635.

Thibaut, J. W., & Kelley, H. H. (1959). *The social psychology of groups.* Piscataway, NJ: Transaction Publishers.

Torelli, C. J., & Shavitt, S. (2010). Culture and concepts of power. *Journal of Personality and Social Psychology, 99,* 703–723.

Trafimow, D., Triandis, H. C., & Goto, S. G. (1991). Some tests of the distinction between the private self and the collective self. *Journal of Personality and Social Psychology, 60,* 649–655.

Treisman, A. (1986). Properties, parts, and objects. In K. R. Boff, L. Kaufman & J. P. Thomas (Eds.), *Handbook of perception and human performance: Vol. 2.* (pp. 1–70). New York: Wiley 35.

Triandis, H. C. (1989). The self and social behavior in differing cultural contexts. *Psychological Review, 96*, 506–520.

Triandis, H. C. (1995). *Individualism and collectivism.* Boulder, CO: Westview.

Tsai, J. L., Miao, F. F., Seppala, E., Fung, H. H., & Yeung, D. Y. (2007). Influence and adjustment goals: Sources of cultural differences in ideal affect. *Journal of Personality and Social Psychology, 92*, 1102–1117.

Tucker, M., & Ellis, R. (1998). On the relations between seen objects and components of potential actions. *Journal of Experimental Psychology. Human Perception and Performance, 24*, 830–846.

Turner, F. J. (1920). *The frontier in American history.* New York: Henry Holt.

Ueda, Y., & Komiya, A. (2012). Cultural adaptation of visual attention: calibration of the oculomotor control system in accordance with cultural scenes. *PloS One, 7*, e50282.

Uskul, A. K., Kitayama, S., & Nisbett, R. E. (2008). Ecocultural basis of cognition: Farmers and fishermen are more holistic than herders. *Proceedings of the National Academy of Sciences of the United States of America, 105*, 8552–8556.

Vallacher, R. R., & Wegner, D. M. (1987). What do people think they're doing? Action identification and human behavior. *Psychological Review, 94*, 3.

Van Baaren, E. R., Horgan, T. G., Chartrand, T. L., & Dijkmans, M. (2004). The forest, the trees, and the chameleon: Context dependence and mimicry. *Journal of Personality and Social Psychology, 86*, 453–459.

Varnum, M. E. W., Grossmann, I., Katunar, D., Nisbett, R. E., & Kitayama, S. (2008). Holism in a European cultural context: Differences in cognitive style between Central and East Europeans and Westerners. *Journal of Cognition and Culture, 8*, 321–333.

Varnum, M. W., Grossmann, I., Kitayama, S., & Nisbett, R. E. (2010). The origin of cultural differences in cognition: The social orientation hypothesis. *Current Directions in Psychological Science, 19*, 9–13.

Vescio, T., Snyder, M., & Butz, D. (2003). Power in stereotypically masculine domains: A Social Influence Strategy × Stereotype Match Model. *Journal of Personality and Social Psychology, 85*, 1062–1078.

Weber, M. (1958). *The protestant ethic and the spirit of capitalism* (Talcott Parsons, Trans.) New York: Scribner (Original work published in 1904–1905).

Weisz, J. R., Rothbaum, F. M., & Blackburn, T. C. (1984). Standing out and standing in: The psychology of control in America and Japan. *The American Psychologist, 39*, 955–969.

Witkin, H., & Berry, J. (1975). Psychological differentiation in cross-cultural perspective. *Journal of Cross-Cultural Psychology, 6*, 4–87.

Witkin, H. A., Dyk, R. B., Faterson, H. F., Goodenough, D. R., & Karp, S. A. (1974). *Psychological differentiation.* Potomac, MD: Erlbaum.

Witkin, H. A., Lewis, H. B., Hertzman, M., Machover, K., Meissner, P. B., & Wapner, S. (1954). *Personality through perception.* New York: Harper.

Witkin, H. A., Oltman, P. K., Raskin, E., & Karp, S. A. (1971). *Group embedded figures test manual.* Palo Alto, CA: Consulting Psychologists Press.

Zanna, M. P., & Fazio, R. H. (1982). The attitude-behavior relation: Moving toward a third generation of research. In *Consistency in social behavior: The Ontario symposium: Vol. 2.* (pp. 283–301).

Zárate, M. A., Uleman, J. S., & Voils, C. I. (2001). Effects of culture and processing goals on the activation and binding of trait concepts. *Social Cognition, 19*, 295–323.

Zemba, Y., Young, M. J., & Morris, M. W. (2006). Blaming leaders for organizational accidents: Proxy logic in collective- versus individual-agency cultures. *Organizational Behavior and Human Decision Processes, 101,* 36–51.

Zhong, C., McGee, J. C., Maddux, W. W., & Galinsky, A. D. (2006). Power, culture, and action: Considerations in the expression and enactment of power in East Asian and Western societies. In E. A. Mannix, M. A. Neale & Y. Chen (Eds.), *Research on managing in teams and groups: Vol. 9.* (pp. 53–73). Greenwich, CT: Elsevier Science Press.

Zhou, X., He, L., Yang, Q., Lao, J., & Baumeister, R. F. (2012). Control deprivation and styles of thinking. *Journal of Personality and Social Psychology, 102,* 460–478.

CHAPTER FOUR

Message Position, Information Processing, and Persuasion: The Discrepancy Motives Model

Jason K. Clark*, Duane T. Wegener†

*Department of Psychology, University of Iowa, Iowa City, Iowa, USA
†Department of Psychology, Ohio State University, Columbus, Ohio, USA

Contents

Abstract

When a person encounters a persuasive appeal, a salient perception of the message is often the extent to which it is relatively proattitudinal or counterattitudinal. Some studies suggest that counterattitudinal communications are processed more deeply than proattitudinal messages. However, other research has found the opposite processing relation. Similarly, various properties of premessage attitudes and attributes of message sources have been shown to affect message processing. Yet, in some cases, these

Advances in Experimental Social Psychology, Volume 47
ISSN 0065-2601
http://dx.doi.org/10.1016/B978-0-12-407236-7.00004-8

findings have appeared inconsistent with one another. We suggest that this variety of findings can be organized and understood by considering the motivational states that guide processing of agreeable and disagreeable information, respectively. When encountering counterattitudinal advocacies, people should often be motivated to defend their views, and variables that influence defense motives should determine the amount of processing. Conversely, proattitudinal information presents an opportunity to bolster the premessage attitude. Thus, variables that affect the degree of bolstering motivation can affect the amount of proattitudinal message processing. In this chapter, we present the Discrepancy Motives Model—an integrative framework for organizing how persuasion variables interact with message position to affect the depth of information processing. In addition to processing differences, we discuss implications that this new account holds for understanding other attitude change phenomena.

1. INTRODUCTION: MESSAGE POSITION AND PERSUASION

Persuasion is an integral part of daily life. From TV spots and web pop-ups, to policy proposals and personal requests, attempts to change our attitudes account for a substantial amount of everyday social influence and interaction. When people encounter a persuasive appeal, one of the most salient initial perceptions may be the position that the communication takes on the issue. Sometimes such perceptions come directly from the title of a message. At other times, the source, the social setting, or a combination of factors can elicit clear expectations that a message will be relatively consistent with (i.e., proattitudinal) or discrepant from the message recipient's currently held attitude (i.e., counterattitudinal).

Across the persuasion literature, this message discrepancy construct has been found to play an important role in several critical processes. In particular, much research has identified the pro- or counterattitudinal position of the message as a determinant of how much attention and processing the communication receives. Some classic research suggests that people think more deeply about counterattitudinal than proattitudinal persuasive messages (e.g., Brock, 1967; Cacioppo & Petty, 1979b; Ditto & Lopez, 1992; Edwards & Smith, 1996). However, there are clear indications that this straightforward view of message position and information processing is insufficient. In particular, several researchers have discovered instances in which exactly opposite effects occur (i.e., greater processing of proattitudinal rather than counterattitudinal messages; e.g., Baker & Petty, 1994; Ziegler & Burger, 2011). These data include a number of recent studies designed to test a more general perspective on when proattitudinal or counterattitudinal messages receive greater scrutiny (e.g., Clark & Wegener, 2009; Clark, Wegener, & Fabrigar, 2008a, 2008b; Clark, Wegener, Habashi, & Evans, 2012).

In our research, a number of factors have yielded processing differences as a function of message position—including several properties of premessage attitudes and characteristics of message sources. At first glance, these influences may seem diverse. However, we believe that the findings point to general motivations related to the processing of agreeable or disagreeable information. For instance, when one encounters a counterattitudinal advocacy, variables that increase motives to defend against the attacking message can enhance scrutiny of that information. On the other hand, variables that elicit a greater need to bolster (i.e., support or strengthen) one's attitude can increase attention to and processing of information that is proattitudinal.

Building from these basic assumptions, we present the Discrepancy Motives Model (DMM). The DMM is a new, integrative framework for understanding when and why a message arguing in one direction may be processed more substantively than a message arguing in the opposite direction. Following brief overviews of classic and contemporary perspectives on message position in persuasion, we present the tenets of the model and review a number of investigations that provide empirical support. In addition, we posit several novel future directions generated by the DMM and then discuss implications that it may hold for understanding phenomena beyond the initiation of message processing.

2. CLASSIC AND CONTEMPORARY THEORIES

2.1. First-generation research: An emphasis on persuasion outcomes

Since the inception of systematic research on persuasion, scientists have been keenly interested in how the perceived pro- or counterattitudinal nature of a message can impact attitude change. Classic, first-generation research linked message position to the overall persuasive effectiveness of the appeal. For example, some early theorists asserted that the degree of attitude change should be an increasing function of how far the position of a message is from a person's current attitude toward the issue (i.e., message discrepancy; e.g., Anderson & Hovland, 1957). Later, with their influential Social Judgment Theory, Sherif and Hovland (1961) qualified and expanded upon this idea. These researchers postulated that the degree of attitude change should increase with message discrepancy, but only if the position of a message fell into a person's *latitude of acceptance* or range of positions they would find acceptable. Conversely, if an encountered message fell into a person's *latitude of rejection* (i.e., the range of disagreeable positions), the amount of persuasion should be a decreasing function of discrepancy.

The findings of several studies supported these general predictions. For example, Bochner and Insko (1966) presented subjects with one of nine messages advocating a certain number of hours of sleep per night (covering all 1-h increments between 0 and 8 h). Subjects were also led to believe that the message source was either a Y.M.C.A. director (low credibility) or a Nobel Prize winning physiologist (high credibility). Results on belief change represented an inverted-U relationship that was largely consistent with Social Judgment Theory. For each source, the amount of belief change toward the message increased to a point and then decreased with additional extremity of the message (with the downturn in persuasive effectiveness occurring at greater extremity when the source was high rather than low in credibility). Although other studies showed similar inverted U-shaped patterns, later research suggested that such findings were not driven by the latitude in which a given message position fell. Rather, contrary to the Social Judgment Theory, these experiments indicated that attitude change was more a function of the width of the person's latitude of acceptance (Eagly & Telaak, 1972; see also Eagly, 1981).

2.2. Second-generation research: A shifted focus toward information processing

As the field of social psychology experienced the cognitive revolution, researchers began to emphasize the role of information processing in persuasion. With the emergence of dual- and multiprocess models (i.e., the Elaboration Likelihood Model, Petty & Cacioppo, 1986; the Heuristic Systematic Model (HSM), Chaiken, Liberman, & Eagly, 1989), one mechanism that received considerable attention is the extent to which variables (such as message position) can increase or decrease motivation to process information. Such effects were postulated to occur when background levels of motivation and ability (determined, e.g., by the level of personal relevance of the attitude object or extent of distraction in the context) are relatively moderate and not constrained to be particularly high or low (Petty & Cacioppo, 1986). Despite specifying conditions in which effects on amount of information processing were likely, these general theories of persuasion did not specify particular effects of message position on depth of thinking.

Rather, they were complemented by theory directly relating the position of the message (as relatively pro- or counterattitudinal) to the amount of scrutiny given to the message.

During this era, the prevailing conceptualization was that counterattitudinal messages were more threatening to one's attitude or sense of self than proattitudinal information. Thus, message recipients should be more motivated to carefully attend to and process counterattitudinal compared with proattitudinal information (Cacioppo & Petty, 1979b; Petty, Cacioppo, & Haugtvedt, 1992). Early evidence consistent with this idea came from work on cognitive responses as a mechanism for persuasion. In one study, college participants were given a message that advocated a tuition increase of one of three possible sizes (Brock, 1967). Message recipients produced more counterarguments as the advocacy championed a larger tuition increase (i.e., as the appeal became more discrepant from recipients' preferences; see also Greenwald, 1968). Similarly, in the context of health persuasion, Ditto and Lopez (1992) found that participants generated more alternative explanations in response to an unfavorable as opposed to a favorable medical diagnosis.

This proposed link to amount of thinking also received support from studies that used other indicators of attention and cognitive processing. For instance, people spent more time evaluating (Edwards & Smith, 1996) and showed greater recall of counterattitudinal compared to proattitudinal message arguments (Cacioppo & Petty, 1979b). Other research obtained physiological evidence. For example, Cacioppo and Petty (1979a) either provided no information about message position or told participants that they would receive a message that was either proattitudinal or counterattitudinal. Consistent with heightened motivation to process, greater electrical activity in oral, speech-associated muscles was found when participants anticipated a counterattitudinal appeal compared with the proattitudinal and no-expectation conditions (for a review, see Cacioppo & Petty, 1981).

To this day, research questions relating common variables to the depth of information processing have dominated the study of persuasion. This is understandable because attitudes formed or changed via relatively high levels of thinking are stronger than attitudes stemming from low levels of processing (for reviews, see Petty & Cacioppo, 1986; Petty, Haugtvedt, & Smith, 1995; Wegener, Petty, Smoak, & Fabrigar, 2004). In particular, more effortful processing of attitude-relevant information has been linked to enhanced persistence of the attitude over time (e.g., Haugtvedt & Petty, 1992), increased resistance of the attitude to attacks (e.g.,

Zuwerink & Devine, 1996; Haugtvedt & Wegener, 1994), and greater influence of the attitude on future behavior (e.g., Verplanken, 1991).

2.3. Third-generation research: Moderated impact of message position on information processing

An emerging body of research challenges the general conceptualization that counterattitudinal messages receive greater processing than proattitudinal information. In fact, the findings of several investigations suggest that the opposite is true in many cases—proattitudinal messages are processed more thoroughly than counterattitudinal appeals. A general acknowledgment that both proattitudinal and counterattitudinal messages can sometimes increase thinking has been a long time in coming. Some early examples of greater scrutiny of proattitudinal than counterattitudinal information occurred when message recipients were in a happy mood state (Wegener, Petty, & Smith, 1995) or when a message was identified as representing a (numeric) minority opinion (Baker & Petty, 1994). At the time, however, such effects were couched narrowly within theories specifically addressing recipient mood or source status, respectively. However, the presence of those effects and others like them makes it clear that the previous "main effect" theory relating message position to the amount of processing is insufficient. More generally, such effects call for a complex account that can predict when proattitudinal appeals receive greater scrutiny and when counterattitudinal messages receive greater scrutiny. Moreover, if the theory is to have broad impact, it would have to address a wide variety of relevant moderator variables, rather than creating a new theory for each factor that is studied.

Over the past several years, we have turned our attention to developing and testing such a theory. As we will review in later sections of this chapter, we have identified a number of characteristics of the persuasion setting that moderate effects of message position on the depth of information processing. Similar to the earlier studies of mood or majority/minority sources, our research has identified moderators that shift the effects from the traditional increases in processing with counterattitudinal messages to opposite patterns of enhanced scrutiny of proattitudinal messages. Unlike that previous research, however, our research is guided by a more general theory capable of organizing effects across a variety of moderator variables, rather than developing a new variable-specific theory for every moderator that is addressed. Before reviewing the various lines of research that identify and document these moderators of message position effects, we discuss the broad theory that motivated the research.

3. THE DISCREPANCY MOTIVES MODEL

Our DMM centers on the motives that may drive the processing of proattitudinal or counterattitudinal messages. When a message recipient encounters a counterattitudinal advocacy, it may well serve to threaten the person's opinion (cf., Cacioppo & Petty, 1979b). If so, the message recipient may be motivated to defend their existing attitude against that threat. It stands to reason, then, that variables capable of enhancing or reducing that perceived threat should be capable of moderating the extent to which the message motivates extensive processing. From this perspective, then, counterattitudinal messages would sometimes prompt effortful scrutiny, but sometimes they would not. At the same time, we suggest that motives related to threat and defense only represent part of the picture. The processing of proattitudinal messages should serve a different set of goals. In particular, when an appeal supports the person's existing view, message recipients may seek out and process that information in an effort to support or bolster the attitude. Therefore, variables that influence the extent to which people want to bolster their attitude or the extent to which the message appears supportive could influence motives to process the proattitudinal information. Thus, as with counterattitudinal messages, there should be some circumstances in which proattitudinal messages receive a great deal of processing, and situations in which they do not. In the following sections, we expand on these general ideas to outline the types of factors that fall under the DMM rationale.

3.1. Defense motives associated with counterattitudinal message processing

When a counterattitudinal message is encountered, message recipients will often be motivated to defend their current attitude against the attack (Chen & Chaiken, 1999). The conceptualization of counterattitudinal messages as threats converges with a diverse base of past research and theory (see Baumeister, Bratslavsky, Finkenauer, & Vohs, 2001; Cacioppo & Berntson, 1994; Rozin & Royzman, 2001). Counterattitudinal information implies that the person is wrong about the topic. Because the desire to hold correct attitudes is a primary motivation for evaluative processing (Festinger, 1954; Petty & Cacioppo, 1986), information suggesting that the person is wrong would likely be experienced as negative and threatening (cf., Cacioppo & Petty, 1979b; Edwards & Smith, 1996). Thus, in an effort to avoid or defend against potential threats, individuals should be motivated to take action

(Taylor, 1991). Consistent with this rationale, encountering negative stimuli has been linked to heightened physiological arousal (Clore & Gormly, 1974) and stronger emotional reactions (Vinokur & Selzer, 1975) relative to positive experiences. Furthermore, paralleling some persuasion findings, negative information has been linked to increased cognitive activity in many contexts including evaluations of the self (Klinger, Barta, & Maxeiner, 1980), others (Fiske, 1980), and social situations (Abele, 1985).

While this negativity-based processing may often be pronounced, a number of common factors should be capable of enhancing or attenuating such effects by increasing or decreasing a person's motivation and ability to defend their attitudes. For example, motivation to defend one's attitude could be affected either by shaping the perceived correctness of the advocated position or by creating expectations that the proposed undesirable outcomes are more or less likely to come to fruition. Similarly, perceptions that one is able to defend their position could be influenced by the extent to which the person believes she or he possesses the requisite knowledge or resources to engage in the defense. With this in mind, one might consider effortful defense as likely when a counterattitudinal message is perceived as a challenge (cf., Blascovich & Tomaka, 1996; Schneider, Rivers, & Lyons, 2009). In this chapter, we use the threat terminology that has been more common in the persuasion literature (e.g., Cacioppo & Petty, 1979b; Edwards & Smith, 1996; Hovland, Janis, & Kelley, 1953). However, we acknowledge that perceived inability to deal directly with a threatening message could change the manner of response to the message (e.g., withdrawing from the message rather than scrutinizing it).

A number of aspects of the persuasion setting could directly relate to motives for active defense against a counterattitudinal appeal. For example, consider the strength of the premessage attitudes held by recipients. Compared to those with a weak premessage attitude on an issue, recipients holding a strong opinion should have greater perceptions that their current view is correct, valid, and reflective of the self—even if the valence of attitudes is the same across levels of strength (see Petty & Krosnick, 1995). For example, to the extent that people are sure what their premessage attitudes are (Petrocelli, Tormala, & Rucker, 2007), confident that they are correct (Gross, Holtz, & Miller, 1995), and/or considering the attitudes as their own (Prentice, 1987), counterattitudinal messages may seem surprising and should constitute more of a threat. Of course, people with strong premessage attitudes are also likely to feel relatively capable of confronting the threat in a direct and active way. As a result, recipients with strong premessage attitudes may often be more motivated to defend their views and effortfully scrutinize the counterattitudinal message. Conversely, if message recipients are relatively unsure what their attitude is, whether it is correct or not, or do not view the attitude as their own, then they may not perceive the message to be as much of a threat. In addition, weak premessage attitudes may also mean that those recipients would not feel as capable of actively defending against any threat that is perceived. Therefore, recipients holding weak attitudes would seem less likely to engage in effortful scrutiny of the counterattitudinal information.

Appraisals of threat or perceived ability to defend may also be influenced by shaping expectations about the likelihood of undesirable outcomes. When a counterattitudinal outcome seems likely, the message should pose more of a threat or elicit more surprise than when the same unfavorable outcome seems less likely. Thus, if a persuasion variable influences the perceived likelihood of the advocated outcome, this could also determine the amount of careful scrutiny. Certain characteristics of message sources seem particularly capable of carrying this potential. If a source possesses attributes that lead message recipients to expect an effective, compelling advocacy, then the proposed outcomes may seem likely to happen. If so, a counterattitudinal message from this advocate should be more threatening and take greater effort to oppose. In other words, when the message is counterattitudinal, stronger expectations of undesirable outcomes should be associated with increased defense motivation. Therefore, if the source is viewed as likely to be effective, message recipients should be highly motivated to carefully scrutinize the merits of the appeal. In contrast, if the source is viewed as ineffective, recipients should have expectations that the information will be specious rather than compelling. In such cases, the proposed undesirable outcomes may be viewed as less likely to happen and, in turn, recipients should be less motivated to scrutinize the message.

In summary, we believe that enhanced motivation to defend one's attitudes should often be responsible for more extensive, elaborative processing of counterattitudinal messages (assuming that the recipient believes they have sufficient ability to deal with a given threat). A number of common variables in persuasion settings can enhance or reduce such motives and therefore influence the extent of scrutiny of counterattitudinal messages. It is important to note that these moderators were not considered within the earlier perspectives attributing greater threat with counterattitudinal relative to proattitudinal messages (e.g., see Ditto & Lopez, 1992; Edwards & Smith, 1996; Petty et al., 1992). In addition, these moderators get all the more interesting when one recognizes that the same variables capable of influencing motives to defend against counterattitudinal appeals may also affect motives more applicable to proattitudinal appeals.

3.2. Bolstering motives associated with proattitudinal message processing

Although negativity effects on processing are supported by much research, we believe that there are many situations in which people seek, process, and rely upon information perceived as positive (proattitudinal) rather than negative (counterattitudinal). For example, in the context of verbal communication, people use positive evaluative words more frequently than negative evaluative words (e.g., Boucher & Osgood, 1969; Matlin & Stang, 1978). Similar biases have been found when individuals form impressions of others. People report more positive than negative traits about others (e.g., Benjafield, 1984; Tuohy & Stradling, 1987). Furthermore, when people draw inferences about others' abilities, perceivers rely more on positive than on negative performance information (because positive information is more diagnostic in these contexts; e.g., Reeder & Fulks, 1980; Skowronski & Carlston, 1987).

Closer to the domain of persuasion, studies of selective exposure to information include many examples of people seeking predominantly attitude-consistent rather than attitude-inconsistent information (see Hart et al., 2009, for a review). Much of this research has been guided by cognitive dissonance theory (Festinger, 1957, 1964). From this perspective, biases toward choice of consonant (proattitudinal) information are propelled by a desire to avoid the inconsistency that comes from free choice of exposure to dissonant (counterattitudinal) information. Especially when experiencing the negative state associated with dissonance (Elliot & Devine, 1994; Losch & Cacioppo, 1990), consonant (proattitudinal) information should be perceived as likely to facilitate one's goal to reduce the discomfort. In contrast, dissonant (counterattitudinal) information would only work against this pursuit (and increase feelings of discomfort). Thus, under these circumstances, people should be motivated to seek out information that is attitude-consistent and to avoid information that is attitude-inconsistent (see Frey, 1986; Smith, Fabrigar, & Norris, 2008).

We believe that similar motives to support or strengthen one's attitude often guide the processing of proattitudinal persuasive messages. A number of factors might influence the level of bolstering motivation that one experiences and the extent to which the message is viewed as likely to advance rather than thwart that motivation. For example, as discussed earlier, a number of strength-related attitudinal properties are associated with perceptions that an existing opinion is already correct (and not in need of additional support, see Petty & Krosnick, 1995). Therefore, recipients with a relatively strong attitude should feel little need to bolster by devoting cognitive resources to information perceived as redundant with existing views. In contrast, when the premessage attitude is weak, recipients may prefer to hold an opinion that is stronger. In some cases, the weakness of the attitude stems from an attitude quality associated with an experience of discomfort (as in attitude ambivalence or uncertainty, Van Harreveld, Van der Pligt, & De Liver, 2009). In such cases, the presence of a proattitudinal message should be perceived as a good opportunity to strengthen one's weak opinion—to increase subjective feelings of correctness (a key motivation underlying attitude formation and change; Petty & Cacioppo, 1986) and reduce any discomfort associated with the weak attitude. Hence, these message recipients should be motivated to engage in careful attention to and effortful processing of proattitudinal information.

One version of a goal to strengthen attitudes was used to explain motivations to process in the HSM (Chaiken et al., 1989). That is, regardless of the position of a message, recipients were said to process information in an effort to increase confidence in their attitude to a point that matched their desired confidence. For the most part, this idea was used to account for differences in processing motivation across levels of issue importance or personal relevance (where the level of desired confidence would be higher for more important/relevant topics). However, some research also suggested that this processing can be selective, based on whether message recipients believe that the processing will, indeed, increase their confidence. For example, Bohner, Rank, Reinhard, Einwiller, and Erb (1998) provided research participants with false feedback about what type of information they could most effectively process (i.e., topic or person information). Later, when lacking desired confidence, those same participants only engaged in increased processing if the available information was of a type that they presumed they could effectively process. We believe that motives to support or strengthen one's attitude would be broader than the construct of confidence and would more generally direct message recipients toward processing of proattitudinal rather than counterattitudinal information.

In addition to attitudinal properties creating bolstering motives, aspects of the communication itself could also influence the existence and strength of such motivation. For example, various characteristics of the persuasive attempt might alter expectations regarding whether the desirable (proattitudinal) outcomes seem likely to occur. When such desirable outcomes seem possible but uncertain, the extent of support for the person's current attitude may seem insufficient or tenuous. In these cases, message recipients might seek information that would reassure them and enhance their perceptions that the favorable outcomes may yet come to fruition.

Consider a proattitudinal message presented by a high-quality source— one expected to supply effective arguments and, thus, one likely to succeed in implementing the proposal. In this case, the message itself should be taken as very nonthreatening, highly supportive, and the positive outcomes espoused should be viewed as likely to come to fruition. Thus, at moderate background levels of motivation and ability to process the message, an active bolstering attempt may seem unnecessary and recipients may choose to conserve resources rather than actively process the information. On the other hand, this same message from a source with dubious credentials or other indicators of ineffectiveness should send a very different signal. This advocate should be viewed as likely to provide inadequate support to one's views and would make the proposed positive outcomes seem relatively unlikely to happen. Because of these shortcomings, recipients' motivation to bolster their position may be substantial. They may be motivated to carefully attend to the message as a means to ensure (or hope) that their own views are indeed "correct" and/or that the outcomes they prefer are still likely to occur.

3.3. Summary and implications of the DMM

In sum, the DMM posits that persuasion variables work in concert with the position of an advocacy to determine the likelihood of message processing. These intersecting influences can be conceptualized in a number of ways that are separately depicted in panels (A)–(C) of Figure 4.1. Each of these panels represents a type of interaction between message position and other persuasion variables that can influence processing through affecting motives to defend or to bolster. Consider panel (A). When an encountered message is relatively counterattitudinal rather than proattitudinal, message recipients may be motivated to defend their premessage attitudes. However, a variety of persuasion variables work in concert with message position to influence the extent of this motive to defend. For example, motives to defend should be strengthened when the attitude is relatively strong rather than weak or when the attacking source is perceived as being relatively effective rather than ineffective. In such cases, heightened defense motivation should increase the amount of information processing.

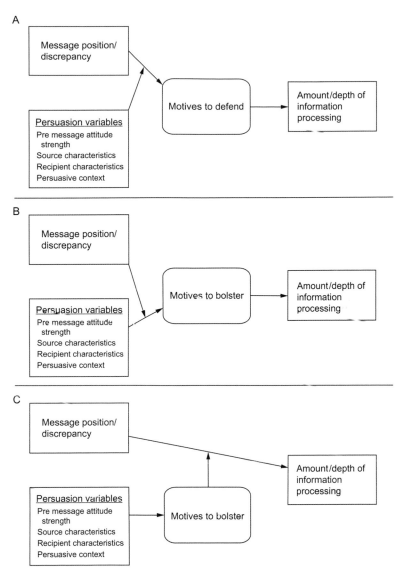

Figure 4.1 Graphic depiction of three conceptual ways (panels A, B, and C) that message position/discrepancy may combine with other persuasion variables to affect the amount of processing of a persuasive message.

Motives to defend are not the only influences on amount of thinking, however. In panels (B) and (C), the key construct is the extent to which the message recipient is motivated to bolster the premessage attitude. As depicted in panel (B), message position is likely to interact with certain persuasion variables to influence the level of this motive. For example, relatively ineffective support for a desired (proattitudinal) outcome could enhance motives to bolster the attitude, but more effective support for that desired outcome could dampen such motivation.

When a combination of message position and other variables creates a motive to bolster, that motive can directly enhance message processing. However, as depicted in panel (C), premessage attitude qualities or other variables can also directly affect the level of bolstering motivation. Because motives to bolster are satisfied more by processing of relatively proattitudinal rather than counterattitudinal information, the level of bolstering motivation should interact with the message position variable to influence the extent of processing. Figure 4.2 presents a summary of the model with the three types of interactions between message position/discrepancy and other persuasion variables from Figure 4.1 labeled as points A, B, and C, respectively.

At least two aspects of the DMM approach are worth emphasizing at this juncture. First, this depiction of the model should make clear that the DMM approach goes substantially beyond a "main effect" theory of counterattitudinal messages receiving greater processing than proattitudinal appeals (cf., Edwards & Smith, 1996; Petty et al., 1992). Such a model would have been represented by the single path from message position to depth/amount of processing (or by the mediational path from message position to defense motivation and from defense motivation to depth/amount of processing). The DMM adds moderators to the traditional message position

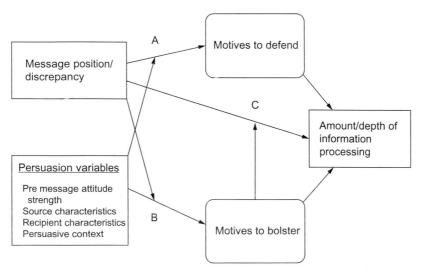

Figure 4.2 Graphic representation of the DMM that combines the types of interactions depicted in the separate panels of Fig. 4.1 (as points A, B, and C, respectively).

effects and adjusts the role of defense motivation to account for interactions between message position and other persuasive variables. In addition, the model adds a new mediator and moderator in the form of motives to bolster.

Another key feature of the DMM is that many variables would be expected to create opposite processing effects across pro- and counterattitudinal positions because they work through more than one of these paths at the same time. For example, consider a characteristic of the premessage attitude—such as its relative strength or weakness. A strong initial attitude could create stronger motives to defend the attitude when encountering a counterattitudinal message (panel A in Figure 4.1 and interaction A in Figure 4.2). According to the DMM, this would enhance processing of the counterattitudinal message relative to a weaker premessage attitude. However, the weaker attitude might also create stronger motives to bolster the attitude, and this would create more extensive processing of a proattitudinal message (panel C in Figure 4.1 and interaction C in Figure 4.2). Thus, key results in studies supporting the DMM will often include opposite processing patterns when messages are relatively proattitudinal rather than counterattitudinal.

4. EMPIRICAL SUPPORT FOR THE DMM

In recent years, research comparing pro- and counterattitudinal message processing has grown by leaps and bounds. Consistent with much research on the scrutiny of persuasive messages, the majority of this work has indexed the level of processing by manipulating the quality of the arguments provided in a persuasive appeal. When the amount of message processing is relatively low, the quality of arguments in the message has little impact on resulting cognitive responses and attitudes. In contrast, when processing of message content is relatively high, the quality of the arguments has a substantial impact on thoughts and attitudes (for a discussion of this method of indexing amount of information processing, see Petty & Cacioppo, 1986). Related to the view from the 1970s to the 1990s that proattitudinal messages receive less scrutiny than counterattitudinal messages, Worth and Mackie (1987) manipulated the quality of arguments provided by a political candidate that was either opposed to or in favor of government controls on acid rain. Argument quality had little impact on postmessage attitudes of people for whom the government control information was relatively proattitudinal. However, the quality of the arguments had significantly greater influence on postmessage attitudes of people for whom the appeal was relatively counterattitudinal.

In the DMM-inspired research, we expected opposite effects of message position on processing across levels of the relevant moderating variables. This appears in studies as Moderator × Message Discrepancy × Argument Quality interactions. The three-way interaction pattern could be decomposed by examining Message Discrepancy × Argument Quality interactions at different levels of the moderating variables or by examining Moderator × Argument Quality effects for relatively pro- versus counterattitudinal messages. For ease of graphing (because of large main effects of pro- vs. counterattitudinal messages), the figures presented in the chapter will depict separate Moderator × Argument Quality interactions for relatively counterattitudinal (where defensive motives should prompt scrutiny) and proattitudinal messages (where bolstering motives should initiate processing).

4.1. Properties of premessage attitudes

Message recipients often bring a great deal to the persuasive setting. Chief among these elements is the attitude the person holds before the message is encountered. Therefore, we start our discussion with research on how qualities of premessage attitudes produce opposite processing effects depending on the extent to which an advocacy is relatively pro- or counterattitudinal. We focus on the variables of attitude ambivalence, accessibility, and certainty. After discussing these variables, we then consider other common factors that may tap similar defense or bolstering motives.

4.1.1 Attitude ambivalence

Over the past two decades, a focus on strength-related dimensions of attitudes has significantly advanced scientific inquiry into how opinions are formed and changed. One key contributor to attitude strength is the degree to which people hold mixed or conflicted opinions. For example, consider a person's attitude toward a proposed government policy. Even if the individual holds favorable views of the advocacy, he or she may realize that there are some unfavorable aspects of it as well. This simultaneous activation of positive and negative evaluations has been termed as attitude ambivalence (see Kaplan, 1972; Olson & Zanna, 1993).

Ambivalent attitudes are characterized as structurally weak and, perhaps even more importantly, as psychologically uncomfortable. Therefore, people who are ambivalent might often be motivated to reduce the discomfort triggered by holding inconsistent evaluations (for a review, see Van Harreveld et al., 2009). Before our research, the prominent view linking premessage attitude ambivalence to message processing was to assert that people experiencing ambivalence would effortfully process attitude-relevant information in order to resolve conflicting evaluations (e.g., Jonas, Diehl, & Brömer, 1997; Maio, Bell, & Esses, 1996).

The DMM perspective on this question would start by suggesting that ambivalence would motivate message recipients to bolster their existing attitude (i.e., to reduce its ambivalence). However, this bolstering motive would not be served equally well by processing all types of information. Instead, pro- and counterattitudinal information should be considered as differentially capable of serving such goals. Therefore, premessage attitude ambivalence should increase the processing of proattitudinal but not counterattitudinal messages. When lacking ambivalence, the premessage attitude is stronger and motives to defend the attitude may be present when encountering a counterattitudinal (but not a proattitudinal) message. Thus, when attitudes are relatively unambivalent, processing should be greater when messages are relatively counterattitudinal rather than proattitudinal.

Clark et al. (2008b) tested these hypotheses. In a pair of studies using message topics of nuclear power and taxation of junk food, the valence and ambivalence of participants' premessage attitudes were measured. Later, participants received either strong (compelling) or weak (specious) arguments supporting the advocacy. Participants' postmessage attitudes were measured on typical evaluative scales (e.g., good/bad; desirable/undesirable), and cognitive responses were collected via a thought-listing task (for specific thought-listing procedures, see Wegener, Downing, Krosnick, & Petty, 1995). In each study, results on both postmessage attitudes and thought favorability supported the DMM predictions (Figure 4.3 presents the postmessage attitude results of the junk food tax study, Clark et al., 2008b, Study 1B). When encountering a relatively counterattitudinal message (where defensive motives would encourage processing), strong arguments were more persuasive than weak arguments when the recipient's premessage attitude was relatively strong (low ambivalence) rather than weak (high ambivalence). However, the processing pattern was in the opposite direction when the message was relatively proattitudinal (and bolstering motives would encourage processing). That is, strong arguments were more persuasive than weak arguments when the recipient's premessage attitude was relatively weak (high ambivalence) rather than strong (low ambivalence).

In a follow-up study, Clark et al. (2008b, Study 2) found additional support for bolstering motives directing processing of proattitudinal information at high levels of ambivalence. In this investigation, high ambivalence

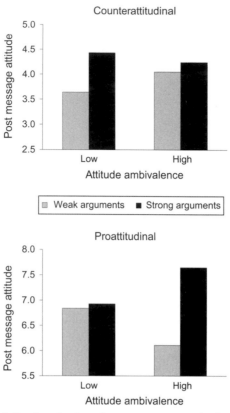

Figure 4.3 Top panel: Predicted values for postmessage attitude as a function of attitude ambivalence (±1 SD) and argument quality when the message was relatively counterattitudinal (−1 SD). Bottom panel: Predicted values for postmessage attitude as a function of attitude ambivalence (±1 SD) and argument quality when the message was relatively proattitudinal (+1 SD). *Adapted from Clark et al. (2008b, Study 1b).*

participants reported that a proattitudinal message would be more likely than a counter appeal to reduce their ambivalence. Furthermore, these perceptions were found to mediate effects of message discrepancy on processing (i.e., the Potential Ambivalence Reduction × Argument Quality interaction remained significant but reduced the Message Discrepancy × Argument Quality interaction when both were in the model).

4.1.2 Attitude accessibility

A variety of other strength-related features of attitudes have been shown to hold important implications for persuasion (see Petty & Krosnick, 1995). Of these properties, perhaps the most widely researched is attitude accessibility—the ease with which attitudes can be retrieved from memory. The degree of accessibility has been hypothesized to reflect the associative strength between a person's mental representation of the attitude object and their evaluation of it (Fazio, 1995). Early research linking attitude accessibility to information processing suggested that higher levels of premessage accessibility were associated with greater message scrutiny (Fabrigar, Priester, Petty, & Wegener, 1998). These findings were originally thought to result from accessibility triggering perceptions of importance/personal relevance (e.g., Roese & Olson, 1994; but see Bizer & Krosnick, 2001) or activating attitude-relevant knowledge (e.g., Wood, 1982). However, later research found higher accessibility to be associated with greater attitude confidence (Holland, Verplanken, & van Knippenberg, 2003)—especially, a greater sense of clearly knowing what one's attitude is toward an object (Petrocelli et al., 2007).

A DMM approach would suggest that a counterattitudinal message would be perceived as more wrong and more of a threat when the message recipients have a clearer idea of what their attitude is. A proattitudinal message might seem redundant and unnecessary when one already has an accessible attitude. However, when one lacks attitude clarity (holding an inaccessible attitude), the proattitudinal message can bolster the attitude and make it stronger.

In an experimental test of these predictions, Clark et al. (2008a, Study 2) manipulated the favorability of participants' attitudes toward a tuition proposal at an unnamed university. Participants later received a message advocating institution of the program. Thus, the message was counterattitudinal for some participants and proattitudinal for others. Following this induction, participants completed a survey in which attitude accessibility was manipulated by expressing the attitude either once or six times (see Fazio, 1995). After the survey, participants received either strong or weak arguments in favor of the tuition plan. The effects on the favorability of message-related thoughts and postmessage attitudes (see Figure 4.4) supported the hypotheses. When the message was counterattitudinal (and processing of the message would be encouraged by defense motives), the quality of the arguments influenced persuasion when premessage attitudes were high but not low in accessibility. The opposite pattern occurred when the message was proattitudinal (and processing of the message would be encouraged by bolstering motives). Argument quality influenced persuasion when premessage attitudes were low but not high in accessibility. An additional study revealed the same Accessibility × Message Discrepancy × Argument Quality interaction

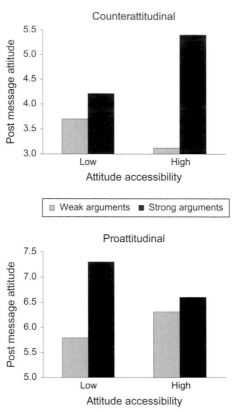

Figure 4.4 Top panel: Postmessage attitude as a function of attitude accessibility and argument quality when the message was counterattitudinal. Bottom panel: Postmessage attitude as a function of attitude accessibility and argument quality when the message was proattitudinal. *Adapted from Clark et al. (2008a, Study 2).*

when the valence and accessibility of premessage attitudes were measured rather than manipulated (Clark et al., 2008a, Study 1).

Prior to this DMM research, the attitude accessibility effects of Fabrigar et al. (1998) did not fit conceptually with the attitude ambivalence effects of Maio et al. (1996). Specifically, accessibility and ambivalence tend to be negatively correlated (e.g., see Krosnick, Boninger, Chuang, Berent, & Carnot, 1993), but high levels of accessibility and ambivalence were both linked to increased message processing. The DMM approach organizes and clarifies these effects. Though the original theories did not treat message position as a moderator, Maio et al. (1996) happened to use a proattitudinal message, whereas Fabrigar et al. (1998) used largely counterattitudinal messages. Indeed, one can see in the DMM research that the Maio et al. (1996) results parallel the Clark et al. (2008b) processing of relatively proattitudinal messages (bottom half of Figure 4.3), and the Fabrigar et al. (1998) results parallel the Clark et al. (2008a) processing of counterattitudinal messages (top half of Figure 4.4). As each DMM study makes clear, however, the Maio et al. and Fabrigar et al. results each constitute only half of the overall picture. In each case, the opposite pattern of processing occurs when the message represents a different level of discrepancy from the premessage attitude.

4.1.3 Attitude certainty

The Clark et al. (2008a) research on attitude accessibility did not directly test for a role of attitude confidence or certainty, though the DMM rationale for those studies would be consistent with such a possibility. Similar to having ambivalence, uncertainty has also been characterized as a psychologically uncomfortable state—one that people should often be motivated to alleviate (see Petty, Briñol, Tormala, & Wegener, 2007). Consistent with this conceptualization, research has shown that low levels of certainty are often associated with increased processing of related stimulus information (e.g., Edwards, 2003; Tiedens & Linton, 2001).

The predominant explanation for these processing effects centered on the notion of social perceivers as "cognitive misers" (Fiske & Taylor, 1984; for a review, see Tormala & Rucker, 2007). Strong feelings of certainty are considered as a signal that one has sufficient knowledge about a stimulus. Thus, there is little need to expend limited cognitive resources in scrutinizing stimulus-relevant information. Conversely, a state of uncertainty signals that more knowledge is needed and effortful processing of additional information serves as a means to gain confidence. This logic is consistent with the sufficiency principle of the HSM—which emphasizes the importance of the discrepancy between actual and desired levels of certainty (Chaiken et al., 1989).

These previous perspectives linking confidence and processing did not consider message position as a moderator. However, a DMM perspective on premessage attitude confidence would suggest that uncertainty leading to processing is likely to be a limited effect. When a persuasive appeal is relatively proattitudinal (and processing would serve motives to bolster the attitude), recipients who are uncertain of their attitude should be more likely to process the message than people who are already certain. However, opposite effects may occur when the message is counterattitudinal (and defense motives would prompt effortful processing). Message recipients who hold their attitudes with certainty should be more likely to process as a means to defend their attitude. In contrast, people holding uncertain attitudes may not be as motivated to defend those attitudes and might perceive themselves as less able to successfully defend their view (which could further dampen motivation to attempt the defense).

These hypotheses were examined by Jules, Clark, Wegener, and Tormala (2012, 2013) in one study that measured existing differences in certainty and another investigation wherein confidence was manipulated (by instructing participants to write about a past instance when they experienced either confidence or doubt, cf., Petty, Briñol, & Tormala, 2002). In each study, the valence of participants' premessage attitudes toward an issue was first measured. After an unrelated task, participants were given a message consisting of either strong or weak arguments on the topic (in favor of more U.S. nuclear power plants in Jules et al., 2012; in favor of a university tuition plan in Jules et al., 2013). In both studies, the key Attitude Certainty × Message Discrepancy × Argument Quality interaction was significant. When the message was relatively counterattitudinal (and processing of the message would be encouraged by defense motives), the quality of the arguments influenced persuasion when premessage attitudes were held with high but not low certainty. The opposite pattern occurred when the message was relatively proattitudinal (and processing of the message would be encouraged by bolstering motives). Argument quality influenced persuasion when premessage attitudes were held with low but not high levels of certainty.

In a follow-up study, Jules et al. (2012) found that participants with low attitude certainty expected a proattitudinal message to be better able to enhance confidence in their opinion compared with a counterattitudinal appeal. These expectations were then found to mediate message discrepancy effects on the extent to which these participants processed a later attitude-relevant advocacy. Taken together, these results for premessage attitude certainty conceptually parallel the earlier results for premessage attitude accessibility (one potential antecedent of attitude certainty; Holland et al., 2003; Petrocelli et al., 2007). Furthermore, it seems likely that certainty can have effects above and beyond accessibility *per se*—given the observed findings when confidence was manipulated via a procedure that is unlikely to influence accessibility of attitudes (i.e., Jules et al., 2013; see Petty et al., 2002).

4.1.4 Summary of premessage attitude (recipient) factors

The research reviewed in this section offers convergent support for the DMM perspective. Across a number of investigations, key premessage attitudinal variables have been found to interact with message discrepancy to determine how much people process information. Furthermore, these processing patterns are consistent with differences in defense motives guiding scrutiny of counterattitudinal appeals and bolstering motives driving the processing of proattitudinal messages. That is, relatively strong premessage attitudes tend to enhance processing of attacking (counterattitudinal) information, but relatively weak premessage attitudes tend to enhance processing of bolstering (proattitudinal) messages. In a number of cases, mediational evidence also supports the proposed role of motives to bolster weak premessage attitudes in processing of proattitudinal information.

Prior theories had related each of the studied premessage attitude properties to the extent of processing of attitude-related information. In each case, initial theories simply predicted more processing with ambivalent, accessible, and uncertain premessage attitudes, respectively. These proposed effects may have appeared to be paradoxical. Accessible attitudes could be held with certainty but were likely to be associated with low rather than high levels of ambivalence. However, the DMM proposed that such effects would be moderated (and would often reverse) across different levels of message discrepancy. In showing support for these predictions, the previous contradictions are resolved, and the conditions are clarified for when each of the previously hypothesized effects occurs.

It is clear that message recipients bring much more than a premessage evaluation to the persuasive setting. That evaluation can be infused with different qualities or experiences that interact with message discrepancy to produce propensities to effortfully process the message. It could well be that additional premessage attitude properties (such as the importance of the attitude, Eaton & Visser, 2008, or the amount of attitude-relevant knowledge, Wood, Rhodes, & Biek, 1995) would combine with message discrepancy in similar ways to influence message processing. It also seems possible that the message recipient could bring a variety of other qualities and experiential states to the persuasive setting, and these qualities and states might also be relevant to DMM theorizing. For instance, one of the early examples of proattitudinal receiving greater scrutiny than counterattitudinal information was when the persuasion context made the recipient happy prior to receipt of a message (Wegener, Petty, et al., 1995). Similar to the DMM-oriented view of bolstering motives related to tenuously held attitudes, Wegener, Petty, et al. (1995) suggested that tenuously held positive states could motivate selective processing of proattitudinal (capable of maintaining the positive state) rather than counterattitudinal information (capable of undermining the positive state). More recent theorizing suggests that when dealing with pro- or counter appeals that are less capable of influencing mood, information that is evaluatively inconsistent with prior mood can be surprising and receive greater scrutiny (Ziegler, in press; Ziegler & Burger, 2011).

Message recipients are also likely to bring general motivational orientations or discrepancy-related individual differences to the persuasive setting. For example, when individuals or recent situations prime a promotion- or prevention-oriented regulatory focus (Higgins, 1998), those orientations might influence the extent to which pro- or counterattitudinal information is processed (e.g., with a promotion orientation leading to enhanced processing of proattitudinal messages and prevention orientation leading to enhanced processing of counterattitudinal information). Similarly, some individual differences might advance processing motives related to the DMM. For instance, people high in preference for consistency (Cialdini, Trost, & Newsom, 1995) might be more likely to bolster any weak existing attitudes and, hence, process pro- rather than counterattitudinal messages. These and other possibilities should be examined in future research.

4.2. Characteristics of message communicators

In addition to message recipient variables, aspects of message communicators would seem capable of influencing motives to process counter- and proattitudinal information. As discussed earlier, perceptions of the extent to which one's current attitude is well versus inadequately supported should be relevant to both defense and bolstering motives. Therefore, features of a communicator that relate to the quality of support the source can offer would seem likely to moderate processing of pro- and counterattitudinal messages. We begin by discussing the credibility or efficacy of individual message sources. Then, we review research on the extent to which a group source is organized, cohesive, and efficacious (i.e., source entitativity).

4.2.1 Source credibility/efficacy

Compared with sources that lack credibility, highly credible advocates should be perceived as more likely to present information that is compelling, valid, or otherwise "correct." Due to these perceptions, early theorists posited that advocacies from credible sources held more potential incentives than those from noncredible communicators. Thus, message recipients should be more motivated to carefully attend to information disseminated by credible advocates (Hovland et al., 1953; Hovland & Weiss, 1951; Kelman & Hovland, 1953). Several previous findings are consistent with this conceptualization (e.g., Heesacker, Petty, & Cacioppo, 1983; Tobin & Raymundo, 2009; cf. DeBono & Harnish, 1988). For example, Tobin and Raymundo

(2009, Experiment 1) gave college participants a counterattitudinal message that argued against extending the length of Spring Break. When the source was described as an expert, participants processed the message more thoroughly compared to when the source was a nonexpert.

The DMM approach suggests that validity-related and similar perceptions would work in concert with the position of the message to motivate processing. That is, perceptions of source credibility and how likely a source will have success with their proposal may combine with the position of the message to trigger various levels of threat or concern over likely outcomes. As previously discussed, counterattitudinal appeals should often represent at least some level of threat and recipients should typically view the message-relevant outcomes as undesirable. When such a message emanates from a credible or efficacious source, these negative perceptions may be enhanced. In this case, knowledge about the source's credibility may not only yield strong expectations that the information will be compelling but also that the proposed negative outcomes will be likely to occur. Hence, recipients should be motivated to carefully scrutinize a counterattitudinal communication from a highly credible advocate. This threat-based explanation aligns with many of the past studies that have linked increased message processing with high credibility sources. In particular, reported data in these investigations indicated that the stimulus messages were indeed counterattitudinal (see DeBono & Harnish, 1988; Heesacker et al., 1983; Tobin & Raymundo, 2009).

Perceptions of high source credibility should not have the same effect when messages are proattitudinal, however. Rather than threatening, these messages should be viewed as supportive and recipients should want the proposed outcomes to come to fruition. With this in mind, a proattitudinal appeal from a highly credible source should be viewed as especially support-ive—because he or she should be expected to provide valid information that resonates with a recipient's opinion on an issue. In this case, there should be little indication that something is amiss and recipients' should feel little need to engage in effortful scrutiny of the message. However, this same favorable advocacy from a source that lacks credibility may be disconcerting. In this situation, the recipient should want the proposal to be successful, however he/she may be concerned that this is unlikely to happen—given that source will likely present arguments that are specious or otherwise ineffective. This perceived lack of support should trigger motives to bolster and recipients' should be motivated to process the message. In this case, increased processing could serve as a means to gain assurance that the merits are reasonable, that preferred outcomes are likely, and that the advocacy might yet be successful—in spite of the low credibility source.

Taken together, the DMM approach suggests that processing of a counter-attitudinal appeal should be enhanced when the source is credible or efficacious rather than noncredible or ineffective (because the effective source increases the need to defend against the attack). In contrast, processing of a proattitudinal appeal should be enhanced when the source lacks credibility or effectiveness (because the ineffectual source creates concern that the desired outcome will not occur, prompting a desire to bolster the attitude).

Research by Clark et al. (2012) tested this DMM conceptualization. In an initial investigation (Study 1), participants' premessage attitude toward the taxation of junk food was measured as part of a large survey. Next, participants were given expertise information about the source of a forthcoming message. In high-expertise conditions, the source was described as "a leading scholar in the field of health and food sciences." Conversely, participants in low-expertise conditions were told that the message source was "a high school junior." Following this manipulation, participants then received a set of either strong or weak arguments that advocated for the institution of junk food taxes in the United States. Results on postmessage attitudes (see Figure 4.5) and the favorability of participants' thoughts supported the predictions. When the message was relatively counterattitudinal, the quality of the message arguments had a significant effect on persuasion when the source was an expert, but not when the source lacked expertise. In contrast, when the message was relatively proattitudinal, argument quality influenced persuasion when the source lacked expertise, but not when the source was an expert. As a more direct test of the motives at work, a follow-up study found that an expert source was associated with greater perceived opposition than a nonexpert when the message was counterattitudinal. On the other hand, relative to an expert, a nonexpert triggered greater perceptions of inadequate support when the message was proattitudinal (Clark et al., 2012, Study 2). In turn, these perceptions accounted for the interactive effects of source expertise and message position on processing.

Other experiments that directly manipulated communicator efficacy showed similar patterns of information processing (Clark & Wegener, 2009, Studies 4A and 4B). In particular, an efficacious source was found to elicit more scrutiny of a counterattitudinal message relative to an ineffectual advocate. However, in response to a proattitudinal message, greater processing was observed when a source was portrayed as ineffectual rather than as efficacious.

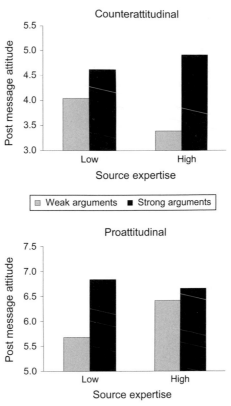

Figure 4.5 Top panel: Predicted values for postmessage attitude as a function of source expertise and argument quality when the message was relatively counterattitudinal (−1 SD). Bottom panel: Predicted values for postmessage attitude as a function of source expertise and argument quality when the message was relatively proattitudinal (+1 SD). *Adapted from Clark et al. (2012, Study 1).*

4.2.2 Source entitativity

In many settings, persuasive communications originate from groups rather than individuals. Regardless of whether the source is an organization, company, or other type of collection, many characteristics of individuals (e.g., credibility) should also be applicable to those group advocates. However, some perceptions may be primarily meaningful in situations where one encounters a message from a group rather than an individual. One such attribute corresponds to the perceived entitativity of a group.

Entitativity is the extent to which an aggregate of individuals is viewed as bonded together to form a coherent, meaningful unit (Hamilton, Sherman, & Castelli, 2002; cf., Campbell, 1958). Perceptions of entitativity differ widely across various collections of people. For instance, friends and families are perceived as having high levels of entitativity, whereas people waiting in a store or at a bus stop have low perceived entitativity (Lickel et al., 2000). Because greater entitativity should be related to stronger perceptions of singularity or consistency, a perceiver should be better able to predict the future behaviors of entitative rather than nonentitative groups. Therefore, in the context of impression formation, it has been postulated that highly entitative groups should initiate deeper, more elaborative processing of target-related information (see Hamilton & Sherman, 1996).

When a group source provides a persuasive message, it seems likely that these perceptions of singularity or cohesion would relate to important DMM-related source characteristics. For example, Clark and Wegener (2009) postulated that perceptions of group entitativity should be associated with perceptions of group efficacy. As opposed to nonentitative groups, highly entitative message sources should be viewed as likely to effectively argue their position and, consequently, likely to bring about the future outcomes they propose. The results of two studies supported this rationale. A strong and consistent relation between perceptions of entitativity and message-related efficacy was found both in response to real groups (Study 1A) and common group characteristics (Study 1B).

According to the DMM, an entitative group should be perceived as especially threatening when presenting a counterattitudinal appeal because the negative outcomes being proposed may seem likely to come to fruition. In turn, these perceptions should motivate message recipients to carefully process the presented arguments. In contrast, a group lacking entitativity (thus lacking efficacy) would not prove much of a threat. The pattern should be different when the message is proattitudinal, however. A highly entitative group should not be perceived as threatening at all. Rather, high source entitativity/efficacy may lead one to view the favorable advocacy as being "in good hands" and that it is unnecessary to expend cognitive resources scrutinizing the appeal. However, a source that lacks entitativity should elicit concern that the group cannot bring the desirable outcomes to fruition. Thus, message recipients may be motivated to carefully process in an effort to find some information that may alleviate their concerns or—in essence—bolster their own position.

Clark and Wegener (2009) found evidence that source entitativity may guide processing differently as a function of message discrepancy. After measuring participants' premessage attitudes toward nuclear power, Clark and Wegener (2009, Study 2) supplied them with information designed to manipulate the entitativity of a group message source. In the high entitativity conditions, the group was described as very organized and its members shared common goals. Conversely, in low entitativity conditions, the group was depicted as loosely organized and its members held separate intentions (adapted from Rydell & McConnell, 2005). Participants then received a strong or weak message in favor of building more nuclear power plants. Results on postmessage attitudes (see Figure 4.6) and cognitive responses showed the predicted effects of entitativity and message discrepancy on processing. When the message was relatively counterattitudinal, argument quality had a significant effect on postmessage attitudes when the source was high rather than low in entitativity. In contrast, when the message

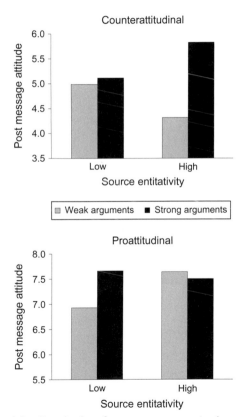

Figure 4.6 Top panel: Predicted values for postmessage attitude as a function of source entitativity and argument quality when the message was relatively counterattitudinal (−1 SD). Bottom panel: Predicted values for postmessage attitude as a function of source entitativity and argument quality when the message was relatively proattitudinal (+1 SD). *Adapted from Clark and Wegener (2009, Study 2).*

was relatively proattitudinal, the quality of the arguments influenced persuasion when source entitativity was low rather than high.

The hypothesized role of concern over likely negative outcomes and
unlikely positive outcomes was also addressed by Clark and Wegener
(2009, Study 3). Message recipients reported high levels of concern both
when entitative sources provided a counterattitudinal message and when
nonentitative sources provided a proattitudinal message. Concern was
low when entitative sources provided a proattitudinal message and when
nonentitative sources provided a counterattitudinal message. Also, the
extent of concern about message outcomes mediated the interactive effects
of source entitativity and message discrepancy on message processing. The
research on efficacious or inefficacious individuals (who were equally high
on entitativity) also supported the role of perceptions of source efficacy in
driving these effects (Clark & Wegener, 2009, Studies 4A and 4B).

It is worth noting that work conducted by other researchers also supports
the DMM approach. In a set of studies, Rydell and McConnell (2005)
found that participants processed messages more deeply when a group source
was perceived as high compared to low in entitativity. Interestingly, among
participants in their samples, the message was viewed as largely counterattitudinal (i.e., advocating comprehensive exams for college seniors; see
Petty & Cacioppo, 1986).

4.2.3 Summary of source factors

Since the inception of systematic research on persuasion, characteristics of
message sources have been some of the most widely studied aspects of communication settings. One of the distinct mechanisms by which sources can
affect persuasion is by determining how much message recipients carefully
think about communications. In this section, we reviewed the extent to
which the source was credible or efficacious and the extent to which a group
source was highly entitative. The evidence corresponding to each of these variables provides strong support that their scrutiny-inducing capabilities are
moderated by the position of the message. In particular, characteristics that
trigger stronger expectations of validity or the ability to facilitate proposed
outcomes have been associated with greater processing of counter- but
decreased processing of proattitudinal information. Conversely, attributes that
lead recipients to anticipate invalidity or an inability to facilitate outcomes
have been linked to enhanced processing of pro- but diminished scrutiny
of counterattitudinal messages. As specified by the DMM, these processing

outcomes and the mediational evidence are consistent with sources influencing motives to defend or bolster one's premessage views.

A variety of other source attributes may produce similar effects on message processing. Indeed, one of the early examples of proattitudinal messages receiving greater scrutiny than counterattitudinal messages was when the source represented a numeric minority (Baker & Petty, 1994; see also Martin & Hewstone, 2003; 2008). Baker and Petty (1994) focused on the surprise that would be involved in learning that one holds a minority position (because people generally assume that most people agree with them). However, in addition to surprise, the DMM suggests that the majority–minority status might affect the perceived threat (and defense motivation) involved with counterattitudinal messages and perceived support (and bolstering motivation) when dealing with proattitudinal messages.

Other source characteristics likely to influence processing of pro- versus counterattitudinal messages might include the sheer number of sources or the extent of similarity between a source and the message recipient. Previous research suggests that messages delivered by multiple sources are processed more than those delivered by a single source (e.g., Harkins & Petty, 1981). Likewise, advocates who are relatively similar to the message recipient elicit more information processing than sources that are dissimilar (Mackie, Worth, & Asuncion, 1990). For each of these variables, differences in processing depth have been attributed to general source-based perceptions of the likely validity of the message—with both multiple and similar communicators postulated to create strong expectations of cogency or accuracy. Of course, as discussed throughout this section, differences in these same perceptions are at the heart of the opposite processing effects we have found across relatively pro- versus counterattitudinal messages. Hence, future research should examine whether these additional communicator variables also produce processing patterns that differ as function of message position.

5. IMPLICATIONS FOR DEFENSE AND BOLSTERING MOTIVES BEYOND THE AMOUNT OF INFORMATION PROCESSING

Thus far, we have discussed how the DMM organizes previous persuasion findings and unveils a number of future research directions concerning determinants of message-related thinking. We believe that this conceptualization holds the potential to enhance understanding of a variety of other attitude change mechanisms as well.

5.1. Selective exposure to information

As discussed in this chapter, a great deal of research on persuasion examines influences on processing of encountered messages. However, in many settings, people actively seek out some pieces of attitude-relevant information and avoid others. Therefore, influences on information seeking are also important. Because information choices represent more behavioral outcomes, such studies also allow us to compare the DMM approach with traditional attitude strength predictions for attitude–behavior relations. That is, properties of attitudes associated with strength (such as low ambivalence or high confidence) would enhance the likelihood of later thinking and behavior being guided by that attitude (Petty & Krosnick, 1995). In turn, this may sometimes create stronger relations between existing attitudes and the extent to which chosen information is attitude-consistent (e.g., see Brannon, Tagler, & Eagly, 2007). However, the current discussion of bolstering motives opens up an alternative possibility. That is, when bolstering motives are strong and people view an action as capable of serving those motives, information choices might be directed more by attitudes with properties traditionally associated with weakness rather than strength.

5.1.1 Doubt and selective exposure

Sawicki et al. (2011) examined links between attitude certainty and selective exposure. In two studies examining exposure to pro- and antinuclear power information, measures and manipulations of attitude doubt (vs. certainty) showed a significant bolstering pattern. That is, attitudes held with relative doubt better predicted the favorability of information chosen in an exposure task (in which participants had 2 min to sample from a list of five pro- and five antinuclear power paragraphs). From the DMM perspective, the stronger relation between prechoice attitudes and the favorability of information chosen when prechoice attitudes were doubtful (rather than confident) could reflect differences in motivation to bolster. It could also be that the more even-handed choices by people holding their attitudes with confidence reflected some presence of defense motivation. However, people with confident attitudes did not prefer counter- over proattitudinal information.

Follow-up work examined the conditions under which this DMM-inspired (bolstering) pattern was most likely and when the opposite (traditional attitude strength) pattern might emerge. In general, the perceived ability of available information to effectively bolster attitudes should be an important limiting factor. In particular, Sawicki et al. (2011) considered the familiarity of the available information. If able to seek proattitudinal information that is unfamiliar, it could add new support to the attitude and effectively bolster it. However, if information is already familiar and doubt still remains, then this information was presumably not enough to remove uncertainty. Furthermore, reminding the person of that familiar information would be less likely to effectively bolster the attitude. Thus, bolstering effects seemed most likely when choosing unfamiliar information.

Traditional attitude strength effects seemed more likely when choosing more familiar information. If attitudes provide an indication of which available information is dependable and correct (the knowledge function of attitudes, Katz, 1960), then attitudes might be perceived as especially useful with regard to familiar information (that helps form the basis of one's opinion). Thus, if people are choosing familiar proattitudinal information, it could be because the attitude was used as a signal for the quality of the information (and attitudes held with confidence rather than doubt should be viewed as providing more valid evaluative input).

With this mind, in a third study, Sawicki et al. (2011) measured attitudes, attitude certainty, and two key perceptions of the chosen information—its favorability and familiarity. When participants reported choosing relatively familiar information, pre-exposure attitudes better predicted the favorability of chosen information when the attitudes were held with certainty rather than doubt (the traditional attitude strength pattern). In contrast, when participants reported choosing relatively unfamiliar information, pre-exposure attitudes better predicted the favorability of chosen information when the attitudes were held with doubt rather than certainty (the bolstering pattern consistent with the DMM).

5.1.2 Ambivalence and selective exposure

Sawicki et al. (in press) examined parallel predictions pertaining to attitude ambivalence. Consistent with the previous rationale about familiarity, research participants reported that unfamiliar (unknown) proattitudinal information would more effectively reduce their ambivalence compared with familiar (known) proattitudinal information. Rather than examine ratings of familiarity after choice, Sawicki et al. (in press) measured research participant's level of reported knowledge about the topic. Two studies produced interactions of knowledge, ambivalence, and attitudes. Higher levels of ambivalence were associated with stronger influences of prechoice attitudes on information choices when topic knowledge was low (a bolstering pattern).

However, lower levels of ambivalence were associated with stronger influences of attitudes when topic knowledge was high (an attitude strength pattern).

5.2. Implications for high- and low-elaboration persuasion

The DMM organizes message position effects on information processing that occur when motivation to process a persuasive communication is malleable (i.e., not constrained to be quite high or low). However, the DMM also has implications for persuasion in high- and low-elaboration settings. Persuasion variables influence attitudes through different mechanisms when motivation and ability to process are constrained to be low or high (see Petty & Wegener, 1998, for a review). For instance, when unmotivated or unable to think, message recipients often rely on some peripheral aspect of a communication as a simple shortcut to persuasion. In contrast, the same persuasion variable might influence attitudes through other mechanisms when message recipients are highly motivated and able to process the message. That is, under particular circumstances, the variable could bias effortful processing, serve as an argument to support or oppose the advocacy, or (in) validate cognitions generated in response to the attitude object (for a review, see Petty & Briñol, 2012).

5.2.1 Differential reliance on peripheral cues and directional biases in processing

A number of variables act as simple cues when motivation or ability is lacking but bias processing when motivation and ability are high (if messages are sufficiently ambiguous). For example, Petty, Schumann, Richman, and Strathman (1993) examined effects of recipient mood across different levels of elaboration. Positive mood led to more favorable postmessage attitudes than neutral mood. However, the favorability of message-related thoughts mediated the effect of mood on attitudes when motivation to process the message was high (consistent with mood biasing processing), but not when motivation to process was low (consistent with mood operating as a simple cue). Other variables such as source credibility (Chaiken & Maheswaran, 1994) have produced similar peripheral cue and biased processing effects.

Many such effects could be driven in part by perceptions of correctness—related to the defense or bolstering motives specified by the DMM. Thus, one implication of the DMM approach may be that defense or bolstering motives would lead to selective impact of variables that serve the motives. For instance, when a message is proattitudinal and, therefore, capable of serving motives to bolster, message recipients may be especially likely to seize on attitude-consistent cues (if motivation or ability is lacking) when premessage attitudes are weak (in need of bolstering) rather than strong. Similarly, when motivation and ability to process are high, processing may be more biased by bolstering-consistent variables when premessage attitudes are weak rather than strong. In contrast, when the message is counterattitudinal, message recipients may be especially likely to seize on attitude-consistent cues (if motivation or ability is lacking) if premessage attitudes are strong (prompting motivation to defend the attitude) rather than weak. Similarly, when motivation and ability to process are high, processing may be more biased by defense-consistent variables when premessage attitudes are strong rather than weak (cf., Giner-Sorolla & Chaiken, 1997). Thus, future research could examine the extent to which the cue and biased processing effects of variables like positive mood or source credibility vary when an advocacy is pro- versus counterattitudinal. This DMM-inspired proposal would represent an interesting new direction for research on high- or low-elaboration persuasion.

5.2.2 Differential validation of thoughts

Over the past decade, persuasion researchers have become increasingly interested in metacognition (i.e., thinking about thinking; Jost, Kruglanski, & Nelson, 1998)—especially the degree to which people are confident in their thoughts about an attitude object (see Petty et al., 2007). According to the self-validation hypothesis (Petty et al., 2002), the amount of confidence that an individual has in their thoughts should carry substantial implications for attitude change. For example, two message recipients could produce the same positive thought in response to a persuasive appeal. However, one recipient may have more confidence in the thought than the other. The self-validation hypothesis posits that the person who has more confidence should view their thought as more valid and hence rely on it more when forming an attitude toward the issue. Consistent with the DMM, we believe that message position can influence the extent to which people are confident in their thoughts, especially when that confidence comes from inferences about the correctness of available information.

To date, a number of persuasion variables have been found to determine thought confidence under certain conditions. First, self-validation has been found primarily when individuals are highly motivated to carefully process a message and thus produce cognitions that could become validated. A second limiting condition concerns the timing of the confidence-inducing factor. In particular, research has shown that variables can primarily validate thoughts when they are encountered *after* recipients have processed a message (for a review, see Briñol & Petty, 2009). For example, learning that a communicator is credible rather than noncredible after a message has been shown to increase thought confidence (Evans & Clark, 2012; Tormala, Briñol, & Petty, 2006; see also Briñol, Petty, & Tormala, 2004; Tormala, Briñol, & Petty, 2007). Similarly, learning that a source is highly efficacious rather than ineffectual (Clark, Evans, & Wegener, 2011) or that the source represented a numerical majority rather than a minority (Horcajo, Petty, & Briñol, 2010) also increases thought confidence. Presumably, these effects are driven by beliefs that credible, efficacious, or majority communicators should present information that is trustworthy and valid. If the source should present the best available arguments, then a recipient can infer that seemingly compelling features of a position are indeed strong and positive. If support for the advocacy is weak, this same communicator can also confirm reactions to these arguments by signaling that no truly compelling arguments can be made. In sharp contrast, a source expected to present invalid information should elicit a lack of trust—leading message recipients to doubt rather than be confident in their own reactions.

Consistent with the DMM, we believe that these different expectations may carry decidedly different validation effects contingent on the position of a message. Moreover, we posit that such influences may be driven by the different goals that people may have when motivated to process pro- versus counterattitudinal information. When carefully processing a proattitudinal message, recipients should often be motivated to verify, confirm, or corroborate the tenets of the appeal (e.g., high bolstering motivation). In this context, source characteristics suggesting that the communicator can be trusted (e.g., high credibility) should better facilitate this goal compared with an advocate whose message validity should be questioned (e.g., low credibility). Hence, source indicators of validity should enhance recipients' confidence in their reactions to a proattitudinal message—as shown in previous research (e.g., Tormala et al., 2006).

However, validity-related characteristics might have the opposite effect on confidence when introduced after a counterattitudinal advocacy. Rather than processing in an effort to find confirmation, message recipients would be motivated to counterargue, refute, and discredit the message (i.e., high defense motivation). Thus, it seems plausible that these message recipients would feel more confident when source characteristics support the invalidity rather than validity of the message arguments. At first blush, this notion seems to conflict with the findings of previous investigations of source influences on self-validation. However, one intriguing aspect to this body of research is that counterattitudinal messages have not been used. Rather, past studies have employed messages that advocated consumer products or other stimuli (e.g., a fictitious company; Horcajo et al., 2010) that likely elicited premessage views that are moderate or favorable as opposed to decidedly unfavorable.

6. SUMMARY AND CONCLUSIONS

People receive persuasive messages every day that vary in the extent to which they are perceived as agreeable (proattitudinal) or disagreeable (counterattitudinal). For more than half a century, the extent to which a persuasive communication is pro- or counterattitudinal has been of keen interest to researchers. One notable way this factor influences persuasion is by affecting the amount of careful scrutiny that people give to the information. For many years, the prevailing view has been that counterattitudinal messages are processed more deeply than proattitudinal messages (e.g., Cacioppo & Petty, 1979b; Edwards & Smith, 1996). Throughout the literature, a number of other common persuasion variables have also been shown to determine the amount of thinking (Petty & Wegener, 1998), although some of these effects have seemed contradictory—as when evidence suggested that both highly ambivalent and highly accessible attitudes increase information processing (Fabrigar et al., 1998; Maio et al., 1996). By focusing on the different motives that guide the processing of agreeable and disagreeable information, however, the DMM offers a comprehensive framework for organizing and understanding these various findings. In particular, the pro- or counterattitudinal nature of a message works in concert with other persuasion variables to influence motives to defend one's attitude against attacks and to bolster one's attitude by processing proattitudinal information.

A significant mass of research supports this new conceptualization. As reviewed in this chapter, an ever-growing number of studies show that properties of the premessage attitude (Clark et al., 2008a, 2008b; Jules et al., 2012, 2013) and characteristics of the message source (Baker & Petty, 1994; Clark & Wegener, 2009; Clark et al., 2012) interact with message position to determine the amount of processing. Strikingly, opposite effects on processing are routinely observed across these moderating variables. Such effects illustrate quite clearly that previous "main effect" theories relating message position or other persuasion variables to amount of message processing are insufficient. Early examples of such findings were narrowly conceptualized in theories relating to the specific moderator variable (e.g., Baker & Petty, 1994; Wegener, Petty, et al., 1995). However, when taken together with evidence directly inspired by the DMM, these previously separate pieces converge to support a broader understanding of how message discrepancy can influence the depth of information processing.

Furthermore, the DMM holds important implications in the literature, beyond effects on amount of processing. In some areas, supportive evidence is beginning to accumulate (as in selective exposure to information; e.g., Sawicki et al., 2011). In other areas, such as low- and high-elaboration persuasion processes, the implications await further research. We look forward to work that addresses these possibilities. Moreover, it is our hope that the current theory and research will fuel future investigations within and beyond the context of message-based persuasion.

ACKNOWLEDGMENT

This chapter was supported in part by a University of Iowa Old Gold Summer Fellowship awarded to J. K. C.

REFERENCES

Abele, A. (1985). Thinking about thinking: Causal, evaluative and finalistic cognitions about social situations. *European Journal of Social Psychology*, *15*, 315–332.

Anderson, N. H., & Hovland, C. I. (1957). The representation of order effects in communication research (Appendix A). In C. I. Hovland (Ed.), *The order of presentation in persuasion* (pp. 158–169). New Haven: Yale University Press.

Baker, S. M., & Petty, R. E. (1994). Majority and minority influence: Source-position imbalance as a determinant of message scrutiny. *Journal of Personality and Social Psychology*, *67*, 5–19.

Baumeister, R. F., Bratslavsky, E., Finkenauer, C., & Vohs, K. D. (2001). Bad is stronger than good. *Review of General Psychology*, *5*, 323–370.

Benjafield, J. (1984). On the relation between the Pollyanna and golden section hypotheses. *The British Journal of Social Psychology*, *23*, 83–84.

Bizer, G. Y., & Krosnick, J. A. (2001). Exploring the structure of strength-related attitude features: The relation between attitude importance and attitude accessibility. *Journal of Personality and Social Psychology*, *81*, 566–586.

Blascovich, J., & Tomaka, J. (1996). The biopsychosocial model of arousal regulation. In M. P. Zanna (Ed.), *Advances in experimental social psychology: Vol. 28.* (pp. 1–51). New York: Academic Press.

Bochner, S., & Insko, C. A. (1966). Communicator discrepancy, source credibility, and opinion change. *Journal of Personality and Social Psychology*, *4*, 614–621.

Bohner, G., Rank, S., Reinhard, M.-A., Einwiller, S., & Erb, H.-P. (1998). Motivational determinants of systematic processing: Expectancy moderates effects of desired confidence on processing effort. *European Journal of Social Psychology*, *28*, 185–206.

Boucher, J., & Osgood, C. E. (1969). The Pollyanna hypothesis. *Journal of Verbal Learning and Behavior*, *8*, 1–8.

Brannon, L. A., Tagler, M. J., & Eagly, A. H. (2007). The moderating role of attitude strength in selective exposure to information. *Journal of Experimental Social Psychology*, *43*, 611–617.

Briñol, P., & Petty, R. E. (2009). Persuasion: Insights from the self-validation hypothesis. In M. P. Zanna (Ed.), *Advances in experimental social psychology: Vol. 41*. (pp. 69–118). Elsevier: New York.

Briñol, P., Petty, R. E., & Tormala, Z. L. (2004). Self-validation of cognitive responses to advertisements. *Journal of Consumer Research, 30*, 559–573.

Brock, T. C. (1967). Communication discrepancy and intent to persuade as determinants of counterargument production. *Journal of Experimental Social Psychology, 3*, 296–309.

Cacioppo, J. T., & Berntson, G. G. (1994). Relationship between attitudes and evaluative space: A critical review, with emphasis on the separability of positive and negative substrates. *Psychological Bulletin, 115*, 401–423.

Cacioppo, J. T., & Petty, R. E. (1979a). Attitudes and cognitive response: An electrophysiological approach. *Journal of Personality and Social Psychology, 37*, 2181–2199.

Cacioppo, J. T., & Petty, R. E. (1979b). Effects of message repetition and position on cognitive responses, recall, and persuasion. *Journal of Personality and Social Psychology, 37*, 97–109.

Cacioppo, J. T., & Petty, R. E. (1981). Electromyograms as measures of extent and affectivity of information processing. *The American Psychologist, 36*, 441–456.

Campbell, D. T. (1958). Common fate, similarity, and other indices of the status of aggregates of persons and social entities. *Behavioral Science, 3*, 14–25.

Chaiken, S., Liberman, A., & Eagly, A. H. (1989). Heuristic and systematic information processing within and beyond the persuasion context. In J. S. Uleman & J. A. Bargh (Eds.), *Unintended thought* (pp. 212–252). New York: Guilford.

Chaiken, S., & Maheswaran, D. (1994). Heuristic processing can bias systematic processing: Effects of source credibility, argument ambiguity, and task importance on attitude judgment. *Journal of Personality and Social Psychology, 66*, 460–473.

Chen, S., & Chaiken, S. (1999). The heuristic-systematic model in its broader context. In S. Chaiken & Y. Trope (Eds.), *Dual-process theories in social and cognitive psychology* (pp. 73–96). New York: Guilford Press.

Cialdini, R. B., Trost, M. R., & Newsom, J. T. (1995). Preference for consistency: The development of a valid measure and the discovery of surprising behavioral implications. *Journal of Personality and Social Psychology, 69*, 318–328.

Clark, J. K., Evans, A. T., & Wegener, D. T. (2011). Perceptions of source efficacy and persuasion: Multiple mechanisms for source effects on attitudes. *European Journal of Social Psychology, 41*, 596–607.

Clark, J. K., & Wegener, D. T. (2009). Source entitativity and the elaboration of persuasive messages: The roles of perceived efficacy and message discrepancy. *Journal of Personality and Social Psychology, 97*, 42–57.

Clark, J. K., Wegener, D. T., & Fabrigar, L. R. (2008a). Attitude accessibility and message processing: The moderating role of message position. *Journal of Experimental Social Psychology, 44*, 354–361.

Clark, J. K., Wegener, D. T., & Fabrigar, L. R. (2008b). Attitudinal ambivalence and message-based persuasion: Motivated processing of proattitudinal information and avoidance of counterattitudinal information. *Personality and Social Psychology Bulletin, 34*, 565–577.

Clark, J. K., Wegener, D. T., Habashi, M. M., & Evans, A. T. (2012). Source expertise and persuasion: The effects of perceived opposition or support on message scrutiny. *Personality and Social Psychology Bulletin, 38*, 90–100.

Clore, G. L., & Gormly, J. B. (1974). Knowing, feeling, and liking: A psycho-physiological study of attraction. *Journal of Research in Personality, 8*, 218–230.

DeBono, K. G., & Harnish, R. J. (1988). Source expertise, source attractiveness, and the processing of persuasive information: A functional approach. *Journal of Personality and Social Psychology, 55*, 541–546.

Ditto, P. H., & Lopez, D. F. (1992). Motivated skepticism: Use of differential decision criteria for preferred and nonpreferred conclusions. *Journal of Personality and Social Psychology, 63*, 568–584.

Eagly, A. H. (1981). Recipient characteristics as determinants of responses to persuasion. In R. E. Petty, T. C. Brock & T. M. Ostrom (Eds.), *Cognitive responses in persuasion* (pp. 173–196). Hillsdale, NJ: Erlbaum.

Eagly, A. H., & Telaak, K. (1972). Width of the latitude of acceptance as a determinant of attitude change. *Journal of Personality and Social Psychology, 23*, 388–397.

Eaton, A. A., & Visser, P. S. (2008). Attitude importance: Understanding the causes and consequences of passionately held views. *Social and Personality Psychology Compass, 2*, 1719–1736.

Edwards, J. A. (2003). The interactive effects of processing preference and motivation on information processing: Causal uncertainty and the MBTI in a persuasion context. *Journal of Research in Personality, 37*, 89–99.

Edwards, K., & Smith, E. E. (1996). A disconfirmation bias in the evaluation of arguments. *Journal of Personality and Social Psychology, 71*, 5–24.

Elliot, A. J., & Devine, P. G. (1994). On the motivational nature of cognitive dissonance: Dissonance as psychological discomfort. *Journal of Personality and Social Psychology, 67*, 382–394.

Evans, A. T., & Clark, J. K. (2012). Source characteristics and persuasion: The role of self-monitoring in self-validation. *Journal of Experimental Social Psychology, 48*, 383–386.

Fabrigar, L. R., Priester, J. R., Petty, R. E., & Wegener, D. T. (1998). The impact of attitude accessibility on elaboration of persuasive messages. *Personality and Social Psychology Bulletin, 24*, 339–352.

Fazio, R. H. (1995). Attitudes as object-evaluation associations: Determinants, consequences, and correlates of attitude accessibility. In R. E. Petty & J. A. Krosnick (Eds.), *Attitude strength: Antecedents and consequences* (pp. 247–282). Hillsdale, NJ: Erlbaum.

Festinger, L. (1954). A theory of social comparison processes. *Human Relations, 7*, 117–140.

Festinger, L. (1957). *A theory of cognitive dissonance.* Evanston, IL: Row, Peterson.

Festinger, L. (1964). *Conflict, decision, and dissonance.* Stanford, CA: Stanford University Press.

Fiske, S. T. (1980). Attention and weight in person perception: The impact of negative and extreme behavior. *Journal of Personality and Social Psychology, 38*, 889–906.

Fiske, S. T., & Taylor, S. E. (1984). *Social cognition.* (1st ed.). Reading, MA: Addison-Wesley.

Frey, D. (1986). Recent research on selective exposure to information. In L. Berkowitz (Ed.), *Advances in experimental social psychology: Vol. 19.* (pp. 41–80). San Diego, CA: Academic Press.

Giner-Sorolla, R., & Chaiken, S. (1997). Selective use of heuristic and systematic processing under defense motivation. *Personality and Social Psychology Bulletin, 23*, 84–97.

Greenwald, A. G. (1968). Cognitive learning, cognitive response to persuasion, and attitude change. In A. G. Greenwald, T. C. Brock & T. M. Ostrom (Eds.), *Psychological foundations of attitudes* (pp. 47–170). San Diego, CA: Academic Press.

Gross, S. R., Holtz, R., & Miller, N. (1995). Attitude certainty. In R. E. Petty, & J. A. Krosnick (Eds.), *Attitude strength: Antecedents and consequences* (pp. 215–245). Mahwah, NJ: Erlbaum.

Hamilton, D. L., & Sherman, S. J. (1996). Perceiving individuals and groups. *Psychological Review, 103*, 336–355.

Hamilton, D. L., Sherman, S. J., & Castelli, L. (2002). A group by any other name. . .: The role of entitativity in group perception. In W. Stroebe & M. Hewstone (Eds.), *European review of social psychology: Vol. 12.* (pp. 139–168). New York: John Wiley.

Harkins, S. G., & Petty, R. E. (1981). The effects of source magnification of cognitive effort on attitudes: An information processing view. *Journal of Personality and Social Psychology, 40*, 401–413.

Hart, W., Albarracin, D., Eagly, A. H., Lindberg, M., Merrill, L., Brechan, I., et al. (2009). Feeling validated versus being correct? A meta-analysis of selective exposure to information. *Psychological Bulletin, 135*, 555–588.

Haugtvedt, C. P., & Petty, R. E. (1992). Personality and persuasion: Need for cognition moderates the persistence and resistance of attitude changes. *Journal of Personality and Social Psychology, 63*, 308–319.

Haugtvedt, C. P., & Wegener, D. T. (1994). Message order effects in persuasion: An attitude strength perspective. *Journal of Consumer Research, 21*, 205–218.

Heesacker, M., Petty, R. E., & Cacioppo, J. T. (1983). Field dependence and attitude change: Source credibility can alter persuasion by affecting message-relevant thinking. *Journal of Personality, 51*, 653–666.

Higgins, E. T. (1998). Promotion and prevention: Regulatory focus as a motivational principle. In M. P. Zanna (Ed.), *Advances in experimental social psychology: Vol. 30.* (pp. 1–46). San Diego, CA: Academic Press.

Holland, R. W., Verplanken, B., & van Knippenberg, A. (2003). From repetition to conviction: Attitude accessibility as a determinant of attitude certainty. *Journal of Experimental Social Psychology, 39*, 594–601.

Horcajo, J., Petty, R. E., & Briñol, P. (2010). The effects of majority versus minority source status on persuasion: A self-validation analysis. *Journal of Personality and Social Psychology, 99*, 498–512.

Hovland, C. I., Janis, I. L., & Kelley, H. H. (1953). *Communication and persuasion: Psychological studies of opinion and change.* New Haven, CT: Yale University Press.

Hovland, C. I., & Weiss, W. (1951). The influence of source credibility on communication effectiveness. *Public Opinion Quarterly, 15*, 635–650.

Jonas, K., Diehl, M., & Brömer, P. (1997). Effects of attitudinal ambivalence on information processing and attitude-intention consistency. *Journal of Experimental Social Psychology, 33*, 190–210.

Jost, J. T., Kruglanski, A. W., & Nelson, T. O. (1998). Social metacognition: An expansionist review. *Personality and Social Psychology Review, 2*, 137–154.

Jules, S. J., Clark, J. K., Wegener, D. T., & Tormala, Z. L. (2012). *Persuasion under uncertainty: Implications for processing of pro- versus counterattitudinal information.* Poster presented at the annual meeting of the Society for Personality and Social Psychology, San Diego, CA.

Jules, S. J., Clark, J. K., Wegener, D. T., & Tormala, Z. L. (2013). *Confidence versus doubt: Differential processing of proattitudinal and counterattitudinal information.* Poster presented at the annual meeting of the Society for Personality and Social Psychology, New Orleans, LA.

Kaplan, K. J. (1972). On the ambivalence-indifference problem in attitude theory and measurement: A suggested modification of the semantic differential technique. *Psychological Bulletin, 77*, 361–372.

Katz, D. (1960). The functional approach to the study of attitudes. *Public Opinion Quarterly, 24*, 163–204.

Kelman, H. C., & Hovland, C. I. (1953). "Reinstatement" of the communicator in delayed measurement of opinion change. *Journal of Abnormal and Social Psychology, 48*, 327–335.

Klinger, E., Barta, S. G., & Maxeiner, M. E. (1980). Motivational correlates of thought content frequency and commitment. *Journal of Personality and Social Psychology, 39*, 1222–1237.

Krosnick, J. A., Boninger, D. S., Chuang, Y. C., Berent, M. K., & Carnot, C. G. (1993). Attitude strength: One construct or many related constructs? *Journal of Personality and Social Psychology, 65*, 1132–1151.

Lickel, B., Hamilton, D. L., Wieczorkowska, G., Lewis, A., Sherman, S. J., & Uhles, A. N. (2000). Varieties of groups and the perception of group entitativity. *Journal of Personality and Social Psychology, 78*, 223–246.

Losch, M. E., & Cacioppo, J. T. (1990). Cognitive dissonance may enhance sympathetic tonus, but attitudes are changed to reduce negative affect rather than arousal. *Journal of Experimental Social Psychology*, 26, 289–304.

Mackie, D. M., Worth, L. T., & Asuncion, A. G. (1990). Processing of persuasive in-group messages. *Journal of Personality and Social Psychology*, 58, 812–822.

Maio, G. R., Bell, D. W., & Esses, V. M. (1996). Ambivalence and persuasion: The processing of messages about immigrant groups. *Journal of Experimental Social Psychology*, 32, 513–536.

Martin, R., & Hewstone, M. (2003). Majority versus minority influence: When, not whether, source status instigates heuristic or systematic processing. *European Journal of Social Psychology*, 33, 313–330.

Martin, R., & Hewstone, M. (2008). Majority versus minority influence, message processing, and attitude change: The source-context-elaboration model. In M. P. Zanna (Ed.), *Advances in experimental social psychology: Vol. 40.* (pp. 237–326). New York: Elsevier.

Matlin, M., & Stang, D. (1978). *The Pollyanna principle.* Cambridge, MA: Schenkman.

Olson, J. M., & Zanna, M. P. (1993). Attitudes and attitude change. *Annual Review of Psychology*, 44, 117–154.

Petrocelli, J. V., Tormala, Z. L., & Rucker, D. D. (2007). Unpacking attitude certainty: Attitude clarity and attitude correctness. *Journal of Personality and Social Psychology*, 92, 30–41.

Petty, R. E., & Briñol, P. (2012). The Elaboration Likelihood Model. In P. A. M. Van Lange, A. Kruglanski, & E. T. Higgins (Eds.), *Handbook of theories of social psychology: Vol. 1.* (pp. 224–245). London, England: Sage.

Petty, R. E., Briñol, P., & Tormala, Z. L. (2002). Thought confidence as a determinant of persuasion: The self-validation hypothesis. *Journal of Personality and Social Psychology*, 82, 722–741.

Petty, R. E., Briñol, P., Tormala, Z. L., & Wegener, D. T. (2007). The role of metacognition in social judgment. In A. W. Kruglanski & E. T. Higgins (Eds.), *Social psychology: Handbook of basic principles* (pp. 254–284). (2nd ed.). New York: Guilford.

Petty, R. E., & Cacioppo, J. T. (1986). *Communication and persuasion: Central and peripheral routes to persuasion.* New York: Springer-Verlag.

Petty, R. E., Cacioppo, J. T., & Haugtvedt, C. (1992). Involvement and persuasion: An appreciative look at the Sherifs' contribution to the study of self-relevance and attitude change. In D. Granberg & G. Sarup (Eds.), *Social judgment and intergroup relations: Essays in honor of Muzafer Sherif* (pp. 147–174). New York: Springer/Verlag.

Petty, R. E., Haugtvedt, C., & Smith, S. M. (1995). Elaboration as a determinant of attitude strength: Creating attitudes that are persistent, resistant, and predictive of behavior. In R. E. Petty & J. A. Krosnick (Eds.), *Attitude strength: Antecedents and consequences* (pp. 93–130). Mahwah, NJ: Erlbaum.

Petty, R. E., & Krosnick, J. A. (Eds.), (1995). *Attitude strength: Antecedents and consequences.* Mahwah, NJ: Erlbaum.

Petty, R. E., Schumann, D. W., Richman, S. A., & Strathman, A. J. (1993). Positive mood and persuasion: Different roles for affect under high- and low-elaboration conditions. *Journal of Personality and Social Psychology*, 64, 5–20.

Petty, R. E., & Wegener, D. T. (1998). Attitude change: Multiple roles for persuasion variables. In D. Gilbert, S. Fiske, & G. Lindzey (Eds.), *The handbook of social psychology* (pp. 323–390). (4th ed.). New York: McGraw-Hill.

Prentice, D. A. (1987). Psychological correspondence of possessions, attitudes, and values. *Journal of Personality and Social Psychology*, 53, 993–1003.

Reeder, G. D., & Fulks, J. L. (1980). When actions speak louder than words: Implicational schemata and the attribution of ability. *Journal of Experimental Social Psychology*, 16, 33–46.

Roese, N. J., & Olson, J. M. (1994). Attitude importance as a function of repeated expression. *Journal of Experimental Social Psychology*, 30, 39–51.

Rozin, P., & Royzman, E. (2001). Negativity bias, negativity dominance, and contagion. *Personality and Social Psychology Review, 5*, 296–320.

Rydell, R. J., & McConnell, A. R. (2005). Perceptions of entitativity and attitude change. *Personality and Social Psychology Bulletin, 31*, 99–110.

Sawicki, V., Wegener, D. T., Clark, J. K., Fabrigar, L. R., Smith, S. M., & Durso, G. R. O. (in press). Feeling conflicted and seeking information: When ambivalence enhances and diminishes selective exposure to attitude-consistent information. *Personality and Social Psychology Bulletin.*

Sawicki, V., Wegener, D. T., Clark, J. K., Fabrigar, L. R., Smith, S. M., & Bengal, S. T. (2011). Seeking confirmation in times of doubt: Selective exposure and the motivational strength of weak attitudes. *Social Psychological and Personality Science, 2*, 540–546.

Schneider, T. R., Rivers, S. E., & Lyons, J. B. (2009). The biobehavioral model of persuasion: Generating challenge appraisals to promote health. *Journal of Applied Social Psychology, 38*, 1928–1952.

Sherif, M., & Hovland, C. I. (1961). *Social judgment: Assimilation and contrast effects in communication and attitude change.* New Haven, CT: Yale University Press.

Skowronski, J. J., & Carlston, D. E. (1987). Social judgment and social memory: The role of cue diagnosticity in negativity, positivity, and extremity biases. *Journal of Personality and Social Psychology, 52*, 689–699.

Smith, S. M., Fabrigar, L. R., & Norris, M. E. (2008). Reflecting on six decades of selective exposure research: Progress, challenges, and opportunities. *Social and Personality Compass, 2*, 464–493.

Taylor, S. E. (1991). Asymmetrical effects of positive and negative events: The mobilization-minimization hypothesis. *Psychological Bulletin, 110*, 67–85.

Tiedens, L. Z., & Linton, S. (2001). Judgment under emotional certainty and uncertainty: The effects of specific emotions on information processing. *Journal of Personality and Social Psychology, 81*, 973–988.

Tobin, S. J., & Raymundo, M. M. (2009). Persuasion by causal arguments: The motivating role of perceived causal expertise. *Social Cognition, 27*, 105–127.

Tormala, Z. L., Briñol, P., & Petty, R. E. (2006). When credibility attacks: The reverse impact of source credibility on persuasion. *Journal of Experimental Social Psychology, 42*, 684–691.

Tormala, Z. L., Briñol, P., & Petty, R. E. (2007). Multiple roles for source credibility under high elaboration: It's all in the timing. *Social Cognition, 25*, 536–552.

Tormala, Z. L., & Rucker, D. D. (2007). Attitude certainty: A review of past findings and emerging perspectives. *Social and Personality Psychology Compass, 1*, 469–492.

Tuohy, A. P., & Stradling, S. G. (1987). Maximum salience vs. golden section proportions in judgmental asymmetry. *British Journal of Psychology, 78*, 457–464.

Van Harreveld, F., Van der Pligt, J., & De Liver, Y. (2009). The agony of ambivalence and ways to resolve it: Introducing the MAID model. *Personality and Social Psychology Review, 13*, 45–61.

Verplanken, B. (1991). Persuasive communication of risk information: A test of cue versus message processing effects in a field experiment. *Personality and Social Psychology Bulletin, 17*, 188–193.

Vinokur, A., & Selzer, M. (1975). Desirable versus undesirable life events: Their relationship to stress and mental distress. *Journal of Personality and Social Psychology, 32*, 329–337.

Wegener, D. T., Downing, J., Krosnick, J. A., & Petty, R. E. (1995). Measures and manipulations of strength-related properties of attitudes: Current practice and future directions. In R. E. Petty & J. A. Krosnick (Eds.), *Attitude strength: Antecedents and consequences* (pp. 455–487). Mahwah, NJ: Erlbaum.

Wegener, D. T., Petty, R. E., & Smith, S. M. (1995). Positive mood can increase or decrease message scrutiny: The hedonic contingency view of mood and message processing. *Journal of Personality and Social Psychology, 69*, 5–15.

Wegener, D. T., Petty, R. E., Smoak, N. L., & Fabrigar, L. R. (2004). Multiple routes to resisting attitude change. In E. S. Knowles & J. A. Linn (Eds.), *Resistance and persuasion* (pp. 13–38). Mahwah NJ: Erlbaum.

Wood, W. (1982). The retrieval of attitude-relevant information from memory: Effects on susceptibility to persuasion and on intrinsic motivation. *Journal of Personality and Social Psychology, 42*, 798–810.

Wood, W., Rhodes, N., & Biek, M. (1995). Working knowledge and attitude strength: An information processing analysis. In R. E. Petty & J. A. Krosnick (Eds.), *Attitude strength: Antecedents and consequences* (pp. 283–313). Mahwah, NJ: Erlbaum.

Worth, L. T., & Mackie, D. M. (1987). Cognitive mediation of positive affect in persuasion. *Social Cognition, 5*, 76–94.

Ziegler, R. (in press). Mood and processing of proattitudinal and counterattitudinal messages. *Personality and Social Psychology Bulletin.*

Ziegler, R., & Burger, A. M. (2011). Mood and the impact of individuating information on the evaluation of ingroup and outgroup members: The role of mood-based expectancies. *Journal of Experimental Social Psychology, 47*, 1000–1006.

Zuwerink, J. R., & Devine, P. G. (1996). Attitude strength and resistance to persuasion: It's more than just the thought that counts. *Journal of Personality and Social Psychology, 70*, 931–944.

CHAPTER FIVE

Implicit Attitudes and Beliefs Adapt to Situations: A Decade of Research on the Malleability of Implicit Prejudice, Stereotypes, and the Self-Concept

Nilanjana Dasgupta
Department of Psychology, University of Massachusetts, Amherst, Massachusetts, USA

Contents

Advances in Experimental Social Psychology, Volume 47
ISSN 0065-2601
http://dx.doi.org/10.1016/B978-0-12-407236-7.00005-X

233

Abstract

In this chapter, I review my program of research on implicit attitudes and beliefs. These attitudes and beliefs are often acquired without individuals' awareness and influence judgments, decisions, and actions without intention. My work seeks to identify circumstances that produce changes in people's implicit attitudes and beliefs toward social groups. Over the course of a dozen years, my collaborators and I have found that implicit attitudes and beliefs are remarkably malleable even in the absence of active attempts at persuasion. I review four lines of research relevant to this issue. Collectively, this work shows that implicit attitudes and beliefs are mirror-like reflections of local environments and communities within which individuals are immersed. Changes in local environments (and sometimes emotions elicited by them) produce corresponding changes in people's implicit attitudes and beliefs. In essence, implicit attitudes and beliefs are better described as situational adaptations or reflections rather than personal possessions acquired and discarded by conscious acts of will.

1. IMPLICIT ATTITUDES AND BELIEFS ADAPT TO SITUATIONS: A DECADE OF RESEARCH ON THE MALLEABILITY OF IMPLICIT PREJUDICE, STEREOTYPES, AND THE SELF-CONCEPT

In a provocative article published a quarter century ago, Bob Abelson observed that in everyday discourse, attitudes and beliefs are often treated as if they are personal possessions that belong to individuals (Abelson, 1986). Attitudes and beliefs are talked about as "things" or possessions individuals acquire in response to life experiences, personal values, and information from the social world. Individuals carry these possessions with them as they navigate various situations in daily life. This metaphor highlights three important assumptions about the nature of attitudes that are latent in the mind of social psychologists and laypeople alike. The first is the assumption that people consciously acquire attitudinal possessions as they navigate life; they reflect on them, speak about them if they so choose, and discard them when they want. The second is the assumption of a sharp distinction between one's own attitudinal possessions and that of others in the broader community around the individual. And the third is the assumption that changing attitudes involves an active act of giving up one's possession or exchanging it for another possession. This possession metaphor captures the way in which attitudes were conceptualized in classic theories of social psychology popular until the 1980s and it continues to be the way in which laypeople think of attitudes in everyday life.

However, the real story of attitudes is far more complicated and interesting. This story has been uncovered through meticulous empirical research and new theories in social psychology over the past two decades. The new story reveals that attitudes are not necessarily consciously acquired possessions. They often accrue passively in individuals' minds without their conscious awareness. Unlike personal possessions, the distinction between one individual's personal attitude and that of others in one's community is remarkably fuzzy. And attitude change does not have to involve an active act of discarding an old possession or changing it for a new one. Attitudes often change in the absence of conscious reflection and active consideration of new information. Expanding the conceptualization of attitudes and attitude change to include new theories and measures is immensely important to social psychology because this construct—attitude—is relevant to almost every topic in social psychology. It is relevant to the self-concept, person perception, intergroup relations, close relationships, social influence, helping, and aggression, just to give a few examples. Equally important is the need to understand the conditions under which attitudes and beliefs change, whether these changes are overt or subtle, and how these changes affect subsequent judgments, decisions, and actions. Expanding the scope of attitude change research promises to enhance the explanatory power of psychological theories to predict social behavior and to generate translational research that applies attitude change interventions to solve real social problems.

My research focuses on this new breed of attitudes and beliefs that are acquired passively without individuals' awareness and that influence subsequent judgments, decisions, and actions without intention or volition. These subtle attitudes and beliefs have been variously labeled *implicit*, *unconscious*, or *automatic*. I examine implicit attitudes and beliefs about *social groups*

(groups defined by race, gender, sexual orientation, nationality, and so on) and how group-based attitudes and beliefs impact group members' *self-concept*. I am particularly interested in understanding the circumstances under which implicit attitudes and beliefs change.

2. SETTING THE STAGE: THE ROLE OF THE UNCONSCIOUS IN SHAPING ATTITUDES AND BELIEFS

A longstanding theme in social psychology is that people's attitudes and behavior are frequently shaped by factors that lie outside their awareness and cannot be fully understood by introspection and self-report. Although we as individuals think of our attitudes and actions as solely guided by conscious intentions and motivations, social psychological research shows that, to the contrary, attitudes and actions are often shaped by situational cues and motivational processes that operate with little awareness on the part of the perceiver (Banaji & Dasgupta, 1998; Bargh, 1994, 1997; Dasgupta, 2004, 2008; Greenwald & Banaji, 1995; Kihlstrom, 1990; Nisbett & Wilson, 1977). When people encounter a person, a group, or an issue they are familiar with, the attitude or belief associated with it pops into mind quickly and automatically in a split second. People may be unaware of attitude activation or only semiaware of it. But once an implicit attitude or belief is activated, it is difficult to inhibit or suppress right away and the activated attitude or belief is more likely to drive subsequent behavior, judgments, and decisions.

Implicit attitudes and beliefs are typically seen as conceptually distinct from explicit, controlled, self-reported, or conscious responses. As these terms suggest, attitudes are considered explicit when perceivers are aware of their evaluations and opinions, able to claim them as their own, and have the capacity to change their attitudes and beliefs given sufficient motivation and effort. Whereas explicit attitudes are measured by directly asking people to consider how they feel about a particular object or issue and report their thoughts and feelings in a deliberate fashion, implicit attitudes are inferred indirectly from people's performance on tasks that, at face value, seem unrelated to attitude measurement. For example, the speed with which people associate certain words or pictures during rapid reaction time tasks is used to infer their implicit attitudes. Similarly, people's choice of words in a word completion task might also be used to infer their implicit attitudes (Petty, Fazio, & Brinol, 2008).

3. IMPLICIT ATTITUDES AND BELIEFS ABOUT SOCIAL GROUPS

Much of the research on implicit attitudes and their effects on social behavior have been conducted in the context of intergroup relations, particularly around issues of prejudice and stereotyping. Research has gravitated in this direction for two good reasons. First, the socially sensitive nature of intergroup prejudice and stereotypes typically raises concerns that people's explicitly reported attitudes toward in- and outgroups may be distorted by self-presentation and impression management concerns. That is, people may not always be willing to report socially sensitive attitudes honestly, especially if those attitudes deviate from social norms. Second, while self-reporting their attitudes, people sometimes make a sharp distinction between their own personal attitudes (their personal possessions) from the attitudes of others in their community or larger society. They might say, for example: "people in my community are prejudiced against Group X, but I am not." Yet, commonly held opinions of social groups are known by everybody immersed in a given community through hearsay, media exposure, and by passive observation of who occupies valued roles and devalued roles in the community. Passive exposure to commonly held attitudes and beliefs register in individuals' minds and get incorporated into their mental representation of a given group without their active consent. As a result, people's implicit attitudes toward social groups often mirror the societal hierarchy of privilege and disadvantage although their explicit attitudes and beliefs are likely to focus on their personal possessions as distinct from that of others.

4. CHANGING IMPLICIT ATTITUDES AND BELIEFS

Empirical evidence that implicit attitudes are automatically activated without awareness and that they have the capacity to drive judgments and behavior regardless of explicit intention and control had, for a long time, led to the conclusion that these attitudes are relatively immutable. Early theories of implicit social cognition argued that implicit attitudes and beliefs are learned early in life and they change slowly only after long-term accrual of new associations and a great deal of training (Bargh, 1999; Devine, 1989; Petty, Tormala, Brinol, & Jarvis, 2006; Wilson, Lindsey, & Schooler, 2000). In other words, the assumption was that conventional persuasion techniques that change explicit attitudes by relying on perceivers' awareness of their attitudes, motivation to reconsider their stance, and willingness to expend effort to consider new information, ought to leave implicit attitudes untouched.

As in the case of attitude change in general, so too prejudice reduction interventions had also been assumed to require conscious mental processes. The working assumption was that perceivers must be aware of their bias (Banaji, 2001; Dasgupta, 2004, 2008); motivated to suppress negative thoughts (Macrae, Bodenhausen, Milne, & Jetten, 1994; Macrae, Bodenhausen, Milne, & Wheeler, 1996); and motivated to change their responses toward outgroups because of personal values, guilt, compunction, or self-insight (Allport, 1954; Devine, Monteith, Zuwerink, & Elliot, 1991; Monteith, 1993; Monteith, Devine, & Zuwerink, 1993; Monteith, Zuwerink, & Devine, 1994; Myrdal, 1944). In some cases, prejudice reduction interventions involved highlighting the discrepancy between people's general egalitarian values and their prejudice toward specific groups and motivating them to align the two (Gaertner & Dovidio, 1986; Katz & Hass, 1988; Katz, Wackenhut, & Hass, 1986; Rockeach, 1973). One of the best tried and tested methods of prejudice reduction involved motivating people to engage in intergroup contact (Pettigrew & Tropp, 2006; Tropp & Bianchi, 2006; Tropp, Stout, Boatswain, Wright, & Pettigrew, 2006). Because changing prejudice and stereotypes was viewed as a conscious relearning process, the research cited above mostly focused on changing explicit attitudes. Until the turn of the new century, few had attempted to modify implicit forms of prejudice and stereotyping because these were seen as inescapable habits that are expressed despite attempts to bypass or ignore them (Bargh, 1999; Devine, 1989). With the advent of the twenty-first century, new research from several research laboratories including mine began to challenge assumptions about the immutability of implicit attitudes (for reviews, see Blair, 2002; Dasgupta, 2009; Gawronski & Bodenhausen, 2006).

5. A ROADMAP OF MY RESEARCH PROGRAM

For the past dozen years, research from my lab has consistently shown that implicit attitudes and beliefs are remarkably malleable both in the short term and over time, without the need to invoke conscious intentions and motivated learning. We started with the working assumption that if implicit attitudes and beliefs about social groups are learned and strengthened through repeated observation of particular classes of people in valued or devalued roles through direct contact, indirect contact, or media exposure in one's local environment, then such attitudes and beliefs ought to remain stable as long as one's local environment and its inhabitants remain constant. On the flip side, these attitudes and beliefs ought to change if the environments and its inhabitants change. If this assumption is true, we hypothesized that seemingly intractable implicit prejudice against historically disadvantaged groups (e.g., racial minorities and sexual minorities) might become less biased if the average person's local environment is changed.

Using this simple logic, in one line of research we focused on measuring or manipulating the types of local environments people are immersed in and who they observe in admired and valued roles. Do they observe admired and well-regarded outgroup members who belong to historically disadvantaged groups (e.g., African Americans, gays and lesbians, and elderly individuals) or are such individuals absent from their local environment? We then examined the effects of inserting such admired counterstereotypic individuals in the local environment on people's implicit attitudes toward the outgroup as a whole. We wanted to determine if relatively small changes in local environments and communities would produce substantial shifts in individuals' implicit attitudes toward disadvantaged outgroups.

In a second related strand of research, we moved beyond implicit *attitudes* (the degree to which people *like* or *dislike* a group) and sought to investigate whether changes in local environments affect perceivers' implicit *beliefs* about ethnic outgroups—particularly, their implicit beliefs about ethnic minorities' nationality. Who is seen as legitimately American and who is seen as a perpetual foreigner? Does exposure to particular types of admired ethnic minorities in one's local environment enhance the implicit perception of their group as legitimately American?

In a third line of research, we examined the malleability of implicit bias as it relates to individuals' *ingroup* and their *self-concept*. An insidious quality of implicit bias is that it functions like an "equal opportunity virus" that gets in the mind of anybody regardless of their own group membership. Even individuals who are members of disadvantaged groups learn and acquire implicit stereotypes about their own group if they are immersed in the same local environment as their advantaged counterparts. We shine a spotlight on the conditions under which changes in local environments shape people's implicit stereotypes about their ingroup, and examine, by extension, if they have downstream consequences on group members' implicit self-concept and life choices.

Local environments shape implicit attitudes and beliefs through passive observation of people and media around us. At the same time, local environments also shape implicit attitudes and beliefs in another more active way—local events arouse specific emotions and motivations in individuals. My collaborators and I have found that strong negative emotions aroused in one local environment can linger in the mind and taint individuals' implicit attitudes toward groups encountered in a different environment even though the source of the original emotion was unrelated to the target being evaluated. Once aroused, negative emotions can unwittingly carry over from one local environment to another and increase implicit prejudice against specific social groups. This is our fourth line of research on the malleability of implicit attitudes.

Collectively, these four lines of research convey the message that implicit attitudes and beliefs are not like personal possessions acquired and discarded by conscious acts of individuals who possess them. Rather they are mirror-like reflections of local environments and communities within which individuals are immersed. Changes in these environments and communities (and sometimes emotions elicited by them) produce changes in implicit attitudes and beliefs about one's outgroup, ingroup, and the self. Put differently, I propose that implicit attitudes and beliefs are situational adaptations. As situations change, so too do implicit reactions.

6. DO CHANGES IN LOCAL ENVIRONMENTS INFLUENCE IMPLICIT ATTITUDES TOWARD DISADVANTAGED GROUPS?

6.1. Local environments influence implicit attitudes toward outgroups

Recall that we started with the assumption that implicit preference for some groups and bias against others are learned associations acquired by passive immersion in an unequal society where people are segregated into disparate roles, jobs, and geographies based on group membership. In everyday life and in daily media, people observe that some types of individuals typically occupy highly valued roles, while others typically occupy devalued roles, and this distinction is often based on group membership. Take, for instance, the reality that in many local environments highly valued community members such as business leaders, educational leaders, and politicians are frequently White and male. Ethnic minorities and women are rarely seen in these roles. When they exist they are not as visible or publicly recognized as their male counterparts. At the other end of the spectrum, less valued members of many communities such as nannies, housecleaners, and laborers are frequently Black or Latino. Through repetition, these observations get passively recorded in the mind and become the basis of implicit attitudes and beliefs. If this is how implicit attitudes develop then such biases should shift when people are immersed in different types of situations where they encounter admired and counterstereotypic individuals who do not fit their prescribed role in society.

To test this hypothesis, we conducted a series of studies to determine if implicit bias against historically disadvantaged groups such as African Americans, the elderly, and gays and lesbians can be reduced by changing the local environment that people inhabit (Dasgupta & Greenwald, 2001; Dasgupta & Rivera, 2008). In our first such study, we brought people into the lab for what they thought would a "general knowledge task" and immersed them in one of three types of media environments in the lab. Participants in one condition were shown images and brief biographies of admired and famous African Americans from various walks of life (e.g., civil rights leaders like Martin Luther King, actors like Denzel Washington, and athletes like Michael Jordan). We also showed them disliked and infamous White Americans (e.g., serial killers like Ted Bundy and Jeffrey Dahmer, and the Oklahoma City bomber, Timothy McVeigh). One might call this the *pro-Black media exposure condition*. Participants who were randomly assigned to a second condition were shown images and biographies of disliked and infamous African Americans (e.g., O.J. Simpson, Marion Barry, Louis Farrakhan) as well as admired and famous White Americans (President John F. Kennedy, actor Tom Hanks, comedian Jay Leno). One might call this the *pro-White media exposure condition*. Participants in the third control condition were shown images and descriptions of strongly positive and negative things but not people (flowers and insects). A little later, under the guise of a different and unrelated experiment, we measured people's implicit racial attitudes unobtrusively, without asking any direct questions about their attitudes. In fact, people were typically unaware that their attitudes were being measured; they viewed the implicit measure as a hand–eye coordination task.

Implicit attitude measures are very different from the common way of measuring attitudes (e.g., surveys, interviews) in which people are asked to report how they feel about a person or group with the assumption that they are both willing and able to report their attitudes accurately. Implicit attitude measures start with the assumption that at its core an attitude toward a social group is simply a mental association between a group and a good or a bad feeling. Such mental associations vary in terms of how quickly they come to mind (i.e., how mentally accessible they are). For example, if a person holds a strong negative attitude toward a group, when he or she sees a member of that group, the negative evaluation should come to mind quickly and automatically. By contrast, if a person holds a weak negative attitude toward a group, when he or she encounters a group member, the negative evaluation should come to mind much more slowly. In other words, the speed with which good or bad evaluations come to mind can serve as an important indirect indicator of people's attitudes toward particular groups without us having to ask them to report how they feel. Based on this logic, implicit attitudes are typically measured using rapid reaction time tasks that capture the speed with which good or bad concepts are associated with particular groups that participants see.

In our study, we used a rapid task called the Implicit Association Test (IAT) to measure people's implicit racial attitudes. This task measured the speed with which people associated African Americans and White Americans (represented by popular first names in each racial/ethnic community) with words that are strongly positive or strongly negative in meaning. Study participants sat at a computer and saw names and positive/negative words flash briefly, one at a time, on a computer screen. Their task was to categorize each name or word by pressing one of two response keys on the keyboard as instructed. We measured the speed with which people did the classification task when Black names and good words were to be classified together using the same response key and White names and bad words were to be classified together using a different response key. We compared these responses to another part of the task where response instructions were reversed: now Black names and bad words were to be classified together and White names and good words were to be classified together. If good thoughts pop into mind more quickly and easily when people think of Whites than Blacks, then they should respond faster on the IAT when White is paired with good and Black with bad than vice versa. And this is what past research has typically found for non-Black participants. The vast majority of participants in past studies showed strong implicit preference for White Americans and relative bias against African Americans on IATs and other similar tasks (Nosek, Banaji, & Greenwald, 2002a).

In our study, we investigated if the magnitude of implicit race bias against African Americans would be substantially reduced if people are first immersed in a pro-Black media environment rather than a pro-White media environment or even a control environment. We also wanted to determine if implicit bias reduction (if it occurred) would endure over time and continue to be revealed the next day if we brought people back into the lab and retested their implicit attitudes 24 hours later. Our results strongly supported our hypothesis. As illustrated in Figure 5.1, study participants who had been

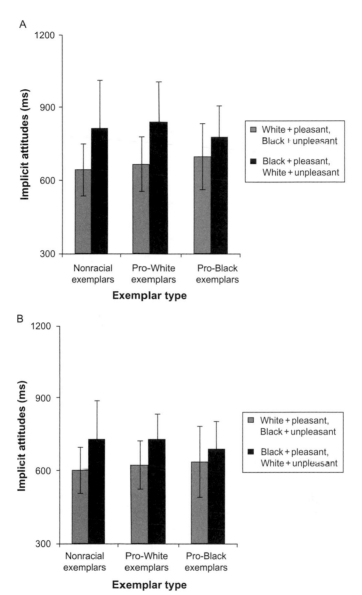

Figure 5.1 (A) Implicit racial attitudes immediately after exposure to pro-Black versus pro-White media images. (B) Implicit racial attitudes 24 h after exposure to pro-Black versus pro-White media images.

immersed in a pro-Black media environment expressed significantly less implicit race bias than others who had been immersed in a pro-White media environment or a nonracial environment. Importantly, the prejudice reduction effect endured for at least 24 hours holding steady when participants' implicit attitudes were measured again the next day without reminding them of the media environment in which they had been immersed the previous day (Dasgupta & Greenwald, 2001, Study 1).

In a follow-up study, we tested the same hypothesis for a different group— the elderly. We wanted to determine if implicit ageism against the elderly could be reduced by placing people in a media environment where they saw admired and famous older people together with disliked and infamous young people (*pro-elderly media environment*) compared to the opposite (*pro-young media environment*). Similar to the previous study, we found a significant reduction in implicit bias against the elderly among people who had been immersed in a local media environment that afforded exposure to admired elderly individuals compared to others immersed in a different media environment that afforded exposure to admired young individuals (Dasgupta & Greenwald, 2001, Study 2).

6.2. How brief media environments and everyday local communities jointly impact implicit bias

The research described above created local environments in the laboratory to determine their impact on implicit attitudes. Another way to examine the power of local environments is to focus on naturally existing communities and measure how often people come in contact with admired members of a stereotyped group in their local community. Does positive contact with such admired members influence people's implicit attitudes toward the group as a whole? What is the combined effect of living in diverse local environments and experiencing diverse media environments on people's implicit attitudes? And finally, how do naturally existing local environments and brief media environments influence behavioral intentions and decisions related to implicit bias?

Luis Rivera and I took up these questions in a study on implicit bias against gays and lesbians (Dasgupta & Rivera, 2008). We recruited adult nonstudent community members in an urban area who varied in the degree of contact they had with gays and lesbians in their everyday local environment. Some participants were embedded in relatively diverse local environment where they had several friends, coworkers, and sometimes family members who were gay or lesbian. Other participants were embedded in a homogeneous local environment (at least with regard to sexual orientation) where they did not know anyone who was gay or lesbian in their community. We randomly assigned these participants to one of two experimental conditions. Participants in one condition were immersed in a media environment where they saw pictures and biographies of admired and famous individuals who were gay or lesbian. These were individuals who were actors and celebrities (e.g., Rupert Everett), authors and writers (e.g., Alice Walker), athletes (e.g., Martina Navratilova), politicians (e.g., Barney Frank), and so on. This media manipulation was conceptually identical to the studies described earlier (Dasgupta & Greenwald, 2001). Participants in the other (control) condition saw positive information unrelated to gays and lesbians (pictures and descriptions of flowers). We hypothesized that participants who did not have any contact with well-liked gays and lesbians in their everyday local environment would benefit substantially from a gay-friendly media intervention, whereas other participants who had frequent positive contact with gays and lesbians in their everyday local environment would not benefit much from a gay-friendly media intervention (Dasgupta & Rivera, 2008).

Consistent with our predictions, and as shown in Figure 5.2A and B, results showed that people whose everyday environments were homogeneous— that is, who did not have any gays or lesbians in their social network—benefited *most* from exposure to gay-friendly media. Specifically, this group showed significantly less implicit prejudice against gays and lesbians and more support for gay-friendly legislation about same-sex marriage, adoption of children, and other civil rights legislation after exposure to a gay-friendly media compared to other positive (but nongay) media. In comparison, participants whose everyday local environment was diverse—who had several gays and lesbians in their social network—did not need gay-friendly media exposure. Their implicit attitudes showed low levels of implicit bias and their voting intentions were relatively gay-friendly regardless of the type of media exposure they experienced in the lab.

6.3. The take-away

Collectively, the research findings described above illustrate that multiple types of local environments can decrease implicit prejudice toward outgroups. These include a person's local community and social network in everyday life— their friends, well-liked classmates, coworkers, and neighbors. Local environments also include brief virtual situations people step into and out of through the books and magazines they read; the TV shows,

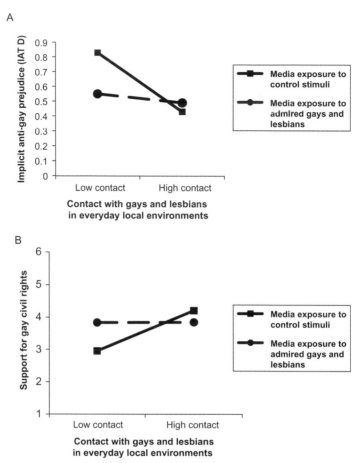

Figure 5.2 (A) Implicit attitudes toward gays and lesbians after exposure to admired gay and lesbian media images and after everyday contact with gay people. (B) Support for gay civil rights legislation after exposure to admired gay and lesbian media images and after everyday contact with gay people.

movies, and online media they watch. Our data show that not only do these various local environments reduce implicit bias in one's attitudes, but they also increase people's support for public policies and legislation focused on fixing structural bias and extending equal rights to all groups.

It is worth noting that in everyday life people may land in these beneficial local environments in different ways. In some cases, people choose counter-stereotypic local environments because of their preexisting attitudes and values, but in other cases, they land in these local environments by happen-stance—for example, if a family member or friend happens to come out as gay or lesbian or if their college or workplace happens to have diverse group members who people get to know and like. Regardless of choice, being embedded in naturally existing local environments that facilitate positive contact with members of stereotyped groups create and reinforce positive implicit associations, thereby counteracting implicit bias. For others who are embedded in relatively homogeneous environments where contact with admired members of stereotyped groups is rare, brief media exposure to such admired members is invaluably effective.

The focus of the above research was on *implicit attitudes*—that is, the degree to which people *like* or *dislike* an outgroup quickly and automatically. But this is only one form of implicit bias. Implicit bias can take other forms as well that are quite different. Take, for example, the implicit assumption that individuals named Jorge Garcia and Hong-Kun Zhang cannot possibly be *really* American, while others named Greg Baker and Emily Walsh are unquestionably American. This example captures implicit bias about nationality. Who is seen as legitimately American and who is seen as a perpetual foreigner? Can implicit bias about nationality be reduced to enhance the recognition that diverse types of individuals are authentically American? These questions lie at the heart of a second line of research described below.

7. DO CHANGES IN LOCAL ENVIRONMENTS IMPACT PERCEIVERS' IMPLICIT BIAS ABOUT NATIONALITY?

Not only do specific local environments change people's implicit attitudes toward outgroups, but they also shape people's implicit beliefs and assumptions about outgroup members' national identity. One strand of my research in collaboration with Kumar Yogeeswaran sheds light on this issue. We ask—who is seen as legitimately American and who is not? How malleable are these beliefs? How can implicit beliefs about nationality be rendered more inclusive? The 14th Amendment of the American Constitution defines American citizenship as follows: "All persons born or naturalized in the United States, and subject to the jurisdiction thereof, are citizens of the United States and of the State wherein they reside." While this legal definition draws a bright line separating who is American from who is not, the psychological boundary defining nationality is fuzzier—driven by social norms, stereotypes, the context in which the question is asked, and who is answering the question.

A growing literature that predates our research suggests that Americans' perceptions of who is authentically American are often driven by who seems prototypical or representative of the country based on dimensions such as race or religion (Devos & Banaji, 2005; Devos, Gavin, & Quintana, 2010; Devos & Ma, 2008; Dovidio, Gluszek, John, Ditlmann, & Lagunes, 2010). People grant American identity more easily to Whites than to Blacks, Asians, and Latinos even if they were born and raised in the United States. Sometimes these beliefs emerge particularly starkly when measured unobtrusively with implicit tasks (Devos & Banaji, 2005; Devos et al., 2010; Devos & Ma, 2008). At other times, they also emerge in self-reports (Cheryan & Monin, 2005; Dovidio et al., 2010). The American-is-White stereotype leads to implicit misattribution of American nationality to celebrities who are clearly not American. For example, European celebrities who are White (e.g., Hugh Grant) are miscategorized as American more readily than African American celebrities are correctly categorized as American (e.g., Michael Jordan; Devos & Banaji, 2005). The miscategorization effect is stronger when perceivers' attention is focused on the famous individuals' race than on their individuality (Devos & Ma, 2008).

The stereotype that American-is-White exists despite widespread societal endorsement of multiculturalism which embraces the idea that there are multiple ways of being American without having to look the same and assimilate into the national melting pot. In our initial research, we sought to examine the behavioral consequences of this stereotype in order to determine whether the implicit stereotype that American-is-White would lead to behavioral discrimination in terms of hiring and employment. To test this hypothesis, we conducted a two-session study. In the first session, participants completed an IAT, a speeded categorization task that assessed people's implicit stereotype about who is "truly" American. During this task, participants saw quintessential American symbols (e.g., the American flag, symbol of the bald eagle, Statue of Liberty) and symbols of other countries (e.g., foreign flag, symbols, and architecture) flashed rapidly on a computer screen one at a time. Interspersed among these symbols were faces of White and Asian individuals. Participants' task was to classify these symbols and faces using two keys on the keyboard. In one part of the task, they were asked to classify White faces and American symbols using the same key (White + American) and Asian faces and foreign symbols (Asian + foreign) using the other key. In another part of the task, key assignment was switched (White + foreign, Asian + American). We unobtrusively measured how quickly and easily participants associated White faces and American symbols compared to Asian faces and American symbols. Faster responses on White + American compared to Asian + American would indicate participants' implicit assumption that quintessential American symbols are linked to Whites more than Asians. Next, after a few filler tasks, we used a survey instrument to measure the degree to which participants thought various ethnic groups (including White Americans and Asian Americans) are patriotic and loyal to the United States, love the United States and are likely to defend America when it is criticized.

One week later, the same participants returned to a different location for what they thought was a different study on employment decisions. During this session, they were asked to evaluate job candidates for an important job in the National Security Agency (NSA) of the United States. Participants read a job description of a forensic investigator at the NSA. The position called for an individual who examines potential breaches to the nation's security by identifying and analyzing forensic evidence from criminal investigations related to national security thereby defending the country from foreign threats. Most elements of the job description were culled from actual jobs listed on the NSA's Web site. We created equally qualified resumes that ostensibly belonged to a shortlist of the top five candidates who had applied for this job. Each resume included demographic information about the candidate (gender, date of birth, place of birth, citizenship), educational background, and employment history. All resumes were matched for age, education, and prior work experience. The only difference was applicants' race which was indicated by their names: two of the candidates had Chinese sounding names (e.g., Sung Chang, Meilin Huang) and three of the candidates had European sounding names (e.g., Allen McMillan, Susan Cutting). In order to ensure that participants knew that the Asian American candidates were U.S. born, we included place of birth in the resumes and all resumes explicitly mentioned that the candidates were American citizens. Participants were asked to evaluate and rank order the candidates in terms of hireability based on their work experience and fit for the job.

As predicted, results revealed the more strongly people held the implicit stereotype that American-is-White the more they doubted Asian Americans' patriotism and loyalty to the United States, which in turn drove them to reject a qualified Asian American candidate and to hire a White candidate instead (Yogeeswaran & Dasgupta, 2010, Studies 1 and 2). A follow-up study replicated this finding and also showed that this hiring bias only occurred for jobs in national security but not for identical jobs outside of national security in the corporate world, indicating again that the bias was driven by doubts about Asian Americans' nationality and patriotism (Yogeeswaran & Dasgupta, 2010, Study 2).

We were interested in taking this work further by investigating whether the restrictive stereotype about who is American would become more malleable and inclusive if study participants are immersed in a local media environment where they are exposed to life stories of admired and well-known ethnic minority Americans. We tested this general idea using a media exposure procedure borrowed from our prior research. Our specific hypotheses in this line of work were informed by political science research which argues that there are two competing representations of American identity. Sometimes American identity is defined in terms of a shared ethnocultural heritage originating in Europe (we call this the *ethnocultural prototype* of who is American). At other times, American identity is defined in terms of Americans' shared commitment to civic responsibility and the public good (we call this the *civic responsibility prototype* of who is American). We hypothesized that highlighting the civic responsibility prototype would make national boundaries become more open and inclusive in one's mind because citizens of all stripes can contribute to the public good and fit this prototype. In contrast, we expected that highlighting the ethnocultural prototype should make national boundaries more restrictive in one's mind because only Americans of European descent can fit this prototype.

To test these hypotheses, we conducted a series of experiments in which research participants were placed in a media environment created in the laboratory where they read life stories of several admired well-known Americans (all Hispanic Americans). We orthogonally manipulated whether these life stories emphasized target individuals' civic responsibility or their ethnocultural heritage (Yogeeswaran, Dasgupta, & Gomez, 2012). For civic responsibility, we manipulated whether target individuals' professional work was framed as serving the national good or serving the local community. This manipulation allowed us to test whether national inclusion of ethnic minorities depends on any public service that exemplifies civic responsibility or whether ethnic minorities have to engage in work that specifically benefits the nation in order to overcome doubts about their patriotism. For example, in the "national service" condition, participants read about Luis Alvarez, a pioneering physicist who is Hispanic American, whose research was described as "helping in the creation of more energy efficient technologies that will reduce America's dependence on foreign oil." In the "local service" condition, participants read about the same physicist whose research was described as "helping in the creation of more energy efficient technologies that will generate grants for the university."

For ethnocultural identity, we manipulated whether individuals in the biographies were described as strongly identified with their ethnic group or no mention was made about ethnic identity. For example, in the strong ethnic identification condition, participants read about the same Hispanic

American physicist, Luis Alvarez, described earlier with the following sentences inserted in his biography: "Some of his fondest childhood memories come from dinner conversations with his parents and siblings in Spanish. As a child, his parents always encouraged him to speak Spanish as a way of preserving his Hispanic heritage." In the other condition where no ethnic identification information was provided, the above-mentioned language was modified as follows: "Some of his fondest childhood memories come from dinner conversations with his parents and siblings. As a child, his parents always encouraged him to grow his vocabulary and communicate effectively." In a final control condition, participants did not read about ethnic minorities. Thus, this study used a 2 (ethnocultural prototype) × 2 (civic responsibility prototype) + 1 (control) factorial design. We then measured whether exposure to these four types of media environments influenced the degree to which participants implicitly viewed ethnic minorities as American using the same IAT described earlier.

As shown in Figure 5.3, results showed that emphasizing Hispanic American individuals' national service (rather than their local service) made their entire ethnic group be seen as less foreign and more American because such portrayals highlighted their fit with the civic responsibility prototype. However, emphasizing Hispanic American individuals' ethnic identity (vs. making no mention of it) made them appear more foreign and less American because such portrayals highlighted their deviance from the ethnocultural prototype of European American heritage. In a subsequent study, we identified the underlying psychological process responsible for these effects. We

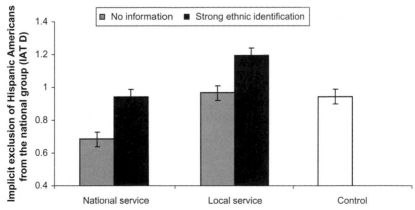

Figure 5.3 Implicit exclusion of Hispanics from being seen as American after media exposure to different types of Hispanic individuals.

found that highlighting minorities' ethnic identity increased concern that American distinctiveness was being threatened and diluted by "foreign influences," which in turn increased the American-is-White bias. In contrast, highlighting minorities' civic contribution to the nation increased pride in American distinctiveness, which in turn decreased the American-is-White bias.

7.1. Public versus private expressions of ethnic identity have different effects on national inclusion

Not all ethnic identity expressions are the same. Extending the above-mentioned research, we proposed that perceivers draw a bright psychological line separating public expressions of ethnic identity from private expressions (Yogeeswaran, Adelman, Parker, & Dasgupta, 2012; Yogeeswaran, Dasgupta, Adelman, Eccleston, & Parker, 2011). We proposed that strong ethnic identity is likely to be accepted when it is practiced in the privacy of one's home but rejected when it is practiced in public life because public expressions openly violate the national prototype of what it means to be American (see Branscombe, Ellemers, Spears, & Doosje, 1999; Marques & Paez, 1994). Consider, for example, situations in which ethnic groups maintain and express their group identity through languages other than English. People may speak their ethnic language with fellow co-ethnics only in the privacy of their home or they may also speak their language in public spheres such as in restaurants, stores, and on the street. We propose that when perceivers learn that ethnic minorities speak a language other than English in public spaces they are more likely to see this group as un-American than when they learn that ethnic minorities speak their language at home. Whereas the former situation challenges mainstream norms and practices and evokes distinctiveness threat, the latter does not.

We also investigated if White and non-White ethnic groups are held to the same standard such that private ethnic identity expression is okay but public expression is not. Given accumulating research showing that the prototypical "true" American is automatically imagined to be White rather than of any other race, we expected that White ethnic groups may be implicitly regarded as American no matter how they express ethnic identity—publicly or privately; but non-White ethnic groups may be implicitly regarded as American *only* if they limit ethnic identity expressions to the home.

Two experiments were conducted to test the above predictions (Yogeeswaran et al., 2011). Participants were immersed in a local environment in the lab where they read life stories of some Americans who were either members of ethnic minorities (e.g., Native American, Chinese American) or members of White ethnic groups (Polish American). All target individuals were portrayed as equally ethnically identified; however, we manipulated whether these individuals expressed their ethnic identity in private only or in both public and private. Ethnic identity expression was-operationalized by individuals' use of their ethnic language. For example, in the public identification condition participants read about a Native American individual who spoke his native language with family and friends in both private and public spheres (e.g., "To this day, Thomas continues speaking Lakota Sioux both at home and in public with his family and friends."). In the private ethnic identification condition, the same individual was described as speaking his native language in private spheres *only* (e.g., "Although Thomas continues speaking in Lakota Sioux at home with his family, he only speaks English when he is out in public."). Likewise other participants read about a Polish American individual who spoke Polish with family and friends in private only (in one condition) or spoke Polish with friends and family in private and public (in the second condition).

Then later, under the guise of a "separate and unrelated study," we measured the effect of this media exposure on participants' implicit and explicit construal of the entire ethnic group as legitimately American. Results indicated that at an explicit level, White and non-White ethnic groups were held to the same standard and construed as significantly less American when members expressed their ethnic identity publicly rather than privately. However, at an implicit level, a double standard emerged: non-White ethnic groups were implicitly rejected as less American if members expressed ethnic identity publicly rather than privately, while White ethnics were implicitly accepted as legitimate Americans no matter how they expressed ethnic identity—publicly or privately.

7.2. The take-away

Collectively, this program of research highlights that local media environments influence the degree to which ethnic minorities are implicitly included as legitimately American. When local media environments define the American people as individuals who work for the public good and provide examples of ethnic minority individuals who fit this prototype, such media enhances the implicit perception that ethnic minorities as a group are genuinely American. However, when local media environments define the American people as individuals who share a common history rooted in

Europe, ethnic minority individuals are hard pressed to fit this prototype especially if they feel identified with their ethnic group. This type of media environment exacerbates the implicit perception that ethnic minorities are perpetual foreigners in America.

Another important take-home message from this research is the cost of ethnic identity expression for minority groups. Specifically, if White Americans encounter ethnic minority individuals in their local environment who express their ethnic identity publicly, such exposure makes perceivers implicitly view ethnic groups as quite foreign. However, if they encounter ethnic minority individuals who keep their ethnic identity private and separate, such exposure leads to more national inclusion.

Thus, the stereotype that the prototypical American-is-White is not a fixed immutable belief, but rather one that changes depending on the type of local environment in which perceivers are embedded and whether or not they see ethnic minority individuals who fit American norms and prototypes. For ethnic minorities, the dilemma is between freely expressing their ethnic identity and potentially being seen as a perpetual foreigner versus limiting their ethnic identity to the private domain and being accepted as American.

The two programs of research described thus far shine a spotlight on perceivers' implicit attitudes and beliefs toward *outgroups*—groups to which they do not belong—with the goal of illustrating that even strongly biased attitudes and beliefs can be attenuated by changing local environments. We now shift focus to people's implicit attitudes and beliefs about their *ingroup*—groups to which they belong—and the impact of those ingroup beliefs on their self-concept.

8. DO CHANGES IN LOCAL ENVIRONMENTS INFLUENCE IMPLICIT STEREOTYPES ABOUT ONE'S INGROUP?

If immersion in counterstereotypic local environments reduces implicit bias against outgroups, will a similar benefit occur for ingroups? This question is important because implicit bias can operate like an "equal opportunity virus" that infects people's unconscious assumptions about their ingroup's abilities and competencies, as well as the outgroup's abilities. Take for example, the gender stereotype that women are less suited for professional leadership roles than men and more suited for caretaking roles than men. This stereotype is shared by women as well as men (Diekman & Eagly, 2008; Eagly & Carli, 2007; Eagly & Karau, 2002; Rudman & Kilianski, 2000; Swim & Hyers, 2008) and has been documented using implicit and explicit belief measures (Dasgupta & Asgari, 2004; Rudman & Glick, 2001; Rudman & Kilianski, 2000). Using the gender-leadership stereotype as the starting point, Shaki Asgari and I sought to determine whether women's implicit beliefs about their group's leadership ability would become less stereotypic if they were embedded in local environments where they encountered professional women in leadership roles (Dasgupta & Asgari, 2004).

Using a multimethod approach, we tested our hypothesis in a pair of studies: one was a controlled lab experiment and the second was a field study that took advantage of natural variations in local environments. In the lab experiment, we randomly assigned female participants to a lab environment where they saw pictures and biographies about famous women who are leaders in their profession such as Ruth Bader Ginsberg (U.S. Supreme Court justice), Madeline Albright (former Secretary of State), Toni Morrison (winner of the Nobel Prize for literature), and Eileen Collins (first American woman to pilot a spacecraft). Other female participants were randomly assigned to the control condition where they read about non-gendered information. Subsequently, we measured all participants' implicit beliefs about gender and leadership using an IAT that assessed how quickly and easily they associated leadership attributes (e.g., ambitious, dynamic, leader) and supportive attributes (e.g., helpful, compassionate, supporter) with female names compared to male names. If people show implicit stereotypes about gender and leadership, we expected they would be much faster at associating male names with leadership attributes and female names with supportive attributes than vice versa.

In the second study, we recruited young women who had recently entered a naturally existing environment where they were more likely to see women in leadership roles (a women's college) or less likely to see women in such roles (a coeducational college). These two colleges were of similar quality and located in the same town. Using a longitudinal research design, we tracked female students from these two types of colleges from the beginning to end of their first year on campus. At the beginning of their first year in college, we assessed participants' implicit beliefs about gender and leadership using the same IAT described in the previous study. We also measured participants' experiences on campus (e.g., what classes they were taking, the gender of their professors, who they viewed as role models on campus, etc.). One year later, at the beginning of their sophomore year, we recontacted the same participants and administered the same measures again. Our goal was to use converging methods to test whether naturally existing local environments that provide exposure to women leaders (type of college campus) and experimentally created local environments that do the same (media exposure in the lab) would both enhance young women's implicit beliefs about women's leadership.

As predicted, results from both lab and field studies revealed that when female students were immersed in local environments where they saw many women in professional leadership roles they were significantly less likely to implicitly assume that men make better leaders than women than female students in comparison environments. The field study further demonstrated that at entry into college female students at both institutions had similar gender stereotypic beliefs; but by the end of their first year their implicit beliefs had diverged substantially as a function of their college campus or local environment. Students at the women's college exhibited no implicit gender stereotypes at all at the end of their first year (i.e., they associated leadership roles equally with women and men), whereas their peers at the coed college exhibited very strong gender stereotypes (i.e., they associated leadership roles with men and supporter roles with women). Importantly, the frequency with which students met professional women on campus (particularly female faculty) mediated the beneficial effect of the women's college. Students who had more female faculty as course instructors during their first year showed less implicit gender stereotyping than others who had fewer female faculty as instructors in the same year. Because the women's college had more female faculty than the coed college, students at the women's college showed reduced implicit gender stereotypes over time compared to their peers at the coed college. Together, these studies reveal the power of local environments in shaping women's implicit beliefs about their ingroup's professional leadership abilities.

9. DO CHANGES IN LOCAL ENVIRONMENTS HAVE SIMILAR EFFECTS ON INDIVIDUALS' IMPLICIT SELF-CONCEPT?

Not only do ingroup stereotypes limit what people think their group can accomplish, but they also constrain individuals' perceptions of their own skills and competencies thereby limiting their academic and professional trajectories. People tend to gravitate toward achievement domains that feel comfortable because they conform to ingroup stereotypes and they gravitate away from other domains that feel uncomfortable because they deviate too far from ingroup stereotypes. Consider the case of girls and women in science, technology, engineering, and mathematics (STEM). Research shows even girls and women who perform well in STEM often feel less confident about their ability than their male peers, express less positivity toward STEM majors and careers, and are less likely to pursue these majors and careers than their male peers (Ceci, Wiliams, & Barnett, 2009; Ceci & Williams, 2011; Eccles, Wigfield, Harold, & Blumenfeld, 1993; Else-Quest, Hyde, & Linn, 2010; Mendez, Mihalas, & Hardesty, 2006; Park, Lubinski, & Benbow, 2007; Robertson, Smeets, Lubinski, & Benbow, 2010; Stout, Dasgupta, Hunsinger, & McManus, 2011). These studies and others suggest that cultural stereotypes alleging that women are less skilled in STEM compared to men implicitly shape girls' and women's self-concept, making them doubt their ability in science and engineering and avoid majors and careers in STEM (Dasgupta, 2011; Nosek, Banaji, & Greenwald, 2002b; Nosek et al., 2009; Stout et al., 2011). How might one inoculate women against these stereotypes so that more women who are talented in math and science consider themselves as potential scientists and engineers in the future?

Just as small changes in local environments affect women's implicit beliefs about their ingroup's ability, similarly small changes in local environments ought to bolster women's implicit beliefs about their own ability in traditionally masculine fields and professions in STEM. Put differently, who women aspire to become is likely to be heavily influenced by individuals they see in successful roles and professions and the degree to which they relate to those individuals, assuming of course a basic foundation of skills in a given achievement domain (Asgari, Dasgupta, & Gilbert Cote, 2010; Asgari, Dasgupta, & Stout, 2012; Dasgupta & Asgari, 2004; Lockwood & Kunda, 1997, 1999). To describe how local environments influence self-concept change, I developed a new theoretical model—the Stereotype Inoculation Model. In this model, shown in Figure 5.4, I proposed that analogous to biomedical vaccines that protect and inoculate individuals' body against viruses and bacteria, so too ingroup experts and peers in high achievement environments serve as *social vaccines* that protect and inoculate individuals' mind and sense of self against pernicious stereotypes (Dasgupta, 2011; Stout et al., 2011).

Four broad predictions emerge from the Stereotype Inoculation Model. First, as shown in Figure 5.4, I predict that contact with successful ingroup experts and peers in high stakes achievement environments will inoculate individuals against self-doubt, especially in early years of academic and professional development and other transitional periods when their self-efficacy is in flux. Such contact will enhance beginners' positive attitudes toward the

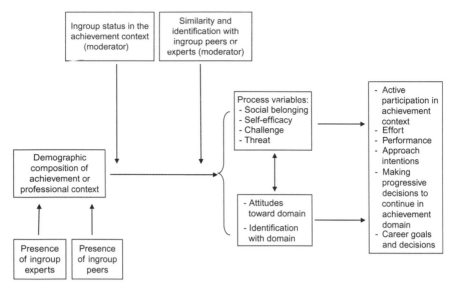

Figure 5.4 Stereotype Inoculation Model.

achievement domain, strengthen their identification with it, enhance self-efficacy, and increase motivation to pursue career goals in the domain.

Second, I hypothesize that contact with ingroup experts and peers will be especially important for individuals whose ingroup is a numeric minority and who are negatively stereotyped in an achievement domain (as is the case for girls and women in science and engineering). Contact with ingroup experts and peers will be relatively less important for others whose ingroup is the majority and expected to succeed by default (as is the case for boys and men in the same fields). For members of a negatively stereotyped group, seeing successful ingroup experts undercuts the negative stereotype and thus enhances their own self-efficacy and motivation to succeed (Blanton, Crocker, & Miller, 2000; Brewer & Weber, 1994).

Third, I expect that exposure to ingroup experts will be most beneficial if individuals feel a subjective sense of connection or identification with those experts because subjective identification makes the path from one's present self as a novice to a future "possible self" as an expert seem more attainable given that one can imagine following the career trajectory of the ingroup member (see Markus & Kunda, 1986; Markus & Nurius, 1986; Markus & Wurf, 1987).

Fourth, I predict that the impact of stereotypes on individuals' self-concept in high achievement domains will be subtle and often unconscious. Individuals themselves may be unaware that the experts and peers they encounter had any effect on their personal academic and professional interests and choices. Yet, the imprint of others ought to be evident in individuals' *implicit* self-conception—making them gravitate toward achievement domains where ingroup members are visible and away from domains where ingroup members are scarce. While individuals' implicit self-concept is often sensitive to people in their local environment, their explicit self-concept may remain relatively stable in the short term. This prediction is informed by theories and research in implicit social cognition, which show people are sometimes unable or unwilling to explicitly report their attitudes accurately because of incomplete awareness of how social contexts affect personal decisions and/or social desirability concerns (Dasgupta, 2004, 2009; Ferguson & Bargh, 2007; Greenwald & Banaji, 1995; Greenwald et al., 2002; Nisbett & Wilson, 1977; Nosek & Hansen, 2008; Petty et al., 2008; Wilson et al., 2000). Applied to the Stereotype Inoculation Model, I expect that contact with ingroup experts and peers will produce small changes in implicit self-conceptions that, initially, may be too subtle to be consciously noticed or reported (Greenwald & Banaji, 1995; Greenwald et al., 2002). Indeed, classic studies on the self-concept show that individuals spontaneously adjust and calibrate their working self-concept to fit with their social context and this is observed when measured indirectly, but not when measured directly by asking individuals to report their self-beliefs (Markus & Kunda, 1986; Markus & Nurius, 1986). At an implicit level, some self-traits become mentally accessible or valued by individuals more than other traits in particular situations, even though the global content of their explicit self-concept remain unchanged across situations.

Finally, I propose that four interrelated processes arc likely to serve as underlying psychological mechanisms responsible for the inoculation process when individuals encounter ingroup experts and peers in high achievement environments: (1) a stronger and more stable sense of belonging in the environment, (2) increased self-efficacy, (3) feeling challenged by difficulty, and (4) less threatened. Thus far, my graduate student collaborators and I have conducted several lab experiments and longitudinal studies test different pieces of this model.

9.1. Local environments implicitly influence women's academic self-concept

In one longitudinal study, we recruited students (both female and male) from a multiple sections of a college calculus class that is a prerequisite for all STEM majors on campus (Stout et al., 2011, Study 3). As a prerequisite or "gateway" course, this is a well-known site of student attrition from

STEM majors. Some of the calculus sections were taught by female professors while others were taught by male professors. Students were tracked from the beginning of the semester (September) to the end (December). At two time points in September and December, we measured students' implicit and explicit attitudes toward mathematics relative to humanities, identification with math relative to humanities, confidence in their math ability as assessed by their expected performance in calculus class, and the degree to which they identified with their math professor. Implicit attitudes were measured with an IAT that captured the relative speed with which participants associated words about math (equation, theorem, computation) versus humanities (poetry, Shakespeare, essay) with strongly positive and negative words (happy, warm, sad, death). Implicit identification with math was also measured with an IAT that captured the relative speed with which participants associated words about math versus humanities with first person pronouns (I, me, myself) compared to third person pronouns (they, them, theirs). As a performance measure, we obtained students' permission to get their calculus course grade from the registrar's office. Finally, to supplement our quantitative findings with qualitative data, we conducted classroom observations to capture student–faculty interactions at the beginning and end of the semester.

Although this was a quasi-experimental study, several important strengths of this study bring it very close to a controlled laboratory experiment. First, students preregistered for specific sections of this calculus class before the semester began—before professors had been assigned to each section. Thus, students could not have self-selected into specific sections based on prior knowledge of course professors including their gender. Second, thanks to unparalleled assistance from the Mathematics Department male and female professors who taught the sections from which we recruited our sample were matched in terms of their teaching skills, stage of career, and fluency in English. Third, professors teaching these sections were yoked to same-sex teaching assistants (TAs) to ensure that in the context of this class participants came into contact exclusively with female experts in mathematics (i.e., a lecture taught by a female professor and a discussion section led by a female TA) or male experts in mathematics (i.e., a lecture taught by a male professor and a discussion section led by a male TA). All instructors and TAs were blind to the real purpose of this study. Fourth, all course sections had identical syllabi and exams; thus, students learned the same material and were tested in the same way regardless of who their professors were. Finally, professors and TAs graded blind to students' identity and grading was shared across sections so that instructors did not necessarily grade their own students' exams. Thus, professors' evaluation of students' exams and their final grade could not have been biased by their preexisting expectations of any student.

The longitudinal design allowed us to assess whether the predicted benefit of contact with same-sex experts for female students takes effect immediately and remains stable across the semester or if it grows stronger over time. It also allowed us to test whether the benefit of same-sex experts endures after students leave class and move to other environments where the experts are not physically present. If the positive effect of contact is confined to the classroom where such experts are physically present, then testing students outside the calculus class in other situations should wipe out the benefit.

Consistent with predictions from the Stereotype Inoculation Model, we found that for female students, contact with female (compared to male) professors enhanced implicit positive attitudes toward math, increased implicit identification with the field, and bolstered their self-efficacy in math (see Figures 5.5A and B and 5.6A). For male students, professor gender had no effect on their attitudes, identification, and self-efficacy in math. Interestingly, even though women's self-efficacy fluctuated as a function of who their professor was, in terms of their final grade in calculus women outperformed their male peers on average across all sections of calculus regardless of the professor's gender (see Figure 5.6B). Despite their superior performance, women's attitudes toward math, confidence in their ability, and identification with the field were substantially lower than that of their male peers when they were in sections taught by male professors. In contrast, in sections taught by female professors, their attitudes toward math, identification with the field, and confidence bounced up to the same level as their male peers. Put differently, strong performance in mathematics was not enough to protect women's academic self-concept in math when they were immersed in a class environment that was stereotypically masculine. Contact with female experts (the professor and TA) was necessary to inoculate and strengthen their self-concept in mathematics. We also found the more women identified with female math professors at the beginning of the academic semester, the higher their self-efficacy in math at the end of the semester. But women's identification with male math professors had no effect on their self-efficacy.

To supplement and enrich the quantitative measurement of students' attitudes and self-concept, we also collected qualitative data on classroom dynamics by conducting in-class observations. Research assistants observed students' behavior in class and coded interactions with their professor once at the beginning and once at the end of the semester. They coded the number of times

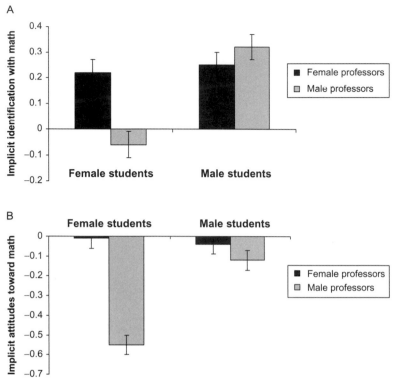

Figure 5.5 (A) Students' implicit identification with mathematics after exposure to a female or male mathematics professor in class. (B) Students' implicit attitudes toward mathematics after exposure to a female or male mathematics professor in class.

students asked questions in class, answered professors' questions in class, and sought help from professors after class. From this, we calculated the percentage of female and male students who engaged in each behavior. These descriptive data revealed that female students became more responsive over time toward their female professors in terms of speaking up in class (this behavior did not change when professors were male). At the same time, they became more avoidant with their male professors over time in that they stopped seeking his help after class (this behavior did not change for female professors). Together, these results suggest that female experts may produce an approach-oriented response in terms of women's motivation to stay in STEM, while at the same time male experts may produce an avoidance-oriented response.

To complement this longitudinal field study, we conducted two other controlled lab experiments which replicated and extended the same pattern of results described above. In one such study, female students majoring in

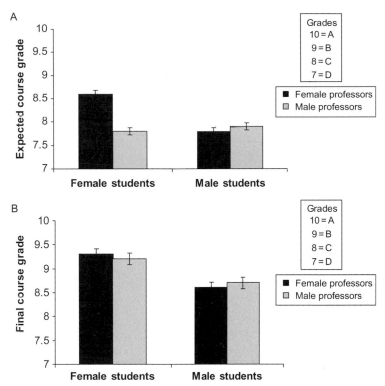

Figure 5.6 (A) Students' expected course grade in mathematics after exposure to a female or male mathematics professor in class. (B) Students' actual course grade in mathematics after exposure to a female or male mathematics professor in class.

STEM disciplines participated in a study on math ability where they were randomly assigned to come to a lab environment where they interacted with a senior math student who was either female or male. After a brief interaction, we measured participants' implicit attitudes toward math, their implicit identification with the field, their performance, and effort on a difficult math test. Results showed that after an interaction with the female math student, female participants showed more implicit positive attitudes toward math, more implicit identification with math, and more effort on the math test compared to other participants who had interacted with a male student majoring in math (Stout et al., 2011, Study 1).

In another study, female engineering students were randomly assigned to a lab-based media environment where they saw pictures and professional biographies of female engineers, male engineers, or they read about engineering innovations without any mention of the engineer's gender. We then measured participants' implicit attitudes toward engineering, subjective identification with the engineers they had read about, self-efficacy, and career aspirations in engineering (Stout et al., 2011, Study 2). Replicating the previous studies, we found that immersion in a media environment that provided exposure to successful female engineers increased young women's implicit positive attitudes toward engineering compared to the other two conditions. Further, the more women identified with female engineers whose biographies they had read the stronger their own self-efficacy in engineering and implicit identification with the field, both of which mediated and predicted more career aspirations in engineering. Identification with male engineers did not predict women's self-efficacy, identification with engineering as a field, or career intentions.

9.2. The take-away

A consistent theme across all these studies is that small modifications in local classroom environments changed the way women implicitly conceived their academic self. Seeing same-sex experts in academic environments enhanced women's implicit attitudes and identification with math and engineering, even though their explicit attitudes and beliefs remained unchanged. Importantly, in talking to participants at the end of the study, it was eminently clear that these women were unaware that the people they came in contact with in class or read about in the lab had any effect on their own academic self-concept and career goals. Like most people, participants described their academic interests as driven mostly by their intrinsic interest and motivation. They were unaware of the profound effects their local environments were having on their intellectual self-concept and career trajectories.

9.3. Same-sex experts in local environments are most effective if framed as similar to the self

While contact with same-sex experts in local environments produces subtle changes in young women's self-concept, our empirical work and theoretical model suggest this is more likely if individuals see themselves as similar to those same-sex experts. Similarity between the self and other makes the path from one's current self as a novice to a future self as a professional leader seem more attainable because one can imagine following the same trajectory as this expert. Instead of being portrayed as similar to the self, if female experts are portrayed as "superstars" who are unique and exceptional, they have little impact on young women's views of themselves (see also Lockwood &

Kunda, 1997, 1999). Some evidence for this prediction comes from studies on women in STEM described earlier where we found that young women who identified more strongly with female experts in math and engineering reported greater self-efficacy and more ambitious career aspirations in math and engineering (Stout et al., 2011, Studies 2 and 3).

Additional evidence comes from our studies on women's self-views as professional leaders. For example, in a longitudinal field study I conducted with Shaki Asgari and Nicole Gilbert Cote, we tracked young women across 1 year in college (Asgari et al., 2010). At the beginning of their first year and again in their sophomore year, we measured women's implicit beliefs about their own leadership ability relative to their male peers using an IAT that assessed how quickly and easily they associated agentic qualities (ambitious, go-getter) versus communal qualities (helpful, nurturing) with the self relative to others. We also recorded the classes participants were taking, the gender of their professors, the quality of their relationship with those professors, class participation as an instance of intellectually assertive behavior, and their career goals. We computed how frequently each participant had come in contact with female faculty members and academic leaders and how much they subjectively identified with those individuals. Results showed that frequent contact with female faculty produced more implicit attribution of leadership qualities to oneself and more ambitious career aspirations—but only when participants subjectively identified with those female faculty. Interestingly, frequent contact with female faculty did not have any effect on young women's self-concept when they did not identify with such female faculty. These findings suggest that changing implicit self-beliefs requires both frequent exposure to counterstereotypic ingroup members and feelings of connection with those individuals (Asgari et al., 2010).

In a subsequent series of lab experiments, we sought to provide a clearer causal test of the prediction that similarity with successful female experts in a local environment causes women's implicit self-beliefs to shift in the direction of leadership. So we manipulated similarity between female students' self-concept and the life stories of successful professional women (Asgari et al., 2012). In one such study, we brought young women into the lab and randomly assigned them to experience one of three media environments (Asgari et al., 2012, Study 3). All media environments involved pictures and biographies of successful women who are leaders in business, law, politics, science, and medicine. The difference between conditions lay in the instructions participants were given prior to media exposure. In one condition, participants were led to believe that these professional women had graduated

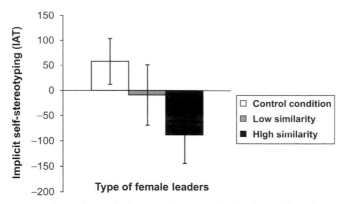

Figure 5.7 Women's implicit beliefs about their own leadership ability after exposure to successful female leaders portrayed as similar to oneself or different from oneself.

from their own undergraduate institution (*high similarity condition*). In a second condition, they were led to believe that the same women had graduated from a very different type of institution (*low similarity condition*). In the third control condition, participants were given no information about these successful women's college affiliation. After media exposure, in all cases we measured how much participants identified with these successful professional women. Then, under the guise of a separate experiment, we measured participants' implicit and explicit self-beliefs and their career goals and aspirations.

As illustrated in Figure 5.7, results showed that young women who were exposed to successful female leaders framed as similar to the self by virtue of their college affiliation implicitly viewed themselves *least* stereotypically feminine, and instead as having more leadership potential than participants in the control condition. The third group of participants who were exposed to the same successful female leaders but were told that these leaders were very different from the self by virtue of the colleges they had attended, did not show any change in their implicit self-beliefs compared to the control condition. In other words, successful women leaders only inspired female students' own leadership self-concept if similarity between them was made salient. Finally, in the case of career aspirations, exposure to successful female leaders framed as very different from oneself had a negative effect on young women. Participants reported significantly *lower* career aspirations after reading about successful women leaders framed as very different from the self compared to participants in the other two conditions. Thus, highly successful ingroup members framed as *dissimilar* from the self *deflate* women's career aspirations.

Two other studies provided converging evidence by manipulating similarity in other ways. In one study, high similarity was manipulated by describing women leaders' success as starting small, growing over time, and as something that is attainable for all women through hard work and persistence. In contrast, low similarity was manipulated by describing the same women leaders' success as driven by their exceptional ability that emerged early in life and is unattainable for most people. In the control condition participants did not see any biographies (Asgari et al., 2012, Study 1). In yet another study, participants were led to believe that their personality was very similar to that of successful women they had read about, or that their personality was very different, or no personality information was provided (Asgari et al., 2012, Study 2). After each of these manipulations, in both studies we measured participants' implicit beliefs about their own leadership ability. Results consistently revealed that young women's implicit leadership self-concept was enhanced if they had been immersed in a local environment where they saw successful women framed as similar to the self. However, when the same women were framed as different from the self, they either had no effect on participants' implicit self-beliefs or sometimes backfired—deflating participants' implicit self-beliefs about leadership (see also Parks-Stamm, Heilman, & Hearns, 2008; Rudman & Phelan, 2010).

9.4. The take-away

A consistent theme across all these studies is that encountering successful ingroup members in local environments inspires young people's self-concept only if similarity between those successful others and oneself is made salient. Successful ingroup members who are described as exceptional superstars often have no effect on ordinary individuals' implicit self-concept. In fact, sometimes their presence can have negative effects, deflating young people's implicit beliefs about what is personally attainable for oneself. The best social vaccines are admired ingroup members who share some important similarities with the self so that their success and visibility in a stereotypic domain makes one's own success seem plausible. Another important theme running through these studies is the finding that exposure to successful ingroup members can change individuals' implicit self-conceptions even though their explicit self-descriptions might not reveal any change.

The various programs of research I have described thus far illustrate the various ways in which passive observations of people and media in one's local environment influence individuals' implicit attitudes and beliefs. However, local environments can also exert an influence in a more active way—by arousing emotions and motivations in the individual. Strong negative emotions aroused in one local environment can linger in the mind and taint individuals' implicit attitudes in a different environment. This is another example of implicit attitude malleability that I examined in my research.

10. DO SPECIFIC EMOTIONS AROUSED IN ONE SITUATION SPILL OVER INTO ANOTHER TO BIAS IMPLICIT ATTITUDES TOWARD OUTGROUPS? WHAT EMOTIONS AND WHAT GROUPS?

In the final program of research in collaboration with David DeSteno, we are pursuing the topic of implicit bias malleability from a different angle—by examining how emotions and motivations activated by one local environment carries over into another, and biases perceivers' implicit attitudes and behavior toward outgroups. This project creates a synergy between implicit social cognition research and emotion research. Emotion theories argue that emotions allow individuals to adapt to obstacles and challenges in the environment (Damasio, 1994; Frijda, 1986; Keltner & Gross, 1999; LeDoux, 1996). These challenges include social interactions between groups. Because membership in social groups, and the benefits and conflicts inherent in those affiliations, play a central role in human life, we expect that appraisals of social groups will be informed by emotions via both automatic (implicit) and controlled (explicit) mental processes. Moreover, emotions that are functionally related to conflictual intergroup relations (e.g., anger, disgust, fear) are more likely to magnify implicit bias than other emotions that are unrelated to intergroup relations (e.g., sadness).

In an early series of experiments, we induced participants to feel angry, disgusted, sad, or neutral by recalling past events that had happened in their life. In a subsequent unrelated situation, we created minimal groups in the lab by giving participants a fake "personality test" and assigning them to one of two personality types allegedly based on their test results. We showed them photographs of people who apparently shared their personality type (the ingroup) and others who had a different personality type (the outgroup). We then measured participants' implicit attitudes toward these fictitious groups using an IAT that measured how quickly they were able to associate good versus bad words with pictures of ingroup and outgroup members. We found that participants who had previously recalled a past event in their life that had made them feel angry or disgusted expressed more implicit bias

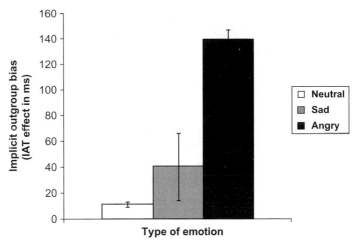

Figure 5.8 Implicit attitudes toward a fictitious outgroup after experiencing anger, sadness, or a neutral emotion.

against this unknown outgroup than others who had previously recalled a past event that had made them feel calm or neutral (see Figure 5.8). In other words, negative emotions carried over from one local environment to another without people's awareness and tainted their evaluations of these previously unknown group (Dasgupta, DeSteno, Williams, & Hunsinger, 2009; DeSteno, Dasgupta, Bartlett, & Cajdric, 2004). Interestingly, sadness had no effect on implicit outgroup attitudes and functioned much like a neutral state. The message here is that all negative emotions do not have the same carry-over effect. Negative emotions associated with intergroup conflict and competition (anger and disgust) carry over and get unconsciously applied to implicit evaluations of outgroups but other negative emotions that are not intergroup in nature (sadness) do not carry over in the same way.

Even though anger and disgust had similar biasing effects on attitudes toward unknown groups, they have very different effects on attitudes toward *known* groups about which people have preexisting knowledge. In a pair of studies, we put people in a mindset where they recalled a past event from a particular environment that had made them feel very angry, or very disgusted, or neutral. Participants had been randomly assigned to one of these three emotion recollection conditions. Subsequently, under the guise of an alleged "unrelated study," we assessed their implicit attitudes toward two known groups in another situation—gay men (Dasgupta et al., 2009, Study 2) and Arab men (Dasgupta et al., 2009, Study 3) using IATs. Our results showed that anger (but not disgust) increased implicit prejudice against Arabs, a group that triggers stereotypes about aggression and terrorism. And disgust (but not anger) increased implicit prejudice against gays and lesbians, a group that evokes stereotypes about moral contamination. In other words, the carry-over effect of negative emotions was remarkably nuanced. Participants' preexisting negative emotion magnified implicit prejudice only when the threat signaled by the particular emotion was applicable to the stereotype of the particular group being evaluated (Dasgupta et al., 2009). In our current research, we are extending beyond implicit attitudes to examine whether negative emotions escalate biased actions against outgroup members like aggression.

10.1. The take-away

Collectively, these studies show that local environments have the potential to cast long shadows. When people recall past events that happened in long-gone local environments, emotions aroused by those past environments become vivid in the present moment. It is easy for thoughts and feelings triggered by the past to color judgments and evaluations in the present. This type of misattribution may be particularly likely for implicit attitudes that are "gut reactions" that happen too fast to allow self-editing.

A second important lesson from these studies is that while many negative emotions broadly relevant to intergroup relations accentuate bias against unknown groups, not all negative emotions have this effect. Sadness, which is more of an interpersonal (rather than intergroup) emotion did not increase outgroup bias. When it comes to known groups about which people hold preexisting stereotypes, emotion-induced implicit biases are more specific. Our ongoing research is beginning to suggest that these biasing effects are not limited to attitudes only; they also extend to aggressive actions.

11. COMMON THEMES, UNANSWERED QUESTIONS, AND FUTURE DIRECTIONS

In this chapter, I have reviewed more than a decade of research conducted in my lab in which my collaborators and I have found that changes in local environments, social networks, and affective states evoke substantial shifts in people's implicit attitudes toward outgroups, implicit beliefs about the ingroup, and their self-concept. This review brings together four programs of research that share a common take-home message: implicit attitudes and beliefs reflect and adapt to social situations fairly effortlessly in the sense that they do not require perceivers' conscious introspection, deliberation, and intentional action. Several common themes and unanswered questions cut across these research programs. These, described below, are promising topics of future research.

11.1. The malleability of implicit attitudes and beliefs: How long does change endure?

Based on our data and theoretical conceptualization, I expect that individuals' implicit attitudes will reflect whatever local environments they are chronically immersed in. If they choose (or, through happenstance, find themselves in) situations and communities that increase exposure to counterstereotypic ingroup and outgroup members repeatedly, then bias reduction will endure. If, however, they briefly pass through counterstereotypic environments and then return to stereotypic local environments for the long term, I expect their implicit bias will reduce momentarily and then return to baseline. It bears repeating that by the term "local environment" I do not mean society at large, but rather the types of people and media representations the individual encounters in daily life—at home, work, and in their social network.

Even though implicit attitudes and beliefs adapt to situations in which the individual is immersed and change if subsequent situations are different, this does not mean that implicit attitude change is so fleeting that it fades away as soon as the person leaves the situation. In support of that position, in Dasgupta and Greenwald (2001), we found that the reduction in implicit race bias brought about by exposure to admired African Americans endured for at least 24 hours after the original experience. Even better, in Stout et al. (2011, Study 3), we found that positive implicit attitudes toward math and self-concept malleability elicited in female students who interacted with a female math professor in class remained even when students were not in that classroom environment nor reminded of it when their attitudes and self-conceptions were assessed in various other situations outside class. In other words, something about interacting with female professors lingered long after class was over and students were back in mostly male environments. What may have helped the durability of implicit self-concept change in this case is that students encountered the female math professor several times a week over the course of the semester. In other words, they had repeated exposure to a same-sex expert in a counterstereotypic local environment.

We are pursuing the durability question more directly in an ongoing study on peer mentoring in engineering. In this longitudinal study, we randomly assign first-year female students to female peer mentors who are advanced students in the same major, or equivalent male peer mentors, or no peer mentors for 1 year. After ensuring mentor–mentee contact for 1 year, we track participants' progress through the year and for the next several years until graduation long after their mentors have left in order to examine whether early contact with a female peer mentor in the first year of college will act as a social vaccine to protect and enhance women's engineering self-concept and success for the next 3 years of college (Dasgupta & Dennehy, 2012). Our hypothesis derived from the Stereotype Inoculation Model is that the first year of college is a critical period during which exposure to successful same-sex peers (or lack thereof) is more likely to "stick" and have a prolonged effect than is typical in other periods of time. As such, this study promises to provide a strong test of how long implicit self-concept change endures.

11.2. What is the mechanism that drives the effect of local environments on implicit attitudes?

Another unanswered question and possible direction of future research involves identifying underlying psychological processes that drive implicit attitude and belief change seen in our research. Recent theories by Sherman, Gawronski, Bodenhausen, and others have argued that implicit responses are driven by a mixture of automatic associations rendered accessible by the local environment and executive control driven by internal states such as goals, motivations, and emotions; these two processes are thought to work independently to influence social behavior (Conrey, Sherman, Gawronski, Hugenberg, & Groom, 2005; Gawronski & Bodenhausen, 2006; Smith & DeCoster, 2000; Strack & Deutsch, 2004). Applied to my research, I propose that increasing the salience of counterstereotypic individuals in local environments will create new implicit associations linking the target group (or self) with counterstereotypic attributes reflected in the local environment (cf. Gawronski & Bodenhausen, 2006). While stereotypic associations are more accessible in default situations or decontextualized experiments, the introduction of counterstereotypic cues in the form of background situational characteristics or counterstereotypic individuals is likely to make alternative associations dominate in that situation. Counterstereotypic situational cues may also suppress stereotypic associations if these attributes are thought to be bipolar constructs that cannot be activated simultaneously (e.g., good–bad, masculine–feminine; see Greenwald et al., 2002). Over time, long-term immersion in counterstereotypic environments may reduce the default accessibility of stereotypes and/or enhance the chronic accessibility of counterstereotypes.

A different process may drive implicit attitude change produced by transient emotional states. Our past studies demonstrating that anger and disgust, exacerbate implicit prejudice may be driven by changes in control processes. Consistent with this idea, prior research shows that changes in cognitive control processes can influence attitude expressions typically thought of as implicit (Conrey et al., 2005; Payne, 2001, 2005; Payne, Lambert, & Jacoby, 2002). These researchers argue that although implicit attitudes are activated without awareness and expressed under time pressure (as demonstrated by studies using speeded reaction time tasks that constrain response time) such responses are not "process pure"; they are guided by a blend of automatic and controlled processes. Thus, it seems reasonable to expect that arousal of anger, disgust, and similar negative intergroup emotions may reduce the motivation to engage control processes and, as a result, increase implicit bias in attitudes and behavior.

11.3. The role of awareness and choice in changing implicit attitudes and beliefs

One of the signature findings of my research is that participants were either unaware of the fact that their attitudes, beliefs, self-conceptions, and choices were systematically shaped by the situation or unaware of which aspects of the situation were producing the change. Cutting across several programs of research, our data often reveal that small changes in local environments elicit systematic shifts in people's implicit attitudes and beliefs even though their explicit responses remain unchanged. Even when informed about the research hypotheses at the end of the study participants typically do not think their own implicit reactions were affected by environmental cues. For example, people assume their academic self-conceptions and career decisions are freely chosen; solely guided by talent and intrinsic motivation; as if these choices are unconstrained by external factors. Yet, as our data have shown, for individuals who are numeric minorities and stereotyped in a field, their implicit attitudes toward science and engineering, identification with these fields, and self-efficacy are heavily influenced by the presence or absence of ingroup experts and peers. It is not a free choice solely determined by talent (Stout et al., 2011). Even though people are often unaware of the impact of stereotypic cues in achievement settings on their academic and professional interests and choices, these cues have profound effects on their intellectual and professional identities and career choices.

Having said that, conscious choice no doubt plays an important role in the selection of local environments and communities in to which people enter. People routinely make decisions about what books and media to read and watch and what others to avoid; whom to seek out as friends and whom to avoid; where to go to college; and how much to engage with coworkers from different backgrounds and in different roles within the workplace hierarchy. Each of these decisions contributes to a unique local environment surrounding a given individual that may be quite different from others living in the same town. Individuals' implicit attitudes, beliefs, and self-conceptions reflect these local environments.

11.4. Full-cycle research

An important theme in my research is that in many cases I do initial hypothesis testing in controlled laboratory experiments followed by replications and extensions of the same hypotheses in field settings to determine if lab-based findings, cause-and-effect relations, and underlying psychological processes apply to real-world social problems I would like to impact. This is consistent with Cialdini's (1980) description of full-cycle research. He suggests that some psychological phenomena, particularly in social psychology, benefit greatly from full-cycle research; testing ideas iteratively in the laboratory and field so that knowledge from both sources enriches understanding of the phenomenon of interest (Cialdini, 1980; Dasgupta & Hunsinger, 2008; Dasgupta & Stout, 2012). Applying this concept to our research, our data testing the Stereotype Inoculation Model combined controlled lab experiments and messier field studies, cross-sectional research designs and longitudinal designs in search of converging evidence of stereotype inoculation and the conditions that make it more or less likely (Asgari et al., 2010, 2012; Dasgupta, 2011; Dasgupta & Asgari, 2004; Stout et al., 2011). Full-cycle research allows controlled tests of cause-and-effect, encourages investigation in theoretically interesting field environments, helps identify differences between lab evidence and field evidence, and increases the chance that we will stumble upon new research questions and hypotheses about ways to change implicit bias in naturally unfolding environments.

REFERENCES

Abelson, R. P. (1986). Beliefs are like possessions. *Journal for the Theory of Social Behaviour, 16*, 223–250.
Allport, G. W. (1954). *The nature of prejudice*. Reading, MA: Addison-Wesley.
Asgari, S., Dasgupta, N., & Gilbert Cote, N. (2010). When does contact with successful ingroup members change self-stereotypes? A longitudinal study comparing the effect of quantity vs. quality of contact with successful individuals. *Social Psychology, 41*, 203–211.

Asgari, S., Dasgupta, N., & Stout, J. G. (2012). When do counterstereotypic ingroup members inspire vs. deflate? The effect of successful professional women on women's leadership self-concept. *Personality and Social Psychology Bulletin, 38*, 370–383.

Banaji, M. R. (2001). Implicit attitudes can be measured. In H. L. Roediger III., & J. S. Nairne (Eds.), *The nature of remembering: Essays in honor of Robert G. Crowder* (pp. 117–150). Washington, DC: American Psychological Association.

Banaji, M. R., & Dasgupta, N. (1998). The consciousness of social beliefs: A program of research on stereotyping and prejudice. In V. Y. Yzerbyt, G. Lories & B. Dardenne (Eds.), *Metacognition: Cognitive and social dimensions*. Great Britain: Sage Publications.

Bargh, J. A. (1994). The four horsemen of automaticity: Awareness, intention, efficiency, and control in social cognition. In R. S. Wyer & T. K. Srull (Eds.), (2nd ed.). *Handbook of social cognition, Vol. 1.* (pp. 1–40). Hillsdale, NJ: Lawrence Erlbaum Associates.

Bargh, J. A. (1997). The automaticity of everyday life. In R. S. Wyer Jr., (Ed.), *The automaticity of everyday life: Advances in social cognition, Vol. 10.* Mahwah, NJ: Erlbaum, pp. 1–61.

Bargh, J. A. (1999). The cognitive monster: The case against the controllability of automatic stereotype effects. In S. Chaiken & Y. Trope (Eds.), *Dual-process theories in social psychology.* New York: Guilford Press pp. 361–382.

Blair, I. V. (2002). The malleability of automatic stereotypes and prejudice. *Personality and Social Psychology Review, 6*, 242–261.

Blanton, H., Crocker, J., & Miller, D. T. (2000). The effects of in-group versus out-group social comparison on self-esteem in the context of a negative stereotype. *Journal of Experimental Social Psychology, 36*, 519–530.

Branscombe, N., Ellemers, N., Spears, R., & Doosje, B. (1999). The context and content of social identity threat. *Social identity: Context, commitment, content.* Oxford, England: Blackwell Science, pp. 35–58.

Brewer, M. B., & Weber, J. G. (1994). Self-evaluation effects of interpersonal versus intergroup social comparison. *Journal of Personality and Social Psychology, 66*, 268–275.

Ceci, S. J., Wiliams, W. M., & Barnett, S. M. (2009). Women's underrepresentation in science: Sociocultural and biological considerations. *Psychological Bulletin, 135*, 261–281.

Ceci, S. J., & Williams, W. M. (2011). Understanding current causes of women's underrepresentation in science. *Proceedings of the National Academy of Sciences of the United States of America, 108*, 3157–3162.

Cheryan, S., & Monin, B. (2005). "Where are you *really* from?": Asian-Americans and identity denial. *Journal of Personality and Social Psychology, 89*, 717–730.

Cialdini, R. B. (1980). Full-cycle social psychology. *Applied Social Psychology Annual, 1*, 21–47.

Conrey, F. R., Sherman, J. W., Gawronski, B., Hugenberg, K., & Groom, C. J. (2005). Separating multiple processes in implicit social cognition: The quad model of implicit task performance. *Journal of Personality and Social Psychology, 89*, 469–487.

Damasio, A. R. (1994). *Descartes' error.* New York: Avon Books.

Dasgupta, N. (2004). Implicit ingroup favoritism, outgroup favoritism, and their behavioral manifestations. *Social Justice Research, 17*, 143–169.

Dasgupta, N. (2008). Color lines in the mind: Unconscious prejudice, discriminatory behavior, and the potential for change. In A. Grant-Thomas & G. Orfield (Eds.), *Twenty-first century color lines: Multiracial change in contemporary America.* Philadelphia, PA: Temple University Press.

Dasgupta, N. (2009). Mechanisms underlying malleability of implicit prejudice and stereotypes: The role of automaticity versus cognitive control. In T. Nelson (Ed.), *Handbook of prejudice, stereotyping, and discrimination.* Mahwah, NJ: Erlbaum.

Dasgupta, N. (2011). Ingroup experts and peers as social vaccines who inoculate the self-concept: The Stereotype Inoculation Model. *Psychological Inquiry, 22*, 231–246.

Dasgupta, N., & Asgari, S. (2004). Seeing is believing: Exposure to counterstereotypic women leaders and its effect on the malleability of automatic gender stereotyping. *Journal of Experimental Social Psychology, 40*, 642–658.

Dasgupta, N., & Dennehy, T. (2012). Effect of peer mentors on women's self-concept and success in engineering. University of Massachusetts. Unpublished data.

Dasgupta, N., DeSteno, D. A., Williams, L., & Hunsinger, M. (2009). Fanning the flames of prejudice: The influence of specific incidental emotions on implicit prejudice. *Emotion, 9*, 585–591.

Dasgupta, N., & Greenwald, A. G. (2001). On the malleability of automatic attitudes: Combating automatic prejudice with images of admired and disliked individuals. *Journal of Personality and Social Psychology, 81*, 800–814.

Dasgupta, N., & Hunsinger, M. (2008). The opposite of a great truth is also true: When do student samples help versus hurt the scientific study of prejudice? *Psychological Inquiry, 19*, 90–98.

Dasgupta, N., & Rivera, L. M. (2008). When social context matters: The influence of long-term contact and short-term exposure to admired outgroup members on implicit attitudes and behavioral intentions. *Social Cognition, 26*, 54–66.

Dasgupta, N., & Stout, J. G. (2012). Contemporary discrimination in the lab and real world: Benefits and obstacles of full-cycle social psychology. *Journal of Social Issues, 68*, 399–412.

DeSteno, D. A., Dasgupta, N., Bartlett, M. Y., & Cajdric, A. (2004). Prejudice from thin air: The effect of emotion on automatic intergroup attitudes. *Psychological Science, 15*, 319–324.

Devine, P. G. (1989). Stereotypes and prejudice: Their automatic and controlled components. *Journal of Personality and Social Psychology, 56*, 5–18.

Devine, P. G., Monteith, M. J., Zuwerink, J. R., & Elliot, A. J. (1991). Prejudice with and without compunction. *Journal of Personality and Social Psychology, 60*, 817–830.

Devos, T., & Banaji, M. (2005). American = White? *Journal of Personality and Social Psychology, 88*, 447–466.

Devos, T., Gavin, K., & Quintana, F. (2010). Say "Adios" to the American dream? The interplay between ethnic and national identity among Latino and Caucasian Americans. *Cultural Diversity and Ethnic Minority Psychology, 16*, 37–49.

Devos, T., & Ma, D. (2008). Is Kate Winslet more American than Lucy Liu? The impact of construal processes on the implicit ascription of a national identity. *The British Journal of Social Psychology, 47*, 191–215.

Diekman, A. B., & Eagly, A. H. (2008). On men, women, and motivation: A role congruity account. In J. Y. Shah & W. L. Gardner (Eds.), *Handbook of motivation science* (pp. 434–447). New York: Guilford.

Dovidio, J., Gluszek, A., John, M., Ditlmann, R., & Lagunes, P. (2010). Understanding bias toward Latinos: Discrimination, dimensions of difference, and experience of exclusion. *Journal of Social Issues, 66*, 59–78.

Eagly, A. H., & Carli, L. (2007). *Through the labyrinth: The truth about how women become leaders.* Boston, MA: Harvard Business School Press.

Eagly, A. H., & Karau, S. J. (2002). Role congruity theory of prejudice toward female leaders. *Psychological Review, 109*, 573–598.

Eccles, J. S., Wigfield, A., Harold, R., & Blumenfeld, P. (1993). Age and gender differences in children's achievement self-perceptions during the elementary school years. *Child Development, 64*, 830–847.

Else-Quest, N. M., Hyde, J. S., & Linn, M. C. (2010). Cross-national patterns of gender differences in mathematics: A meta-analysis. *Psychological Bulletin, 136*, 103–127.

Ferguson, M. J., & Bargh, J. A. (2007). Beyond the attitude object: Implicit attitudes spring from object-centered contexts. In B. Wittenbrink & N. Schwarz (Eds.), *Implicit measures of attitudes* (pp. 216–246). New York, NY: Guilford Press.

Frijda, N. H. (1986). *The emotions.* Cambridge, England: Cambridge University Press.

Gaertner, S. L., & Dovidio, J. F. (1986). An aversive form of racism. In J. F. Dovidio & S. L. Gaertner (Eds.), *Prejudice, discrimination, and racism* (pp. 61–89). New York: Academic Press.

Gawronski, B., & Bodenhausen, G. V. (2006). Associative and propositional processes in evaluation: An integrative review of implicit and explicit attitude change. *Psychological Bulletin, 132,* 692–731.

Greenwald, A. G., & Banaji, M. R. (1995). Implicit social cognition: Attitudes, self-esteem, and stereotypes. *Psychological Review, 102,* 4–27.

Greenwald, A. G., Banaji, M. R., Rudman, L. A., Farnham, S. D., Nosek, B. A., & Mellott, D. S. (2002). A unified theory of implicit attitudes, stereotypes, self-esteem, and self-concept. *Psychological Review, 109,* 3–25.

Katz, I., & Hass, R. G. (1988). Racial ambivalence and American value conflict: Correlational and priming studies of dual cognitive structures. *Journal of Personality and Social Psychology, 55,* 893–905.

Katz, I., Wackenhut, J., & Hass, R. G. (1986). Racial ambivalence, value duality, and behavior. In J. F. Dovidio & S. L. Gaertner (Eds.), *Prejudice, discrimination, and racism* (pp. 35–60). New York: Academic Press.

Keltner, D., & Gross, J. J. (1999). Functional accounts of emotion. *Cognition and Emotion, 13,* 467–480.

Kihlstrom, J. F. (1990). The psychological unconscious. In L. A. Pervin (Ed.), *Handbook of personality: Theory and research* (pp. 445–464). New York: Guilford Press.

LeDoux, J. E. (1996). *The emotional brain.* New York: Simon & Schuster.

Lockwood, P., & Kunda, Z. (1997). Superstars and me: Predicting the impact of role models on the self. *Journal of Personality and Social Psychology, 73,* 91–103.

Lockwood, P., & Kunda, Z. (1999). Increasing the salience of one's best selves can undermine inspiration by outstanding role models. *Journal of Personality and Social Psychology, 76,* 214–228.

Macrae, C. N., Bodenhausen, G. V., Milne, A. B., & Jetten, J. (1994). Out of mind but back in sight: Stereotypes on the rebound. *Journal of Personality and Social Psychology, 67,* 808–817.

Macrae, C. N., Bodenhausen, G. V., Milne, A. B., & Wheeler, V. (1996). On resisting the temptation for simplification: Counterintentional effects of stereotype suppression on social memory. *Social Cognition, 14,* 1–20.

Markus, H., & Kunda, Z. (1986). Stability and malleability of the self-concept. *Journal of Personality and Social Psychology, 51,* 858–866.

Markus, H., & Nurius, P. (1986). Possible selves. *American Psychologist, 41,* 954–969.

Markus, H. R., & Wurf, E. (1987). The dynamic self-concept: A social psychological perspective. *Annual Review of Psychology, 38,* 299–337.

Marques, J. M., & Paez, D. (1994). The black sheep effect: Social categorization, rejection of ingroup deviates, and perception of group variability. In W. Stroebe & M. Hewstone (Eds.), *European review of social psychology, Vol. 5,* (pp. 37–68). Chichester, England: Wiley.

Mendez, L., Mihalas, S., & Hardesty, R. (2006). Gender differences in academic development and performance. *Children's needs III: Development, prevention, and intervention.* Washington, DC: National Association of School Psychologists, pp. 553–565.

Monteith, M. J. (1993). Self-regulation of prejudiced responses. Implications for progress in prejudice-reduction efforts. *Journal of Personality and Social Psychology, 65,* 469–485.

Monteith, M. J., Devine, P. G., & Zuwerink, J. R. (1993). Self-directed vs. other-directed affect as a consequence of prejudice-related discrepancies. *Journal of Personality and Social Psychology, 64,* 198–210.

Monteith, M. J., Zuwerink, J. R., & Devine, P. G. (1994). Prejudice and prejudice reduction: Classic challenges, contemporary approaches. In P. G. Devine, D. L. Hamilton &

T. M. Ostrom (Eds.), *Social cognition: Impact on social psychology*. San Diego, CA: Academic Press.

Myrdal, G. (1944). *An American dilemma: The Negro problem and modern democracy*. New York: Harper.

Nisbett, R. E., & Wilson, T. D. (1977). Telling more than we can know: Verbal reports on mental processes. *Psychological Review, 84*, 231–259.

Nosek, B. A., Banaji, M. R., & Greenwald, A. G. (2002a). Harvesting implicit group attitudes and beliefs from a demonstration web site. *Group Dynamics: Theory, Research, and Practice, 6*, 101–115. Special issue: Groups and the Internet.

Nosek, B. A., Banaji, M. R., & Greenwald, A. G. (2002b). Math = male, me = female, therefore math ≠ me. *Journal of Personality and Social Psychology, 83*, 44–59.

Nosek, B. A., & Hansen, J. J. (2008). The associations in our heads belong to us: Searching for attitudes and knowledge in implicit evaluation. *Cognition and Emotion, 22*, 553–594.

Nosek, B. A., Smyth, F. L., Sriram, N., Lindner, N. M., Devos, T., Ayala, A., et al. (2009). National differences in gender–science stereotypes predict national sex differences in science and math achievement. *Proceedings of the National Academy of Sciences of the United States of America, 106*, 10593–10597.

Park, G., Lubinski, D., & Benbow, C. P. (2007). Contrasting intellectual patterns predict creativity in the arts and sciences: Tracking intellectually precocious youth over 25 years. *Psychological Science, 18*, 948–952.

Parks-Stamm, E. J., Heilman, M. E., & Hearns, K. A. (2008). Motivated to penalize: Women's strategic rejection of successful women. *Personality and Social Psychology Bulletin, 34*, 237–247.

Payne, B. K. (2001). Prejudice and perception: The role of automatic and controlled processes in misperceiving a weapon. *Journal of Personality and Social Psychology, 81*, 181–192.

Payne, B. K. (2005). Conceptualizing control in social cognition: How executive functioning modulates the expression of automatic stereotyping. *Journal of Personality and Social Psychology, 89*, 488–503.

Payne, B. K., Lambert, A. J., & Jacoby, L. L. (2002). Best laid plans: Effects of goals on accessibility bias and cognitive control in race-based misperceptions of weapons. *Journal of Experimental Social Psychology, 38*, 384–396.

Pettigrew, T., & Tropp, L. R. (2006). A meta-analytic test of intergroup contact theory. *Journal of Personality and Social Psychology, 90*, 751–783.

Petty, R. E., Fazio, R. H., & Brinol, P. (2008). *Attitudes: Insights from the new implicit measures*. New York: Psychology Press.

Petty, R. E., Tormala, Z. L., Brinol, P., & Jarvis, W. B. G. (2006). Implicit ambivalence from attitude change: An exploration of the PAST model. *Journal of Personality and Social Psychology, 90*, 21–41.

Robertson, K. F., Smeets, S., Lubinski, D., & Benbow, C. P. (2010). Beyond the threshold hypothesis: Even among the gifted and top math/science graduate students, cognitive abilities, vocational interests, and lifestyle preferences matter for career choice, performance, and persistence. *Current Directions in Psychological Science, 19*, 346–351.

Rockeach, M. (1973). *The nature of human values*. New York: Free Press.

Rudman, L. A., & Glick, P. (2001). Prescriptive gender stereotypes and backlash toward agentic women. *Journal of Social Issues, 57*, 743–762.

Rudman, L. A., & Kilianski, S. E. (2000). Implicit and explicit attitudes toward female authority. *Personality and Social Psychology Bulletin, 26*, 1315–1328.

Rudman, L. A., & Phelan, J. E. (2010). The effect of priming gender roles on women' implicit gender beliefs and career aspirations. *Social Psychology, 41*, 192–202.

Smith, E. R., & DeCoster, J. (2000). Dual-process models in social and cognitive psychology: Conceptual integration and links to underlying memory systems. *Personality and Social Psychology Review, 4*, 108–131.

Stout, J. G., Dasgupta, N., Hunsinger, M., & McManus, M. A. (2011). STEMing the tide: Using ingroup experts to inoculate women's self-concept in science, technology, engineering, and mathematics (STEM). *Journal of Personality and Social Psychology*, *100*, 255–270.

Strack, F., & Deutsch, R. (2004). Reflective and impulsive determinants of social behavior. *Personality and Social Psychology Review*, *8*, 220–247.

Swim, J. K., & Hyers, L. L. (2008). Sexism. In T. D. Nelson (Ed.), *Handbook of prejudice, stereotyping, and discrimination*. Philadelphia, PA: Psychology Press.

Tropp, L. R., & Bianchi, R. A. (2006). Valuing diversity and interest in intergroup contact. *Journal of Social Issues*, *62*, 533–551.

Tropp, L. R., Stout, A. M., Boatswain, C., Wright, S., & Pettigrew, T. F. (2006). Trust and acceptance in response to references to group membership: Minority and majority perspectives on cross-group interactions. *Journal of Applied Social Psychology*, *36*, 769–794.

Wilson, T. D., Lindsey, S., & Schooler, T. Y. (2000). A model of dual attitudes. *Psychological Review*, *107*, 101–126.

Yogeeswaran, K., Adelman, L., Parker, M. T., & Dasgupta, N. (2012). In the eyes of the beholder: White Americans' national identification predicts differential reactions to ethnic identity expressions. Manuscript under review.

Yogeeswaran, K., & Dasgupta, N. (2010). Will the "real" American please stand up? The effect of implicit stereotypes about nationality on discriminatory behavior. *Personality and Social Psychology Bulletin*, *36*, 1332–1345.

Yogeeswaran, K., Dasgupta, N., Adelman, L., Eccleston, A., & Parker, M. (2011). To be or not to be (ethnic): The hidden cost of ethnic identification for Americans of European and Non-European origin. *Journal of Experimental Social Psychology*, *47*, 908–914.

Yogeeswaran, K., Dasgupta, N., & Gomez, C. (2012). A new American dilemma? The effect of ethnic identification and public service on the national inclusion of ethnic groups. *European Journal of Social Psychology*, *42*, 691–705.

INDEX

Note: Page numbers followed by "*f*" indicate figures, and "*t*" indicate tables.

CONTENTS OF OTHER VOLUMES

Volume 16

Volume 17

Volume 18

Volume 19

Volume 29

Volume 30

Volume 31

Volume 32